BY ZECHARIAH CHAFEE, JR.

The Blessings of Liberty

Freedom of Speech

The Next War (*part author*)

The Inquiring Mind

Report on Lawlessness in Law Enforcement
(*part author*)

State House v. Pent House

Free Speech in the United States

Government and Mass Communications

Documents on Fundamental Human Rights

How Human Rights Got Into the Constitution

Freedom of Speech and Press

Three Human Rights in the Original Constitution

THE BLESSINGS OF LIBERTY

WE, THE PEOPLE of the United States, in Order to . . . secure the Blessings of Liberty to ourselves and our Posterity, do ordain and establish this Constitution for the United States of America.

ZECHARIAH CHAFEE, JR.

THE BLESSINGS
OF
LIBERTY

J. B. Lippincott Company
Philadelphia and New York

Acknowledgments

My thanks are due to many periodicals and other enterprises for originally making possible and publishing what I wrote or spoke, and for kindly permitting its use in this book. The articles and addresses, from which the successive chapters are taken and now much revised, are as follows:

I. WATCHMAN, WHAT OF THE NIGHT? Most of this chapter was published in the *Atlantic Monthly* (May 1956) under the title, "The Encroachments on Freedom." A few passages are taken from an address with the same title at the Honors Day Convocation at Brown University, November 25, 1947, published as *Brown University Papers, XXI*. A few paragraphs are taken from "Protecting Civil Liberties in the United States," *Columbia Daily Spectator*, Sunday, October 31, 1954, Special Biennial Issue on "What Will Tomorrow Bring?" (Copyright 1954 by Columbia Daily Spectator). A paragraph comes from a book review in 47 *Northwestern University Law Review* 270 (May-June 1952). (Copyright 1953 by Illinois Law Publishing Corp.; now owned by Northwestern University School of Law.)

II. WHY I LIKE AMERICA. Commencement Address with same title at Colby College, May 21, 1944, printed in abridged form in the *Colby Alumnus*, July 1944. Supplemented from unpublished lecture at Brown University in winter of 1940-1941 on "What Democracy Means to Me," with paragraphs from the Brown address used in Chapter I.

III. FORTY YEARS WITH FREEDOM OF SPEECH AND OF THE PRESS. Mainly from an address at Columbia University, March 12, 1952, under the auspices of the Roger N. Baldwin Civil Liberties Foundation. Published by the Foundation in a pamphlet, "Thirty-five Years with Freedom of Speech" (May 1952). This was reprinted with the same title in 1 *Kansas Law Review* 1 (November 1952). (Copyright 1952 by Kansas Law Review, Inc.) A few paragraphs come from a book review in 62 *Harvard Law Review* 891 (March 1949). (Copyright 1949 by The Harvard Law Review Association.)

IV. DOES FREEDOM OF SPEECH REALLY TEND TO PRODUCE TRUTH? Portions of unpublished address on "Freedom and Truth" at Aspen, Colorado, August 5, 1952, in the Conference on Human Freedom, held by the Aspen Institute for Humanistic Studies.

V. FREEDOM AND FEAR. Harvard Phi Beta Kappa Oration, June 20, 1949. This address made extensive use of my mimeographed statement against the Mundt-Nixon Bill (now the McCarran Act) filed with the Senate Judiciary Committee on June 4, 1949, and repeated with additions in a mimeographed statement filed with the House Committee on Un-American Activities on March 15, 1950, and also sent to President Truman before he vetoed the bill in September 1950. The address was printed with the same title in abridged form in the *Harvard Alumni Bulletin*, July 9, 1949. (Copyright 1949 by Harvard Alumni Bulletin.) It was reprinted in full in 35 *Bulletin of the American Association of University Professors* 397 (Autumn 1949). The subsequent statement to the House Committee was published by the American Civil Liberties Union in a pamphlet, "The Free and the Brave" (April 1950). Most of the part of this chapter dealing with the registration of Communist-front organizations was not in the Harvard address, but is based on paragraphs in my statement to the House committee; this discussion was separately published as "The Registration of 'Communist-front' Organizations in the Mundt-Nixon Bill," 63 *Harvard Law Review* 1382 (June 1950). (Copyright 1950 by The Harvard Law Review Association.)

VI. Purges Are for Russian Lawyers, Not American Lawyers. First published in *Harvard Law School Record* (November 1 and 8, 1950) under title, "Chafee Criticizes Resolution of A.B.A. Requiring Loyalty Oaths From Lawyers"; and reprinted by me in offset in a four-page leaflet for distribution to the bar under title, "A Statement to My Fellow-Lawyers Who Have Sworn to Uphold the Constitution of the United States Urging Painstaking Scrutiny and Long Deliberation on the Resolution of the American Bar Association to Require Every Lawyer to Take Periodic Oaths." Address under same title as chapter to Pennsylvania Bar Association at Pittsburgh, January 19, 1951; printed in *Philadelphia Legal Intelligencer* (January 23, 1951) and *Pittsburgh Legal Journal* (February 7, 1951).

VII. The Right Not to Speak. A small part is based on a joint statement by my colleague Arthur E. Sutherland and myself first published in the *Harvard Crimson* (January 8, 1953), and distributed in mimeographed form, receiving considerable publicity at the time. Most of this chapter has never been published.

VIII. The Freedom to Think. Address at Founders Day, University of Oregon, October 18, 1954, under title, "If the Salt Have Lost His Savour—". Published under the title of the chapter in the *Atlantic Monthly* (January 1955). (Copyright 1954 by The Atlantic Monthly Company; now owned by Zechariah Chafee, Jr.) The address was later included under its original title in "Charter Day Addresses, Delivered at the University of Oregon, October 18-19, 1954."

IX. With Full Liberty in Religious Concernments. Address to New England Library Association at Swampscott, Massachusetts, October 12, 1951. Published in 77 *Library Journal* 379 (March 1, 1952). It was reprinted in the *Christian Register* (May 1952). (Copyright 1952 by The Christian Register.)

X. Strengthening Liberty in All Countries. This is mainly based on a paper read to American Philosophical Society on April 20, 1951, under title, "Some Problems of the Draft International Covenant of Human Rights," and at the University of Florence in April 1953 as "Quelques Problèmes du Pacte International Relatif aux Droits de l'Homme." Published in 95 *Proceedings of the American Philosophical Society* 471 (October 1951). Some passages are taken from "Legal Problems of Freedom of Information in the

United Nations," 14 *Law and Contemporary Problems* 545 (Autumn 1949). (Copyright 1949 by Duke University.) Other passages come from "Federal and State Powers Under the UN Covenant on Human Rights," [1951] *Wisconsin Law Review* 389, 623. (Copyright 1951 by the University of Wisconsin.)

XI. FREE SPEECH IN THE UNITED NATIONS. Commencement Address at Radcliffe College, June 9, 1948. Abstracted in *Radcliffe Quarterly* (August 1948). (Copyright 1948 by the Radcliffe College Alumnae Association.) It was fully printed under title, "Channels and Chances for World-Wide Growth of Understanding," in *Dun's Review* (December 1948). (Copyright 1948 by Dun's Review.) The two last paragraphs are taken from "Watchman, What of the Night?" the Brown address also used in Chapter I.

Also I am very grateful to the following persons for permission to make various quotations in the headings of several chapters and in the text. These are: Henry D. Edmunds, Archivist, and Alfred A. Knopf, Inc., for the quotation from Henry Ford in the heading to Chapter II, which was published in *Henry Ford* by Roger Burlingame (copyright 1954 by Roger Burlingame). Archibald MacLeish for quotations in Chapters II and V (copyright by him 1933, 1948). The Atlantic Monthly Company and Walter Pritchard Eaton for the quotation from him in the same chapter (copyright 1930 by The Atlantic Monthly Company). The Viking Press Inc. for the quotation from Charles A. Beard's *The Republic* in the same chapter (copyright 1943 by Charles A. Beard). Charles Scribner's Sons, for the quotation from *Leaven of Malice* by Robertson Davies in the heading to Chapter III (copyright 1955 by Charles Scribner's Sons). Harper & Brothers and Frank Knight for the quotations from his book, *The Ethics of Competition,* in Chapter IV. Judge Samuel H. Hofstadter for the quotation in the heading to Chapter VII. The Macmillan Company, New York, for three quotations from Edwin Arlington Robinson's *Collected Poems:* from *The Three Taverns* (1920) in the heading to Chapter IX; from *The Master* (1910) in the text of Chapter IV; from *Nicodemus* (1937) in the text of Chapter VIII (copyright by The Macmillan Company, New York, at the respective dates). Mark Antony DeWolfe Howe for the quotation in the heading to Chapter X (copyright 1924 by Mark Antony DeWolfe Howe).

This book is affectionately dedicated

to

JAMES LAWDER GAMBLE

COMPANION DURING FIFTY YEARS

Eager in his laboratory to understand

the causes of health

Eager outside it

to spread happiness

CONTENTS

THE BLESSINGS OF LIBERTY

1 Watchman, What of the Night?

Held we fall to rise, are baffled to fight better
——BROWNING, *Epilogue to Asolando*

The Constitution is not just a fence which Congress must not climb over. It is also a flag.

True, if Congress goes beyond the extreme limits fixed by the Bill of Rights, the Supreme Court will defend our freedoms. Yet that rarely happens—only five times since 1937 when its power to check unconstitutional legislation was barely saved by Chief Justice Hughes.[1] Now the fence is set far out and inside it Congress can range at will over a wide field, controlled (except for an occasional Presidential veto) only by public opinion and by itself.

The Constitution is a flag flying over the wide field of law-making. "Let us raise a standard," said George Washington in the final hour of the Philadelphia Convention—"a standard to which the wise and honest can repair." If Senators, Representatives, and the citizens who choose them are inspired by the Constitution with a determination to make the fundamental freedoms, which are there emblazoned, enter into the detailed provisions of statutes and official action, then and only then will the blessings of liberty be secure.

It is very important to remember that the clauses in the document of 1787 and the amendments of 1791 safeguarding basic human rights are much more than technical rules of law, which judges are sometimes unable to apply to contemporary situations unforeseen by the men who wrote those clauses. Regardless of their precise legal boundaries, the words of the Constitution need to be deeply felt by each one of us as ideals of fairness, sound government, and happiness for our own perplexing times.

This book is written because, so far as in me lies, I want to make my fellow-citizens care more about these ideals. No doubt, liberties sometimes have to be cut down to preserve the nation. We have

[1] See page 323 and following for footnote references.

been passing through very troubled years since Germany and Japan surrendered. Instead of returning to a happy period of unbroken homes and business as usual, for which everybody longed, we faced almost immediately the threat of Communist power abroad, which broke into actual and protracted fighting in Korea. This unceasing tension in foreign affairs was aggravated by fears of Soviet sympathizers in our midst. Therefore, it is not surprising that influential persons and groups urged various kinds of abridgements of liberty. Nevertheless, I hope to let readers see how many sacrifices of freedom have taken place, and to set them questioning whether these sacrifices were all necessary to save the country. Were they planned wisely? Did they really lessen the dangers from disaffection in the United States? Or were these restrictive measures often adopted in careless haste or out of personal vindictiveness and thirst for popularity? This introductory chapter is not the place to answer such questions, but they ought to be asked. The great ideals and traditions of liberty are in the Constitution because Englishmen and American colonists thought and worked, decade after decade, and were ready to risk prison and death. Shall we abandon them blithely?

When I try to envisage the future of civil liberties in this country, I recall Philip Cabot's remark, "For me fifteen years is eternity." So I do not look beyond 1970. Trying to see even that far ahead is a risky task. If a writer in 1920 amid the hysteria of the Red Menace, when Charles Evans Hughes was vainly opposing the disfranchisement of left-wing radicals, had predicted that Hughes would before 1935 be leading the Supreme Court in vigorously upholding freedom of speech, this would have been ridiculed as an iridescent dream.

Nevertheless, I audaciously look forward to a future by no means wholly black. What may be called the tangible civil liberties will be better protected in 1970 than now. The recent Segregation Cases in the Supreme Court [2] have begun the destruction of the last legal barriers against citizens who have a strain of color not white. Those who wanted to solve gradually the problems of the descendants of slaves may recognize by 1963 that a century after the Emancipation Proclamation is long enough. The eventual disappearance of legal differentiations based on race or color will come not only by judicial nullification and legislative repeals, but also—what is more important—through notable alterations in public opinion. Common sacrifices in war and other disasters and the experience of working and living together will make Americans regard themselves increasingly as a single people.

Other tangible rights acquiring greater solidity are those giving a fair trial to all persons who have to stand before judges and juries and face the possibility of being punished for crimes. Convictions obtained by mobs dominating the courtroom no longer stand.[3] The Supreme Court has recently strengthened the right to counsel; and provisions for defenders paid out of taxes or community chests are making it easier to obtain a reputable lawyer without great pecuniary sacrifices. The presence of a lawyer in the courtroom greatly increases the practical value of all the constitutional rights of a prisoner on trial.

Abuses of his rights before trial such as the brutality called the "third degree"[4] are likely to diminish with the striking progress in police organization and police methods. Even prolonged questioning of a person in custody may be subjected to more regulation.[5]

There is much more cause for apprehension, however, when I think of the future of the more subtle freedoms proclaimed by the First Amendment, those concerned with our believing, our thinking, our expression of our thoughts by voice and print, and our association with others to exchange or promote ideas.

Freedom of religion now appears safe for any man who holds any variety of faith in the supernatural, however heterodox, at least when it does not make it immoral for him to go to war.[6] But what about the atheist or agnostic? The men of fluid beliefs who participated in the Constitution intended to protect him, too. Although a churchman myself, I regard it as vital to our national life that a man's right to hold public office should never be affected by what he believes about his relation to the totality of being.

Bribing men into a profession of faith is monstrous. Yet we may be moving that way. Frequent allusions to "atheistic communism" are tending to identify free-thinking with disloyalty. The law may remain as now, but in practice atheists and agnostics may be virtually ineligible as candidates for election or appointment to public office. Though no statute is likely to require church membership as a qualification for teachers in public schools, the same result can conceivably be attained by determined school committees.

A community is likely to be happiest if Church and State are careful to keep away from each other, except by commonly recognized ways of working together like having chaplains in the armed forces and Christmas songs in public schools.[7] Chapter IX of this book sets forth some of the lessons of history showing how, when governmental authorities get close to religion, the outcome is bitterness and hatred, which religion ought to abhor. "Then I saw that there was a way to hell, even from the gates of heaven." [8]

When we go outside religion, freedom of thought and discussion about controversial issues will, I expect, have to be defended against frequent incursions for many years ahead. This book pays little attention to the future of the Communist Party of America. It has no future. Yet in our fear of domestic Communists and our eagerness to identify heterodoxy with spying and sabotage, we have developed vague legal concepts like "subversive" and "disloyalty" which will trouble us for a long time to come. Our present national policy of driving Communists underground will spread suspicion into new quarters.

Disputes about the proper ways to deal with radicals in our midst are largely caused by a sharp divergence of opinion about the extent of the danger. One group thinks the country to be in great peril. The other group has confidence in the heartfelt devotion of the American people to our form of government and in their ability to sift good ideas from bad ideas through their own intelligence and common sense without needing legislators and officials to do that job for them. Both groups are obliged to form their opinions without knowing badly needed facts. The $64,000 question in every program of laws against domestic radicals is: How big a danger do they create, beyond what can be met by the ordinary processes of reasoning by voice and print?

It is high time that some authoritative group of dispassionate persons gave us a trustworthy answer to that question.

Meanwhile, there is one elementary principle which all thinking Americans would do well to keep in mind, namely, that the denunciations of "Reds" are really directed against four quite different kinds of persons:

(1) Spies and saboteurs, whose bad acts fall under plenty of existing laws, and who are very much the concern of the Federal Bureau of Investigation. There is little reason for believing that novel methods are either needed or useful for unearthing them. For example, Seth Richardson, the first chairman of the Loyalty Review Board, reported in 1950 while evaluating the loyalty program after three years, "Not one single case, or evidence directing toward a case, of espionage has been disclosed . . . [in more than 10,000 cases given a field investigation] not one single syllable of evidence has been found by the FBI, efficient as they are, indicating that a particular case involves a question of espionage." [9] And despite all the talk about spies in the laboratory at Fort Monmouth, all the charges growing out of the Senate committee investigation involved only affiliations alleged to be Communistic, but no espionage.

(2) Desperate revolutionaries, who whether they carry Communist cards or not are ready to injure this country for the sake of helping the Soviet Union. An accurate estimate of their number is sorely lacking.

(3) The mass of enrolled members of the Party, not over fifty thousand at any one time,[10] who drift in and out of it with an astonishing turnover and who may conceivably be reabsorbed into the ranks of ordinary citizens by the use of wise methods other than force.

(4) A far larger number of persons who incline to the left on particular issues, but who for the most part share the ideas and occupations of common or garden people.

Each set calls for considerations all its own. It is a bad blunder to exaggerate the danger by bundling these four sets of persons into an indistinguishable mass.

The last great group of non-Communists are my main concern.

In this opening chapter, I shall list briefly several of the encroachments on the ideals of freedom of speech, press, and assembly which have taken place since 1945, without expressing any judgment as to whether or not they were required by national safety. I leave that question to my readers, and in some cases for discussion in later chapters. I also ignore issues of constitutionality. My only purpose now is to show what is going on.

First. The Smith Act of 1940[11] was little used before V-J Day, but since then the government has prosecuted top-string Communists and second-string Communists. About one hundred persons who were active in the organization have been sent to prison, often for five years. If there be an actual plot to take over the nation by revolutionary violence, it seems rather odd that nobody has been prosecuted under a severe statute of 1861 for conspiracy to overthrow the government by force.[12] Banding together to start a revolution seems more wicked than assembling to talk about a revolution.

Second. In 1950 Congress passed the Mundt-Nixon Bill, usually called the McCarran Act. It sets up a body of officials called the Subversive Activities Control Board, which, on finding that groups have specified objectionable purposes, can order them to register with the Attorney General and incur very disagreeable legal consequences. The full discussion of this law in Chapter V shows that it goes far beyond Communists. The machinery of the McCarran Act operated so slowly that, when nobody had registered by 1954, Congress got impatient. It jumped over the heads of the Board and, by the Communist Control Act, decided that the Communist Party of America had to register and made it an outlaw.[13]

Third. Aliens are more and more made deportable by Congress for what they have said, or because of ideas expressed not by them but by other men in groups they have joined. It makes no difference how long an alien has been in this country or how deeply he has put down his roots. The laws began by throwing out anarchists and Communists, but since 1945 many new categories of objectionable ideas have been added.[14] The vital decisions are all made by government officials. These laws apply the same tests of orthodox thought to temporary visitors as to prospective settlers. Chapter VIII of this book tells how greatly we are harming ourselves by making it hard for distinguished scientists and scholars to obtain visas in order to give Americans the benefit of their knowledge in our universities and scientific conferences.

Fourth. Officials can lock the frontier on both sides. They frequently deny American citizens a passport, which is indispensable for going to Europe but has been treated as a gracious favor from the State Department, to be withheld whenever it did not like the cut of a man's mind. Recently the prospective traveler has been able to get help from the courts [15] if he wants to use the crowded weeks between engaging his passage and boarding the steamer for a lawsuit and pay a lawyer some of the money he had been saving for the Alps and Italy.

Fifth. The frontiers have also been closed by officials against books and magazines.[16] The Customs Bureau has managed to by-pass the valuable law of 1929, which was intended to end their long practice of destroying at will whatever imported books and art they chose to consider indecent.[17] It transferred the control to the courts and thus made possible Judge Woolsey's famous decision admitting Joyce's *Ulysses*. Afterwards the Treasury referred to Huntington Cairns, the secretary of the National Gallery in Washington, all cases where exclusion was possibly required by law.[18] His wise rulings have been so satisfactory to all parties that it was unnecessary to call on the courts. Now, however, the customs officials have joined forces with the postal authorities, and, with very dubious statutory authority, are freely seizing incoming material which is neither obscene nor revolutionary simply because they think it is undesirable "political propaganda" for Americans to read. A high customs official told a Congressional committee about instructing all collectors "on this border-line stuff where we don't feel we have a real law, to seize it, to detain it, . . . and if the Federal Bureau of Investigation officer in the district feels that it should not be released, we more or less strong-arm it to prevent it from going. . . ." Samples of what this new Index Librorum Prohibitorum includes are *Lenin's Selected Works* and *Happy Life of Children in the Rumanian People's Republic*.[19]

Sixth. Congressional investigations into radicalism were occasionally conducted after 1917, but became continuous in 1938, when the House Committee on Un-American Activities was organized. In 1945 it was changed from a special into a permanent committee.[20] Hopes that the Senate was repelled from imitating what was going on in the House have been dashed since the end of the war. Indeed, the Senate now has two committees busy unearthing radicals. The Subcommittee on Internal Security in the Judiciary Committee seems adequate to guard the nation against real dangers, but that is not the view of the Permanent Subcommittee on Investigations of the Senate Committee on Government Operations. This committee (until 1952 entitled Expenditures in the Executive Departments) [21] is charged with all proposed legislation and other matters relating to budget and accounting measures (except appropriations); examining reports of the Comptroller General; studying the operation of government activities at all levels with a view to determining its economy and efficiency; reorganizing the legislative and executive branches; and studying intergovernmental relationship between the nation and states or municipalities, and between the United States and international organizations. One would suppose that these vast ramifications of public affairs would give the committee a gigantic task, but it prefers to spend much of its time investigating workers in private factories and teachers at Harvard.

These three Congressional investigating committees have received more attention in the news than any other method by which our government has been restricting freedom of expression by American citizens, either singly or in groups. Some of their work has been devoted to the Communist Party and real Communists, but a great deal to so-called Communist-front organizations, subversive individuals, fellow-travelers, and so on. For example, the most flamboyant and widely publicized hearings were held at Washington in October 1947 to investigate the motion-picture industry.[22] Representative Rankin, the moving force, spoke of "the loathsome, filthy, insinuating, un-American undercurrents that are running through various pictures." [23] A notable film, *The Best Years of Our Lives*, was condemned because a banker was shown as hesitating to give a loan to a veteran (who eventually got it). If an occasional misleading radical photoplay gets past the gauntlet of producers, banker pressure, the Hays-Johnston Office, and the Catholic National Legion of Decency, will the harm be very great? We need creative art, not controlled art. Leave that to the U.S.S.R.

No doubt, bodies which hold so many sessions as these three committees do must occasionally run across something of value, but the voluminous press reports are mainly concerned with their resemblance to circuses and publish very little carefully considered information from them about the extent of the Communist danger. The impression is left that a large amount of the money of American taxpayers has been spent fishing in dirty waters for cast-off rubbers and battered tin cans.

Seventh. In the spring of 1953, the State Department, at the behest of staff-members of a Senate investigating committee, took hundreds of books out of our very serviceable Information Libraries in foreign cities and junked them, not because of anything these books said, but because their authors were alleged to be subversive. It was considered perilous for foreigners to read books like Alan Barth's *The Loyalty of Free Men* and Dashiell Hammett's *Maltese Falcon*, a thrilling crime story as remote from politics as Sherlock Holmes. While the State Department was thus alienating European lovers of liberty, President Eisenhower told the students at Dartmouth, "Don't join the book-burners." [24]

Eighth. The loyalty and security-risk program came into extensive operation in April 1947 through an executive order by President Truman. It called for every federal official to be investigated by the F.B.I. and his superiors, so that disloyal or untrustworthy persons might be weeded out of the public service.[25] There was a good deal to be said for screening men in sensitive positions like work for the Atomic Energy Commission, but the job did not stop there and it did not stop with possible Communists. Everybody had to stand before the searchlight and let it play over his whole life, his opinions, his family and friends, the books and magazines he read, and the opinions he held. Thus when it was discovered that the mother of a bootblack in the Pentagon had given ten dollars to the Scottsboro Defense Fund before he was born, seventy interviews by the F.B.I. were required to find him worthy to shine the shoes of army officers.

After immense work and the outlay of millions of dollars, a very small percentage of the total number of officials were dismissed and the rest were cleared. Yet there were grave doubts whether the program had accomplished either of Mr. Truman's declared objectives in his order, that "[1] maximum protection must be afforded the United States against infiltration of disloyal persons into the ranks of its employees, and [2] *equal protection from unfounded accusations of disloyalty must be afforded the loyal employees of the government.*" [26] His opponents showed no confidence whatever in the first objective. When Mr. Eisenhower came to the White House, he issued a different order and then pretty much the whole thing was gone through again. And some of the best men in public service have felt that the government is slighting the second objective of "protection from unfounded accusations of disloyalty." Dr. Vannevar Bush, the head of the Office of Scientific Research and Development in the Second World War, told the House Government Operations Committee in October 1954 that the security-risk program had demoralized the scientific community and hindered the nation's program of research into weapons.[27] He testified that the mutual respect between the military services and the scientific community achieved during the Second World War has been "almost destroyed, and one of the primary reasons was the security system." He added that, although scientists are still continuing to serve the military department, their morale is so low that they are doing the job "without enthusiasm and without fruitful inspiration. They go on working, but they feel that they are not welcome; that they are regarded with suspicion; that some of the men who led them through the war are now being questioned and their security and loyalty are in doubt."

Apart from important questions as to procedure of the loyalty-security program (to be mentioned when I come to speak of current encroachments on the great ideals in the Sixth Amendment) the main point for the government and the public to remember is that any possible risk from retaining a man who has performed good service in the past is not the sole consideration; it should always be balanced against the sure loss his dismissal will cause, by cutting off his future contributions to the national welfare. Most of the reasons given for denying J. Robert Oppenheimer access to classified information about nuclear physics related to events in his life before 1941. If the men who ousted him from public service in 1954 had been exercising authority at the time of Pearl Harbor, there would have been no danger from Dr. Oppenheimer and no atomic bomb.

Directors of the American Association for the Advancement of Science do well to insist[28] that it is just as important to ask: "What risk of delayed progress and diminished achievement is incurred in not employing a person?" as it is to ask: "What security risk is incurred in employing such person?"

The current satisfaction of politicians over the number of federal employees who have been dismissed for disloyalty is badly misplaced if in a considerable fraction of those cases the charges were improperly proved or insubstantial and the government has thrown out honest citizens. Somebody ought to count the number of devoted public servants who have resigned in disgust. Nobody can count the much larger number of able men who have decided not to enter government departments during the years since the loyalty-security program began because, as is the way of able men, they preferred to be part of an enterprise which is built on trust.

Ninth. The Attorney General's list [29] took shape under President Truman as an auxiliary to the loyalty-security program:

> Activities and associations of an applicant or employee which *may be considered* in connection with the determination of disloyalty *may include one or more of the following:*
> f. Membership in, affiliation with or sympathetic association with any foreign or domestic organization, association, movement, group or combination of persons, designated by the Attorney General as totalitarian, fascist, communist, or subversive, or as having adopted a policy of advocating or approving the commission of acts of force or violence to deny other persons their rights under the Constitution . . . , or as seeking to alter the form of government of the United States by unconstitutional means.[30]

Although the Executive Order made this list only one piece of evidence against an official, it is not so treated in the administration of the loyalty program; instead it usually raises a *prima facie* case of his disloyalty. Moreover, the list was compiled only to guide this federal program, and yet it has been widely employed by states and cities and even by private organizations as proof of the disloyalty of teachers and employees. The radio industry has accepted it as a basis for canceling the contracts of its performers. The list has accordingly become a powerful weapon for injuring any group there named or any individual who belongs to such a group.

Nevertheless, the reliability of this list is seriously undermined by the fact that most of the organizations on it were singled out by government officials as they pleased without giving the organization any notice or any hearing. Thus there was no chance for the heads of a group to state objections, to offer evidence, or to examine the Attorney General's evidence and argue against its trustworthiness or value. An able federal judge declared [31] that "the list is a purely hearsay declaration by the Attorney General . . . which has no competency to prove the subversive character of the listed organizations. . . ."

On April 30, 1951, the Supreme Court severely condemned the procedure used for listing.[32] The Attorney General waited until May 5, 1953, before making a new regulation, which did call for a notice and hearing.[33] However, this did no good to the numerous organizations which had gone out of existence, several of them just temporary committees to collect signers on a petition filed in accordance with the First Amendment, for or against some pending measure. Their names constantly remain on the list to the damage of persons who belonged to them long ago, often without knowing they were on the list, for it is not placarded in post-offices or otherwise publicized. Furthermore, it is by no means clear that existing organizations get hearings when they ask for them. A court case in 1955 indicates that a hearing was sought in vain for six years by the Independent Socialist League (formerly the Workers Party), which, notwithstanding, is listed as subversive and worse.[34]

Since the Attorney General's list is my only point of personal contact with contemporary restrictions on freedom of speech, some firsthand information may not be out of place. Occasionally somebody calls me a member of the Citizens Committee to Free Earl Browder, which is on this list as Communist.[35] Hence I am said to be a bad security risk and next door to a Communist. Here is what happened. Around 1941, some people whose names I have forgotten wrote asking me to sign a petition to Attorney General Biddle for Browder's release from prison. I replied that I would not sign it because it said that Browder ought not to have been convicted. He had lied to his government on a passport application,[36] and I believe that a citizen ought to tell the truth to his government. However, I thought four years in prison a very severe punishment for one word, "No." Browder had already served over two years, which seemed to me tough enough. I never knew Browder, but I was reliably informed that he was not a violent revolutionary and that his release would help our relations with the Soviet Union, then our ally, which were in a ticklish state. So I sent these views in a personal letter to Francis Biddle, the Attorney General, whom I knew and who was charged by the Constitution with the duty of advising the President on legal matters. I do not know whether Mr. Biddle mentioned my request to Mr. Roosevelt; but I do know that the President under Article II, section 2, of the Constitution has "Power to grant Reprieves and Pardons for Offenses." And President Roosevelt did pardon Browder. If this be treason, make the most of it!

Tenth. Thus far I have dealt only with restrictions by the national government on freedom of thought and speech. Meanwhile, the legislatures of numerous states have been imitating Congress by passing all sorts of anti-Communist laws and setting up their own investigating committees. I have not the space to relate what has been going on under these state laws,[37] but it is an important question whether the time has not come for state legislatures to give up concerning themselves with subversive activities, and entrust the whole matter of the safety of the nation to the government of the nation.[38] Obviously, nobody has the slightest chance of overthrowing the government of Massachusetts by force and violence unless, at the same time, he succeeds in overthrowing the government of the whole United States. Although Senators and Representatives with large powers to cut down our fundamental freedoms are a serious cause for anxiety, the petty imitators who follow in their train are even worse. At all events, the investigating committees of the two Houses of Congress are controlled by a legislature which has to some extent a nation-wide point of view, and they are subject to scrutiny by a nation-wide press and public. State investigating committees create the risk of proliferation of local meddlers with speech and press who have less sensitivity to public opinion.

Eleventh. Combined national and state attacks on objectionable ideas have produced a mass of restrictions which reach into almost every human activity. Loyalty oaths have been required of candidates for election,[39] occupants of public offices,[40] teachers in public schools,[41] labor union officials bargaining under the Wagner Act,[42] students in state colleges and universities,[43] applicants for unemployment compensation,[44] and prospective jurors.[45] California requires such oaths from all institutions seeking exemption from taxes.[46] The unsuccessful attempt to impose a nation-wide loyalty oath on lawyers is fully discussed in Chapter VI. Congress has excluded from federal housing projects "a person who is a member of any organization designated as subversive by the Attorney General," [47] and thousands of occupants have been required to furnish certificates of non-membership. One court had difficulty in seeing how the efforts of subversives would be combatted "by compelling them to live in slums." [48] Pennsylvania denies poor relief to persons actively seeking to change the form of government by unconstitutional means, perhaps thereby making unhelped paupers see the benefits of the existing system.[49] California tried to prohibit the use of public schoolhouses by "subversive" groups, though opening them for other meetings.[50] William Carlos Williams, the poet, was prevented from taking a lectureship in the Library of Congress for lack of security clearance.[51] The Georgia Board of Education allows local school authorities to revoke, perhaps for life, the license of any teacher who supports the idea of non-segregated schools or agrees to teach in such a school.[52] In 1953, the legislatures of Alabama and Texas required all school textbooks to bear certificates that the authors were not Communists or ex-Communists and whether they had belonged to an organization on the Attorney General's list.[53] And any schoolboy in Louisiana who advocates the violent overthrow of the government will be expelled.[54]

As a striking example of what is going on, a doctor was suspended from practising medicine in New York because he had served six months in jail for failing, on advice of counsel, to produce papers to the House Un-American Activities Committee relating to the activities of his organization in rescuing and healing victims of the totalitarian government of Spain. So the New York state authorities reduced him to idleness for six months more. The highest court in New York and the Supreme Court of the United States were helpless to give him relief.[55] But Justice Douglas observed:

> So far as I know, nothing in a man's political beliefs disables him from setting broken bones or removing ruptured appendixes safely and efficiently. . . . When a doctor cannot save lives in America because he is opposed to Franco in Spain, it is time to call a halt and look critically at the neurosis which has possessed us.

Twelfth. After all this legislation, the government of the United States is like the daughters of the horseleech calling, "Give, give." The General Counsel of the Department of Defense calls it a deplorable gap in the security structure that workers in defense plants cannot now be discharged, without proof that they have done anything wrong, simply because they might commit espionage or sabotage in a crisis.[56] Inasmuch as nearly every factory has some conceivable relation to national defense, this proposal would give a few officials power to decide whether most of the skilled workmen in the United States would go on earning a living or starve.

The zeal of those in power to protect the nation from ideas they detest has imperiled more than the First Amendment. It has weakened great policies which underlie several other parts of the Constitution. Here again, this opening chapter leaves aside the necessity and legal validity of what has been done, and just tells how much our nation has been throwing away the blessings of liberty.

The strongest safeguard of human rights in the Constitution is the Habeas Corpus Clause.[57] It protects liberty of the person by usually enabling a judge to release an imprisoned man at once, unless he has been convicted or ought to be held to stand trial for a crime. Thus it prevents officials from jailing anybody because they think he might possibly commit a crime some day. According to Justice Robert Jackson,[58] "Imprisonment to protect society from predicted but unconsummated offenses is unprecedented in this country and fraught with danger of excesses and injustice." The Constitution specifies only two emergencies which will justify the suspension of habeas corpus—"Rebellion or Invasion." The McCarran Act of 1950 by-passes this clause. It produces the effect of suspending habeas corpus by allowing American citizens who have committed no crime to be shut up in a concentration camp in any war, even if it be a localized conflict thousands of miles from our shores without the slightest danger of an "Invasion." [59]

The President and the Attorney General can imprison any person "as to whom there is reasonable ground to believe that [he] probably will engage in acts of espionage or sabotage" or will conspire with others for that purpose. Other officials can review this decision, but there is very little likelihood that any court can reverse it.[60] In 1942 civil and military officials tore scores of thousands of American citizens of Japanese descent from their homes because, so the officials asserted, they might commit sabotage and spying. Yet "not one person of Japanese ancestry was accused or convicted of sabotage after Pearl Harbor while they were still free." [61] Here is a sample of official reasoning:

> The very fact that no sabotage has taken place to date is a disturbing and confirming indication that such action will be taken.[62]

Officials whose minds work like that will easily find a "reasonable ground to believe" that anybody whose views they happen to dislike is a potential spy or saboteur.

Bills of attainder in both Congress and the states were prohibited because our ancestors hated legislative condemnations without any determination of guilt by judges. Although it is uncertain how far penalizing specified persons otherwise than by prison and fines is unconstitutional,[63] the policy against bills of attainder was ignored when Congress in 1954 outlawed the Communist Party of America.[64] Furthermore, loyalty oaths force a man to condemn himself to lose his job without ever being tried by a court. We are coming very close to the oaths exacted from possible Confederate sympathizers after the Civil War, which were held to be bills of attainder.[65]

Although the *ex post facto* clauses render only retroactive criminal punishments unconstitutional, the ideal they express is abandoned when a law makes personal conduct before it was passed cause consequences like deportation after long residence [66] or expulsion from one's chosen profession, which most men would regard as far worse than considerable fines or substantial terms in jail.

The Fourth Amendment against unreasonable searches and seizures does not apply to wire-tapping, under a five to four decision, but Holmes in dissenting called it a "dirty business" and thought it "a less evil that some criminals should escape than that the government should play an ignoble part." [67] The ideal of the Amendment is that a man's house is his castle. A telephone is as much a part of his home nowadays as his desk. When a man cannot ring up his family and friends without having officials overhear all he says, the invasion of his home is like policemen in his dining-room without a search warrant. It is just as poisonous to his life as if his personal letters were opened and read by the police. Indeed, Congress has recognized all this by enacting that "No person" shall without the sender's consent intercept any communication and divulge the contents to "any person"; [68] and "person" at either end of this illegal disclosure includes federal policemen.[69] Yet, in spite of the unlawfulness of wire-tapping, it is done all the time, notably in cases against radicals. In one case, a lawyer's telephone conversations with his client while she was awaiting trial were tapped by the F.B.I. with the Attorney General's approval,[70] thus undermining the constitutional right "to have the Assistance of Counsel." No doubt, it would be harder for the F.B.I. to catch and convict offenders if it undertook to obey the law. Here, as often, "Liberty brings with it many advantages, but it certainly does not tend to enable men in office to lead an easy life. . . ."[71]

In the Fifth Amendment, which Chapter VII will discuss in other connections, we are departing from the tradition that no person shall "be twice put in jeopardy" for the same offense. Technically, of course, the clause applies only to criminal prosecutions. Still, the human values are just as great when any other serious penalty is involved. You get a happier civilization if a man who has been forced to go through a gruelling legal proceeding in order to keep his job can say, after being acquitted of wrongdoing, "That's over," and then go back to untroubled work. Serenity is impossible if he knows that he may have to rebut the same charges and go through all the agony again, perhaps even many times. Yet that is the situation under the loyalty program. Nobody is ever really cleared.[72] In a recent case reported to the Hennings committee,[73] a naturalized Austrian was dismissed by the State Department for close association with his wife, although he had been cleared on substantially the same charges the year before. This man had been officially cited for standing up under Nazi tortures, from which he escaped through barbed wire. There is no lasting escape through red tape.

Look next at the Eighth Amendment. "Excessive bail shall not be required," but no bail at all can be obtained by a suspected alien if a government official orders him locked up for a long time until he boards the boat for Europe.[74] For instance John Zydok, a Pole of fifty-six, had been in this country since he was seventeen.

His wife and children were American citizens. During the Second World War, he had two sons in the armed forces, gave his blood seven times to the Red Cross, and as waiter in a restaurant, sold the eaters $50,000 in war-bonds. In 1949, he was charged as deportable for joining the Communist Party and holding a minor office. Then the immigration officials put Zydok in jail. The judge found that he was "not likely to engage in any subversive activities" if at large. Meanwhile, several top-string Communists, convicted under the Smith Act, were out on bail during their appeal.[75] Yet the uncontrolled discretion of the Attorney General kept Zydok in prison. Even the Supreme Court of the United States could not let him be at home with his family until he was put on trial and actually decided to be deportable.[76]

By the same Amendment, "cruel and unusual punishments" shall not be inflicted. Being torn like Zydok from wife and children who are American citizens and shipped to a country known only as a youngster, is no longer "unusual" but it is "cruel." It may be law, as judges say, that deportation is not punishment but a rearrangement of the population, yet cruelty is a fact. What a queer distinction! The Bill of Rights prevents the government from being cruel to criminals; it can be as cruel as it pleases to men who are not criminals.

Our cruelty is not confined to aliens. We have been creating a new kind of second-class citizens out of naturalized Americans. More and more they are denaturalized and then deported. The final step was to strip citizenship from native-born Americans. In 1954 Congress turned everybody convicted under the Smith Act into a Man without a Country.[77]

Finally, where the radical opinions of citizens and their affiliations are concerned, we are abandoning the American ideals of a fair trial, proclaimed by the Sixth Amendment. Of course, it begins "In all criminal prosecutions," and hence its provisions are not constitutionally applicable to Congressional investigations or the loyalty program. Nevertheless, a loyalty board can deprive a public employee of his livelihood, and a Congressional committee frequently takes away a man's good name and perhaps his job too. These consequences may be worse than a fine or a jail sentence. Conclusions which are so damaging to a citizen ought to be reached with the utmost care to determine the truth.

Under the Tudors and Stuarts criminal trials were often conducted without opportunities for a fair defense.[78] Gradually proper safeguards were worked out, and these are embodied in the Sixth Amendment. They are essentials of decent procedure in any inquiry which may result in punishment. Consequently, even though this Amendment is not binding in a departmental or legislative inquiry, it is wise that the same essentials should be substantially observed in order to prevent unfairness and grievous mistakes.

Two essential principles in the Sixth Amendment are especially desirable in departmental or Congressional inquiries into a man's loyalty.[79] First, he ought "to be informed of the nature . . . of the accusation." Chapter VII of this book shows the intensity with which our ancestors objected to answering roving questions. Second, it is of the highest importance that the suspected man should "be confronted with the witnesses against him." Perhaps the most besetting sin in non-judicial trials is for the deciding officials to make use of information which is not communicated to the person whom they have power to condemn. For instance, in the Dreyfus case the army officers on the court-martial read secret army papers which were kept back from Dreyfus.

One important benefit from confronting the suspect with his accusers is the opportunity to cross-examine them and rigorously test any dubious statement.[80] As old Sir Matthew Hale says, it "beats and boults out the truth much better." Add to that the old-fashioned value of putting people face to face out in the open.[81] Accusers who secretly confer in private with an official or two and a couple of clerks may, as in Hale's time, "oftentimes deliver that which they will be ashamed to testify publicly." An honest witness may feel quite differently when he has to repeat his story looking at the man whom he will harm greatly by distorting or mistaking the facts. He can now understand what sort of human being that man is. As for the false witness, the tribunal can learn ever so much more by looking at him than by reading an F.B.I. abstract of his story. The pathological liar and the personal enemy can no longer hide behind a piece of paper.

No doubt, police are helped by concealment of the names of the men who supply evidence used by Congressional committees and loyalty boards. Still, the question is whether official secrecy excuses unjust condemnations. No such excuse for hiding spies and tale-tellers will be listened to by a judge in a criminal prosecution. Either the informant must take the stand and be cross-examined, or what he said cannot be used in the trial at all. Is an inquiry which may take away a man's lifetime job or his good name really different?

President Eisenhower said in November 1953 at Washington:

> I was raised in a little town of which most of you have never heard. But in the West it's a famous place. It's called Abilene, Kansas. We had as our Marshal for a long time a man named Wild Bill Hickok. . . .
>
> Now that town had a code, and I was raised as a boy to prize that code. It was: Meet anyone face to face with whom you disagree. You could not sneak up on him from behind, do any damage to him without suffering the penalty of an outraged citizenry. If you met him face to face and took the same risk he did, you could get away with almost anything, as long as the bullet was in the front.
>
> In this country if someone dislikes you or accuses you, he must come up in front. He cannot hide behind the shadows, he cannot assassinate you or your character from behind without suffering the penalties an outraged citizenry will inflict.[82]

These words, like the "book-burners" speech at Dartmouth [83] are among the noblest expressions of liberty in our time.

Put these words beside what Mr. Eisenhower's Attorney General told the United States Supreme Court:

> A large area of vital government intelligence depends on under-cover agents, paid informers, and casual informers who must be guaranteed anonymity. Thus, evidence which would be rejected under established legal doctrine in a criminal proceeding could well be the compelling reason for dismissal of an employee on loyalty grounds. . . .
>
> Professional undercover agents of continuing utility not in one but in many cases and situations, casual informants in individual cases who would withhold information if confronted by the exigencies of appearing as witnesses in trials on the merits, highly confidential sources of information consisting of confidential government and non-government files, information obtained under a

pledge of confidence—all these vital sources of information, and others, might well dry up, to the detriment of the basic security of the country, if petitioner's contention as to his overriding rights of confrontation and cross-examination were to be honored.[84]

Marshal Bill Hickok is not Attorney General. Mr. Eisenhower's Cabinet rates the Abilene code at zero. Still, it is good to have a President who does not preach what his subordinates practise.

This book will not take up all the problems I have been listing. My *Free Speech in the United States* tried to make a systematic presentation of the crises and issues of liberty of speech and press until 1941, but I am not now bringing that book down to date. Instead, I have gathered together a number of spoken and written discussions [85] of some significant problems raised by the Bill of Rights, mostly since 1945, and by plans to strengthen liberty in all countries. I have thoroughly remolded everything. This book gives my reflections at the close of 1955. Some of its statements may become inaccurate before it is published, because the Supreme Court will have decided several important pending cases. Still, an author has to stop sometime.

Is it right to conclude that the inroads on freedom described in this introductory chapter and in the rest of my book ought to be extrapolated like a geometrical curve into the indefinite future? If so, I can predict more indirect and subtle suppressions. Hardly anybody will be exempted from loyalty investigations, because most occupations have government connections or somehow affect public safety. Teachers in endowed schools and universities will be kept in line by threats to take away tax exemptions and government research grants, essential to institutional solvency. Science will aid snooping. Wire-tapping will be supplemented by some invention enabling informers to overhear whatever a man says on the street or in his home. A new kind of X-ray will let postal officials read letters without bothering to steam them open. Now that the Chief Justice of the United States has to be passed by the Federal Bureau of Investigation, why take any chances on the President who appoints judges? The next logical step is for the loyalty of every candidate to be thoroughly investigated and certified by a board of officials before voting starts in the Republican and Democratic conventions.

Still, politics is not mathematics. Pronounced trends suddenly reverse themselves, as in the Presidential elections of 1801, 1860, and 1932. So with civil liberties.

My great confidence in the American people, in their love of liberty and their good sense, makes me believe that their fit of tantrums about disloyalty among our fellow-citizens will end long before 1970. Even though relations with the Communist countries continue strained, as seems probable, we may appreciate the advantages of a united nation and stop increasing suspicion of each other. And, in government as in any sensibly run business, we may learn to trust the judgment of the men who select officials and the wisdom of the superiors who are in close contact with the work of subordinates day in and day out. Once more we shall be content to meet bad talk, not with force but with plenty of good talk.

The blessings of liberty, though weakened, are ours if we want them, to hold and make strong. The flag still flies, and the city is not yet fallen.

II Why I Like America

> I will build a motor car for the great multitude.
> It will be large enough for the family but small
> enough for the individual to run and care for. It
> will be constructed of the best materials, by the
> best men to be hired, after the simplest designs that
> modern engineering can devise. But it will be so low
> in price that no man making a good salary will be
> unable to own one—and enjoy with his family the
> blessing of hours of pleasure in God's great open
> spaces.——HENRY FORD, about 1907 *

For many reasons I am happy to be an American though I had
nothing whatever to do with being born in Providence, Rhode
Island. This is no mood of complacent satisfaction. Each of my
hopes is matched by fears. Whether the nation changes for better
or worse will depend on the readers of this book and its writer
and people like us. What kind of country do we want to serve in
the years ahead?

First, I like America because of the land itself. Although American scenes have not brought me quite so much happiness as those
of Europe, here I have much to remember and long to see again.
I recall the Parapets of Mount Madison in late afternoon, Northwest
days off the Maine coast, the Connecticut Valley anywhere above
Holyoke, the Hudson River from the Cloisters, Aiken pines, Point
Lobos in the swirling fog, the silence of the Grand Canyon, the
unbroken poppy-fields which stretched in my boyhood from Pasadena to the foothills of the Sierra Madre. Aside from such rewards
of long journeys, beauty lies within reach of an afternoon or a
weekend from most of our crowded cities. On a more utilitarian
level, the fullness and variety of our natural resources bring the

* Roger Burlingame, *Henry Ford* (New York: Alfred A. Knopf, Inc., 1955),
p. 62.

exhilaration felt in Archibald MacLeish's account of the Lewis and
Clark expedition:

> Many men will have living on these lands.
> There is wealth in the earth for them all and the wood standing
> And wild birds on the water where they sleep.
> There is stone in the hills for the towns of a great people. . . .[1]

We can never be thankful enough that Fate brought our ancestors
to these shores.

Yet all this can easily go the way of the buffalo and the passenger
pigeon. The poppy-fields north of Pasadena have vanished and today I can barely see the Sierra Madre in the smog. We have suddenly been aroused to the evils of redwood stumps and topsoil
forever lost. Only vision and hard work will keep the riches we
were given for the asking.

Nor can we separate the land from what we have put on the land.
Buildings and roads can be as satisfying as mountains. Witness the
University of Virginia and U.S. 202. Or they can be as meaning-
less as the imperial frigidity of Constitution Avenue in Washington,
as ugly as the factory on the Sheepscot River below Wiscasset.
And it is for us to decide whether our main highways shall multiply
Walter Pritchard Eaton's description of the Mohawk Trail:

> Most of its length it is a swiftly moving steel and rubber river be-
> tween banks of "hot-dog" kennels, fried clam stands, filling stations,
> and other odoriferous and ugly reminders of this progressive age.[2]

I refuse to believe that progress is incompatible with beauty. The
great advance in housing for those of moderate means, the New
York sky-line, the San Francisco bridges, the Trailridge Road in
Colorado, the hillside drive above Bar Harbor, all show what can be
done. Surprisingly little money is sometimes enough to save a
delightful landscape or building, but it has to be saved now or never.

Second, our heritage from the men of the past. Our settlers were
neither conquistadores nor convicts. They were men and women
with a deep sense of the purposefulness of life. We were especially
fortunate in having the founders of the United States free from
faults which might later infect our ideals. The nation was not based

on Bismarck's "blood and iron" like Germany, or like Italy on the craftiness of Cavour. Our first leader willingly laid down his military command and later his power as President. We disagree but we do not hate. The adherents of Hamilton admire Jefferson, the adherents of Jefferson recognize Hamilton's greatness. The South honors Lincoln, the North honors Lee. We have been spared the calamity of the French where the heroes of half the nation are monsters of depravity to the other half.

At one time our national heroes seemed likely to become plaster saints, but the lights and shades with which they have been painted lately make them more impressive than before. There is a risk that our pride in Americans of the past may make us ignore the benefits brought us by later-comers from abroad, always excepting of course the group which included our own ancestors. The immigrants outside that group are regarded as "foreigners" whose descendants had better cut themselves loose from their European heritage as fast as possible.

Third, the pooling of peoples for freedom and friendliness. Class distinctions no longer seem permanent as they did before the Depression. When I visited the South after an absence of thirty years, I felt a marked decline in racial antagonism. This seems partly caused by the higher economic level on which both races are living. When there is money to go around, people get along better with each other. And the equally shared sacrifices during the Second World War made us increasingly conscious of the injustice of withholding other equalities.

Yet disquieting factors persist. The situation of the Negroes continues to be our biggest single domestic problem. I anticipate that desegregation will spread southward from state to state until defiance of the Supreme Court is confined to a few isolated areas, where eventually the white people will get weary of banging their heads against a stone wall. We shall be lucky if those who rejoice in resisting the inevitable do so peacefully. Again, general condemnations of religious intolerance are likely to be futile unless the specific causes of intolerance are frankly and wisely faced. Yet any attempt to examine a definite issue is likely to produce a free-for-all fight participated in by many who show very little wisdom.

Fourth, Americans have a healthy attitude toward the family. Perhaps I like our prevailing ideals of marriage and parenthood just because I was brought up among them, but I should hate to have to adjust myself somehow to polygamy or the complete legal subjection of women. I am glad my wife is not to be burned alive on my funeral pyre if I should die first, and it is pleasant to be able to take a walk without seeing the bodies of exposed female infants as in China or the Athens of Pericles. Coming closer to our own civilization, I prefer our norm of a married couple who "live happily ever after," despite its occasional absurdities, to the Parisian norm of the Eternal Triangle. I should not want marriages arranged by the parents as in France. The demands of the frontier for youthful independence and enterprise freed us centuries ago from the traditional subordination of children to parents which lasted in England until after 1850. It is good that Thanksgiving, our most characteristic festival, symbolizes the essential unity of the procession of the generations.

We have a sound norm, but we deal stupidly with departures from this norm. When the varied relationships between men and women are sought to be explored sincerely and thoughtfully in a radio program or a motion-picture produced in the United States all sorts of obstacles are raised. Yet at the same time, an actual scandal, with no lessons except the general messiness of immorality, is recounted at length on the front pages of newspapers. Broken homes are bound to occur, but they are handled by divorce laws which are a conglomerate of inconsistencies and hypocrisies. We deliberately prolong and intensify the unhappiness of unhappy marriages and fool ourselves into the belief that this will make happy marriages more frequent.

Fifth, opportunities for productive enterprise at all the essential stages. In the past the situation was excellent for inventors and men who wanted to start new businesses, but too many people were just cogs in the industrial machine. During my lifetime I have seen purely manual labor almost disappear with the advent of new devices. There is a much greater opportunity than formerly for all who work to feel themselves part of a creative process and contributing to a satisfying product. Also the constant warfare between employers and unions has to a considerable extent been transformed into something approaching an orderly adjustment of disputes.

These improvements, however, are overcast by the curse of bigness—big corporations, big unions, big government agencies, each of them inclined to make its own decisions for its own benefit. The old-fashioned, enterprising, hard-working citizen feels lost in this play of enormous economic forces, in the same way that his vote seems insignificant in the great electorate of today. He just does not count. Frankly, I do not see the way out. The Socialists tell us that these gigantic groups are the last step to an all-absorbing state. That would not relieve us from the curse of bigness. We should merely get something still bigger.

Sixth, we now have abundant leisure with abundant opportunities for its fruitful use. Leisure until very recently was the privilege of only the favored few, but in the United States today leisure belongs to everybody. The normal forty-hour week in factories, stores, and offices is less than a quarter of the whole week of 168 hours. In homes and on farms, labor-saving devices and machinery have similarly released many hours of free time. All this would have brought little enjoyment to our ancestors. Only a few recreations were open to them, especially in cities. Rich men could drive fast horses and educated men could read, but the working man whose schooling had been cut short was largely limited to the poolroom and the saloon. In 1870, drunkenness and street-fighting were so prevalent in Boston that there were more crimes in proportion to the population than now. What else was there to do in a man's spare time? He had no access to the wide range of enjoyment which has since been opened by inventiveness and organization and by the knowledge of literature and art made possible through the great increase of enrollment in high schools.

Yet even now, the existence of leisure carries no guarantee that it will be used fruitfully. The knowledge how to employ it must come in part from formal education. On this account the current demand for vocational training at the expense of the humanities seems to me particularly calamitous. We are determined to give more training for work at the very time when work is a smaller part of a man's life than ever before.

Seventh, freedom for the life of the mind and the spirit. The hope of Roger Williams for "full liberty in religious concernments" has been realized all over the United States, as a later chapter will tell. Equally precious are freedom of speech, press, and assembly, which are also assured by the First Amendment. These are peculiarly sensitive to insidious attacks, and freedom is in large measure indivisible. When liberty of speech was lost in Nazi Germany, liberty of the person soon became gravely impaired. So we ought to cling resolutely to the primary freedoms of the mind.

Nevertheless, liberties of speech, press, and assembly which were universally cherished by Americans in my boyhood have been eroded during the past forty years by law after law, and only scattered protests have been heard. Much of the rest of this book will show how the whittling away of these liberties has increased notably during the last decade. Just as truly now as in Jefferson's day: "Eternal vigilance is the price of liberty."

Eighth, our courageous response to crises. We rose to the emergency of Fort Sumter and Pearl Harbor. We were much more baffled by the Depression of 1929, but when we had been shown by Mr. Roosevelt what we might do to end it, we did with determination whatever we were asked to do.

There is more doubt of the wisdom of some of our responses and of our ability to work out solutions for ourselves. Thus we were completely at a loss from 1929 until 1933. Sometimes we have a predilection for over-simplified solutions and cling to them with prolonged obstinacy as in the case of Prohibition. To use good old New England words, we have more guts than gumption.

Ninth, I am proud of the honorable part which America has, on the whole, played in the world. Here again our nation has been peculiarly fortunate. Much of our expansion has been accomplished without attacking our neighbors, a fate denied to most nations. There were regrettable phases of our history, such as breaches of faith with the Indians, but these are so far in the past that they have left no running sores to bother us now. We have no Alsace-Lorraines. We have not acted the bully.

The difficulty now is, of course, that we can no longer pursue a policy of benevolent isolation, whether we want to or not. The only question is whether we shall belong to a struggling mob or a town meeting. The fact that our people and our Congress have never before been forced to think so much about other national governments makes it hard for us to participate patiently in a world organization. We shall have to learn as we go along.

Tenth, and last, the satisfying nature of the governmental framework. I like the separation of national and regional problems by the device of federalism; the division of governmental powers among three distinct groups of men; and the safeguards of liberty in the Bill of Rights.

The trouble is that we are like a boy who has outgrown his clothes, and nobody lets them out. The main features of our government seem to me as sound as ever; but, because of new conditions, details have gone wrong at several points. This leads to plenty of grumbling, but there is very little systematic effort to discover and adopt suitable remedies for the maladjustments. I am especially troubled by the lack of popular confidence in the agencies of government which are closest to the people, for example, Congress and city governments. A French writer says that a country is in danger when the voters hate and despise the very men for whom they vote. Sighs of relief go up whenever Congress adjourns, and editorials in thoughtful newspapers denouncing municipal inefficiency and corruption often sound uncomfortably like what Hitler used to say against democracy.

Beard wrote of Congress in his stimulating little book, *The Republic*:

> The framers of the Constitution expected . . . that Congress should be the dominant branch of the Federal Government. They put it first in order in the Constitution. . . . They gave it the power of the purse and the power of the sword—the two mighty engines of government.[3]

If the President rather than Congress occupies the dominant place today, may not Congress itself be partly to blame? I do not mind that Congress should differ from the President. God forbid that any single man should be thought entitled to have everything his own way in these United States. The historic function of the legislature since the days of the Stuart kings is to make the popular will operate as a check on the power of the Executive. What disturbs me is that in these clashes the President seems to be closer than Congress to what the people want. The fault is not mainly, I believe, with the calibre of the men who get elected. I know from long experience the ability and devotion of many men in both Houses. But their ability is not canalized so as to work responsibly and effectively.

Nobody can read a dozen pages of the *Congressional Record* straight through without feeling either ridicule or shame. I have sometimes thought of rewriting a day of the debates in the Constitutional Convention of 1787 as if they took place in the United States Senate in 1955. Three times in the same morning, delegates at Philadelphia would stop all business as follows: [4]

> MR. X. Mr. President, I suggest the absence of a quorum.
> THE PRESIDENT. The clerk will call the roll.
> The clerk proceeded to call the roll [showing far more than a quorum, as was obvious to anybody with eyes].
> MR. X. Mr. President, I ask unanimous consent that the order for the quorum call be rescinded.
> THE PRESIDENT. Without objection, it is so ordered.

The discussion of the conflict between large and small states would be interrupted by the request for leave to print a rabble-rousing speech of Sam Adams to the Boston wharf rats on the anniversary of the Boston Tea Party. Then some member from New Hampshire would talk for an hour on the bravery of the New Hampshire soldiers at the Battle of Bennington, winding up with a glowing eulogy of Molly Stark.

The most striking example of our distrust of democracy is the City of Washington. Taxation without representation and government without the consent of the governed prevail within sight of the Capitol. This was not always so. Until 1871 Washingtonians chose their own mayor and council, who (it is said) rivaled the Tweed Ring in New York. After a few years of appointed and elected officials combined, Congress established the present system in 1878. For over three-quarters of a century Washington has been under a triumvirate about as absolute as Caesar, Pompey, and Crassus. Congress did not even try to make Washington safe for democracy. Nor does it appear that the inhabitants, then or subsequently, cared very much about their loss.

How many other American cities, I wonder, would willingly abandon self-government if in return they could get rid of padded payrolls, endlessly dug-up streets, and a $65 tax rate?

While discussing each of my first nine reasons for liking America, I have in the end expressed confidence that my hopes will prevail over my fears. I feel considerably more anxiety about the actual operation of our national, state, and local governments. Although I am by no means discouraged, this anxiety leads me to reflect at greater length on our ideals of government than on the other matters with which this chapter deals.

Woodrow Wilson described our political institutions and our hopes for their future by the single word "democracy." Although some influential Americans have recently insisted that our country is a republic and not a democracy,[5] it can be both. No doubt, "democracy" is one of the words which the Soviet bloc has tried to take away from us and transform into something else. All the more reason why we should hold on to it and understand better what makes it precious to us. The best way to protect democracy against insidious onslaughts is to give this ideal solid substance to which our minds can firmly attach themselves. That will put us on guard when anybody is persuading us to give some of it away.

What is this democracy which most Americans have long wanted to preserve and strengthen? Everybody knows that it comes from two Greek words meaning "people" and "rule" or "govern," but this is just a start. Who are the people and how are they to govern?

Take a test case: Is Great Britain a democracy, although it is surely not a republic? Many American students of politics and history would answer "Yes," at least if they do not go back of the Reform Bills of the Nineteenth Century. Yet much depends on what definition of "democracy" is chosen. Turn to the highest authority in England, the Oxford Dictionary in many volumes. Here the principal definition of "democracy" begins: "Government by the people; that form of government in which the sovereign power resides in the people as a whole, and is exercised either directly by them (as in the small republics of antiquity) or by officers elected by them." So far, this may include England, but look at the next sentence: "In modern use often more vaguely denoting a social state in which all have equal rights, without hereditary or arbitrary differences of rank or privilege." Surely this does not apply to a nation with a royal family, hereditary nobles and baronets, and a House of Lords. The second definition in the same dictionary raises even more perplexities: "A state or community in which the government is vested in the people as a whole." Was there ever such a government, where even babes in arms were carried to the polls? More satisfactory is the Funeral Oration of Pericles: "We are called a democracy, for the administration is in the hands of the many and not of the few." And yet a century later we find Aristotle using "democracy" to describe mob rule in contradiction to "commonwealth." According to him, the United States is a commonwealth, as Massachusetts, Pennsylvania, Virginia, and Kentucky call themselves. A definition of "democracy" with a thrill to it is Mazzini's: "Progress of all through all, under the leading of the best and wisest." Excellent though rare. Contrast Lord Byron's diary, "What is democracy?—an aristocracy of blackguards."

All this brings about my chief conclusion. Democracy is not a single thing like oxygen. There are several kinds of democracies just as there are several kinds of beauty. Possibly there is a least common denominator which inheres in all the different kinds, but it is by no means easy to frame a definition which will include them all.

Nevertheless, as a convenient starting-point, political democracy will be loosely defined as any system of government in which a considerable portion of the population exercises a substantial control. Then to bring out the wide range of such systems and the limits at which a government ceases to be a democracy, I shall consider in detail three questions: Control by whom? Control over what? Control for what?

Who exercises control? We think of democracy as government by the people, but who are the people? If they be the whole population of the territorial unit, then it is plain that a good many of

them do not do any governing. A very large number of citizens
cannot vote, namely, persons under twenty-one. Of course, some of
them do not know how to talk, but the bright boys of sixteen know
more than most of us ever will again. Even if the voting age is
reduced to eighteen, as is now proposed, the younger teen-agers
will still be disfranchised. They may fairly argue that they are
affected by the expenditure of a big fraction of the public revenue
on schools and are subjected to stricter regulations than the rest of
us. At any rate, youths will become adults if they go on living,
but women will never be anything else than women. Must we say
that democracy did not exist in the United States until 1920 except
in Wyoming and a few other western regions which opened voting
booths to pioneering wives? Or that Switzerland is not a democracy
today? And if we can surmount these obstacles by the dubious
argument that voting men represent their families, we still have to
decide whether democracy is possible when males are barred by
drastic property qualifications like those at the time of the Constitution or by failure to pay poll taxes or pass literacy tests.

Now comes another point. No official who serves is the choice of
the entire electorate. A substantial minority of those who voted
wanted somebody else. And many citizens stayed away from the
polls. For example, it would be very unusual for the winning candidate in a Presidential election to receive sixty per cent of the popular vote or for the votes cast to run much over sixty per cent of
the electorate. It is convenient and, I believe, desirable to say that
government by the President thus elected is government by the
people, but the bare fact is that he was named by only about a third
of the qualified voters and by a much smaller fraction of the whole
population of the United States. No doubt, those who fail to register a choice have themselves to blame, but the smallness of the vote
often deprives an election of some of the impressiveness we like to
attach to it. This is especially true of votes on the ratification of
amendments to a state constitution, which sometimes attract much
less attention than contests over minor offices and yet are treated as
the highest manifestation of the will of the people of the state.

Finally, we ought never to forget that some of the citizens who
are concerned with the acts of a government cannot possibly vote
with reference to such acts. Edmund Burke described constitutional

government as "a partnership between those who are living, those who are dead and those who are to be born." [6]

Thus the phrase "the people" can be used to describe at least five different groups of persons in a political community: (1) the whole body of inhabitants past, present, and future; (2) the entire population at the time of speaking; (3) the electorate; (4) those who actually vote at a given election; (5) the victors at that election. Theoretical defenders of democracy are tempted to obscure the important distinctions between these groups. The idea of all the men, women, and children in a nation or state or city glows in our imaginations and rightly so, especially when it embraces the dead who made possible so much of our happiness, and the unborn generations for whom we plan and sacrifice. But there is nothing sacred about the individuals who happened to be on the winning side at the last election. Yet by sliding the word "people" hither and thither, writers and orators contrive to surround the momentary majority with a bright halo.

Talk about "the will of the people" makes eloquent perorations, but persons subject to the actual strains of campaigning and being governed are bound to disbelieve it. The voter who sees his honest candidate for mayor defeated by a crook knows very well that he and his associates are not identical with the majority. Large taxpayers are constantly indignant about the burdens imposed on them by citizens who are taxed little or nothing.

In truth, the relation between the momentary majority and the whole population is a central problem of democracy. The two are not the same and yet they ought to be closely linked. The manner in which the connecting cord is woven determines the strength of self-government in that nation. The whole system really rests on the willingness of the losers to accept the decision against them and carry it out loyally. When this willingness breaks down, serious trouble is likely, as during National Prohibition. It is true that stable governments could hardly exist if men felt that their consciences entitled them to disobey whatever laws they disliked, and yet there is a limit to what the majority can safely try to do in coercing opponents. The outstanding example of this is the repeated failure of religious persecutions. One of the chief purposes of the Bill of Rights is to prevent the momentary majority from undertaking legal action which diverges widely from the deep-seated desires of the rest of the population.

The foregoing discussion of the question: Who controls? leads me to three further reflections. In the first place, since the electorate is always smaller than the whole body of persons affected by government, it follows that voters, like legislators, are representatives. They do not act merely for themselves, but for others—the living who cannot or do not vote, the dead, the unborn. The voter, like the legislator and the officeholder, is a trustee for the public. Like them, he has duties as well as rights, and is bound by grave responsibilities—not just out to get what he can like the sinecurists of old.

Secondly, democracy is consistent with varying extensions of the franchise. The whole body of citizens never governs, and those who do may be more or fewer without the government's ceasing to be democratic. There are limits, however. Democracy becomes doubtful when the right to hold office or to vote is based on rank or inheritance, although we still have to allow for the House of Lords and remember that slavery was extensive in two of the greatest of democracies—ancient Athens and the United States of America until 1865. Democracy also becomes questionable when the franchise is based on property beyond what almost every citizen can probably acquire by moderate diligence. Furthermore, although control is never actually exercised by everybody, the opportunity to share in control must be open at least to all or nearly all heads of families, even if women be disfranchised. So democracy is evidently a single name for several types of popular government.

It may also be regarded as a term of degree like "hot." A government is said to become more democratic as the right to vote and hold office is widened. Are we bound to conclude that because democracy is good, the more the better? That line of reasoning is not valid for some other things like mince pie or small babies. For example, it is arguable that a citizen must prove his fitness to vote by his ability to save two dollars a year for a poll tax to help support his community or by learning to read and write. However, fitness is only part of the story. The poor and the uneducated may need the ballot to protect themselves from exploitation. Another argument for a wide franchise at some sacrifice in fitness is that no community can afford to let a considerable part of its working strength nourish resentment at being permanently deprived of privileges.

In short, the exact point at which the franchise should stop is a question for sound judgment. Still, the American experience throws a heavy burden of proof on those who urge disqualifying citizens for any reasons except immaturity, mental disease, or conviction for a really serious crime.

My last point about the franchise is its immense educational value. John Stuart Mill emphasized this as the great argument for representative government. Except for jury service, voting is the only opportunity most men have for directly engaging in the business of governing. Furthermore, the prolonged discussion before elections on the part of most voters is a strong mental stimulus. On the other hand, deprivation of the ballot encourages intellectual sluggishness and the feeling that one is not really part of the community. Even if we could obtain more efficient government by diminishing the electorate, we might very well refuse to stop the teaching which the ballot gives.

Look, for example at the effects of women suffrage. Its supporters who prophesied that skirts at the polls would bring housecleaning into politics and peace for the world were as sadly wrong as the anti-suffragists who predicted the disintegration of the home if women left it on election-day. Nobody foresaw that the greatest visible gain from the Nineteenth Amendment would be the League of Women Voters, which does a job of public education men were not bright enough to plan and too busy with their own affairs to carry out.

Our second main question is: Over what do the people exercise control? Of course, they have considerable influence through refusing to re-elect officials and through public opinion, but I am asking now about actual power. How far do they govern directly in a democracy? Here again there are plainly many different types of democracies. The share taken by the electorate in the management of the state may vary widely.

At one extreme lies ancient Athens where the citizens did most of the business of government themselves. The whole body of qualified voters could throng to the market-place for the purpose of enacting laws. They administered justice as large juries without any judges. They did delegate executive power, but only for brief periods running as short as a day. With this rapid rotation and the choice of many officers by lot, any citizen might look forward to being an official. So we can almost say that the executive functions were also in the hands of the electorate. At all events, the Athenian voters made important decisions of military policy which, in this country, would be made by the President with the advice of the Joint Chiefs of Staff. Thus Alcibiades brought about the disastrous expedition to Sicily by a popular referendum. Then, just as it was about to start under his command, the voters recalled Alcibiades and put in another general to take its great fleet to ruin.

In Rome there was somewhat more stability. The executive power was delegated to consuls and judicial power was exercised by judges, sometimes with small juries of knights. Still, such powers were kept in close check by annual elections and by the queer Roman custom of giving almost every job to two or more persons, from consuls down. Moreover, great masses of Roman citizens enacted statutes. This shifting system conquered the world, but probably because a permanent balance-wheel was supplied by the Senate, composed of past officials who sat for life.

When Roman citizenship was extended over the whole of Italy, the system broke down. Everybody realized that things were wrong, yet nobody did anything about it in the way of permanent, unselfish remedies. Tiberius Gracchus was a lone exception, and he was soon put to death for his unusual inventiveness. Cicero had the most capacity to devise a solution, but he was too timid and he never commented on the Gracchi except to denounce them. All he could suggest was to go back to the good old days. There is no way back out of political crises, only forward. So long as the population of all Italy was entitled to make or reject laws by traveling hundreds of miles to gather in a city square too small to hold more than a fraction of them, any decision was bound to depend on accident and manipulation. The only solution which would have preserved the Roman Republic was representative government. This had been used in the Achaean League. Yet the Romans did not even consider it. The truth is that political inventiveness is a very rare quality. This fact entitles the Philadelphia Convention of 1787 to great praise.

Not until democracy was supplemented by representative government, was it able to succeed over large areas. The Dominican Order thought up this device when its scattered monasteries sent delegates to its councils. Afterwards, in the later Middle Ages, many European countries had assemblies of estates, but only the English Parliament kept power into modern times. In the rest of Europe powerful nobles were the chief rivals of the monarch, but the English nobles rendered a great service to democracy by killing each other off during the Wars of the Roses. This left a clear field in England for the King and Parliament, either to work together or to struggle for power. Thus, by the time the American colonies were settled, it was a matter of course for the inhabitants to send delegates to a law-making body roughly resembling the House of Commons.

With the invention of representation, citizens once more participated directly in government although their functions were obviously much more limited than in ancient Athens and Rome. Most of the decisions were not made by them, but by the men they elected. The voters had a wider scope in a considerable part of this country because they could go to town meetings, fix taxes, authorize public works, and generally supervise the governmental affairs which come closest to men's lives. However, the direct political powers of American citizens shrank during the Nineteenth Century as towns grew into cities. The urban population could do no more law-making, only electing.

The Twentieth Century brought a fresh expansion of the powers of the electorate. By the recall, citizens can take a man out of office as well as put him in. By the initiative and referendum they can enact laws. The desirability of these new devices is fiercely debated; but in Massachusetts at least, the voters have made some good decisions on important issues which the legislators lacked courage to touch. For example, the censorship of motion-pictures was defeated, and labor union officials were required to file annual financial reports. The high-water mark of the new tendency was the demand, some years ago, that war should be declared only after a national referendum. The Gallup Polls have made it practicable to refer almost any question to a popular vote. The radio and the progress of electronics might enable every voter each morning to press a black or a white button in order to decide about the enactment of every bill in the state legislature, whether income taxes should be lowered, how many billions are to be spent on the Air Force, and whether a prominent general ought to be retired.

Once more, we are confronted with the argument that if we favor democracy we ought to have as much of it as possible. Hence there should be popular election of federal judges and more and more referenda. Here too, however, it may be true that you can have too much of a good thing. We have to consider sound finance—the people may be inclined to eat up the seed corn. Governmental efficiency, fruitful negotiations with foreign nations, the welfare of groups like business corporations or labor unions which may be temporarily disliked by a great many voters, the freedom of individuals who happen to be in a small minority—these are all desirable purposes which have to be weighed alongside the advantages of increased democracy. Moreover, it is well known that election-days are subject to the law of diminishing returns. The more often people are asked to vote, the fewer votes you get, as time goes on. The size of the dinner must be limited by the capacity of the stomach, else indigestion follows. Experience suggests the wisdom of confining the voter's annual task to choosing between candidates for a few important offices and to answering a very few questions about the adoption or defeat of measures, and, further, that such questions will not be satisfactorily decided unless they call for a plain "Yes" or "No."

The lesson of all I have said, is that democracy is not enough. It must be supplemented by numerous political devices and practices to make it effective. Of this truth the framers of our government were well aware. Safeguards to prevent a government from being too strong are indeed desirable, but it is also important not to have it too weak. "The first business of a government is to govern." If the rules on paper do not permit this, one of two things is bound to happen. One possibility is that a many-headed and inefficient government will break down in a crisis or even be unable to cope with ordinary routine, like that of Poland in the Eighteenth Century. With the commoner alternative, the pressure of hard facts causes concentration of power in somebody without regard to the rules on paper.

To illustrate this last situation, I recall that Athens, despite its extreme democracy, came under the leadership of Pericles and then of Cleon the sausage maker, neither of whom held an official position. And I think of my native state of Rhode Island during the closing years of the Nineteenth Century. The state constitution set up two headless branches of the General Assembly and a governor who had no veto and no genuine power to appoint anybody. Although nominally chief of the state, he could really do nothing except preside over a joint session of these two branches. Thus the rules on paper left power as little concentrated as it possibly could be. Nevertheless, power was concentrated in fact in a single man, Charles R. Brayton, the blind boss,[7] for whom the constitution made no provision whatever.

The phenomenon of the American boss like Brayton can, I believe, be somewhat explained as the devious effort of facts to cure a bad defect in the existing rules on paper. Of course, there were other causes like the prevalence of bribery and corruption among voters, legislators, and officeholders and the opportunities for looting public funds. Things are not perfect today, but nobody under the age of forty can possibly realize what the political atmosphere was in many states and cities during my boyhood. Still, the bosses were in part a response to genuine needs of the community which the rules on paper had failed to satisfy.

I like America in its governmental aspects much better than I did fifty years ago, leaving out of consideration for the moment deprivations of liberty which are discussed elsewhere in this book. We have got rid of the disgusting pretense that states and cities were governed by the men who were elected or appointed to legally created offices, whereas in fact (as most citizens knew) they were governed by a very different set of men unknown to the law. We owe this enormous improvement in government during the past half century to the tireless work of scores of men who combined vision with hard heads. Not content with slogans like, "Turn the rascals out," they changed the rules on paper so as to confer real power on executive officers whom the voters chose and on the associates chosen by these officers. And at the same time more and more men emerged, like Alfred E. Smith, Robert M. LaFollette, and Tom Johnson (to name only a few), who were capable of exercising power with wisdom and bravery. All this shows the importance of supplementing democracy by making it possible that the genuine needs which used to be taken care of by bosses and party machines can be adequately met by the established governments of states and cities. Let me run over some of these needs.

First and foremost, a focus of power has to exist. Somebody must really be able to do something.

Second, modern regulation of business, labor, and other important elements in our complex industrial communities gives rise to a sort of collective bargaining between such private groups and government, or perhaps it may better be called negotiation. There needs to be some outstanding representative of government to whom a power company or a labor union or an association of parents or some other group can go to present its claims, some of which are likely to be legitimate even if others selfishly ignore the interests of the rest of the community. A weak executive and a headless legislature do not take care of this real need. It was met by a boss, at least in response to groups who could make some return for his services. It is met far more satisfactorily by a governor or mayor with power, or by the head of a properly organized department who possesses wide and definite authority over a specific section of governmental activities.

Third, the regulations of a modern government affect all sorts of people very intimately. Yet the organization of various bureaus and departments of a city or state—and this is even more true of the numerous alphabetical agencies in Washington—has become so complex and overlapping, that the ordinary citizen who wants to oppose or obtain governmental action is completely baffled. He is in a bewildering labyrinth. Consequently, he looks eagerly for some kind of information bureau, which will straighten out his perplexities and put him in touch with the right officials. The boss was such an information bureau, and so was welcomed by honest as well as dishonest citizens. Might it be worth while for any government to recognize this persistent need, and establish such a bureau itself?

Fourth, the need for a different kind of information bureau has been created by the length of the modern ballot. On election-day a voter is asked to express his judgment about filling a dozen or more offices. No citizen who works hard at his own job can possibly acquire for himself adequate information about two or more candidates for each of these numerous positions. Nowadays he is still more bewildered by several requests at the bottom of the ballot for his opinion about rather complicated laws on all sorts of subjects outside his own range of knowledge. He may vote by guesswork or not vote at all—either course is a breakdown of democracy. Or else he has to go to somebody to learn how to vote. The boss and his subordinates have always taken great pains to supply this information. Today the need is partly met by the more disinterested methods of the League of Women Voters. Yet I believe that, so long as a voter is confronted with an indigestible mass of choices, his genuine exercise of political judgment is impossible. Here is a strong argument for the short ballot which would in state and local elections resemble a federal election. Most voters might be glad to concentrate their attention on the few most important offices, leaving the rest to be filled by appointment just as the President selects his Cabinet and other national officials. It is harder to find a good way to cut down the number of measures submitted by initiative and referendum.

Finally, there is the need of the less fortunate members of the community for help—help in getting jobs, in being kept going while out of work, in finding legal defense, and so forth. In the old days, the orthodox view was that all this was none of the government's business except in cases of extreme poverty. So the help was obtained from the boss and his machine, largely at the expense of the taxpayers. They still foot the bill, but do so through the established government. There have been mistakes and waste, no doubt, but the great change in policy has given us a better country. A citizen participates in the government with a stronger sense of obligation when he knows that it will protect him from major disasters, like mass unemployment, against which he can do very little to guard.

The foregoing discussion of the extent to which citizens should be able to make decisions themselves about public affairs has necessarily been imperfect, but I want to stress factors which have to be considered as possible limitations on democracy. One is the need for concentration of power. The other cannot be stated so simply. Any person who governs in any way ought to be able to put his mind and heart into his particular job of governing. Voting is a kind of governing. Therefore, a ballot becomes wrong when it asks the voter to make choices into which he does not put his mind and heart—choices which are perfunctory, haphazard, or made for him by others.

The essentials of democracy are plainly compatible with a wide range of political structures—republics or constitutional monarchies as in most of Europe and the British Dominions, nations with a permanent executive officer like our President or executive officers chosen by the legislature like the British Cabinet, with or without a written constitution, with or without judicial power to invalidate statutes, and colonies like our own before the Revolution. There are many different ways in which peoples have learned to govern themselves, directly or indirectly. Each has come to fit pretty well the country in which it developed, but this does not prove it would operate successfully if transplanted to another soil.

Our last question about democracy is: Control for what? The purposes of government are manifold; a democracy faces pretty much the same tasks as any other system. Still, the ideal of government for the people requires it to work for the general welfare and not for that of a few. Thus a danger is presented by groups which are organized for political pressure. Since most elections are carried by a margin of less than ten per cent, the result would be changed by a shift of five per cent. Consequently, any group comprising five per cent of the voters stands a good chance of getting whatever its leaders want because of the assumption by politicians and legislators that everybody in this group will follow its leaders' orders and vote solidly against a candidate who has failed to comply with their demands. Yet the occasional man who will not give in to such pressure and steadily pursues the course he believes right often finds himself re-elected. My classmate Robert Taft put through the Taft-Hartley Act against the wishes of the leaders of powerful labor unions and then carried Ohio by half a million votes. Regardless of the merits of the Act, it was good to see the assumption of group solidarity shot to pieces. Politicians underestimate the admiration of American citizens for courage.

Unorganized small minorities, on the other hand, are especially vulnerable in a democracy because of the craving for conformity, which was noted here by De Tocqueville a century ago. Fortunately, realization of this danger led to the Bill of Rights. Perhaps freedom of religion, speech, and assembly are not inevitable accompaniments of democracy, but they have often gone with it since the Sixteenth Century. This has been true in Switzerland, Holland, and modern England, as well as in the United States, where, Justice Brandeis said,[8] "Those who won our independence believed that the final end of the state was to make men free to develop their faculties."

Having tried to show very sketchily what democracy is, I shall go on to say why I like it.

In the first place, I cannot conceive of any alternative which would be tolerable. No doubt, Plato's theory that permanent control should be vested in "the wise" has always been tempting to many. Thus Van Bibber, the man about town in amusing stories by Richard Harding Davis, wanted the Mayor of New York to be elected by graduates of Harvard College. There are great differences of opinion about who are "the wise," and the misery through which recent dictators have dragged their countries shows that men who possess absolute power are likely to make more disastrous mistakes and commit far greater wrongs than the least estimable products of democracy. Such terrible experiences re-enforce homely sayings that it is better to count heads than break them and to govern by ballots instead of bullets.

However, the argument that we must turn to democracy as a last resort, because, whatever its faults, everything else would be still worse, may be sound but arouses no enthusiasm. A man falls in love with a girl for what she is and not by deciding that all the other girls are even more disagreeable. This argument is not enough to make men die for democracy, or—what is perhaps harder—live for democracy.

Something of what we need was said by Robert Burns:

> A man's a man for a' that.

The differences between men count for less than what they have in common. Those who favor setting up the few "wise" as rulers invariably expect those few to include themselves, or at least their friends. The multitude whom they want to leave out would look at the matter quite differently. When you strip off the non-essentials of inherited or accidental possessions, attempts to create different levels of power become either arbitrary or ridiculous. I am reminded of the time a Columbia professor took me for a swim in a pool where bathing suits are ignored. While we were all standing around as nature made us, a student engaged my friend in some sort of scholarly conversation, in which I joined. Afterwards my friend apologized for not introducing me, but I remarked that such formalities were superfluous between people who had no clothes on.

Thus far I have spoken mostly about political democracy, and said little about social and economic democracy, which have their own crop of problems. The three types are not coextensive, but they do help each other. Equal political power tends to diffuse the means of subsistence and control over the conditions of work. The absence of hereditary rank removes some of the barriers to association, friendship, and marriage. On the other hand, the undemocratic political thesis of the Nazis contemplated voteless millions living in serfdom and ghettos. The converse is also true, that social and economic democracy tend to produce political democracy. Many of us look forward to a classless society in the United States without many very rich or very poor, where everybody will have the opportunity to get as much education as he needs and then obtain work into which he can put the best of himself, and with a widespread distribution of the material things which make for a happy and fruitful life. It is hard to think of such a society tolerating an undemocratic form of government. Men with an approximately equal chance of earning and achieving in their work would not long consent to be outlawed politically.

It is no accident that democracies have arisen in communities with a strong religious consciousness, in the broadest sense of religion to embrace all kinds of faith in the brotherhood of men and their equality before the Spirit of the Universe, however conceived. Forgetting differences, we turn to each other for help and strength in a cause which belongs to all of us and not just to a few.

The biggest danger from communism is the possibility that it will win masses of men away from democracy, here and in Western Europe and Asia. I regret the fashionable phrase "the cold war" because it has made us feel as if we were in a real war and confine our thinking to military might and catching spies, whereas the contest with communism is in large measure a contest of ideas. Ideas and the emotions which give ideas their drawing-power have to be met with stronger ideas possessing a stronger emotional force.

So far as I can judge the attraction which communism has had for some law-abiding men and women, it filled a void in their minds and hearts. A man becomes resentful over conditions he regards as unjust and degrading. He is disillusioned by the claptrap of both our major parties. So he turns to communism because it promises a new earth, if not a new heaven. The oppression which actually takes place in Russia or China today is for him irrelevant—the man is converted by a vision.

Yet Jefferson and Lincoln had a great vision. It also promised to remedy injustices and degrading inequalities. During the Nineteenth Century, it drew millions to our shores. If democracy has lost some of this former vitality, the fault (I believe) is in us, its adherents, and not in democracy. The best way for Americans to combat the ideas of communism here and in the rest of the world is to give increased drawing-power to our great traditions of democracy and freedom. We must show how much they mean to us.

This task requires stirring reaffirmations of our faith. The vision of Jefferson and Lincoln will not be revealed to men with disturbed minds through catchwords like "the American way" and "free enterprise." Only memorable sentences, close to their experience and their dreams, will make them see the vision of democracy and freedom. Nor is it enough for us to repeat the Declaration of Independence and the Gettysburg Address. Noble words lose something of their biting edge with time. In order to win over men of the Twentieth Century, we have to use the language of the Twentieth Century.

The trouble is that we ourselves are not fully aware how much can be said for our ideals. About twenty years ago a *Soviet Primer* was widely sold in this country. I wish we might get out a *Primer of Democracy*. A short book could contain stirring expositions of self-government and freedom, from the Funeral Oration of Pericles down to statements by men and women of today. In it might be David Lilienthal's reply to those who opposed his appointment as head of the Atomic Energy Commission:

> I conceive the Constitution of the United States to rest—as does religion—[upon] the fundamental proposition of the integrity of the individual; and that all government and private institutions must be designed to protect the integrity and the dignity of the individual. . . . The tenets of democracy . . . grow out of this central core of a belief that the individual comes first, that all men are the children of God and their personalities are therefore sacred. . . .⁹

Such a book might reprint the statement of Secretary of State George Marshall to a conference at Moscow about what "democracy" means to us:

> We believe that human beings have . . . rights that may not be given or taken away. They include the right of every individual to develop his mind and his soul in the ways of his own choice, free of fear and coercion—provided only that he does not interfere with the rights of others. . . . To us, a society is not free if law-abiding citizens live in fear of being denied the right to work or deprived of life, liberty and the pursuit of happiness.¹⁰

Without ignoring past shortcomings, we Americans ought to stress our progress and our hopes, so as to make the great vision of democracy shine before the eyes of multitudes at home and abroad who are now disheartened by these troublesome times.

III Forty Years with Freedom of Speech and of the Press

> In spite of all the hogwash that is talked about the freedom of the Press, and in spite of the nauseating slop which the newspapers sometimes write about it, the freedom of the Press is a damned important thing.——CLEREBOLD WARBOYS, publisher of the *Salterton Evening Bellman* *

It is one hundred and sixty-five years since the United States Constitution was first amended, to declare "Congress shall make no law . . . abridging the freedom of speech, or of the press. . . ." For a century and a quarter, however, the meaning of these words remained conjectural. There was hot discussion at long intervals—over the Sedition Act of 1798 and the exclusion of Abolitionist pamphlets from the mails and the treatment of Copperheads—and legal treatises did some speculating, but nobody knew what the First Amendment did or did not protect. Such knowledge could come only from court decisions, and there was little occasion for these until the day when the United States declared war against Germany for the first time. The forty years, almost, since April 6, 1917, have given us all the authoritative judicial interpretation of freedom of speech and press we have, and they have also brought forth a host of restrictions on open discussion, which, whether constitutional or not, were never dreamed of in the United States before we went to war to save freedom.

It happens that my career as a law teacher is spanned by the same forty years. I have chanced to be an observer of the whole constitutional development of freedom of speech. Consequently, it may be interesting to describe these events and trends as seen through one man's eyes.

* In *Leaven of Malice*, a novel by Robertson Davies (New York: Charles Scribner's Sons, 1955)

As I look back, the development of free speech in the United States since 1917 falls roughly into four periods. The dividing lines are blurred, but it is convenient to place them in 1920, 1930, and 1945. First came the Period of Struggle and Criminal Prosecutions, running from the outbreak of the First World War until 1920. Second was the Period of Growth, ending in 1930. The third period of a decade and a half until about V-J Day was the Period of Achievement. Now we are in the midst of a Period of Renewed Struggle and Subtle Suppressions. After passing each of the first three periods in review, I shall concentrate on the last. This most deserves our attention because it is the only one we can do something about.

THE PERIOD OF STRUGGLE AND CRIMINAL PROSECUTIONS, 1917-1920

Misfortunes never come singly. Problems of war are bad enough, not only its purely military aspects but also innumerable questions connected with civilian activities and the ends which ought to be achieved after peace. It is very hard, in the agony of fighting, to keep working toward wise solutions of such unmilitary questions through the fruitful formation of public opinion. Yet on top of all these problems of war were heaped almost immediately the problems of the Russian Revolution. Thus the traditions of free speech which had come down to us from John Milton and Thomas Jefferson were subjected to a double strain. It was just as if the controversy between supporters and opponents of the Civil War had occurred at the same time as the excitement over the French Revolution which produced the Sedition Act of 1798.

No free speech problem can be satisfactorily solved by men who think only of the risks from open discussion. It is indispensable to balance against those risks the deeply felt realization that one of the most important purposes of society and government is the discovery and spread of true facts and sound judgments on subjects of general concern. It is indispensable to remember that every restraint on speaking and printing hampers that important purpose, especially when the unrestrained views are unpopular and may be easily overlooked unless heard. No doubt, some sacrifice of discussion is occasionally required. After careful balancing, the scales may tip in favor of other purposes of society, like protection from disorder and foreign conquest. Nevertheless, it is essential that such careful balancing shall take place in men's minds and that the great social values of open speech and an untrammeled press shall weigh very heavily in the scale. The First Amendment gives binding force to this principle of political wisdom.

During the years from 1917 to 1920, such careful balancing rarely took place. The vivid danger of a German victory and the vivid danger of internal uprisings in response to the contagion of revolutionary doctrines which attacked private property at its foundations encountered no deeply felt realization of the precious values of discussion. The First Amendment had no hold on people's minds because no live facts or concrete images were then attached to it. Like an empty box with beautiful words on it, the Amendment collapsed under the impact of terror of Prussian battalions and terror of Bolshevik mobs. So the emotions generated by the two simultaneous cataclysms of war and revolution swept unchecked through American prosecutors, judges, jurymen, and legislators.

It is the fashion nowadays to say that those were times of little danger from heterodox discussion, and hence the eventual judicial opinions which condemned the suppression during this war and the Red Menace which followed it are said to have no application to the real dangers of our times. Thus the author of the recent Maryland Sedition Act writes: "It is . . . true that the dangers from subversive organizations at the time of World War I were much exaggerated . . . [but] we are no longer in the days of T-model socialism of World War I." [1] And Chief Justice Vinson, in sustaining the conviction of the eleven Communist leaders under the Smith Act, brushed aside the strictures of Holmes and Brandeis on the conviction of Gitlow in 1920 under a similar New York statute for publishing the doctrines of Marx and Lenin: "The situation with which [these two Justices] were concerned was a comparatively isolated event, bearing little relation in their minds to any substantial threat to the safety of the community." [2]

But that was not the way the authorities during the First World War and the Red Menace looked at the people they were suppressing. As to Gitlow, the majority of the Supreme Court said his utterances were "endangering the foundations of organized government" and imperiling New York's "existence as a constitutional State." [3] It was then almost a hopeless task to try to convince any solid citizen that the danger was small. A bomb exploded under the window of the Attorney General of the United States. Another bomb exploded at the corner of Wall Street between the New York Stock Exchange and the office of J. P. Morgan. The newspapers were filled with discoveries of great caches of arms and ammunition in cellars. A score of sedition bills were introduced in the Senate and House and supported by lurid descriptions of the national peril if they were not passed. Attorney General Palmer said of the left-wing pamphlets he wanted suppressed:

> The continual spread of the seeds of evil thought, the continual inoculation of poison virus of social sedition, poisonous to every fiber and root, to every bone and sinew, to the very heart and soul of all that by our standards is integrity in citizenship or personal character cannot help but foster frightfully the revolutionary disease. Is there no . . . Government policy . . . that can stand effectively for social sanitation?

In the New York Assembly, the men who succeeded in expelling Mr. Louis Waldman, now a respected lawyer and bulwark against communism, and his four Socialist colleagues described their party as

> having the single purpose of destroying our institutions and government and substituting the Russian-Soviet government . . . an antinational party whose allegiance is given to the Internationale and not to the United States.

The Lusk Committtee's 1920 collection of radical documents from Karl Marx's *Communist Manifesto* down, to prove the urgent need for immediate suppression of Socialists and Bolsheviks, closely resembles the American Bar Association's 1951 "Brief on Communism, Marxism-Leninism."

Reading what everybody now agrees about the panic-stricken alarmists of 1920, I wonder what will be said thirty-five years from now about the alarmists of 1950-1955.

Lest we forget what was done in those years in the name of

national safety, I quote this brief summary of what was done by trial judges and appellate United States courts during the First World War:

> It became criminal to advocate heavier taxation instead of bond issues, to state that conscription was unconstitutional though the Supreme Court had not yet held it valid, to say that the sinking of merchant vessels was legal, to urge that a referendum should have preceded our declaration of war, to say that war was contrary to the teachings of Christ. Men were punished for criticizing the Red Cross and the Y.M.C.A., while under the Minnesota Espionage Act it was held a crime to discourage women from knitting by the remark, "No soldier ever sees these socks." It was in no way necessary that these expressions of opinion should be addressed to soldiers or men on the point of enlisting or being drafted. Most judges held it enough if the words might conceivably reach such men. They have made it impossible for an opponent of the war to write an article or even a letter in a newspaper of general circulation because it would be read in some training camp where it might cause insubordination or interfere with military success. He could not address a large audience because it was liable to include a few men in uniform; and some judges held him punishable if it contained men between eighteen and forty-five, since they might be called into the army eventually; some emphasized the possible presence of ship-builders and munition makers. . . .
>
> One judge even made it criminal to argue to women against a war, by the words, "I am for the people and the government is for the profiteers," because what is said to mothers, sisters, and sweethearts may lessen their enthusiasm for the war, and "our armies in the field and our navies upon the seas can operate and succeed only so far as they are supported and maintained by the folks at home." [4]

The task of the scattered handful of lawyers who tried to give some real meaning to the First Amendment through this time was indeed hard. The view that prevailed in courts as long as the fighting lasted was that, although previous censorship of publications (except by exclusion from the mails) was unconstitutional, there was no limit upon what could be done under a statute after a speech was delivered or a pamphlet published except the faint hope of the jury's acquitting. Bad tendency, however remote from success, was the sole official test of guilt. It might be tendency to interfere with the war, or a tendency to bring about an eventual violent revolution through the spread of opinions which had been knocking around Europe since 1848. The speaker had to take his chances with a jury and could look for no help from the constitutional guaranties of freedom of speech and press.

To overcome such an attitude, Walter Nelles and his associates in the National Civil Liberties Bureau, which later grew into the American Civil Liberties Union, had to build from the ground up. With almost no prewar cases in point, Nelles in his book of *Espionage Act Cases*[5] displayed a remarkable insight into the relation between the free speech problem and the old problem of criminal attempts. If I gather a few sticks and buy a can of kerosene for the purpose of starting a fire in a house ten miles away and do nothing more, I cannot be punished for attempting to commit arson. However, if I put the sticks beside the wall of the house and pour on some kerosene and I am caught before striking a match, I am guilty of a criminal attempt. The fire is the main thing, but when no fire has occurred, it is a question of the nearness of my behavior to the wished-for outbreak of a fire.[6] So under the First Amendment, lawless acts are the main thing. Speech is not punishable for its own sake, but only because of its connection with those lawless acts, whether they occur or not. But more than a remote connection is necessary here, just as in the case of the attempted fire. The fire must be close to the house; the speech must be close to the lawless acts. So long as the speech is far away from action, the Constitution protects it.

By such reasoning did Nelles lay the foundation for the famous statement of Justice Holmes in the Schenck case, not quite four months after the Armistice:

> The question in every case is whether the words used are used in such circumstances and are of such a nature as to create a clear and present danger that they will bring about the substantive evils that Congress has a right to prevent. It is a question of proximity and degree.[7]

You can easily see the parallel between these words and my case of the man who wants to burn down a house.

Alexander Meiklejohn[8] has vigorously attacked Holmes for not maintaining the complete immunity of all speech on public questions under the First Amendment. Even if Holmes had been thus willing to throw overboard the whole law of libel, which is largely irreconcilable with Meiklejohn's position, he would have been no more than a lone dissenter. Holmes' inestimable service to free speech consisted in his getting a unanimous Supreme Court to accept his test of guilt, which placed a great area of discussion beyond the reach of the government. At last the First Amendment had been given an informative interpretation by the Supreme Court. It came too late to prevent the merciless agony of the war prosecutions in which 1,956 persons had to face prosecution and 877 were convicted.[9] And over eight years would go by before a majority of the Court would apply Holmes' test so as to let anybody out of prison.[10] Still, the "clear and present danger" test did eventually reverse many convictions, and no doubt it staved off many prosecutions which would otherwise have taken place both in peace and during the Second World War.

Perhaps the clear and present danger test is not the best possible formulation of the line between constitutionally protected speech and speech which is punishable if legislatures, prosecutors, and juries so desire. I still like better Judge Learned Hand's phrase in 1917 in the suit to get the *Masses* back into the mails, "direct incitement to violent resistance," [11] or my own suggestion written in 1918: "In wartime, speech should be free, unless it is clearly liable to cause direct and dangerous interference with the conduct of the war." [12] Yet these are only minor variations. The point is that instead of the old line between forbidden previous censorship and wholly permissible subsequent punishment, there is a new line as to punishment. Censorship still remains prohibited by the Constitution, and in addition punishment is prohibited, too, for all words which are not closely connected with dangerous acts. The law does indeed not say, as some would wish,[13] that only overt acts can send a man to prison. That may be a wise policy to be pursued in crises, but the Constitution does not require it to be chosen. The choice depends on wisdom, good judgment, common sense, and the resourcefulness which knows how to make use of better methods than force in order to persuade opponents or counteract them with better arguments. Some speech can be punished by authorities who are unable to think of any better way of handling it, but the First Amendment entitles most speech to be let alone.

When the fighting was over and the Germans were out of the way, the Russians and their numerous sympathizers in this country still remained. The flames of suppression soared too high for any court decision to extinguish them. Eagerness for restriction spread from federal courts to state courts. Syndicalism acts multiplied as fast as the victims of Spanish influenza. An old New York law against advocating the overthrow of the government by force and violence,[14] passed after the assassination of President McKinley by an anarchist and never used, was suddenly revived and directed against Socialists, although they are at the opposite pole of political thought. Federal deportation statutes were amended to stigmatize the same advocacy of overthrowing by force and violence,[15] and were used by Attorney General Palmer to seize thousands of aliens for deportation during the night of January 2, 1920. My sole appearance in court in a free speech case, along with the present Justice Frankfurter, was to get a good many of these prisoners released for lack of a fair hearing.[16] The thirst for suppression reached its height on January Seventh, in the refusal of the New York Assembly to seat five duly elected Socialist members.

Then the tide turned. Charles Evan Hughes, facing unpopularity and the opposition of many of his friends in the Association of the Bar of the City of New York, persuaded the Association to try to keep the Socialists in their seats. He lost the battle because they were excluded despite all he could do, but he won the war. The nation began to realize how foolish it had been, and he left for use in future crises these wise words:

> If there was anything against these men as individuals, if they were deemed to be guilty of criminal offenses, they should have been charged accordingly. But I understand that the action is not directed against these five elected members as individuals but that the proceeding is virtually an attempt to indict a political party. . . . This is not, in my judgment, American government. . . .
> If public officers or private citizens have any evidence that any individuals, or group of individuals, are plotting revolution and seeking by violent measures to change our Government, let the evidence be laid before the proper authorities and swift action be taken for the

protection of the community. . . . But I count it a most serious mistake to proceed, not against individuals charged with violation of law, but against masses of our citizens combined for political action. . . ."[17]

THE PERIOD OF GROWTH, 1920-1930

Let me introduce this period by a personal digression. My first book, *Freedom of Speech*, was published in the autumn of 1920. As I was reading the last page proofs, I spotted a statement of mine about unlawful searches and seizures [18] and was sure it was "just plain wrong." What should I do? I had already exhausted my first royalties and delayed and embarrassed my publishers by an interminable series of proof corrections designed to keep the book in step with the rapid succession of current free speech cases. I did not have the heart or the financial resources to order this erroneous paragraph reset. So I said to Mrs. Chafee, "I'll just have to let this mistake stand as it is, and when the critics jump on it, I'll frankly confess my error." Three months after my book was published, the United States Supreme Court decided squarely in agreement with this statement which I had longed to strike out,[19] and it was the only thing in the book with which the Court agreed for years and years.

Despite such discouragements, the next decade was a time of hope. The early 1920s saw new examples of suppression, but the forces of tolerance grew still faster. Congress rejected all the proposed peacetime sedition laws after they had been strongly opposed by the press and the American Federation of Labor; its attorney, Jackson H. Ralston, took an active part at the hearings and Samuel Gompers testified against these bills with great effect. Aside from deportations and censorship in the customs, there was little more federal suppression. Some states still ran rampant, notably New York under the leadership of the Lusk Committee and California in its attacks on the Industrial Workers of the World; but state governors began to check these excesses, and in 1925 the United States Supreme Court asserted its power to nullify state infringements of freedom of speech.

This decision in Gitlow v. New York [20] was the most significant event in the second period. Benjamin Gitlow was a leader of the left-wing Socialists, who preceded the Communist Party of America. He printed thirty-four tedious pages bringing the *Communist Manifesto* of 1848 down to date, and the Lusk Committee got him convicted under the revived Anti-Anarchy Act, along with his chief associates. The highest court in New York sustained the conviction, but Judge Cuthbert Pound dissented with Cardozo and spoke these memorable words:

> Although the defendant may be the worst of men . . . the rights of the best of men are secure only as the rights of the vilest and most abhorrent are protected.[21]

Walter Heilprin Pollak was retained to carry the case to the United States Supreme Court. He had a hard uphill fight. When we talked together, I was very doubtful whether Walter could persuade the Court that any right under the United States Constitution was involved. The First Amendment, "*Congress* shall make no law . . ." gave no help by itself. The only hope of victory lay in part of the Fourteenth Amendment, adopted after the Civil War: ". . . nor shall any State deprive any person of . . . *liberty* . . . without due process of law. . . ." The technical phrase at the end had long meant arbitrarily, by outrageous restrictions, etc., but the vital question was: What is "liberty"? It surely included many business and pecuniary freedoms like making contracts and running a laundry. Yet could Walter get the Court to read into "liberty" the purely personal liberties of the First Amendment? Several earlier attempts to persuade it to do so had not got far. Nowise discouraged, he plunged ahead. Like Hughes for the New York Assemblymen, Pollak lost the battle for Gitlow but won the war for free speech. The Justices unanimously agreed that "we may and do assume that freedom of speech and of the press . . . are among the fundamental personal rights and 'liberties' protected . . . from impairment by the states. . . ." Walter Pollak is gone from us, but because of him the Supreme Court wields a sharp sword to defend the ideals of Jefferson and Madison against local intolerance.

The majority of the Court did go on to uphold Gitlow's conviction on the ground that his soporific manifesto was too violent talk to come within "liberty" of speech and press. But this defeat did not bother Gitlow. He was immediately pardoned by Governor Alfred E. Smith, who had already released the other left-wing leaders from prison. Indeed, it was all Gitlow's friends could do to hold back Al from pardoning him before the Supreme Court had a chance to pass on his case.

That brings me to a second encouraging feature of the Period of Growth—the notable contributions of Al Smith to freedom of speech and thought. When he was first Governor in 1920, he vetoed all the legislation drafted by the Lusk Committee. These Lusk Bills were of a sort very familiar to us today. They were designed to detect revolutionary conspirators through special investigations, test the loyalty of teachers, and regulate the schools and school courses with the object of preventing the corruption of youth by radicals. Then Smith was defeated for re-election by Nathan Miller, and the Lusk Bills became law. In 1923 Al got back to Albany again, and obtained their repeal. I am going to quote a few extracts from Al Smith's messages about this legislation, not as ancient history, but because his wise and pungent words apply directly to much that is going on today.[22]

Veto of a bill to set up a group of investigators with power to question persons suspected of revolutionary ideas:

> There is no just cause for providing any different method for enforcing the criminal anarchy statute from that employed in enforcing the other penal laws of the State—through the agencies of the grand jury, the magistrate and the district attorneys of the respective counties of the State. . . . The traditional abhorrence of a free people of all kinds of spies and secret police is valid and justified and calls for the disapproval of this measure.

Veto of a bill to oust teachers with objectionable views:

> The test established is not what the teacher teaches, but what the teacher believes. . . . No man is so omniscient or wise as to have entrusted to him such arbitrary and complete power not only to condemn any individual teacher, but to decree what belief or opinion is opposed to the institutions of the country. . . . Every teacher would be at the mercy of his colleagues, his pupils, and their parents, and any word or act of the teacher might be held . . . to indicate an attitude hostile to some of "the institutions of the United States" or

of the State. The bill ... deprives teachers of their right to freedom of thought; it limits the teaching staff of the public schools to those only who lack the courage or the mind to exercise their legal right to just criticism of existing institutions.

Message on signing the repeal of the Lusk Laws:

Under the laws repealed, teachers, in order to exercise their honorable calling, were in effect compelled to hold opinions as to governmental matters deemed by a State officer consistent with loyalty; and further, no private school could be maintained in this State unless its teachings were similarly satisfactory to certain officials of the State. Freedom of opinion and freedom of speech were by these laws unduly shackled, and an unjust discrimination was made against members of a great profession.

A third significant event of this decade was the solid establishment of the American Civil Liberties Union. Without such an organization, arrested speakers and writers would have found it very difficult to get efficient lawyers or sometimes any lawyers at all. The constitutional provision entitling the accused "to have the Assistance of Counsel for his defence" might have remained just empty words on paper. An ordinary lawyer fears the effect of unpopular cases upon his practice. Lawyers who did defend obnoxious persons were threatened with disbarment then as now, and some were disbarred. Moreover, free speech cases are a specialized branch of the law and call for knowledge and experience which lawyers in general lack. Therefore, it was a great service to the administration of justice in the United States when in many cities a law office, staffed with trained and conscientious men, was available to help courts reach proper decisions in civil liberties cases. An institution has been called "the lengthened shadow of one man." Without meaning to underestimate what their numerous associates did, I think of the American Civil Liberties Union as the lengthened shadow of two men—Walter Nelles, the lawyer, and Roger Baldwin, the organizer and inspiring guide.

Before I move out of this period, I want to speak of two of its disturbing features. Both concern the I.W.W., and both are very pertinent to our present situation.

The California Syndicalism Law[23] made the American people

familiar for the first time with what had long been an odious feature of political trials in Europe—the renegade as a chief witness for the government. The state used to trot out two former members of the I.W.W. in almost every prosecution. One of them "admitted participation in numberless atrocious offenses" and was judicially characterized as "one of the most reprehensible characters thinkable." Other renegades appeared very frequently. The testimony of such men sent dozens of migratory workers to prison for years and obtained an injunction to break up the whole I.W.W. organization. At last even jurymen ceased to believe these renegades and convictions stopped.

Another disquieting aspect of these I.W.W. prosecutions was their reliance upon force as the sole remedy for a deep-seated evil. The revolutionary labor union called the Industrial Workers of the World was plainly the product of the disorganized situation of migratory workers. They had no homes of their own, and few opportunities to join labor unions of the usual kind. So they drifted aimlessly into a particularly objectionable sort of union. Unquestionably, the farmers of the Central Valley and their supporters had considerable provocation. They were afflicted with sabotage of agricultural machinery, crop-burning, and other flagrant practices. Since it was difficult to detect the perpetrators of these criminal acts, demands spread for vigorous proceedings against words about such acts—and then against words which did not mention such acts but might conceivably lead somebody to commit them. The behavior and leaflets and speeches of the I.W.W. were bad symptoms of a bad disease.

What I find most disturbing is that the people of California were content with attacking the symptoms and did little about the disease. Until the economic and social disadvantages of the migratory workers, which caused their bitter discontent, were dealt with directly, the use of the tremendous power of the state on behalf of employers, although it might produce a superficial weakening of revolutionary unionism, was sure to intensify the workers' hostility to the state and their belief that government was only the organ of capital. It is a mistake to spend upon mosquito-killing the energy which might be used in draining the swamps where the insects breed. The I.W.W. prosecutions and injunction may have put an end to the

I.W.W., but the same sort of workers showed up later as Communists. And the suppressions left the problem of migratory labor just as it was. What did solve that problem was the New Deal measures, which gave some of the common incidents of normal human life to laborers who are indispensable.

All this offers a lesson for the treatment of Communists today. A blind confidence in the use of force against individuals may do something to lessen harm, but it stops inquiry into peaceful remedies which might be still more effective. The question which ought to have been asked by Californians in 1920 was: Why do people join the I.W.W., and what can we do to make them want to get out of it and live law-abiding lives? The question which ought to be asked all over the country in 1955 is: Why do people join the Communist Party of America and what can we do to make them want to get out of it and lead law-abiding lives? Driving Communists out of their chosen occupations and putting a stigma on them which makes it almost impossible to obtain any other useful employment, will not turn such persons into decent American citizens. Instead, they will have no means of keeping alive except to become agitators of a dangerous sort.

The Period of Achievement, 1930-1945

On February 3, 1930, President Hoover appointed Charles Evans Hughes as Chief Justice of the United States. Under his leadership Holmes and Brandeis, who had gone down fighting over and over again with inspiring proclamations of the great American tradition of freedom of speech, now became part of the majority of the Court and sometimes had all the Justices with them. One state suppression proceeding after another was struck down as unconstitutional—a California conviction for raising a red flag with a hammer and sickle at a children's camp; a Minnesota injunction against the further publication of a scandal-sheet; a Louisiana tax on the gross receipts of large newspapers; an Oregon conviction of a speaker at a Communist meeting; the use by Georgia of an old statute from the days of slavery about attempting to incite insurrection, in order to lock up for eighteen years a Negro Communist not (I surmise) because he was likely to overthrow the United States Constitution but for fear that he might get it obeyed in Georgia; [24] city ordinances designed to stifle the peculiar activities of Jehovah's Witnesses; [25] and the efforts of several states to hinder peaceful picketing. [26] The American Bar Association, during a surprising interlude of enthusiasm for the First Amendment, established a Special Committee on the Bill of Rights in 1938. It helped obtain from the Supreme Court decisions preventing Mayor Hague in Jersey City from forbidding all meetings which he did not approve [27] and upholding the right of school children to refuse to engage in a daily flag-worshipping ceremony if they considered it detestable or meaningless.[28]

The Flag Salute case is a significant illustration of the recent expansion of constitutional protection beyond discussion of political issues, which had occupied the Court before 1930. It was also made to cover religious controversy,[29] statements by labor unions against employers,[30] and severe criticisms of judges by newspapers.[31] This broad interpretation of freedom of speech and press thoroughly accords with the historical background of the First Amendment. It is true that untrammeled speaking and printing about candidates and issues had come to be regarded before our Revolution as an essential part of the process of self-government, but the men who strove to establish liberty of the press also cared greatly about science, art, drama, and poetry. No doubt, the Zenger trial and the controversy over Wilkes and Junius in England did associate the struggle for freedom of speech to some extent with popular discussion of political questions, but the struggle was also related to the abolition of the censorship of books of any sort. Milton's *Areopagitica* advocated freedom for much else besides political tracts. The Continental Congress in its address of 1774 to the People of Quebec, said that freedom of the press, in addition to its political values, is important for "the advancement of truth, science, morality and arts in general." Jefferson's vigorous support of the Philadelphia bookseller, Dufief, when Dufief was arrested for selling a French book on the creation of the world, shows how closely Jefferson connected freedom of the press with freedom of religion and of all thinking.[32] He said on another occasion, "I have sworn upon the altar of God eternal hostility against every form of tyranny over the mind of man." [33] The men who wrote "the freedom of speech, or of the press" into the Bill of Rights included politicians, lawyers, scholars, churchgoers and *philosophes*, scientists, agriculturists, and wide readers. They used that phrase to embrace the whole realm of thought.

Another important expansion of constitutional protection during the years after 1930 related to the methods of suppression which were nullified. Earlier cases usually concerned convictions by juries under criminal statutes and exclusion from the mails. Under Hughes and his successor Stone, the Court also condemned a conviction for the common law crime of disturbing the peace,[34] a statute fettering the press by burdensome taxes,[35] some sweeping court injunctions,[36] and several judicial proceedings for contempt of court.[37]

The onset of the Second World War did not change the attitude of the Court, and the policy of the Department of Justice under Attorney General Biddle contrasted sharply with its policy during and after the First World War. Although the Espionage Act of 1917 was still on the books, and a new sedition statute had been added in 1940 (of which I shall speak later), the only periodical suppressed, so far as I know, was Father Coughlin's *Social Justice*,[38] an act which evoked protests from people who violently disagreed with him, and there were only seven reported criminal prosecutions for anti-war speeches and publications. In one of these, a five-to-four decision of the Supreme Court set aside the conviction of Hartzel [39] for reasons which would certainly have not affected a majority of the Justices who sent Debs to Atlanta. During most of the fighting in the First World War, a local United States attorney could decide all by himself whether to prosecute or not, and community sentiment often urged him to go ahead; so the fact that in 1941 the Washington authorities kept the entire control of such questions was an important factor in keeping prosecutions from running wild again. Perhaps not everything done was wise, but certainly the Second World War brought far less damage to open discussion than its predecessor.

A personal reminiscence may not be out of place. In 1924 Harlow Shapely, on behalf of a club of Harvard graduate students, arranged a symposium on "The Next War" with three speakers.[40] A chemist foretold the horrors of gas warfare. An international lawyer predicted that the aims with which the next war started would be completely changed by the time it was over. And I lamented that, this time, freedom of speech would be irreparably ruined. You remember how Mark Twain said he had known many bad things during his life and most of them never happened.

THE PERIOD OF RENEWED STRUGGLE AND SUBTLE SUPPRESSIONS, SINCE 1945

The closing years of the Period of Achievement gave several indications of a bad time ahead for freedom of discussion. The inspiring opinions of the Supreme Court under Hughes were not having much effect on the man in the street. Perhaps Americans had not become more tolerant than in 1920, but were merely more indifferent and less frightened. When fear returned, suppression might return with it. As in the opening years of the Period of Growth, the forces of suppression and the forces of freedom were both increasing, but this time the forces of suppression were increasing faster and eventually they got ahead.

The year 1938, which produced the Bill of Rights Committee of the American Bar Association, also gave the country a very different committee in the House of Representatives. Today this House Committee on Un-American Activities is flourishing like the green bay tree, while the Bill of Rights Committee did little during several years of suppressions except render a legal opinion in favor of the McCarran Subversive Activities Control Act.[41] In 1940, Congress passed the first peacetime federal sedition law [42] since the detested Act of 1798. The Smith Act contained practically everything which A. Mitchell Palmer wanted at the height of the Red Menace. Soon afterwards came Pearl Harbor. As in the First World War, we were faced with two staggering sets of problems. Again we had to defend ourselves against German military might, with the Japanese added; and again we were perplexed by the revolutionary rulers of Russia. For four years it was essential to cement the coalition with the Soviet Union against Hitler, which is now commonly forgotten when any American is denounced for the merest gesture of friendship in 1942 or 1943. After the fighting was over, apprehensions about Russia flared, as in 1919, into panic and suppression.

This alarm about our national safety was increased by our recent acquisition of the strongest weapons we ever possessed—the atom bomb and then the H-bomb. Instead of making us less fearful, this made us more fearful, because we have been constantly worried about losing the deadly secrets. We have behaved like LaFontaine's cobbler, who sang gaily so long as he was poor but was made silent by getting some gold coins.

> *Le sommeil quitta son logis:*
> *Il eut pour hôtes les soucis,*
> *Les soupçons, les alarmes vaines.*
> *Tout le jour il avait l'œil au guet; et la nuit,*
> *Si quelque chat faisait du bruit,*
> *Le chat prenait l'argent.*

All the water that ran under the bridge after 1917 began rushing back in waves of intolerance. Again we were seeking to fight objectionable ideas with long prison sentences and heavy pecuniary penalties. Again we borrowed suppressive methods from our enemies. We were constantly urged to fight a land riddled with secret police by increasing our own secret police, to contend against people who would not talk with foreigners by dismissing the head of the Bureau of Standards because he talked with foreigners, to teach Europeans to hate Russian censorship by weeding hundreds of volumes from the shelves of our Information Libraries abroad, so that any book which happened to displease some member of Congress or his zealous aides would not harm the minds of Europeans.

So we are in a Period of Struggle once more. The old arguments for restrictions are repeated. Jefferson, Holmes, and Hughes again need quoting in reply. Yet the present situation differs from conditions in 1919-20 in at least four ways.

First, the danger of bad acts is greater. Communism is no longer the political philosophy of an embryonic government beset on all sides by civil war, but is backed by one of the most powerful nations on earth. As for internal bad acts, the techniques of espionage have improved enormously during thirty-five years, and the opportunities for spying and stealing secrets are vastly greater because there are many more secrets to steal.

Yet these new objective perils do not *ipso facto* call for suppression of ideas. Foreign attack is a matter for generals, and spies can be handled, like other regular criminals, by trained federal and state police. There has been no authoritative statement that we are help-less to combat such dangers unless we create new political crimes. When Mr. Truman vetoed the McCarran Act, he said that neither the F.B.I. nor the various agencies of intelligence and defense favored this law.[43]

Second, and much more important in considering sedition laws, the internal danger from unrest seems to me very much less than it was thirty-five years ago. In 1920, with a much smaller national population, the two Communist parties were judged to aggregate 40,000 to 90,000 while Eugene Debs got a million votes for Presi-dent. As of June 30, 1955, J. Edgar Hoover, the head of the F.B.I., estimates that the Communist Party has 21,500 members.[44] This in-dicates a big decrease in extremist radicals. Moreover, in 1920 I observed at forums what a great drawing-power the Russian Revolu-tion had for American workmen when it began. Since then, purges, labor camps, and other ugly facts in the Soviet Union have largely disillusioned idealists. What was especially serious in 1919 and 1920 was the enormous amount of discontent. While we were in the throes of a big steel strike and labor unions were underdogs and farmers discouraged, bad outbreaks of violence seemed really pos-sible. All these old reasons for discontent have been greatly lessened by the New Deal legislation, whether one likes it or not, and by the high wages and other benefits paid out by employers since 1941. The spiritual health of the nation is far better than in 1919 and it has a much greater immunity to revolutionary radicalism.

Third, although the reasons for suppression are weaker today than during the Red Menace, resistance to suppression is weaker too. Alistair Cooke remarks that "liberty is not in our time a markedly American passion." [45] It was not only outstanding men like Holmes, Brandeis, and Hughes who upheld American traditions of freedom of speech thirty-five years ago. There were a lot of good old Jeffer-sonians around, and many survivors of "the forward-looking men and women" who elected Woodrow Wilson and formed the Pro-gressive Party. Despite many panic-stricken patriots, I found when I talked against sedition bills that I could count on a ready response from plenty of solid citizens in any audience. As the emotions of war died out, freedom of speech acquired a stronger hold on men's minds than it has today. Samuel Gompers and leading newspapers spoke out against the federal sedition bills of 1920, but the Smith Act of 1940 met with no similar opposition [46] and the McCarran Act [47] sailed through in 1950 without any conspicuous support for President Truman's veto.

Fourth and last. The most striking difference from the earlier Period of Struggle lies in the subtlety of the suppressions now employed. During and after the First World War, the chief method for controlling the speech and publications of American citizens was criminal trials. These trials often ran wild, as everybody now agrees,[48] but at least they had several safeguards against abuses. Determination of guilt in a criminal prosecution is made by a jury, and reviewed by judges; and the test of guilt is defined in a statute with considerable clearness. All these safeguards are conspicuously lacking in the novel methods of suppression which have recently sprung up. We do still have criminal trials, with an even wider scope than in 1920 because of the Smith Act and the new McCarran Act crime of facilitating a totalitarian dictatorship; [49] but there is ever so much more suppression today through proceedings which have no juries, no substantial supervision by judges, and vague definitions of wrongdoing.

Ever since the Zenger case in colonial New York, Americans have insisted it is essential to freedom of speech that only a jury should be able to punish a man for expressing questionable views. Even if the jury acquits in disregard of the letter of the law, this is accepted as right, because a man ought not to suffer for saying what a cross-section of the community believes the community has a right to hear. And if the jury goes too far the other way and convicts the man improperly, its action is subjected to substantial supervision by judges, up to the Supreme Court of the United States.

Any proceeding was abhorrent to our ancestors which allowed active members of the government in power to determine the wrongfulness of speech and printing so as to impose various types of penalties. For this reason our ancestors detested censorship by officials and taxes on knowledge imposed by legislatures.

Run rapidly over some of the current methods of suppression and see what persons do the deciding and penalizing instead of jurymen. In legislative investigation, the denouncing and ousting from jobs is done by legislators with an eye on re-election and party axes to grind. Loyalty and security programs in federal and state governments are run by administrative officials, who can drive men out of their chosen careers and often make it hard for them to get any private work. If those programs are extended to industry, the decision is made by businessmen who are often afraid of losing government contracts. In public schools and universities, the loss of a career is inflicted by educational officials, who are sometimes threatened by the statute with being severely punished themselves if they decide the teacher is innocent and are afterwards ruled to have been mistaken. Many efforts are made to extend the same system to private schools and colleges. The outlawing of organizations contemplated by the McCarran Act is to be done by a board of five men specially selected as watchdogs of sedition. Administrators can also stifle organizations by choking off the financial contributions which are essential to their existence; they can deprive potential givers of exemptions from income taxes and sometimes threaten them with prosecution if they give money to a red-listed group.[50] The denial of passports was left until very recently to the uncontrolled discretion of one official in the State Department.[51] If a war or proclaimed emergency exists, administrators will decide who shall be sent to concentration camps under the last part of the McCarran Act.[52] And over and above all these penalties imposed on American citizens by officials is the constant smearing of them by single speakers on the floor of the legislature and single columnists, who now exercise the power to take away any man's good name and blackmail his customers and sponsors with threats of boycotts and very likely ruin his chances of supporting himself, his wife and his children.

Not only do jurymen have almost nothing to do with the suppressions just listed, but judges, too, are pretty much out of the picture. The importance of active judicial supervision over governmental restrictions on speech and press is obvious when we remember what the Supreme Court did under Hughes. Nevertheless, the McCarran Act gives judges little more than perfunctory tasks,[53] and we cannot yet be confident that a majority of the Supreme Court Justices will give substantial protection to freedom of thought and expression from legislative investigations, loyalty programs, purges of teachers, and test oaths.[54] In criminal prosecutions, too, the Court has nearly abdicated the control over sedition laws which it exercised under Hughes. This is to me the most disquieting feature of the Dennis case,[55] which held the Smith Act constitutional. It cut down the First Amendment to mean just about this: Congress shall make no law abridging the freedom of speech and of the press unless Congress does make a law abridging the freedom of speech and of the press.

Anybody who has studied the enactment of the Smith Act [56] and subsequent sedition statutes can see that the indispensable balance of the values of free speech against the danger of violent acts, etc., does not take place in a legislature today. Instead, free speech gets little attention and the dangers are everything. The legislative judgment is not reached "after due deliberation." [57] So the indispensable balancing will have to be done by the courts or not at all. If judges cannot or will not review suppressions, then legislators and officials are left free to penalize speech and even thoughts as much as they may desire, and they desire a great deal.

The definitions of wrongful speech and assembly in the new kinds of suppression since 1945 are very much broader than in the legislation before we entered the Second World War. The state sedition laws during the Red Menace and the Smith Act of 1940 penalized advocating the overthrow of the government by force and violence.[58] Although this phrase was often loosely construed, it was aimed only at Communists. The new legislation goes much farther. It was indeed put through by arguments that it was badly needed to get rid of Communists. Yet it rarely stops with Communists or other violent revolutionaries.

Look at the authoritative definition of "subversive activity" by a House committee as the basis for throwing federal officials out of their jobs: "Subversive activity . . . derives from conduct intentionally destructive of or inimical to the Government . . . which seeks to undermine its institutions, or to distort its functions, or to impede its projects, or to lessen its efforts . . . the ultimate end being to overthrow it all." [59] This goes far beyond support of violent revolution. The same is true of the vague characterization of "Communist-front organizations" in the McCarran Act, which I shall discuss in Chapter V. This Act also allows citizens to be sent to concentration camps without having committed any crime at all. Citizens can be put behind barbed wire for years merely because some official has "reasonable ground to believe" that they will commit or conspire with others to commit espionage or sabotage.[60] Such an official belief can of course be based on all sorts of heterodox opinions, etc., which would never support a conviction in a criminal trial. The tests of wrongdoing which will throw federal officials out of their jobs are "disloyalty" or "a poor security risk." The American Bar Association has called for disbarment proceedings against any lawyer who, without having the remotest connection with the Communist Party, is suspected of embracing "Marxism-Leninism," [61] a doctrine which may mean to his accusers something quite different from what it means to economists. An American citizen, at least until recently, could be denied a passport for no other reason than that his "travel abroad at this time would be contrary to the best interests of the United States." [62]

Perhaps the most extreme departure from the old criminal law tests of guilt appears in the recommendations of a California investigating committee for barring textbooks from public high schools. Books on American life were labeled as "subversive" because they stated that grazing by cattle and sheep could cause soil erosion, or spoke about the adverse criticism of Lincoln for arresting civilian opponents of the Civil War and putting them in military prisons, or contained photographs of slums and dust storms. And often a book was condemned, apart from anything expressed by the author, because of a casual reference to Senator Frank P. Graham, who belonged to groups listed by somebody or other as "Communist-front" or because the textbook had a bibliography which included anything written by any member of such a group or anybody else whom the committee considered "subversive." Among the various red-listed writers who were unfit for California high school children even to know about were Louis Adamic, Sherwood Anderson, Charles A. Beard, Stuart Chase, Morris Ernst, Dorothy Canfield Fisher, Arthur Garfield Hays, Oliver La Farge, Robert S. and Helen M. Lynd, Lewis Mumford, Sigmund Spaeth, Lincoln Steffens, and Sidney and Beatrice Webb.[63]

In short, anything which is found to be "subversive" can be penal-

ized in some way or other, and "subversive" is rapidly coming to mean anything which the powers that be don't like.

The prevailing current belief that this is the way to defend American freedoms against totalitarianism recalls nothing I know of in history since the hysteria over the Popish Plot in England around 1680. I have sometimes wondered what thoughtful, loyal Englishmen did during that time. Probably they simply kept quiet and hoped the storm would ride itself out. Perhaps this is all that thoughtful, loyal Americans can do today. Still, it is important during this crisis to have three general guides for our thinking.

In the first place, there is a strong need for everybody to keep firmly in mind both sides of the balance, which I described early in this chapter as essential to the proper solution of all free speech problems. On one side are the great values of open discussion, and we ought to start with them. If we begin with the vivid dangers, it is easy to stop there. However, people who are devoted to the First Amendment should avoid the opposite error of ignoring the genuine dangers which confront the nation today. The ruling groups in the Soviet Union and its satellites seem determined not to maintain any normal human relations with other countries. During my experiences in the United Nations, it was impossible to get anywhere with them. The chief impression I carried away was of men who had masks instead of faces. And they have despicable, clever allies in our midst, as several spy cases prove.

Supporters of freedom of speech who adequately understand such dangers will be better able to correct exaggerated versions of them by which the advocates of suppression are scaring the American people into throwing overboard our most cherished liberties. They will be better able to show how those dangers can be combatted effectively by other weapons than sedition laws. This existence of good alternatives is constantly getting overlooked. For example, Chief Justice Vinson gave as a main reason for sustaining the constitutionality of the Smith Act: "We reject any principle of governmental helplessness in the face of preparation for revolution. . . ." [64] Yet there was no helplessness if the Smith Act had been set aside.

Suppose there were real preparation for revolution. (I don't mean just talking about a revolution some day or other, which was safely left alone for 150 years before the Smith Act.) The government could crush a revolutionary plot at once by using the Conspiracy Act of 1861, which sends to prison for six years any two or more persons who conspire "to overthrow, put down, or to destroy" the government of the United States by force. The same severe punishment can be inflicted on conspirators who plan the use of force to oppose the authority of the government or to prevent or delay the execution of any federal law.[65] This old statute carried us safely through the terrible dangers of the Civil War, the unrest of the Red Menace, the suffering and resentment of the Great Depression. Yet, almost any argument for the necessity of the Smith Act or the McCarran Act is written as if the Conspiracy Act of 1861 did not exist. Therefore, it is essential to keep emphasizing this and other normal defenses, and line them up against our actual internal dangers.

The second important principle is more complex. Just because you think a certain kind of person or speech or organizational activity is very objectionable, it does not necessarily follow that force and suppression are the right ways to deal with the situation. For example, people ask, "Do you want an extreme Marxist to teach your children?" And when you answer, "No," they regard this as a conclusive reason why you should acquiesce in a test oath or inquisition for all schoolteachers in order to get rid of a few Marxists, if they should thus be turned up. The trouble is that only part of the situation has been stated. I don't want my children to be run over by automobiles, and I could keep them completely safe by never letting them go out of doors. Yet the losses would obviously far outweigh the gain. I am also anxious to have my children grow into active, courageous, and useful citizens. So I must take chances of automobile accidents, and minimize those chances in some better way. That was exactly Jefferson's method for dealing with heterodox agitators and teachers. In both his First Inaugural [66] and his statement to prospective teachers at the University of Virginia, he spoke of not being afraid "to tolerate error so long as reason is free to combat it." [67] Moreover, suppression will often do more harm than good. Thus, after zealous patriots had thrown the University of California into months of turmoil in order to get rid of a score of professors who were not Communists at all, a dean remarked: "No conceivable damage to the university at the hands of the hypothetical Communists among us could have equaled the damage resulting from the unrest, ill will, and suspicion engendered by this series of events." [68] Aside from the fact that students don't absorb all they hear anyway, there were plenty of orthodox professors available to offset the teaching of occasional heretics, to say nothing of parents, newspaper editors, and numberless other influences off the campus. Nor is what is proposed for suppression always an unmixed evil. The most vigorous critics of Karl Marx recognize that *Das Kapital* called attention to grave evils in English factories and slums. A Communist professor of mathematics may teach the differential calculus ably. The fallacy of the prevalent notion that you ought to get rid of a bad thing without looking at anything else involved is best brought home by pungent phrases—"Throwing out the baby with the bath water" and "Susy, get the hammer—there's a fly on baby's head."

Third, what is constitutional may still be very unwise. Most people have fallen into almost exactly the opposite attitude. Every time the Supreme Court refuses to upset one more kind of suppression, this decision is regarded as a green light to dash ahead. Yet nobody acts on the idea that everything constitutional is good when he is discussing income tax rates or the size of old age benefits or the regulation of collective bargaining. There constitutionality is sure, but we talk much about wisdom. We insist one plan will work well and another plan will work badly. We are all aware of many sorts of conflicting interests that require careful consideration.

So it ought to be when we are dealing with free speech problems. The reluctance of the Supreme Court to block loyalty programs, investigating committees, etc., simply puts constitutional objections out of the way. Other very serious objections to what is actually done under the law may still remain and call urgently for careful consideration.

Take legislative investigating committees. So far as the Constitution goes, "no holds are barred." Because their proceedings are not criminal trials, they are not bound by several of the procedural safeguards of prosecutions in the Sixth Amendment. Nevertheless, the First and Sixth Amendments set forth principles of wisdom which are highly relevant to legislative investigations. Therefore it is very regrettable that almost nothing has been done until very recently by Congress or the American bar to work out rules of decent procedure for investigating committees.

What I have been saying about the desirability of stressing practical consequences rather than constitutional issues, proved helpful to me while endeavoring to oppose suppressive measures, in print and at public hearings. I have found it best to keep on the level of wisdom and policy as much as possible. In the situation which now confronts us, we have to start by recognizing that a considerable number of decent people want more suppression of speech and opinions because they are sincerely afraid of the dangers of communism within the United States. The best practical hope is to persuade them that this danger is smaller than they think—small enough so that the risks of toleration are negligible in comparison to the losses to the American way of life which would inevitably follow from a systematic legal campaign against "dangerous thoughts." The First Amendment comes into the discussion chiefly as a powerful means of persuasion. If persuasion fails, then the First Amendment will be invoked in the courts, but that is a last resort. Once a measure is enacted, a large amount of suppression always occurs before it reaches a test in the courts, and plenty of harm is done even if the law is eventually declared unconstitutional. So the most important thing is to prevent the enactment of an unwise measure if possible. And that enactment is most likely to be prevented if a majority of the legislature and of active members of the public can be persuaded that it is undesirable.

It is much more difficult to conduct the argument on a constitutional level when you are appealing to the public or to a legislative committee. What you are really saying then is that they ought not to pass the measure even though they are not persuaded that it is undesirable. Whatever they think about it (you are arguing) the Supreme Court will annul it and so it will be useless. But this argument will fail unless you can convince your hearers that the Court will in fact be against the measure. In order to do this, you have to turn aside from the reasons about desirability which are part of everybody's thinking and stick to the kind of language which lawyers use. You have to be absolutely sure of your ground, for if other lawyers (on the legislative committee or elsewhere) can raise plausible doubts about the validity of your constitutional position, you will get nowhere. And you always have to reckon with the stubborn fact that your solid assertion a law is unconstitutional can be turned into dish-water by five Justices.

Because of my principle about the need for scrutinizing the wisdom and practical consequences of suppressive measures regardless of their constitutionality, I am going to ignore constitutional law for the rest of this chapter. There is no time to review in detail the operation of the various novel types of suppression. I shall attempt to state some aspects of what has been going on for over ten years which disturb a man who loves the kind of country in which he grew up and fears that that kind of country will soon disappear unless present trends are checked.

I am disturbed by the gradual erosion of many fundamental human rights which were cherished by the Americans of 1791. It is not just a question of inroads on freedom of speech and press, freedom of assembly, and freedom of petition (through the deterring effect of red-listing). Equally disquieting is what those inroads are doing to our traditions of a fair trial. A person who is subpoenaed into a legislative investigation, where his reputation and perhaps his livelihood are at stake, is denied much of the protection long enjoyed by those who risk imprisonment or a fine.[69] He is not told what he is charged with before he prepares his defense and starts answering questions; the investigators have a roving commission to find out anything whatever that will damage him. He cannot demand to be confronted with the witnesses against him, for they may be spies whose identity the secret police do not want disclosed.[70] So he may not know who his accusers are, and in any event he cannot cross-examine them. The normal right to counsel is denied. Sometimes he cannot even bring a lawyer into the room with him. When a lawyer is graciously admitted, he must usually be just a bystander with no chance to conduct the defense. Investigating committees even propose the disbarment of lawyers who defend persons suspected of subversive activities.

One frequent line of questioning by investigating bodies is to me abominable. After the investigated person has been asked whether he ever belonged to some "subversive" organization—remember that the range goes far beyond the Communist Party—the next question may be, "Name your associates," or "Were X and Y also in this organization?" The law, of course, gives no privilege against betraying one's friends, and yet no decent American would request such a betrayal, so long as no heinous crime is involved. It is ingrained in schoolboys not to "peach" on a comrade, and any schoolteacher who asked them to do so is not fit for his job.

Nearly three centuries ago, an obscure Englishman named Francis Jenkes was haled before Charles II and his Council for presuming to criticize royal policies at a public meeting. After he had frankly admitted his speech, the King asked him, "Who advised you in this matter?" Jenkes replied:

> To name any particular person (if there were such) would be a mean and unworthy thing, therefore I desire to be excused all farther answer to such questions.[71]

But because of his silence he stayed all summer in prison, and his stubbornness helped bring about the great Habeas Corpus Act of 1679.

It is this "mean and unworthy thing" which investigators are now trying to force citizens to do, in the name of Americanism.

Congressional committees who fling around frequent threats of committing such reluctant witnesses for "contempt of Congress" would do well to remember the old story of a Justice of the Peace. He met on the street a man against whom he had lately decided a case. The defeated litigant started to upbraid the J.P., who said he would sentence him for contempt. "You're not in your court. What I say on the street isn't contempt. You can't punish me." "Yes, I can. A Justice of the Peace is always an object of contempt."

I am disturbed by the growing number of perjury prosecutions which look as if they were brought to put men in prison, not really for lying, but for some long-past personal activities or utterances which could not themselves be punished.[72] Several of the questions involved in the prosecution of Owen Lattimore, for example, were so trivial or general that the only obvious reason for asking them was to crowd a distinguished historian, who had as yet done nothing criminal or unlawful, into giving answers which might cause a jury to convict him for perjury.[73] Many such cases give me the impression that the questioners do not want to get information—they want to "get" the witness and have him locked up.

I am also troubled by the way perjury prosecutions by-pass the Statute of Limitations. One of the main purposes of this statute is to protect innocent persons who might not be able to defend themselves against a charge of an antiquated crime, because of the difficulty of digging up recollections and documents about events a dozen years old, especially when they seemed of no importance at the time. Getting a man prosecuted for perjury if the grand jury happens to disagree with his memory of events long buried appears to be legally valid but it is nothing to be proud of.

There are disquieting aspects of double jeopardy in the cases of many public officials who keep getting attacked after loyalty boards have cleared them. So also in the repeated attempts our government has made ever since 1938 to throw Harry Bridges out of the country, by deportation while he was an alien, by denaturalization after he became a citizen, but always on the same charge of joining the Communist Party.[74] Of course, none of these persons was technically covered by the double jeopardy clause, which applies only to criminal proceedings. Dismissal for disloyalty after years of service, loss of citizenship, deportation—these are not punishments (judges say) though they are more to be dreaded than most fines and terms in jail. Still, beyond law there is still fair play. Hounding a man after he is cleared may be constitutional, but it is not the way I was brought up.

I am disturbed by the common assumption that deprivation of a job connected with the government is not a substantial loss of freedom. The theory is that governmental work is a special sort of thing and not a general privilege; hence the ousted individual is simply thrust out of a small corner of life, with plenty of other places left open to him. Thus, in sustaining the New York Feinberg Law, the Supreme Court reasoned that a schoolteacher is not deprived of freedom of speech and assembly when he is thrown out of the public schools.[75] In short, when a teacher can think and talk as much as he likes by merely giving up a government job, this is freedom.

Such a theory seems to me to assume what is not so. The man

was trained to be a public schoolteacher and to spend his life in that profession. Since thinking and talking are his business, restrictions on them as a condition of holding his job are peculiarly repugnant, while it is like cutting off his hand for him to go elsewhere. And where else? Private schools are fully staffed and unlikely to take a man who has quit in a controversy. A schoolteacher is not prepared for a trade and he is too old to make a fresh start. The Court's reasoning would logically make out that disbarment of a lawyer with heterodox opinions is no infringement of freedom of speech and thought.

And there is still larger fallacy in this attitude. It was all very well for Justice Holmes to say in 1892 that a New Bedford policeman, who was thrown off the force for soliciting money on a political campaign, "may have a constitutional right to talk politics, but he has no constitutional right to be a policeman." [76] Policemen are a small fraction of the population. But as soon as you begin to apply loyalty tests to everybody connected with the government, you embrace an enormous range of activities. The number of federal, state, and municipal employees is a substantial part of the working population. Add workmen in factories with government contracts and professors teaching in universities with an R.O.T.C. or a government grant for scientific research or an assigned unit from the Army or the Navy, and hardly anybody is left out. If millions of Americans lose freedom of speech and assembly by the mere act of earning a living, the First Amendment becomes a mockery.

Moreover, the astonishingly wide extent of federal employment and federal relationships greatly increases the hardship of dismissal for words or membership in peaceable organizations. Bring in the ramifications of state and municipal work, and the hardship becomes enormous. The brawny New Bedford policeman discharged in 1892 could easily get all sorts of other jobs. Not so a highly trained man today, like a public schoolteacher or a scientist in the Department of Agriculture, who in middle age is thrown out of work and branded as disloyal or a poor security risk because he exercised the rights which the Constitution gives to American citizens. Public employment is closed to him; few private employers will use him, and even then for tasks which he has no experience. While he and his family face poverty or ruin, judges blandly assure him that he has nothing to complain about, because he made his choice between working for the government and being free. Are public servants second-class citizens outside the Bill of Rights?

Remember, too, that a mistaken decision can be made. Such hardship may not justify the abandonment of all loyalty tests, but it is certainly a fact which ought to be faced frankly. It should be weighed in the balance against whatever benefits are expected to accrue from such tests. It might be a reason for concentrating the program on sensitive jobs. At all events, the possibility of unjust hardship ought to bring about a very careful scrutiny of the procedure used and the fitness of those who make the decisions.

I am disturbed by the growing inclination to turn spies into heroes. One of the earliest lessons learned by children is, as I have already said, that talebearing on one's comrades is a dirty business. No doubt, there are several long-recognized crimes very harmful to the community, like counterfeiting, where convictions would often be hard to obtain without stool-pigeons and spies. Here the need for the betrayer's evidence is so great as to outweigh the evils of spies. But when one is considering a novel crime, it is a question whether the game is worth the candle. The use by employers of spies in labor unions shows what can happen. And when political utterances are made crimes, secret police, spies, and eavesdroppers are necessary to discover that a crime has been committed at all. Historians of the Popish Plot and sedition laws in England during the French Revolution have demonstrated that spies were a black blot on such affairs.[77]

Spies sometimes become *agents provocateurs*, who incite the very crimes they are hired to report. In Russia years ago the spy Aseff, to make sure that the Czarist secret police saw the necessity of employing him, became one of the most dynamic and successful leaders of the Social Revolutionary Party; and to make sure that the Social Revolutionaries trusted him, he organized the assassination of the Minister of the Interior and of a grand duke. Though I do not believe that anything so bad as that is going on in the United States, it is very disquieting to read the evidence against the eleven top-string Communists in New York in 1949 by at least three spies, working under the direction of the F.B.I., who joined the Communist Party and served on its recruiting committees.[78] Thus these government employees were actively inducing American citizens to become members of a criminal conspiracy against the United States.

A still more pervasive evil of spies is the breakdown of confidence in social and family life. Intercourse is poisoned when one never knows if his fellow-guest at dinner is going to report his casual statements to the secret police. One would suppose we had heard enough of what went on in Germany under the Nazis or what goes on in Russia today to beware of this kind of thing.

The worst spy of all is the renegade. He has already double-crossed the community by engaging in wrongdoing and then double-crossed his associates by deserting them and helping to punish them. After such an experience, truth-telling does not come naturally. The renegade has to make a good story in order to obtain immunity for his own admitted misconduct. Hence there is a great temptation to exaggerate or falsify the behavior of his former associates.[78a] And since it is often his word against theirs, he has magnificent opportunities for gratifying personal spites or getting his rival in business or a love-affair put safely out of the way in jail. Do we get enough good out of many of these suppressive measures to make it worth while to pay this price?

I want to make absolutely clear my position about spies as witnesses against men accused of political crimes. I am not saying that such spies will tell nothing in court except lies. Undoubtedly, some of them will do their best to tell the truth during their whole testimony while many others will mix a good deal of truth with falsehoods. What I do say is that there is a much greater risk of false testimony from spies than from ordinary men. Every witness, no matter how honest, is naturally inclined to make a good showing for his own side. I know this from my own experience in will cases. But, in the case of most witnesses, any risks from this inclination are offset by several checks. Truthfulness is a requisite of most normal occupations from bookkeeping to the practice of medicine. An ingrained habit of telling the truth is carried on to the witness-stand. And the ordinary witness knows that any lack of veracity may be detected when he testifies, as he usually does, about matters which are capable of objective proof or on which he can be contradicted by disinterested eyewitnesses of the facts.

But when spies appear in court, such checks operate in a much weaker way. The very nature of a spy's work requires lying. He has to deceive his associates into thinking him one of themselves. The longer he does spying, the greater the tendency for the boundary between truth and falsehood to be blurred. You can never be sure that Dr. Jekyll has not changed into Mr. Hyde. You may get a man shifting so often from revolutionist to spy and back again that he does not know himself which he is. Readers of Conrad's *Secret Agent* and *Under Western Eyes* will have no doubt of this. We are witnessing altogether too many switches from Communists into spies without any assurance against further switches in the reverse direction. And the subject-matter of a spy's testimony in political cases is often incapable of neutral verification. He has enormous power to imagine words which were never said. The only other possible eyewitnesses of the transactions he narrates are usually the suspected person he is helping to punish and other members of the alleged conspiracy. It is impossible to let in the light of day upon these dusky happenings.

The trouble is not that you can be sure a spy is lying. The trouble is you cannot be sure he is telling the truth. The risk of false testimony is tremendously increased.

Therefore, the fact that it is hard to obtain convictions for political crimes without the use of spies is not an argument for using spies. It is an argument against having political crimes.

I am disturbed by the strong tendency to establish an American party-line. Loyalty and integrity are more and more getting tested by qualifications about what is in a man's mind which go far beyond the old-fashioned determination to support and defend the Constitution of the United States. For instance, a prominent lawyer asserts that the Constitution "contemplates a free enterprise system" [79] and hence everything inconsistent with that system deserves condemnation. The trouble is that the competition of small farmers and shopkeepers which the Founding Fathers knew was not quite the same as a nation of giant corporations. There is no definition of "free enterprise" suitable for application in any sort of legal proceedings. Such a vague phrase can mean what anybody wants it to mean. For some Americans "free enterprise" implies that whatever liberty is good for Joe Doakes is also good for the Aluminum Corporation of America. For some it is a way of asserting that particular governmental activities are bad. Thus the words are occasionally used to describe a system in which government dredges rivers but does not dam them, subsidizes steamships and not housing, supplies drinking water and not water power, puts a tariff on wool but makes no loans on cotton, grants tax exemptions to private plants without ever operating public plants, and hires doctors to treat the diseases of elderly veterans but not the diseases of children. For other Americans, including myself, "free enterprise" is the chance for a young man or woman to select an occupation and ac- quire a home; the probability of promotion for good work either in private industry or public service without interference by poli- ticians; the opportunity to reap a considerable reward for producing more and better things; and the incentive to effort which comes from being able to pass on a competence to one's children, with the hope that they will feel morally obligated to use it in making their lives more serviceable to the community.

In any event, "free enterprise" is an ideal constantly reshaped by experience and discussion. It is wholly unfit to be a legal test for banning textbooks in schools and colleges or taking away privileges from propagandist organizations.

It is a deviation from the American party-line to want democracy. "Ours is a republic. Under a democratic government the major party can put the minority into slavery," said the chairman of the California investigating committee to Florence Eldridge, the actress, before he red-listed her as "typical of the individuals within the various Stalinist orbits." [80] It is becoming a tenet of the American party-line that there was only one right policy in the frightful tangle of Chinese affairs. A cartoon by Herblock pictures a new recruit in the State Department holding up his right hand and swearing to defend the Constitution of the United States and Chiang Kai-shek. Belief in natural law is becoming essential to the American party- line. This is a highly controversial philosophical doctrine, as to which devoted and law-abiding citizens hold contrary views. Yet because Justice Holmes did not believe in natural law, he is now denounced as a totalitarian.[81]

In short, honest differences of opinion are treated like moral differences. The common framework of discussion is getting torn to pieces. Instead of an orderly and enlightened search for facts and sound judgment, public opinion is framed by coercion and intrigue and insinuations. Government by representation has been giving away to government by misrepresentation.

CONCLUSION

The Period of Subtle Suppressions after the Second World War has lasted far longer than the restrictions on speech and press which accompanied and followed the First World War. Ten years have passed since the Japanese surrendered, but not a single sedition law has been repealed or made less sweeping by amendment. Prosecutions and deportations are frequent, the public service is still losing many able, devoted men and women, and all sorts of other curbs on thought and expression remain in operation.[82] Nevertheless, I believe that the Period of Subtle Suppressions is approaching its end.

Many straws are blown by a fresher wind. A perjury prosecution was dropped because the indictment was procured through fraudulent statements to the grand jury by an informer. Another informer, on whom the government repeatedly relied, lately announced that he had given false testimony against several persons. Whether he lied in his accusations or in his recantation, the fact is plain that a government star witness is a liar.

We have arrived, I think, at the same absurd stage of fear which the previous Period of Suppression reached by January 1920 in the expulsion of the five duly elected Socialists from the New York Assembly. When over a million tenants in federal housing projects are forced to take loyalty oaths with the result that only a few are evicted, when a government expert is dismissed as a disloyalty risk by the Department of Agriculture and then found fit for an important job by the Foreign Operations Administration, when a brilliant graduate of notably high character in the Merchant Marine Academy is for several months refused a commission because his mother had been a Communist until he persuaded her out of it, when Indiana requires loyalty oaths from boxers and wrestlers, we are in a situation where any change must be in the direction of common sense. Especially encouraging is the frequent expression of opinions in leading newspapers that such acts are folly.[83]

Meanwhile, the cogent dissenting opinions of Justices Black and

Douglas have done for faith in liberty what the dissents of Holmes and Brandeis did thirty years before. Other members of the Supreme Court have insisted on orderly procedure in determining that individuals or organizations are subject to repressive statutes. And the Supreme Court shows an increasing tendency when the Communist Party is not involved, to question the validity of governmental restrictions on opinion and intellectual activity. For instance, a gratifying series of recent decisions brings motion-pictures under the constitutional protection of "freedom of speech and of the press." [84] In 1955 the Court at last intervened in a departmental loyalty investigation, where the man was not told who his accusers were. The unanimous judgment removed the stigma of disloyalty from a distinguished Yale specialist in diseases of the heart.[85] Although the unimpressive reasoning of the Court will not quicken anybody's pulse, what judges do is sometimes more important than what they say. The decision serves notice on the government to pay more regard to the customary safeguards in the Bill of Rights against unjust or mistaken punishments when it seeks to deprive an official of his job and his good name.

Lower courts have also done much during the last year or two to uphold the liberties of non-Communists, for instance, against vague charges of perjury and arbitrary denials of passports.[86]

However, the termination of an era of repression cannot be effected by judges, except in rather limited ways. The cases which do get to court are necessarily decided after a long lapse of time during which irremediable harm may be done, and many acts of suppression never come before judges at all. For the most part, the reinstatement of liberties depends on the Executive Departments and Congress. Therefore, the most hopeful signs of a new spirit are the recent action of Congress in almost unanimously establishing a commission to survey the whole matter of loyalty and security, the increasing activity in planning rules for the conduct of legislative investigating committees, and the fact that the Senate Standing Subcommittee on Constitutional Rights, under the chairmanship of Senator Hennings of Missouri, is making a wide inquiry into invasions or erosion of the Bill of Rights and possible needs for legal changes.

Though mindful of the old saying: "Don't holler till you're out of the woods," I begin to see the light through the trees.

What can we as plain citizens do to help turn this nation back toward the freedoms which Englishmen and Americans attained through centuries of struggle and privations and hard thinking? For years to come, I fear, there is a very small chance of our being able to affect decisions in specific cases or the enactment of sedition laws or the behavior of subversive control boards and legislative investigating committees. Little can we do there, but much can we do to aid in the formation of a sounder public opinion, which will revert to the courage of Thomas Jefferson.

Free speech problems are arising constantly in private lives. They are not limited to courtrooms and Congressional offices. Shall I let my child read this book? Shall I sit silent while the school committee dismisses an unpopular teacher? Shall this meeting take place in a local hall or on a vacant lot? Shall I vote against a man because some Senator calls him subversive? Am I reading both sides of a controversy? Those are questions presented to common or garden people all the time, and the way they are answered can give us more freedom or less.

And it is very fruitful to keep discussing, in season and out of season, the great advantages of open discussion. Of all the arguments in favor of freedom of speech, the strongest of all (I have come to think) is that it gives us a better country to live in, with fewer suspicions, animosities, informers, heresy trials, and more scope for initiative and originality.

A people gets sooner or later as much freedom as it wants. This want is partly created by prophets on or off the bench, but partly by constant discussion from plain citizens like us. The best safeguard against inroads on freedom of speech lies in the ferment in the thoughts of the young and of those who will not let themselves grow old.

IV   Does Freedom of Speech Really Tend to Produce Truth?

> And though all the winds of doctrine were let
> loose to play upon the earth, so Truth be in the
> field, we do injuriously by licensing and prohibiting
> to misdoubt her strength. Let her and Falsehood
> grapple; who ever knew Truth put to the worse,
> in a free and open encounter?——MILTON, *Areo-
> pagitica*

Those of us who believe that no idea is so sacred as to be immune from inquiry ought not to shrink from trying in the fire of discussion our cherished faith in the inestimable value of discussion. Does truth really emerge from the conflict of ideas, as Milton said, or was he voicing an eloquent illusion?

The oldest and commonest attack on open discussion assumes that it is not needed to produce truth, because truth is already possessed by those in authority. Hence freedom to express other opinions would spread untruths. Thus Plato in his *Republic* was going to have all-wise Guardians who could punish writers for telling lies. An English law of 1401 which stayed in force for nearly three centuries ordered that anyone who taught or wrote anything "contrary to the decisions of Holy Church" should be burned before the people in some prominent place, so as to "prevent such erroneous opinions from being supported." [1] The same view inspired our Sedition Act of 1798, through which the Federalists sent many editors of Jeffersonian newspapers to prison for "false, scandalous and malicious writings." [2] Thomas Carlyle said that "it is the everlasting privilege of the foolish to be governed by the wise." [3] The view that a few men are good enough to decide what is bad for a great many people has plenty of vitality today.

Not much will be said here about this authoritarian view because I have marshaled many arguments against it in my *Free Speech in the United States* [4] and great writers have magnificently set forth the dangers to society when its rulers establish a monopoly of ideas. The whole of Milton's *Areopagitica* assails censorship of the press and Mill on *Liberty* opposes all the methods of suppressing thought and discussion. It will be enough for me to mention two of the weaknesses in the authoritarian view. First, it is almost impossible to find men with the wisdom and incorruptibility which are essential for the task of controlling the minds of everybody else and killing bad ideas *en masse*. Second, men in authority are tempted to identify their own policies with truth and to make opposing ideas criminal as a means of perpetuating those policies and their control of the government. Consequently, as Andrew Hamilton said in his defense of Peter Zenger:

> All freemen have a right publicly to remonstrate against the abuses of power in the strongest terms, to put their neighbors upon their guard against the craft or open violence of men in authority, and to assert with courage the sense they have of the blessings of liberty. . . .[5]

THE SCEPTICAL ATTACK ON FREEDOM OF SPEECH

What I chiefly want to take up in this chapter is a recent and quite different attack on free speech, which in my opinion is much harder to repel than the authoritarian attack just described. Here discussion is attacked, not as false and evil, but as worthless. The supporters of this view deny the validity of Milton's assertion that truth emerges from the clash of ideas. According to them nothing emerges. An argument merely ends in a deadlock, with each side sticking obstinately to its own position.

This view forces us to re-examine the whole process of argument and counter-argument instead of taking its success for granted. A relentless prober of the process is Frank Knight, an economist at the University of Chicago, who likes Liberalism and wishes it could last, but reluctantly believes it doomed to disappear along with the pioneer conditions and the small communities in which political individualism flourished. Contrast the quotation from Milton at the head of this chapter with the following passages from Knight's essay:

The settlement of issues by free general discussion is at best a costly process in time and mental effort and patience, even when the group is very small. . . . It is much simpler to have someone in charge. Reflection on what happens in the simplest cases—say the discussion of presumably scientific problems by two social scientists—is hardly conducive to faith in the possibilities when larger groups and more tangible difficulties are involved.

In fact, "discussion" needs little formal suppression. There is little evidence that any large mass of people ever wanted to discuss or to attend to discussion, of serious issues, involving real intellectual effort.

Interest in winning [a game] and the interest in the game tend to run into conflict; too much interest in winning first spoils a game and then breaks it up altogether, converting it into a quarrel. . . . Discussion seems to manifest in an especial degree the tendency of games to deteriorate . . . first into ill-will, and ultimately into disruption or even violence. From this point of view, the history of intellectual activity . . . is surely far from encouraging. The specialized professional intellectuals have shown little enough capacity to maintain the spirit of discussion, even in small groups and under what should be extremely favorable conditions; and of their ability to settle issues and solve serious problems by discussion among themselves, it is more pleasant not to speak. . . . In the field of morals and politics—to say nothing of religion—it is questionable whether the net result has been progress toward consensus or the multiplication of controversy.[6]

Are things quite so bad as all that, even though much of what Knight says is undoubtedly so? Each of us regrets his heated participation in many arguments which got nowhere. Yet is every argument fruitless? Before endeavoring to answer this question, I am going to consider what sort of fruit we expect a discussion to bring forth.

What Do We Mean by "Truth"?

Without presuming to answer Pontius Pilate's famous question: "What is truth?" I shall try to show that the "truth" which freedom of speech is said to promote is not a single unified concept. Instead of thinking just of the word "truth" it may be helpful to ask what Justice Holmes had in mind when he said "that *the ultimate good desired* is better reached by free trade in ideas." [7] There are three rather different kinds of "ultimate good" which, we hope, will be produced by freedom of discussion.

First. When Milton spoke of Truth as victorious in a free and open encounter, he mainly referred to what Plato called the highest matters—the existence and nature of God, the purpose of the universe, our relations to God and the universe and our fellowmen, our reasons for living. Truth in this sense is especially furthered by freedom of religion. The persecutions and struggles of the past over freedom of expression were mostly in this area, and we can be happy that the victory of freedom has been so largely won. Let us trust that the search for truth in our understanding of the highest matters will continue to be untrammeled.

Second. The ultimate good desired from open discussion may be an accurate presentation of facts. Walter Lippmann in his *Public Opinion* showed the enormous importance, in the conduct of affairs, of having the pictures in our heads correspond to facts—those stubborn things in the external world, which are obvious to the five senses. The best argument I know for freedom of speech in order to attain this kind of truth is a story by Benjamin Constant:

> A sailor related that he was once on board a vessel with a passenger who had frequently made the same voyage. This passenger told the captain about a rock ahead which was hidden beneath the waves, but the captain would not listen to him. On his insisting on it, the captain had him thrown into the sea. This energetic measure put an end to all remonstrances, and nothing could be more touching than the unanimity which reigned on board. Suddenly the vessel hit the reef and was wrecked. They had got rid of the giver of the warning, but the rock remained. [8]

Facts as such are rarely offered to the public. Occasionally a signed document just can't be denied. But all that is usually available is evidence, somebody's say-so, or inferences from other facts. The passenger could not show the submerged rock; he merely stated his recollection as evidence of the fact of the rock. Now, evidence may be mistaken or deliberately falsified. The public cannot be sure of the facts themselves till it has gone through a lengthy sifting of conflicting statements and inferences. Fortunately, the necessity of this process is pretty well realized in the United States, and there is widespread insistence that evidence may be given without serious risk of penalties. This is so even when the facts in issue are very disagreeable to the people in power, like corruption among federal tax-collectors. It is rare to have the situation before the Supreme Court in 1931,[9] where the very district attorney whom a journal charged with being in league with houses of prostitution almost succeeded in putting the journal out of business on the ground that it was a scandal-sheet.

There is, however, an increasing tendency to discourage and perhaps penalize the disclosure of evidence on two types of facts. One is defense secrets, like the number of atomic bombs or the number of F.B.I. agents. Of these I say nothing now, except to point out that the area of facts subtracted by law or public opinion from open discussion is constantly growing larger.

The other type consists of issues of fact of unfamiliar sorts—not like charges of political corruption. When evidence on a particular side is distasteful to a considerable mass of Americans, it is becoming more and more perilous for anybody to offer it. Hence we are getting a lopsided presentation of information on issues of facts as to which the American people badly need to reach sound conclusions; for instance, the real size and fighting strength of Chinese troops at the disposal of Chiang Kai-shek or the real opinion of Spanish workers about the government of Franco.

Third. A very important result expected in much open discussion is what the Persian prince in Herodotus had in mind when he said:

> It is impossible, if no more than one opinion is uttered, to make choice of the best; . . . but if opposite speeches are delivered, then choice can be exercised.[10]

For example, when a voter decides between two candidates for Congress, he is making a value-judgment. The issue is not "What exists?" but "What shall we do?" A sound decision is more probable if men can safely say what they believe or wish. Pericles told the Athenians in their black days that "we think discussion an indispensable preliminary to any wise action at all." [11]

The value of open discussion is most frequently realized when it is preliminary to political action, but it is by no means confined to governmental controversies. As was pointed out in the preceding chapter,[12] the same policy extends to the making of sound decisions and value-judgments in other matters of public interest, such as art, literature, education, and the relations between men and women. This wide scope of freedom of speech was recognized by the Supreme Court when it sustained artistic freedom against state censorship of the movies in the recent case of the *Miracle*.[13]

Talking and writing on the heterodox side about political or social action and value-judgments raise more difficulties in our time as to the proper range of permissible discussion than does discussion about the other two kinds of truth. The bitterness which used to prevail in religious controversies has now been transferred to political and social disputes. Although nobody has yet been put to death in America for expressing non-religious ideas, a good many men in the last forty years have gone to prison or lost their jobs through legal proceedings because they presumed to differ from the opinions accepted by a majority of their fellow-citizens, and scores of aliens have been deported for speaking or even thinking heretically. Since 1945 the methods of enforcing intellectual uniformity by law have grown rapidly in variety and vigor.

Therefore, the problem of this chapter is whether freedom of speech really tends to produce a better understanding of the highest matters and more knowledge of facts and sounder decisions.

Some Obstacles to the Attainment of Truth in Open Discussion

After reading Frank Knight, I can no longer think of open discussion as operating like an electric mixer, which is the impression left by Milton and Jefferson—run it a little while and truth will rise to the top with the dregs of error going down to the bottom. There are at least three obstacles to the automatic emergence of truth from the contest.

The first is the increasing tendency for the most effective instrumentalities of communication to be owned and shaped by persons who are often on one side of many public questions. The Commission on the Freedom of the Press, of which Robert M. Hutchins was chairman, gave a great deal of thought to this matter and proper remedies for it.

For instance, we pointed out in our report on *A Free and Responsible Press* [14] that when the First Amendment was adopted in 1791 anybody with anything to say had little difficulty in getting it published. A journeyman printer could set up a newspaper if he could borrow a few dollars. Each large town had many newspapers which, taken together, represented nearly all of the conflicting viewpoints on public issues. Contrast the press today, which has been transformed into an enormous and complicated machinery and consequently has become big business. There is a marked reduction in the number of newspapers relative to the total population. These facts led our report to state:

> The right of free public expression has therefore lost its earlier reality. Protection against government is now not enough to guarantee that a man who has something to say shall have a chance to say it. The owners and managers of the press determine which persons, which facts, which versions of the facts, and which ideas shall reach the public. . . .
> The press must be free from the menace of external compulsions from whatever source. . . . The press must, if it is to be wholly free, know and overcome any biases incident to its own economic position, its concentration, and its pyramidal organization.

In other words, so far as law goes, freedom of the press is only the right to be let alone. The law itself does nothing affirmative. It leaves the whole task of promoting truth in the hands of authors, editors, reporters, publishers, broadcasters, motion-picture producers, and the rest of the communications people. Unless *they* do something worth while, not a mite of truth has been attained or communicated. All that has happened is that a bunch of outsiders with official titles and police badges has been reduced to inaction. The law is kept away, but is truth any farther ahead?

Thus the First Amendment and other parts of the law erect a fence inside which men can talk. The law-makers, legislators and officials stay on the outside of that fence. But what the men inside the fence say when they are let alone is no concern of the law.

It is, however, the concern of American citizens, and it ought to be the still greater concern of the men inside the fence. Freedom ought to be affirmative for the writers and newspaper publishers and motion-picture producers and operators of radio or television who are immune from legal interference. Nobody can blame the men who own and operate the instrumentalities of communication for seeking to make money. Neither publishers nor professors are called upon to serve God for naught. Yet the question remains: What are their other purposes, or have they no other purposes?

The defects found by the Commission on the Freedom of the Press would not be remedied, we said, by lessening the legal freedom of the press. What we did conclude was that this legal freedom ought to carry with it more moral responsibility to give the people of the United States what they need to get from the press. It is not enough to ask: "Freedom *from* what?" A much bigger question, we insisted, is: "Freedom *for* what?"

> The press must be free for the development of its own conceptions of service and achievement. It must be free for making its contribution to the maintenance and development of a free society.
>
> This implies that the press must also be accountable. It must be accountable to society for meeting the public need and for maintaining the rights of citizens and the almost forgotten rights of speakers who have no press.

Another obstacle to the attainment of truth is the multiplicity of issues and arguments which are thrown at any American all day long until he becomes satiated and the reasoning process which Milton and Jefferson presupposed begins to choke and stop. Is it any longer possible to discover truth amid the clashing blares of advertisements, loud-speakers, enormous headlines, gigantic billboards, television screens, party programs? To sift the truth from all these half-truths drenched with emotion seems to demand a calmness beyond human attainment and a statistical investigation beyond anybody's time and money.

The third obstacle is nothing new, and here we cannot throw the blame on inventors, propagandists, press magnates, or anybody except ourselves. Knight puts his finger on the weakness of each man of us:

[A man] set thinking . . . is as partial to his own ideas as he is to his own children. . . . There is in our field [of the social sciences] no objective test for separating either truth from opinion or the urge to promote an opinion "believed" to be true from the craving for personal aggrandizement. . . . Love of truth is humanly inseparable from the wish to spread the belief in what one believes to be true.[15]

The older writers were not confronted with some of the causes of friction impeding the free flow of discussion, and they paid too little attention to those they did know about. The market for trading in ideas, of which Justice Holmes spoke, is not perfect any more than the market for goods. Yet we ought not to throw up the sponge, but we do have to recognize that the task of attaining truth through freedom is harder than we thought. Reason plays a smaller part in human affairs than we used to believe, but it still remains the best guide we have, better than our emotions, better than tradition, better than any few men in places of authority, however exalted.

Exploration of the Way Opinions Are Formed Out of What Is Said During Discussion

A fuller understanding of the way discussion operates will keep us from being entirely discouraged about its outcome. The great writers did mislead us a little, because their inspiring words made us expect too much from discussion and too soon. Also I suspect we have gone astray by thinking of an argument between two sharply opposed antagonists, like the Lincoln-Douglas Debates, as characteristic of most discussion. After all, we say, Lincoln did not convince Douglas, and Douglas did not convince Lincoln, so neither of them was any closer to the truth than before. This pessimism is mistaken in stopping with the two chief participants. It ignores thousands of listeners and readers; many of them may have reshaped their half-formed views because of what Lincoln and Douglas said. A more important and more subtle mistake consists of overlooking the fact that discussion of a public issue is usually ever so much more unsystematic, informal, prolonged, fluid, far-flung, than this famous series of speeches by two men. Ordinarily the contest between truth and error bears no resemblance to a prize fight with a chance for bystanders to yell, "May the best man win!"

An utterly different metaphor is helpful to me in picturing what goes on while the conflicting statements of individuals are getting transformed into a satisfactory basis for public action: a bay with thousands of waves, piling up on the shore and then pulling back, sometimes higher, sometimes lower. We know that the tide is either coming in or going out, but we do not have a tide-table. The immeasurable motion appears aimless, but time will show the main course of the sea.

One thing I am sure of, that an alteration in our opinions very rarely comes right after an argument in which we have vigorously taken one side. Even so, perhaps two or three facts put forward by our opponent didn't quite fit into our own set-up. They stick in our minds. We observe other facts ourselves which re-enforce these. "A flying word from here and there" [16] makes us uneasy about our conclusion. A friend we especially admire expresses a rather contrary opinion. Some extreme application of our own view occurs in real life and shocks us. In the end we may not go the whole way, but we have greatly shifted from our old position.

Not only does free discussion sometimes lead us to change our minds, but also it very often helps us to make up our minds on issues about which, previously, we did not care one way or the other. Suddenly we realize their importance and the necessity of taking sides.

All this shaping and reshaping takes time, and a good deal of it is not deliberate reasoning like solving an algebraic equation. What matters greatly is a willingness to receive impressions from many different sources and the opportunity for such impressions to reach us. "The wind bloweth where it listeth."

Now, if into this delicate process the government injects threats of penalties and perhaps actual suppression, the disastrous consequences are easily realized. The powerful emotion of fear impedes the process at every point. The multitudinous sources of our impressions begin to dry up; the impressions no longer come near us or if they do, their entrance into our minds is impeded by the barriers of anxiety. Everybody down the line, including you and me, tends to replace the vital question: "Do I believe this?" by

asking, "Is this illegal or disloyal or liable to hurt me, perhaps a year
or two hence in some way I can't now foresee?" As Kant says:

> It is absurd to expect to be enlightened by Reason, and at the same
> time to prescribe to her what side of the question she must adopt.[17]

The foregoing survey of the complicated interchanging of facts
and ideas shows, I hope, that a good deal of what is said one way
and the other does eventually enter into the conclusions we accept
as the basis for action or for the conduct of our lives.

SOME OF THE INDIRECT BENEFITS OF FREEDOM OF SPEECH TO TRUTH

The objection is often raised by the supporters of suppressing a
given speech or pamphlet that what is said therein cannot possibly
contribute anything to truth. It is all worthless. Nothing whatever
is lost by junking it. Leaving out the possibility that an opponent
is not the best judge of the merits of what his antagonist says, I
do feel that a large portion of the output of radical extremists involved in the many free speech cases I have studied was so wordy,
shopworn, and vituperative as to make reading it a complete waste
of time. An example of this was the mass of material issued thirty
or forty years ago by the Industrial Workers of the World.

Nevertheless, these I.W.W.s had grievances. They were homeless
and uprooted, with their wages and working conditions largely
determined by a succession of farmers who employed them for one
crop here and another crop miles away. Their wild speeches and
handbills called attention to their grievances. The remedies they
proposed themselves were probably foolish, but they showed the
need for *some* remedy. Eventually the Roosevelt Administration did
a good deal about the problem of migratory agricultural labor.

Thus the voicing of a minority position is desirable even when
stated with much error. "Those who are unhappy have no need
for anything in the world except people capable of giving them
their attention." [18] Freedom increases the chances of attention. Thus
it contributes indirectly to truth by hastening a sound decision on
a public issue.

The educational value of free choices to the people is stressed by Milton in contrast with "a fugitive and cloistered virtue," and Mill ably shows how contact with error strengthens the presentation of truth. If, instead of silencing domestic Communists by mass prosecutions, we would engage in public debates with them, the noble gospel of American freedom would be enriched by fresh applications to current problems. As I said in Chapter II, we cannot make our tradition contagious for Europeans and Asiatics by merely repeating our great documents of the distant past. Into the old bottles must be put new wine.

The harm to truth from suppression does not come merely from the inability of the public to hear what the particular men would say, who are imprisoned or driven from their jobs. Very often they are loud-mouthed, unattractive men whose evidence and ideas are rather worthless. One of the evils of suppression is that such persistent trouble-makers are the only men with sufficient courage and energy to conflict with the law, so that freedom of speech becomes identified with unscrupulous pamphleteers and ranting soapbox orators. Consequently, it is widely assumed that the loss to the world of thought has been very small. But the governmental attack on the loud-mouthed few frightens a multitude of cautious and sensitive men, who do not dare to imperil their wives and children. It upsets their tranquility, which is essential to productive writing. We cannot know what is lost through the effect of repression on them, because it is not prosecuted but simply left unsaid. The agitator's contest is waged on behalf of these thoughtful men as well as for his own sake, and, if he wins, the gain to truth will usually come more from their writing than from his.

Freedom creates an atmosphere of happiness and mastery of one's work of thinking and writing, which is very favorable to the attainment of truth. Suppression, as Spinoza says, is "paring down the state till it is too small to harbour men of talent." [19] Since exile is not very feasible for American citizens, the best course is to write on safe subjects and keep away from problems which arouse hostility. Those happen to be the very problems on which the nation most needs light.

THE PROPRIETY OF LEGAL LIMITATIONS ON SPEECH

It follows from all I have been saying that the freer free speech is, the better the complicated process of discussion is going to work so as to discover and spread the truth. Because of inevitable elements of friction, truth comes with greater imperfections and delays than we used to think; but if freedom be lessened it comes still more imperfectly and slowly. The delicate machinery for the interchange of facts and ideas begins to slip gears and chatter and run wild.

Every sedition law or other novel restriction on speech seriously hinders the attainment of truth. Every individual case of suppression risks the loss of truth. Anybody who supports such measures is asserting in effect that something else is worth more than truth.

Nevertheless, the search for truth cannot be absolutely immune from legal interference. The settled recognition of damage-suits for slander and libel negatives such a doctrine. The seriousness of a tarnished reputation and the possibility of fights are thought to outweigh the risk that the jury will mistakenly penalize truth. Judges can punish newspapers for publishing evidence which has not been admitted at the trial, and thus influencing the jury; here the proper place for the contest between truth and error is the court-room, and special rules apply. Plans of battleships and atomic energy formulas cannot be passed out to the public; the truer they are, the worse the disclosure. In short, the attainment of truth is not the only purpose for which the community exists. Truth may have to be sacrificed to some more important social need, just as the drafted soldier is required to sacrifice his right to personal liberty and perhaps to life for the sake of national safety.

Without trying to map out all the legitimate limitations on open discussion, I venture to state four guiding principles:

First. Those who are considering such measures should begin by reading and reflecting a good deal upon the importance to society of unrestricted talk, and be very sure that the nation will really be in great danger if the proposed limitation is rejected. The feasibility of alternative remedies for objectionable ideas ought to be carefully canvassed. It would be a good plan to have the relevant passages of Jefferson's First Inaugural read aloud in the Senate and the House of Representatives at the beginning of every debate on a sedition bill or a deportation bill. As Burke, who was no radical, cautioned:

> It ought to be the constant aim of every wise public counsel to find out by cautious experiments, and rational, cool endeavors, with how little, not how much restraint the community can subsist.[20]

Second. Much attention ought to be paid to the capacity of a given tribunal to discriminate accurately between truth and error. Because twelve men from the street are trusted to apply standards of common sense in determining the falsity of a defamatory statement specific in nature, like a charge of stealing bank funds, it does not follow that jurymen are also suited to appraise the injuriousness of unfamiliar political and economic doctrines. And the fitness of a legislative committee of politicians with an eye on re-election to sift truth from error in such matters is far from plain.

Third. A restrictive law is especially objectionable when it has to be enforced through spies and informers. They are not needed in actions for libel or slander, because the plaintiff quickly finds out for himself that he has been defamed. But when political utterances are made crimes, secret police, spies, and eavesdroppers are necessary to discover that a crime has been committed at all. And, as I have already shown,[21] spies have enormous power to imperil truth.

Fourth. Suppressions are much more questionable when the conceivable interference with truth will be extensive than when it will be slight. A law against profanity in public places hinders the communication of facts and ideas very little. A libel upon an individual may concern nobody else. See how obscenity laws illustrate this principle. Punishing the sale of gross pornography to school children does not block truth much; but the consequences are far more serious when such laws are used to ban *Strange Interlude* and *Strange Fruit*, and thus prevent the public from receiving new ideas about changes in marriage and interracial relations.

The conscription of truth should never be undertaken lightly. The men who propose suppressions, in Congress and elsewhere, speak much of the dangers against which they are guarding, but they rarely consider the new dangers which they are creating or the great value of what they are taking away.

V Freedom and Fear

> Those who won our independence by revolution
> were not cowards. They did not fear political
> change. They did not exalt order at the cost of
> liberty—Louis Dembitz Brandeis *

It is late winter in 1801. For less than six months Washington has
been the seat of government of a twelve-year-old union of sixteen
states, cooped up within the eastern third of the continent by the
Mississippi. Across that river for its entire length and in firm control
of its mouth is France, the most powerful nation on earth, ruled
absolutely by the greatest of military geniuses, a man of unbounded
ambition in command of a gigantic army and a navy not yet sunk
at Trafalgar, able to bring troops seasoned in a score of campaigns
across the Atlantic, through our few vessels, to confront only militia
when they land on our shores. The country has recently been torn
by conflicting ideas and passions engendered by the French Revolution and by a bitter Presidential election, which had to be settled by
Congress. Now the winner in that contest, a slight man dressed in
plain clothes, walks from his lodgings through the muddy and
almost houseless streets, without a guard or servant. He reaches the
Capitol, an embryonic structure with one wing and no dome. At-
tended only by a crowd of citizens, he ascends the steps to become
the third President of the United States, and before long is speaking
these words:

> If there be any among us who wish to dissolve this union, or to
> change its republican form, let them stand undisturbed, as monu-
> ments of the safety with which error of opinion may be tolerated
> where reason is left free to combat it. I know indeed that some
> honest men have feared that a republican government cannot be
> strong; that this government is not strong enough. But would the
> honest patriot, in the full tide of successful experiment, abandon a

---

* Concurring in Whitney v. California, 274 United States Reports 357 (1927)

government which has so far kept us free and firm on the theoretic
and visionary fear that this government, the world's best hope, may,
by possibility, want energy to preserve itself? I trust not. I believe
this, on the contrary, the strongest government on earth.

It is late winter in 1949. The sixteen states have trebled and the
five million citizens of 1801 have multiplied in 148 years to well over
148 millions, filling the natural boundaries which the United States
attained a century ago. Our only neighbors now are two peaceful
and friendly nations, and our people are the most prosperous in the
world. Indeed, we are the only large country which is prosperous
at all, for the rest are impoverished, devastated, struggling in
austerity. The thirty-second President, Harry S. Truman, is sworn
in before more than one hundred thousand of his fellow-countrymen
and honored by the greatest parade in the long history of the national capital, watched by a million persons. The pageant passes
before the reviewing-stand for almost three hours, beginning with
the scarlet-coated United States Marine Band. There are the men
from West Point and Annapolis, marching with their famous preci-
sion. There are General Eisenhower and General Bradley, Admiral
Nimitz and Admiral Halsey. An armada of airplanes roars above.
And these are only a small portion of our armed forces which have
exterminated a despot ruling a vaster territory than Napoleon,
fought two mighty enemies at the same time, and reduced them
to ruin. Millions of other Americans trained and hardened in warfare are ready to take up arms again at a moment's notice should
any foe threaten attack. Nor is this all, for the scientists whom
Jefferson encouraged have handed on their patient and resourceful
skill to many more scientists, who have given this nation the most
deadly weapon ever wielded by man.

Once again the national spirit of the moment is voiced in words.
This time it is not by the newly-elected President, but by three
Senators who are inserting in bills, which they will introduce in
Congress in a month, the basic political theme of 1949 and the
subsequent years:

> The recent successes of Communist methods in other countries
> and the nature and control of the world Communist movement itself
> present a clear and present danger to the security of the United

States and to the existence of free American institutions, and make it necessary that Congress, in order to preserve the sovereignty of the United States as an independent nation, . . . enact appropriate legislation recognizing the existence of such world-wide conspiracy and designed to prevent it from accomplishing its purpose in the United States.

THE MCCARRAN ACT OF 1950—GENERAL OUTLINE

That "appropriate legislation," built around the prevailing national principle of fear, will be the subject of this chapter. The new sedition law started in the spring of 1949 as the Mundt-Nixon Bill, because it was sponsored by Senator Carl Mundt of South Dakota and Richard M. Nixon, chairman of the House Un-American Activities Committee, who is now Vice-President. It passed the House of Representatives by a big margin and faded away in the Senate. Next year it might have suffered a similar fate but for the outbreak of the fighting in Korea. The excitement caused by our giving battle to Communists carried this anti-Communist bill triumphantly through both Houses of Congress. By then it had been renamed the McCarran Bill after Senator Pat McCarran of Nevada. Mr. Truman vetoed the bill as unnecessary and objectionable, but it was repassed with little opposition in either House on September 23, 1950, and thus became the third peacetime sedition law in our national history.[1] Its predecessors were the Sedition Act of 1798, which expired long ago, and the Alien Registration Act of 1940 still in force, of which the best-known part is called the Smith Act.[2]

The 1950 sedition law is officially entitled the Subversive Activities Control Act of 1950 but commonly called the McCarran Act, and I shall so speak of it.

By this time Congress had acquired a thirst for sedition laws, which was not slaked by the Smith Act of 1940 and the McCarran Act ten years later. Within four years it had to have still another. The Communist Control Act of 1954 was enacted almost unanimously, and signed by Mr. Eisenhower with a fruitless request for Congress to improve it at the next session. Many provisions of this 1954 law are so incomprehensible[3] that I shall say nothing about it, except when I occasionally have to deal with points in the 1950

Act which were amended in 1954. One sedition law at a time is quite enough. This chapter will deal only with the McCarran Act. Furthermore, I shall take up just the portion of that Act which developed from the Mundt-Nixon Bill, and ignore provisions on other subjects, for instance, to make deportation more severe and to enable American citizens to be put in concentration camps during war or proclaimed emergency without any charge of crime, when the Attorney General thinks they might commit espionage or sabotage if left loose.[4]

The main features of the legislation discussed in this chapter need to be briefly described right away, so that my readers will know what I am talking about. Later, after asking whether we need such a law, I shall examine some of its provisions in detail.

This new sedition law covers twenty-six pages of the United States Code Annotated. It starts with a long preamble, part of it already quoted, in which Congress undertakes the venturesome task of writing contemporary history in a statute. After many definitions of terms used later, the Act creates an entirely new political crime punishable by ten years in prison. Then it embarks on its main job of setting up an elaborate system for registration and public disclosure for groups and to some extent for individuals, whenever these are ruled to be closely or remotely linked with the world Communist movement.

The central feature of the scheme is a Subversive Activities Control Board of five men. This is empowered to classify any group of persons, whether incorporated or not, which is permanently or temporarily associated together for joint action on any subjects, as belonging to either of two types of "Communist organizations." [5]

The first type is the "Communist-action organization," which is defined as any organization in the United States, other than an accredited diplomatic mission, which is substantially directed, dominated, or controlled by the foreign government (presumably the Soviet Union) or the foreign organization, *e.g.*, the Comintern, controlling the world Communist movement, and which operates primarily to advance the objectives of that movement. This definition was, of course, meant to reach the Communist Party of America.

More important to freedom are the provisions of the McCarran Act about the second type—the "Communist-front organization." Here, as elsewhere in this book, I am mainly concerned with the effect of legal restrictions upon persons who are *not* Communists. This type is defined as:

> any organization in the United States which (A) is substantially directed, dominated, or controlled by a Communist-action organization, and (B) is primarily operated for the purpose of giving aid and support to a Communist-action organization, a Communist foreign government, or the world Communist movement.

If the group is determined to be a "Communist organization" of either type, then the Board must order it to register in the Department of Justice—with drastic punishments[6] and damaging consequences if it doesn't and with the same damaging consequences if it does. Assume that a group classified as a "Communist-front organization" has registered. Here are the damaging consequences to it and to its officers and members:

1. *Filing reports.* Within thirty days after the order to register and each year thereafter, the "Communist-front organization" must file a report with the Attorney General, containing a list of all its officers with their addresses and a full financial statement giving the sources of all contributions received and the purposes of all expenditures. (A "Communist-action organization" must also include the names and addresses of all its members.[7]) These reports are to be open for public inspection. If any report is not filed on time or is considered to be untruthful, a criminal prosecution can take place against either the organization or the officers who were responsible for the report. The top penalties are a $10,000 fine and five years in prison for every day the report is delayed, every name wilfully left off the list, and every item which is found by the jury to be deliberately falsified or omitted.[8]

2. *Denial of passports.* If any member of a "Communist-front organization" who knows it has registered applies for a passport or uses one already obtained, he can be punished by five years in prison and a $10,000 fine.[9] Since these propagandist groups have no formal elections and no regular dues, membership is a very loose and uncertain affair, as I shall show later at length;[10] consequently law-

abiding citizens may not realize they belong to a "Communist-front organization" until their plans for an important trip abroad are suddenly wrecked and perhaps they find themselves facing criminal prosecution as well.

3. *Denial of tax benefits.* Charitable, educational, and social enterprises are usually exempt from the federal corporate income tax, but this advantage is taken away from a "Communist-front organization." And an individual cannot deduct contributions to such an organization from his own federal income tax.[11] This strikes a deadly blow at the plainly legitimate activities which the stigmatized group may have been conducting, such as furnishing medical care to refugees from Fascist tyranny and supplying legal defense for radicals in prosecutions and deportation proceedings.

4. *Use of mails and the radio.* After a charitable, educational, social, or propagandist organization has been classified as "Communist-front," it is a crime to send out by mail (or in any way across state lines) any publication, including a letter intended to be read by two or more persons, unless the publication and the outside of the envelope bears the printed words:

Disseminated by—————————, a Communist organization.

It is also criminal to broadcast over radio or television any material sponsored by such a group unless it is announced by similar language. The punishment may be a $10,000 fine for each violation, and any individual concerned may also go to prison for five years.[12]

5. *Barriers against employment.* The most damaging and far-reaching provision of the McCarran Act makes it criminal for a member of a registered "Communist-front organization" to "hold any nonelective office or employment under the United States";[13] and it also renders it difficult for many men to obtain work within their training and capacities under private employers. For this provision goes on to force them, under threat of five years in prison and a $10,000 fine, to disclose their membership in any such organizations in order to seek, accept, or hold employment "in any defense facility."[14] That phrase is very broadly defined to include factories, harbors, laboratories, and about every other place of work, so long as it appears on a list of "defense facilities" which the Secretary of Defense is directed to compile and publish in a way which

will be readily accessible to everybody. Any private business which has been put on this list will be very reluctant to hire or retain an employee after being told by him that he belongs to a group which is considered so dangerous by Congress and government authorities that it has to be dealt with by a vast scheme of registration, penalties, and prison sentences.

In view of what I have shown in a previous chapter [15] about the very wide scope of federal jobs and relationships at the present time, almost anybody who joins or remains in an organization which has been classified as "Communist-front" subjects himself and his family to the disaster of prolonged unemployment, or at best unfamiliar work and a sharp reduction of income.

Thus the provisions of the McCarran Act about "Communist-front organizations" energetically discourage, in many different ways, the expression of ideas which are not criminal but happen to incur the grave displeasure of government officials. Regardless of constitutionality, the great traditions and policies behind the First Amendment throw a heavy burden on those who want such a sedition law kept on the statute book, to show that it is necessary and desirable today and in the years immediately ahead. If not, these provisions of the Act, at least, ought to be repealed as soon as possible.

Is the McCarran Act Necessary?

In 1950 Mr. Truman vetoed this law after consultation with the security and intelligence agencies of the government.[16]

> The Department of Justice, the Department of Defense, the Central Intelligence Agency, and the Department of State have all advised me that the bill would seriously damage the security and intelligence operations for which they are responsible. They have strongly expressed the hope that the bill would not become law. . . .

After summarizing his principal objections, the President said:

> Legislation with these consequences is not necessary to meet the real dangers which communism presents to our free society. These dangers are serious and must be met. But this bill would hinder us, not help us, in meeting them. Fortunately, we already have on the books strong laws which give us most of the protection we need

from the real dangers of treason, espionage, sabotage, and actions looking to the overthrow of our Government by force and violence. Most of the provisions of this bill have no relation to these real dangers.

Nothing has happened during the five years since September 1950 to make this law any more necessary to preserve us from internal dangers than when it was enacted.

Let me begin by reviewing the "strong laws" which, if the McCarran Act were repealed, would protect our government and our institutions from attacks through revolutionary violence or other unlawful action.

First, a statute enacted in 1861 punishes conspiracy "to overthrow, put down, or to destroy by force the Government of the United States," or forcibly hinder the execution of any federal law. This was thought adequate to protect the government when the Confederate Army was within one hundred miles of Washington. Another statute of 1867 punishes conspiracy to commit an offense against the government with any overt act, no force being required. These two statutes [17] kept us safe from any serious consequences of internal disaffection through the Panic of 1873, the Panic of 1893, the Panic of 1907, and the Great Depression of 1929-1933.

Still, in 1940 Congress wanted more than the old conspiracy statutes. So it created two new types of criminal offenses. To begin with, it made the Espionage Act of 1917 applicable in time of peace, so as to punish anybody who advocated insubordination or disloyalty in the armed forces.[18] This measure was urged as essential to protect the Army and Navy from Communist organizations. Yet the only significant case under it was the unsuccessful blanket prosecution, in Washington in 1944, of about thirty writers and propagandists, who were charged with conspiring to stir up mutiny by stuff like "Public officials are controlled by Communists, International Jews and Plutocrats."

The other 1940 statute, commonly called the Smith Act, has been already mentioned [19] as the first peacetime sedition law since the ill-fated Act of 1798. The Smith Act makes it a serious crime to advocate the overthrow of any government in the United States by force, or to be an organizer or a member of any group of persons which advocates such overthrow. It has been upheld by the Supreme Court and vigorously enforced to put dozens of Communists in prison. It goes very far toward reaching anybody who belongs to what the McCarran Act defines as a "Communist-action organization." I have always felt that the country would have been just as safe after 1940 as it was before under the old law of 1861, which punishes any two or more men who try to start a revolution; we could go on ignoring a man who tried to overthrow the government all by himself, as well as men who merely talk about starting a revolution in the distant future.[20] At all events, the 1861 Act and the Smith Act of 1940 together ought to be enough and plenty to enable any really dangerous radicals to be prosecuted and locked up. This seems more effective than having them register, which (Mr. Truman remarks) "is about as practical as requiring thieves to register with the sheriff."

Much has been said about the dangers from spying and sabotage by Communists. Certainly there ought to be effective legal protection against these bad crimes, but we have a great deal of it without the McCarran Act. The Espionage Act of 1917 punishes many kinds of actual spying and disclosure of secret documents or other information.[21] It made wartime spying a capital offense, and it has been amended since the McCarran Act was passed so that spies during peace can be put to death. Statutes give the President and the military authorities wide powers to make regulations governing civilians while they are on military reservations, naval vessels, and defensive sea areas; these impose penalties for violation.[22] Sabotage in war or peace is reached by an Act of Congress in 1940.[23] Many states have criminal statutes against sabotage or advocating it, and practically every state punishes the malicious destruction of tangible property. What reason is there to expect that the men who are not stopped by these drastic laws will be deterred by the McCarran Act? Anybody who is wicked enough to be a spy and hardy enough to brave the electric chair will not be bothered about evading a statute which requires him to be registered as a Communist.

One provision in the McCarran Act punishes with ten years in prison any federal employee who, without authorization, communicates any classified information affecting national security to a member of any "Communist organization," [24] which includes all the non-Communists who belong to "Communist-front" groups. Of course, government secrets ought to be kept secret, but why is it so much more important to hide them from so-called fellow-travelers and parlor pinks than from Fascists, columnists, and ladies at large? This country contains many more blabbers than conspirators.

If the present laws against spying and sabotage are defective, the proper remedy lies in new legislation aimed directly at these vicious crimes, and not in roaming all over the lot to catch thousands of people, most of whom would never dream of being spies or saboteurs. Indeed, the provision of the Act [25] which requires the Secretary of Defense to put in the Federal Register a public catalogue of defense plants, laboratories, and other vital facilities no matter how secret is an open invitation to spies and saboteurs. Mr. Truman here displayed the humorous American shrewdness which most politicians seem to lose the moment they consider anti-Communist bills. "I cannot imagine," he said, "any document a hostile foreign government would desire more. Spies and saboteurs would willingly spend years of effort seeking to find out the information that this bill [now law] would require the government to hand them on a silver platter."

The postal provisions of this Act are unnecessary to prevent the transmission of really dangerous communications, because existing statutes make matter non-mailable for violating the Espionage Act or advocating treason, insurrection, forcible resistance to a law of the United States, arson, murder, or assassination; deny the second-class mailing privilege to such matter; and make imported books, etc., of this sort seizable in the customs.[26]

Finally, before the McCarran Act was passed, we already had two statutes [27] which require registration by anybody who acts as the agent of a foreign government (except diplomats, consuls, etc.), and also by any organization "subject to foreign control" if it is engaged in political activity or if it aims to control, seize, or overthrow the government of the United States by force. Whoever fails to register before acting incurs severe criminal penalties. Now, if the Communist Party of America or any other group in this country really satisfies the definition in the McCarran Act of a "Communist-action organization," then we do not need that Act to make the Communist Party register. It could be compelled to do so under the two statutes just mentioned.

Yet those statutes have never been enforced against the Communist Party or its leaders, before or after 1950. It is much more sensible for the government to go straight at individuals who are thought to be dangerous revolutionaries than to let them get lost in the crowd in a mass registration proceeding.

To sum up in two sentences this survey of other parts of the United States Code:

> If American Communists and fellow-travelers are as dangerous as the supporters of the McCarran Act made out, then there are enough other statutes with teeth to take ample care of these people; so this Act is not needed.

> If, on the contrary, those other statutes are not violated by what these people are saying and doing, then they can't be very dangerous; so the McCarran Act is not needed.

Let us now turn from the law to the facts. How many Communists are there in the United States? No more, probably, than thirty-five years ago when they left the Socialist Party. The United Press said 70,000 in 1947, and a considerable decline is probable for various reasons. Still, take the top estimate of 70,000 Communists out of a total population in the 1950 census of 150,697,391. That makes the Communists form less than one-twentieth of one per cent of all the people in the country.[28] The odds are over 1,999 to 1 in favor of free institutions.

Suppose the Harvard stadium filled with 40,000 people. The chances are that twenty of them would be Communists and 39,980 would not. Remember, too, that it is not a question of twenty dynamiters or twenty men with concealed weapons, for then they could be arrested at once under the ordinary criminal laws. Just twenty unarmed persons who have not violated any existing federal or state law outside sedition laws or conspired to violate any such existing law. But they have learned bad ideas about politics from foreigners and foreign books, they are thinking bad thoughts about these bad ideas, they are telling them to each other and to any outsiders who are willing to listen. What can we do to prevent them from harming the other 99.95 per cent of us, who have on our side only the city and state police, almost every newspaper and school-teacher and professor and preacher, the Federal Bureau of Investigation, the Army, the Air Force, and the Navy, never forgetting the Marines?

Shades of Valley Forge and Iwo Jima! If we no longer want to be the land of the free, at least let us be the home of the brave.

I fully recognize that the Communist Party in Czechoslovakia was a danger to the freedom of Czechoslovakia, and the same is probably true of Italy and some other countries. It does not follow that the inclusion of less than one-twentieth of one per cent of our population in a Communist Party here is a real danger to our institutions and our freedom under the very different conditions in this country. We have a very strong government equipped with existing legislation and efficient federal police. Our government does not need any such novel law as this in order to deal effectively with any actual conspiracy against its existence or any actual effort toward violent revolution. It is not enough that Communists are pestiferous people or indulge in big talk about taking over our government. The question is whether they are within a million miles of doing so. Where *inside this country* are the facts which justify the establishment of unheard-of regulatory machinery, the expenditure of large sums of money in its operation, and the severe punishment of American citizens because somebody or other has not filled out a piece of paper?

It is now more than thirty-five years since my work as a student of freedom of speech led me to pay considerable attention to the activities of Communists in this country. My considered opinion is that they are far less dangerous today than they were in 1919-1920, soon after the Russian Revolution. During those early years that revolution was to many Americans the symbol of a better world. To idealists it at last appeared possible that men might build a fruitful society without having to seek their own profit. Few of those who now dream of a City of God can ignore the ugly facts in Moscow. Also social and economic conditions in this country have vastly improved since 1919. The reasons for revolutionary discontent which then existed have been greatly lessened by the legislation begun under Mr. Roosevelt, the high wages paid during the war and since the realization that Americans of every sort fought and suffered side by side during the war. Consequently, as stated in Chapter III, we have a much greater immunity to revolutionary radicalism.

Sometimes I wonder whether the supporters of measures like the McCarran Act have been worrying so much about Communists that they have forgotten what freedom-loving Americans are like. They are the last people to fall easy victims to the ideology of a country where nobody can speak his own mind unless he agrees with the ruling class, where there is only one party convention and only one man to vote for at an election, where labor unions are state-run bureaus, where men can be grabbed out of their beds in the dead of night with no charge against them and be hidden away from their families for weeks, where hordes of people are moved from their old homes at the will of some official and ordered to live and work in some barren place two thousand miles away. Although communism now has behind it a powerful nation, which was not the case thirty-five years ago, this makes military problems more serious but I believe it decreases whatever attraction it has had for American citizens. If there is one thing American history teaches, it is that most of our citizens intensely detest any possible foreign influences over our own political policies. The very fact that joining the Communist Party means constantly taking sides with a foreign government against our own government is enough to keep most American radicals from having anything to do with that Party. And then there are more material considerations, though by no means sordid. Think of the billions of dollars invested in life insurance and savings banks, the pride a man has in knowing that he is giving his children a better start in life than he had himself, the satisfaction of acquiring a home, a car, a motorboat, a little cottage on the beach. These bulwarks against communism are infinitely stronger than all the inquisitions and prosecutions that could ever be devised.

The only possibility of Communistic control of this country, leaving aside the chance of foreign conquest, would come, I believe, from the destruction of this confidence which the great mass of our citizens now have in their own future and that of their children

and their community. Imagine a prolonged period of enormous unemployment; the dollar buying what a dime buys now, and perhaps
worth a nickel next week, who knows; ever-mounting taxes; the
national revenue heavily mortgaged for decades by unwise commit-
ments to groups of the aged at the expense of active men and women
and their children; voters hating and despising the men they themselves have put in office because they had nobody better to choose
from. That is when communism might grow by leaps and bounds,
not because of what 70,000 Communists say but because of what
the hopeless facts say. Maggots live in rotten meat.

This is not the first time when fear of the infiltration of revolutionary radicalism from Europe has led earnest men to demand
drastic laws against speeches and publications. A hundred and fifty
years ago patriots terrified of the French Revolution got Congress
to enact the Sedition Act of 1798. It is commonly regarded as one
of the greatest follies in our history. Again, after the First World
War, Congress was repeatedly urged to pass a new peacetime sedition law. Revolutionary groups were much more vocal than now.
Violent acts occurred like a bomb exploded near the house of the
Attorney General. Still, Congress refused to do anything, and nobody now regrets that refusal. The years that followed proved that
the law which eminent men said was indispensable to save the country was not needed at all. The names of the men who supported
the bills of 1798 and 1919-1920 have long ago slipped into oblivion,
but we remember Jefferson, Holmes, Hughes, and Al Smith for
their courageous insistence that we must trust open discussion to
bring us safely through.

That courage, we were told by proponents of the McCarran Act,
is out of date. The United States never had to face Stalin before.
But in 1798-1801 it had to face the French Revolution and Napoleon.
And in 1919-1920 it had to face Lenin. His army was not so big as
Stalin's, but he was a far abler master of revolutionary tactics. The
lawyers who drafted the Sedition Act of 1798 and the judges who
enforced that law were firmly convinced that they were stamping
out a foreign menace fully as dangerous as the foreign menace
which confronts us today. Indeed, they used much the same arguments as those urged for this Act of 1950, with France the villain

instead of Russia and Switzerland replacing Czechoslovakia as the victim to forecast the fate of our own republic if we did not save ourselves by passing a sedition law.

Listen to the dire prophecies with which, in 1799, a committee of the House of Representatives urged the continuance of the Sedition Act for two years more:

> If it be asserted . . . that our security arises from the form of our Constitution, let Switzerland, first divided and disarmed by perfidious seductions, now agonized by relentless power, illustrate the consequences of similar credulity. . . .
>
> France appears to have an organized system of conduct toward foreign nations; to bring them within the sphere, and under the dominion of her influence and control. It has been unremittingly pursued under all the changes of her internal policy. Her means are in wonderful coincidence with her ends; among these, and not the least successful, is the direction and employment of the active and versatile talents of her citizens abroad as emissaries and spies.[29]

As late as January 1801, after the Federalists had lost the Presidency, one of them was still trying to get the House to prolong the statute, by charging French agents with buying several American newspapers with foreign money for the purpose of spreading disaffection.

In 1919-1920 you can find the same kind of fears as today eloquently expressed in House and Senate hearings and in the New York Assembly. Some of these outbursts of fright were quoted in a previous chapter.[30]

Everybody agrees now that these fears of subversive organizations in 1798-1801 and 1919-1920 were much exaggerated. Probably this is just as true of the fears expressed today by the supporters of the McCarran Act. Its solemn assertion of its necessity "to preserve the sovereignty of the United States as an independent nation" will sound as queer in the future as the passages I have been quoting.

Every great war, especially a war accompanied by revolutions, is followed by a difficult settling-down period. The anxieties and strains of war do not die out the moment hostilities stop. People go on being worried because they have been worried so long, and all sorts of economic and social adjustments caused by the dislocations of war bring new reasons for anxiety. It took over ten years for us to get back to normal after our own Civil War. The constant tension breaks out in all sorts of queer ways, and one frequent manifestation of it is fear of internal disaffection. The English went through a terrible period of this sort after the long Napoleonic Wars; they enacted any number of suppressive statutes, and soldiers shot down workmen who were attending a peaceful meeting at Peterloo. We experienced the same kind of thing in a milder form after the First World War during the Red Menace.[31] In such times of disturbance and anxiety, sedition laws were demanded as indispensable, but soon the tension began to relax, the fears proved unwarranted, and the country went on safely with its traditional freedoms.

We have been going through such a settling-down process ever since Japan surrendered in August 1945. It has been particularly difficult for all sorts of causes—the magnitude of the devastation, the diverse character of the victorious nations, the unprecedented formation of a world-wide permanent union, and so on. We have had plenty of real worries, and it is quite natural that they should be reflected in some false worries as well. All the more reason for keeping our heads.

It is like waking up at two in the morning and trying to solve all your problems at once. A wise man tells himself that some of those problems won't amount to much in daylight. He faces the immediate tangible tasks squarely, and stops tearing himself to pieces over vague, remote, conspiratorial perils. Usually they vanish next morning. If not, they shrink into concrete problems which can be taken up when they actually arise as part of the ordinary course of life.

I have read a good many regrets that particular sedition laws were passed. Never, given the lapse of two or three years, have I known anybody to regret that a sedition law was rejected or repealed.

The final reason for believing the McCarran Act unnecessary is that the nation got along very well without this peacetime sedition law, not only during the thirty-three years between the Russian Revolution and its enactment in September 1950, but also for all practical purposes during the five years after 1950. The law was passed in the emergency of the Korean fighting, because (according to its supporters) unless the Communist Party and Communist-front groups were made to register right away and undergo all the restrictions in the Act, the country would go to rack and ruin. The Korean War lasted over two years more; it ended over two years ago. Yet during these five years and more until December 1955, when I write, not a single organization has registered or even received a final order to register. The nation would have been just as safe all this time if the McCarran Act had never been passed.

President Truman predicted exactly what has happened in his veto message of September 1950. After describing the elaborate registration machinery in the McCarran Bill, he said:

> All these proceedings would require great effort and much time. It is almost certain that from two to four years would elapse between the Attorney General's decision to go before the Board with a case, and the final disposition of the matter by the courts.
> And when all this time and effort had been spent, it is still most likely that no organization would actually register.

The failure of the Act to accomplish anything for five years is the fault of the Act and not of the members of the Subversive Activities Control Board. These five men have performed their duties with fidelity and diligence.[32]

In November 1950, soon after its organization, the Board began considering a petition against the Communist Party of America as a "Communist-action organization." The hearing lasted fourteen months and filled 14,413 pages, with 507 documents added. In April 1953, two and a half years after proceedings began, the Board gave a decision of 218 pages ordering the Party to register. The Party appealed to the Court of Appeals of the District of Columbia. Another year went by before the case was argued in April 1954. The following August, Congress tried to remedy the sluggish operation of the registration procedure it had created by deciding itself, in the Communist Control Act,[33] that the Communist Party is a "Communist-action organization" and automatically subject to the pertinent provisions of the McCarran Act. Regardless of this close imitation of a bill of attainder, the Court of Appeals went ahead with the issue. After another year, by a two to one vote, it upheld the Board and the constitutionality of the 1950 Act as applied to Communists.[34] The case is likely to be decided by the Supreme

Court in the spring of 1956, after registration proceedings have been going on for somewhat more than five years.

If the government wins again and the requisite final order to register is made, it remains to be seen whether the Communist Party will register or still another prediction in Mr. Truman's veto message will be fulfilled:

> The simple fact is that when the courts at long last found that a particular organization was required to register, all the leaders of the organization would have to do to frustrate the law would be to dissolve the organization and establish a new one with a different name and a new roster of nominal officers. The Communist Party has done this again and again in countries throughout the world. And nothing could be done about it except to begin all over again the long dreary process of investigative, administrative, and judicial proceedings to require registration.
>
> Thus the net result of the registration provision of this bill would probably be an endless chasing of one organization after another, with the Communists always able to frustrate the law enforcement agencies and prevent any final result from being achieved.

After over two years of hard work were required for the Board to decide that the Communist Party of America came within the definition of "Communition-action organization," which had been worded by Congress for the express purpose of reaching this Party, the Board started in the autumn of 1953 upon the more delicate and, in my opinion, more important task of determining whether the loose definition of "Communist-front organization" applied to a wide range of enterprises. These were engaged, at least in part, in adult education, the formation of public opinion, combatting Fascists, furnishing counsel, and other activities which have been customarily regarded in this country as legitimate; and many of their beneficiaries, promoters, and financial supporters were admittedly not Communists.

For example, consider three groups which were summoned before the Board. The Joint Anti-Fascist Refugee Committee rescued from death in Spain and gave medical care to the victims of a Fascist dictator closely associated with Mussolini and Hitler. The National Council of American-Soviet Friendship was formed while Russia was allied with the United States and exhausting Hitler's resources in what was for us the gloomiest period of the war; its original members included United States Senators, distinguished generals, and other admired leaders; some of those original members stayed on during the cold war with the hope of doing something to lessen frictions which might easily produce World War III. The American Committee for Protection of Foreign Born has supplied competent lawyers to many aliens arrested on deportation charges, who might otherwise have been defenseless and who had ever so much to lose from mistaken decisions. Whatever objections can be made to some of the activities or backers of enterprises like these, it is plain that if the government pulls up the tares, it will pull up a good deal of wheat too.

Up to June 30, 1955, Attorney General Brownell had filed petitions with the Subversive Activities Control Board against fourteen groups as "Communist-front organizations," including the three examples just named. Proceedings against the Anti-Fascist Refugee Committee and three other organizations [35] were dismissed because those groups had dissolved. During the two years since "Communist-front" petitions were filed, the Board has ordered two out of the remaining ten groups to register—the Jefferson School of Social Sciences, whose hearings fill 3,525 pages, and the Labor Youth League, with 4,729 pages. Their appeals to the courts still have to be argued. In three more cases, hearings are finished. The respective panel chairmen in charge of these hearings have recommended to the Board that the National Council of American-Soviet Friendship (5,265 pages) and the Veterans of the Abraham Lincoln Brigade (4,584 pages) be ordered to register. The Board has these recommendations under advisement. No action has yet been taken as to the Civil Rights Congress (6,515 pages). In a sixth case, against the American Committee for Protection of the Foreign Born, hearings began in June 1955 (1,169 pages thus far). That leaves four organizations [36] to be heard during the fiscal year 1956.

If there be any real danger to our security and our free institutions from revolutionists, it ought to be met vigorously and effectively. Those words do not describe a law which after five years of steady labor has produced for the protection of the United

States three administrative orders still under review by the courts, no final orders, no registrations, and 40,200 pages of testimony.

Eventually of course, if the "Communist-front" provisions of the McCarran Act are held constitutional, the Board will succeed in forcing some existing organizations to register and perhaps also a new crop, if it springs up, of unpopular educational, social, and propagandist groups. Moreover the threat of proceedings may play some part in making other groups dissolve, many of which would fold up anyway before long. The practical question remains, however, whether such results and the laborious accumulation of facts, which the F.B.I. knows already, are worth the continued outlay year after year of about a quarter of a million dollars and the full time of over thirty persons,[37] who might otherwise be serving the public in more constructive ways or doing productive work in industry. More important still is the point which will be discussed during the rest of this chapter that vigorous enforcement of the registration provisions will impair cherished liberties long after the end of the Korean crisis, which brought about its enactment.

Sacrifices of normal liberties are sometimes required in periods of danger, as a later chapter shows at some length,[38] but it is an essential safeguard of freedom that emergency measures ought to be carefully confined to the emergency and not operate as everyday laws. The "clear and present danger" rule often stressed by the Supreme Court is designed to prevent liberties from being taken away long *before* any real danger. It is equally vital that liberties should not go on being cut down long *after* the danger is over. The Constitution recognizes the double-ended nature of this essential safeguard when it forbids suspension of the writ of habeas corpus "unless when in Cases of Rebellion or Invasion the Public Safety may require it." [39] One effective method to prevent restrictions on liberty from lasting too long is—make the statute expire by its own terms at a fixed date not more than a year or two ahead. This was always done by the British Parliament when habeas corpus was suspended, for example, on May 23, 1794, for fear of domestic outbreaks during the war with Revolutionary France; [40] the Act was to end on February 1, 1795. This practice of a time-limit requires the legislature to reconsider the deprivations of liberty peri-

odically in the light of possibly changed conditions. If the danger
still persists, the law can be renewed with modification of any provisions which have proved futile or unduly harsh. But if the situation is safer and calmer, the restrictions just die when they have
outlived their usefulness without the trouble and uncertainties of
repeal. Some legislators are reluctant to support the repeal of a
repressive law against unpopular opinions and persons, and yet these
same legislators are too sensible to vote to re-enact that law after
it has worked badly or has become unnecessary. The Sedition Act
of 1798, an emergency measure passed when war with France
seemed imminent had, despite its many shortcomings, one notable
merit. It expressly ran for only two years. Unfortunately, this desirable idea of a time-limit has not been used in our contemporary
sedition laws, although they, too, were enacted during great anxiety
and excitement—the Smith Act in July 1940 after Hitler had entered
Paris, and the McCarran Act in September 1950 in the urgency of
Korea.

Still, the absence of a time-limit in the McCarran Act does not
alter the fact that it would be wise for Congress to reconsider it
after several years, like other emergency measures. It is always in
order to reinstate liberties when they do not need to be taken away.

The principles which Jefferson used to allay apprehensions in his
time are equally valid in our time. Meet unlawful action with action; proceed against real spies and real plotters as he prosecuted
Aaron Burr and approved the dismissal of Genêt. Meet objectionable ideas from abroad by living up to our own ideas—give increased
drawing-power to our great traditions of democracy and freedom.

How Is It Possible to Fit the McCarran Act into the Bill of Rights?

This question, too, should be asked by Congress, now that a
calmer atmosphere prevails. It ought to be asked especially about
the "Communist-front" provisions where, as Mr. Truman pointed
out in his veto message, the language is "so broad and vague that it
might well result in penalizing the legitimate activities of people
who are not Communists at all but loyal citizens." It needs to be

asked even if the Supreme Court declines to upset any part of the Act as unconstitutional.[41] Such a decision does not dispose of the Bill of Rights, so far as Congress is concerned. The Court is reluctant to invalidate federal legislation because, it often says, Senators and Representatives are sworn to uphold the Constitution including the Bill of Rights, and judges must not interfere with the way they exercise their powers except in very outrageous situations. This judicial determination to keep hands off throws on all the members of Congress a very heavy responsibility to guard our liberties, for if Congress fails to do so nobody else will.

Take the analogy of a federal tax law. Almost any tax Congress imposes will be sustained by the Supreme Court, no matter how heavy. Yet neither Congress nor the public assumes that any constitutional tax is *ipso facto* wise. On the contrary, great care and energy are exerted to prevent every tax law from taking away property in harmful ways. Surely, it is far more important to be sure that a sedition law does not take away liberty in harmful ways. The signers of the Declaration of Independence pledged their fortunes to preserve their freedoms.

While purporting to be necessary to preserve "free American institutions," the McCarran Act gravely impairs some of the most precious of those institutions, freedom of speech and press and assembly, which our ancestors put at the very head of the Bill of Rights. In Mr. Truman's words:

> It would put the United States into the thought-control business. It could give government officials vast powers to harass all of our citizens in the exercise of their rights of free speech.

It is a vital principle in the great American traditions that the law deals primarily with acts, and with words only when governmental interference is plainly necessary in order to prevent them from ripening into acts. Perhaps this principle is not fully embodied in the First Amendment; some Supreme Court decisions have sustained legislation penalizing bad words which are pretty remote from bad acts. Still, whatever the constitutional situation, observance of the principle is always wise and essential if freedom is to be a living force. An especially strong claim to immunity is possessed by speeches and publications concerning political issues and candidates for office, because they are an essential part of the process of self-government. Thomas Jefferson wrote this principle into the Virginia Statute of Religious Toleration:

> To suffer the civil Magistrate to intrude his powers into the field of opinion, and to restrain the profession or propagation of principles on supposition of their ill tendency, is a dangerous fallacy . . . because he being of course judge of that tendency, will make his opinions the rule of judgment, and approve or condemn the sentiments of others only as they shall square with or differ from his own. It is time enough for the rightful purposes of civil government, for its officers to interfere when principles break out into overt acts against peace and good order.[42]

Judge Learned Hand set forth the same principle,[43] which many other judges unhappily disregarded during the First World War:

> Detestation of existing policies is easily transformed into forcible resistance of the authority which puts them in execution. . . . Yet to assimilate agitation, legitimate as such, with direct incitement to violent resistance, is to disregard the tolerance of political agitation which in normal times is a safeguard of free government. The distinction is . . . a hard-bought acquisition in the fight for freedom.

And Mr. Truman's veto message shows how the principle has been again disregarded in the McCarran Act:

> In a free country, we punish men for the crimes they commit, but never for the opinions they have. And the reason this is so fundamental to freedom is not . . . that it protects the few unorthodox from suppression by the majority. To permit freedom of expression is primarily for the benefit of the majority because it protects criticism and criticism leads to progress.

The numerous disagreeable consequences which this Act imposes on "Communist-front organizations" and their members (not to speak of the other proscribed groups) do not resemble long-established legal situations penalizing the use of words because these are closely connected with acts and with rather definite injuries within the common experience of juries, like telling another man how to murder a third man or slanderous speeches which may provoke an immediate bloody fight and will at once harm the defamed person's chances of getting work. By contrast, the compulsory registration of "Communist-front organizations" restricts normal educational activities and processes of forming views on public questions because of the expression and exchange of opinions without any necessary relation to any unlawful action.

A still more novel feature of this law is that the penalized individual need not have uttered the opinions himself or even approved them. It is enough if other persons did so with whom he was loosely associated, often for quite different objectives. The barriers to getting or keeping a job in a defense plant are not based upon any past unlawful act by the workman or by anybody else in the registered group, or upon proof that members of that group have planned or been trained to do their work badly. The burdens on the use of the mails have no relation to any past or probable unlawful acts or to the harmful nature of the language in the letters or printed publications sent through the post-office. The passport section of the McCarran Act inflicts a repulsive loss of freedom of movement [44] on an American citizen who has *bona fide* reasons for going abroad. It keeps him within this country with no consideration of his own fitness to travel outside it and with no evidence whatever of anything he has ever done or might do except his belonging to a group which also included men of specific political views which he may not share at all—quite the contrary.

On top of all these restrictions of freedom of speech, press, and assembly in the McCarran Act, an amendment in 1954 added still another, requiring every registered "Communist organization" to include in its periodic reports: [45]

> A listing . . . of all printing presses and machines including but not limited to rotary presses, flat bed cylinder presses, platen presses, lithographs, offsets, photo-offsets, mimeograph machines, multigraph machines, multilith machines, duplicating machines, ditto machines, linotype machines, intertype machines, monotype machines, and all other types of printing presses, typesetting machines or any mechanical devices used or intended to be used, or capable of being used to produce or publish printed matter or material (insofar as such machines are in the possession, custody, ownership, or control of the organization) or its officers, members, affiliates, associates, group, or groups in which the . . . organization, its officers or members have an interest.

This extraordinary conception of liberty of the press evoked not a peep that I have heard from the Association of American Newspaper Publishers or any of the other groups of newspapermen who raise a great outcry about invasions of that liberty whenever the government seeks to compel newspapers to bargain with their employees like business concerns or to stop owning radio stations or to open the services of a press association to any outsider ready to pay the regular price.

Going back to the McCarran Act, I wonder what was in the minds of the Senators who put into its opening section: [46]

> Nothing in this Act shall be construed . . . in any way to infringe upon freedom of the press or of speech as guaranteed by the Constitution. . . .

Perhaps this is just lip-service from Congress to the First Amendment— "I have been faithful to thee, Cynara! in my fashion." Or it may be a meaningless statement that anything is unconstitutional which would be held unconstitutional without this clause. However, these words really add something to the law if they are regarded as allowing courts to go farther than is usual in protecting liberty of speech and press. The clause makes sense if in effect it directs judges: "Be careful to refuse to enforce any provision of this Act which, in your opinion, conflicts with the First Amendment. You don't have to defer to the judgment of Congress this time—it's *your* judgment that Congress wants."

Still, it is by no means certain that a few lines in a very long statute would be given such a far-reaching effect by the courts. The only safe and sure way to guard the Bill of Rights is for the numerous provisions which infringe it in the McCarran Act to be repealed as soon as possible before they do great harm at home and abroad.

Vigorous enforcement of this statute would disastrously impair our influence over other freedom-loving peoples. If we leave aside military considerations, the best way to combat the spread of communism in Western Europe and elsewhere is to give increased drawing-power to the great traditions of democracy and freedom.

These war-torn countries want more than weapons, more than food and machinery. They are eager for ideals to strengthen the spirit and make life worth living. More than words is needed. Unless our acts show that we believe in our democratic ideals, we lessen the chance of winning wavering men to democracy.

In my experience with foreigners in the United Nations, I have been constantly impressed by the way our prevailing adherence to the ideals of our Bill of Rights helps to close up the ranks of freedom-loving countries in opposition to undesirable measures. On the other hand, I have seen how much harm is done whenever we conspicuously depart from our professed basic principles. It lays us open to damaging charges of hypocrisy and pretense, which are hard to meet. There is no doubt that such attacks based on concrete facts do impress men from many countries whose support we need, and sometimes they are thus pried apart from the United States delegation on critical votes.

Freedom of speech and press means a very great deal to citizens of countries where censorship and every sort of gross suppression prevailed in recent years. So the way we maintain that freedom or the way we depart from it is bound to have a tremendous effect, for good or ill, upon those countries.

Consequently, if we really start inflicting the damaging consequences of registration under this law and prosecuting individuals for failure to register, our professions of love for open discussion will ring hollow in the ears of our natural friends in the free world. When the newspapers are full of stories of skilled workmen thrown out of their jobs, passports denied to many travelers, mail opened, lists gone through with a fine-tooth comb, law-abiding citizens imprisoned for long terms, and all the rest of it, we cannot defend ourselves against the sneers of our opponents and still less against the distrust of our friends. Frenchmen, Belgians, Dutchmen, Norwegians, Danes have had years of experience with that sort of thing under totalitarian occupations and it leaves a stench in their nostrils.

> Your countrymen who could have hurled
> Their freedom like a brand
> Have cupped it to a candle spark
> In a frightened hand.[17]

The way for us to spread abroad freedom of speech is to live up to it ourselves.

THE NEW POLITICAL CRIME IN THE McCARRAN ACT

Now I turn aside from general questions about the McCarran Act and consider the operation of some of its particular provisions.

One of the early sections, 4 (a), has nothing to do with the registration of "Communist organizations." It threatens with ten years in prison anybody who commits a novel and vague political crime:

> It shall be unlawful for any person knowingly to combine, conspire, or agree with any other person to perform any act which would contribute to the establishment within the United States of a totalitarian dictatorship, . . . the direction and control of which is to be vested in, or exercised by or under the dominion or control of, any foreign government, foreign organization, or foreign individual.

However, it is not an offense to propose a constitutional amendment.

Whatever this crime means, it goes far beyond the speech which has hitherto been punishable, even under the Smith Act. Nobody knows how unexpectedly a sedition law can be construed unless he has studied into such matters. The draftsman and the legislators have some specific situations in mind, but the actual use of the statute may be against some kind of conduct they never dreamed of. Thus a New York statute which was passed after the assassination of President McKinley to punish anarchists has never been used against an anarchist, but it was drastically enforced against Gitlow and other Communists, who are at the opposite pole of political thought from anarchists. So you cannot tell what sort of people will ever be punished for agreeing to aid in establishing a totalitarian dictatorship, but you can be sure that they will be very different people from anybody Congress had in mind in the summer of 1950.

We came through the perilous months between the fall of France and Pearl Harbor without needing any such peacetime sedition law to protect us against the mighty totalitarian dictatorship of Hitler, and we certainly do not need this fantastic law now.

THE MACHINERY OF REGISTRATION

The procedure of registration operates in two successive stages:

1. The Subversive Activities Control Board of five members receives a petition from the Attorney General against the organization alleged to be "Communist-action" or "Communist-front," holds public hearings with benefit of counsel, and either dismisses the case or orders the organization to register. Individuals may also be ordered by the Board to register if not listed by the "Communist-action organization" to which they are found to belong. In addition, a method is provided for an organization or a listed officer or member to get off the register.

2. Either side can get judicial review in the Court of Appeals in the District of Columbia, and after that in the Supreme Court if it is willing to bother with the case. After the courts have upheld the Board (or no appeal has been filed) the order to register becomes final. Then the disagreeable consequences of registration go into effect.

It is my well-considered opinion that the Board is going to do the real deciding in most cases against "Communist-front organizations." Except for passing on constitutional issues, judicial review is not likely to be of much value to a group which has lost its case in the Board. In the first place, going to court is expensive. The financial resources of these propagandist enterprises, schools for adult radicals, etc., are often small anyway; and they will be further crippled by the denial of income tax advantages under the Act, which is likely to scare off contributors as soon as proceedings start, without waiting for the final order. Second, all the evidence against the attacked group or on its behalf will be taken before the Board.[48] No judge will hear any witnesses. Now, any lawyer knows that the way in which testimony shapes up depends considerably upon the competence, experience, and fairness of the person or persons conducting the actual trial. Third, even if a condemned group can afford to appeal, the courts will not have much of a chance to reverse the Board's decision, unless on some constitutional ground. The definition of a "Communist-front organization" in the Act is so wide and vague that it will be hard for judges to say that the Board was wrong in bringing the group within that definition. Busy judges will probably be reluctant to substitute their own judgment for the judgment of the officials who heard the testimony which fills thousands of pages.

Therefore, the way the McCarran Act will operate depends very largely on the five persons composing the Subversive Activities Control Board. What are they going to be like down the years? They are appointed by the President for staggered terms of three years, confirmed by the Senate, and eligible for reappointment. Not more than three can belong to the same political party. Despite the short term, some measure of independence is assured by the provision that they cannot be removed for any reason except neglect of duty or malfeasance in office. The salary is $15,000 a year, and they are not to "engage in any other business, vocation, or employment." [49]

I do not mean to question in any way the character and competence of the present members of the Subversive Activities Control Board.[50]   Harry P. Cain deserves especial credit for warning the country in a public address [51] that "in an effort to keep our Nation secure at home, we have constructed an apparatus which can destroy us if we don't watch out." Yet we have to remember that a new broom sweeps clean. The personnel of the Federal Trade Commission and many other federal or state administrative bodies has tended to run downhill, after the first few years when able men were attracted by the opportunity to get new work started. The future composition of the Subversive Activities Control Board will present the same risk.

Enormous powers over the lives of private citizens are possessed by the five men on this Board. They can shape political action, blast reputations, make government employees and workmen lose their jobs with small hope of getting other employment.

Only a terrible danger to the nation could justify Congress in placing these enormous powers in the hands of five men who do not have the training and experience of judges or the life-tenure which the Constitution considers essential to assure the independence of men who make vital decisions. Does such a terrible danger really exist?

THE REGISTRATION OF "COMMUNIST-ACTION ORGANIZATIONS"

Perhaps something can be said for requiring all political parties to register, and all organizations which are somehow associated with politics; but the McCarran Act singles out particular political groups to bear heavy burdens from which the rest are wholly free. Imagine what it would mean if the Republican Party alone or the Democratic Party alone had to file the names and addresses of all its members with the Department of Justice, and repeat this full list every year, while for every omitted name or address the party officers would go to prison.

But those are good parties, say the supporters of this Act; it hits only bad parties. By the American tradition, sifting bad parties from good parties is the job of the voters, and not the job of Congress or government officials. We have hitherto had confidence that most of the voters would recognize a bad party when they saw it and keep away from it. The fate of the Know-Nothing Party, which incited prejudice against recent immigrants, and the failure of the Communist Party to win an election to any federal, state or city office for years and years, show that this confidence in the voters is amply justified.

Nevertheless, in 1950 and 1954, while France and Italy were managing to recover from devastating defeats in spite of scores of Communists in their national legislatures, the Congress of the victorious United States rushed through two long and complicated laws in order to outlaw a political party which is so nearly dead that it has not nominated a candidate of its own for President since 1940. As Senator Carter Glass remarked, "What's the use of wasting dynamite when insect-powder will do?"

It is argued that, although the Communist Party amounts to nothing in elections, it still exists as an organization making policies and spreading propaganda of a bad sort, and hence it is necessary to break it up completely. No doubt, this purpose will be accomplished if the Supreme Court affirms the Board's registration order. There will no longer be any organization called the Communist Party of America. Yet how much good will that really do? The present actual Communists will be no less harmful than they are now. They will continue to have the same ideas. The prime cause of all dangerous political agitation is discontent, and outlawing men does nothing to remove their discontent. Quite the contrary.

There is no reason to expect that the order of five government officials is going to stop Americans who are Communists at heart from meeting together in some way or other. Anybody who has studied the history of Irish societies in the days of Daniel O'Connell can tell pretty well what will happen. Every time a particular society was declared unlawful, it was promptly dissolved and its former members started a new society for exactly the same purposes. The Communist Party may reorganize under a different name, as Mr. Truman predicted, or perhaps it will split into a number of Shakespearean Societies, Dante Institutes, chess clubs, indoor baseball associations, etc. Whatever occurs, the Subversive Activities Control Board will have to engage in a series of wild-goose chases. And, meanwhile, we shall no longer know whether there are 70,000 Communists or 700,000.

Moreover, this law merely scratches the surface of the biggest danger from the presence of Communists inside a free country. That danger comes, not from the mass of Party members, but from embittered and fanatical individuals who, regardless of carrying cards in any organization, are eager to engage in wicked and desperate acts which will aid the Soviet Union. The Report of the Canadian Royal Commission on atomic spies shows how much harm a few men can do. The more recent Report of the Australian Royal Commission in 1955, which investigated the documents from Moscow turned over by Petrov after he left the Soviet Embassy in Canberra, also tells much about the Communist spy system. This report shows how spies operated under the direction of M.V.D. officials in the Embassy, who were specifically charged with espionage, and that the system had very slight connections with the Communist Party of Australia:

> Quite apart from the known Party member, the auxiliary force [of Australians] comprises some persons whose role it is to conceal their Communist affiliations and sympathies and to operate in the guise of ordinary loyal Australian citizens. This class provides the most dangerous pool of helpers in fifth-column and espionage work, and it is amongst this class that the Moscow Centre [the headquarters for the conduct of espionage work abroad] usually looks for aid.

[From] the material before us we think it unlikely the Australian Communist Party, as a Party, had any connection with Soviet espionage here.

Generally speaking, the M.V.D. [the Ministry of Internal Affairs, in charge of non-military espionage outside the Soviet Union] is disinclined to use the known and prominent Communist Party member as a direct agent. His use is chiefly as a "talent spotter." The prominent Party member is likely to be known to counter-intelligence organizations, and the risk of compromising the Communist Party is one not lightly to be taken. It is the secret or "under cover" Party member or the sympathizer, who is not a member of the Party who is preferred, because his activities are less likely to be subject to the scrutiny of counter-intelligence. There is evidence that latterly the rule against using the known Communist has become more strict.[52]

Aren't we barking up the wrong tree when we worry so much about publicly known Communist organizations and their meetings? The entire government testimony against the eleven top-string leaders at the 1950 trial before Judge Medina in New York City, as reported in the *New York Times*, contains a lot of silly talk at meetings, of a very exasperating sort, but nothing was said or done which would make any sane citizen lie awake at night a single minute. Spies and saboteurs do not make speeches at such affairs. If they meet at all, it is only in very small groups by secret arrangement. The registration or outlawing or dissolution of an organization of thousands of talkative comrades is not going to remove the evil from the minds of men who are ready to brave prison and death out of hatred toward their own government.

The "Communist-action" provisions of the McCarran Act are a bad precedent for future legislation. No major party is likely to try to wipe out the other major party, as the Federalists did in 1798; but both major parties may be tempted to join forces in order to cripple or kill a third party with enough strength to be annoying, especially in state or city elections. For the first time in our history, we have written into law an ingenious device to accomplish this object. The people in power in the two major parties frame a definition of a bad political party. They do this by picking characteristics of an objectionable sort which are possessed by some members of the party they want to smash. Then they brand the whole party with those objectionable characteristics, and consequently make it carry a heavy load in the political race against competing parties which run unburdened.

Now, this may seem very clever when it is used against parties with a Communistic tinge, but it is a game anybody can play at. Once this law gets people accustomed to the method of having officials sift out "bad" parties instead of letting the voters do it themselves, other laws can be drafted with new definitions of badness to hit some party which has nothing to do with communism. There is no logical limit to the possibility of this proscribing an opposition party, for every party has some members with qualities capable of arousing intense and widespread detestation. Even the Republican Party in its early years included many prominent Abolitionists who had vigorously advocated violations of the Fugitive Slave Law, and some of them had overthrown the operation of the law by force and violence in the streets of Boston. The Democrats and the Southern Whigs would have found the device in the McCarran Act very useful for strangling the Republican Party in its cradle. And it can easily be used in the future to get rid of some new third party to which many honest and patriotic citizens belong. In order "to preserve our free institutions" and the processes of self-government, Congress and the American people ought to repudiate the vicious device once and for all.

THE REGISTRATION OF "COMMUNIST-FRONT ORGANIZATIONS"

Inasmuch as this part of the McCarran Act is likely to reach many groups whose purposes are cultural as well as political and who are engaged in exchanging ideas rather than winning elections, the interference with the lives of private citizens is much more extensive than in the case of the "Communist-action" provisions.

Here again, there is something to be said for a general registration law requiring all groups which attempt to influence public opinion to disclose the pertinent facts about themselves through systematic procedures. The harmfulness of non-disclosure is by no means confined to "Communist-front organizations." For instance, virulent anti-Semitic circulars and pamphlets falsely and libelously accusing long lists of well-known, decent citizens of disloyalty are often widely mailed by organizations with high-sounding names,[53] which frequently take good care not to mention their authors and the men who put up the money. A broad statute to break through this vicious anonymity of defamers of every sort is recommended in the 1947 Report of the President's Committee on Civil Rights.[54] On the other hand, I seriously question whether such a statute will be a desirable remedy for this evil; it is likely to be enforced inefficiently and in a haphazard way, and to stifle more good views than bad views.[55] At all events, if Congress thinks a compulsory disclosure law for propaganda is needed, than it is needed for all sides of political, racial, and religious controversies. Such a law should seek to force into broad daylight all the enemies of democracy and not just a particular portion of them as in the McCarran Act, leaving the rest to remain in the darkness they love, "because their ways are evil."

Leaving the lopsidedness of this part of the Act for later attention, let us see what effect registration of a group as "Communist-front" will have upon its capacity to do effective work. Take a labor school as an illustration. Every teacher, every student, every contributor to its support has good reason to expect that the law will treat him as a "member" of the organization.[56] Hence, as already stated, any person who is asked to teach or study at this labor school or to give it some money knows that, if he does so, he will encounter difficulties in getting or holding a job with the government or in a defense plant. He cannot go abroad for lack of a passport. His contributions to the school will not be deductible for income tax purposes. When pamphlets or form letters come to him from the school, the envelopes will be labeled "*Communist Organization*," which will make a very bad impression on any business associates or fellow-tenants in his apartment-house who happen to glance at his mail. This novel stigma on enterprises which have violated no law recalls the practice of medieval princes to require Jews to wear special marks or colors on their coats.

So after the labor school registers, very few people will be willing to teach or study there or give it one cent.

Even those who gave money to a social or propagandist enterprise *before* registration or who no longer participate in its work may still be classed by the law as "members." This is often done by Congressional investigating committees, and there is no formal procedure, either in ordinary life or in the McCarran Act, for terminating one's loose relationship with such enterprises.[57] This uncertainty as to how you get out, once you become a member, is likely to make prudent people refuse to have anything at all to do with enterprises which might conceivably be ordered to register. And as soon as the Board starts a proceeding to compel an organization to register, many former contributors, if they are prudent, will try to announce as publicly as possible that they will have no further dealings with the organization.

All this virtually outlaws whatever groups are asked to register. Even if an enterprise is able to survive, it will have lost most of its moderate members and be wholly in the hands of extremists who don't care. Its unobjectionable activities will be crippled. Whatever it still does will be more radical than ever.

First, I should like to point out the great dangers of thus interfering by law with freedom of discussion through organizations. The Act proposes to twist out of all recognizable shape one of the leading traditions of American life: the possibility of freely forming associations for all sorts of purposes—religious, political, social, and economic.

If we look back over our national history, we see that many of the most significant political and social changes began with the efforts of some small informal group disliked by the ordinary run of citizens. The abolition of slavery grew out of Garrison's Antislavery Society and similar associations. The Nineteenth Amendment is the culmination of the activities of a few unpopular women in the middle of the last century. The popular election of Senators, the federal income tax, and several other reforms largely originated with the Grangers and the Populists. American political, social, and economic institutions have developed to a very large extent through the interaction of propagandists groups. The appearance of a group favoring one side of an issue often aroused a group of opponents, and the public profited from its opportunity to judge between the competing presentations of both sides of an important national problem. Under modern conditions, freedom of speech under the First Amendment is likely to be ineffective if it means only the liberty of an isolated individual to talk about his ideas. Indeed, from the very beginning, freedom of speech has involved the liberty of a number of individuals to associate themselves for the advocacy of a common purpose whether they exchange ideas in a hall or by mail like the Committees of Correspondence before the Revolution. Thus, freedom of speech and freedom of assembly fit into each other. They are both related to the possibility of petitioning Congress and the state legislatures for redress of grievances, which is only part of the wider freedom to submit the views of the individual or the group to the people at large for judgment.

It may be argued, however, that the so-called "Communist-front organizations" present an entirely new problem because they have objectionable purposes and include objectionable persons in their membership. This brings me to my second point. It has always been true of a great many propagandist organizations that their purposes were denounced by numerous law-abiding citizens and that their memberships included some extremists whose actions or ideas were open to serious adverse criticism. The books are full of denunciations by prominent citizens of abolitionists, women suffragists, labor unions, Populists, etc., which would more than match anything which has been written about the Joint Anti-Fascist Refugee Committee or the National Lawyers Guild or any of the other contemporary organizations classed as "subversive" by the House Un-American Activities Committee and the Attorney General's list.

The membership situation is much the same now as it has always been. Propagandist organizations are not likely to be made up of men and women with conventional ideas. The very nature of a propagandist organization is that it wants to change something; obviously, then, it is likely to be made up of the kind of people who do want change. Such people vary a good deal. The core of the propagandist organization often consists of those whom Woodrow Wilson described as "forward-looking men and women," who disagree with the complacency of the ordinary run of citizens about some issue but still are fairly moderate in the changes they desire and so do not seriously offend their neighbors. Yet these are rarely the only members of a propagandist organization; it is likely also to include what Theodore Roosevelt called "the lunatic fringe."

The organizations opposed to slavery had members who urged violations of law, such as rescuing fugitive slaves and transporting them to Canada on the Underground Railway. Some of them even favored or participated in the attempt of John Brown to start a slave-rising in Virginia. Time and again the whole labor movement has been denounced as lawless because some unionists undoubtedly engaged in violence against their employers and non-union workers. Saloons were smashed by some prohibitionists, like Carry Nation. It is plain that there is nothing new in the adherence of extremists to organizations with desirable or at least legitimate purposes.

Hence, we should not be surprised or frightened if some contemporary organizations for upholding the rights of minorities get some members who are more in sympathy with communism than the rank and file of the organization like. It is equally possible that organizations for upholding free speech or a fair trial or other fundamental constitutional rights may attract extremists whose interest is not in constitutional rights but in getting a Communist off. In short, it is inevitable that the membership of organizations formed to bring about change should include some persons who want a great deal of change.

The supporters of this law assume that the moderate members of an organization always have an obligation to oust the extremists or else resign themselves. But this is by no means plain. Throughout the history of this country, the propagandist organizations which I have been describing were engaged in a hard fight against determined opponents. Their chances of winning this fight would clearly have been weakened if they had also waged an internal war with their own extremists or if moderates had got out and stopped supporting the cherished purpose of the organization. The practical question must have arisen hundreds of times: Was it better to put up with the extremists and continue the fight for an important cause, or disrupt the organization and probably kill the cause?

Now, what would have happened in the history of our country if the policy of the McCarran Act had been embodied in law during the Nineteenth Century? There would have been different tests, of course, aimed at the kind of organization whose purpose was hated by the authorities of the particular period. Yet the general principle would have been exactly the same. The idea is to condemn an organization because of the objectionable ideas or conduct of its extremists and thus make it difficult for the moderates in the organization to accomplish their basic purpose. For example, suppose that the standards of permissible membership in anti-slavery societies had been fixed by a board chosen by slaveowners and the owners of Northern cotton mills. Again, suppose that the associations of employers and their friends in Congress had been able to set up a board to outlaw a trade union affiliated with men devoted to industrial violence.

When the membership and policies of an opinion-forming organization can be judged and controlled by outsiders with governmental power, all sorts of opportunities for the suppression of legitimate ideas arise. The officials, being outsiders, may be rather unsympathetic with the legitimate purposes of the organization. There is a tremendous temptation to opponents of those legitimate purposes to influence the selection and the behavior of the controlling officials. The presence of extremists can easily be made an excuse for outlawing an organization when *the real reason for getting rid of it is not fear of the extremists but hatred of the legitimate purposes.* The organization is suppressed, not because it might promote a revolution but because it might win elections and produce legislation.

There are many important questions to be settled in this country today, with much to be said on both sides. Take four illustrations: (1) Should we (a) favor the transfer to a different government (or perhaps the abolition) of one of the permanent seats on the United Nations Security Council, or (b) support its occupancy by the government of Chiang Kai-shek as one of the five Great Powers? (2) Should we (a) stop economic aid to Franco in Spain unless he establishes free and unfettered elections and liberty of the press and religion, or (b) keep on paying millions of dollars to help a totalitarian regime? (3) Should we (a) force states which still want racial segregation in schools and places of entertainment to get rid of it very soon, or (b) allow them to end it very gradually when local public opinion is willing to accept a change? (4) Should we (a) repeal the McCarran Act, or (b) enforce it vigorously and bring about a great many registrations of groups as "Communist-front organizations"? These are vital questions, on which honest and reasonable men differ. They cannot be wisely decided unless individuals and opinion-forming organizations on one side are as free to present their views as are those on the other side.

The significant thing is that in every one of these questions an organization which takes the (b) side cannot possibly be touched by the Act, while any organization which takes the (a) side can conceivably be outlawed. Although there are plenty of honest reasons why many patriotic American citizens stand for the (a) side, it happens in every case that this side coincides with the views of the Soviet Union and its supporters, whose reasons are quite different. One of the factors which the Subversive Activities Control Board can take into consideration in determining whether an organization is "Communist-front" is:

> (4) the extent to which the positions taken or advanced by it from time to time on matters of policy do not deviate from those of any Communist political organization, Communist foreign government, or the world Communist movement . . .[58]

Thus, this Act leaves organizations on the (b) side untouched, no matter if they include Fascists, anti-Semites, and advocates of religious and racial hatred, and also greatly aids them by silencing a large number of their most vigorous opponents. Insofar as there are errors on the (b) side, the law will be increasing public danger enormously by making it very difficult for those errors to be combatted by reason.

Mr. Truman said that, because of the clause just quoted, the McCarran Act "can be the greatest danger to freedom of speech, press, and assembly, since the Alien and Sedition Laws of 1798."

> This provision could easily be used to classify as a Communist-front organization any organization which is advocating a single policy or objective which is also being urged by the Communist Party or by a Communist foreign government. . . . Thus, an organization which advocates low-cost housing for sincere humanitarian reasons might be classified as a Communist-front organization because the Communists regularly exploit slum conditions as one of their fifth-column techniques.

Actual experience amply justifies the expectation that the vague characterization of "Communist-front organizations" in this law [59] will be used to cripple or suppress many organizations which serve very desirable purposes, even if they do include some leftist people among their supporters. The ease with which a very useful organization can be condemned under a similar loose definition on the basis of very thin evidence is shown by Professor Walter Gellhorn of Columbia in an article relating to the wholly unfounded red-listing of the Southern Conference for Human Welfare by the House Un-American Activities Committee.[60]

Remember always that everything depends on the five men who make up the Subversive Activities Control Board as the years go by. Equally important is the attitude of the Attorney General for the time being. Just by filing a petition against any enterprise he dislikes, he can put it under a black cloud which will scare off contributors and force it to interrupt its normal activities in order to defend itself for months before the Board at the cost of thousands of dollars. This is enough to wreck almost any group even though it eventually escapes registration.

Thus the McCarran Act has a lopsided effect on the formation of public opinion. It creates a tremendous risk of outlawing a considerable number of groups of law-abiding people with inquiring minds, engaged in furthering some end which they believe to be in the very best interests of the United States. And, on the other hand, this law will encourage those who hate the purposes of such groups to do all they can to suppress or hamper them by influencing the selection of new members of the Subversive Activities Control Board and by bringing pressure of every sort upon the officials on the Board. The "Communist-front" provisions violate the fundamental principle of self-government that the persons in power for the time being ought not to be able to shape public opinion in their favor by force.

Very likely propagandist groups do exist among us for the support of measures which would hurt the nation if they were adopted. Yet that has always been true in our history. If we wipe out the law requiring "Communist-front organizations" to register, we can rely, as in the past, on the good sense of the American people to choose among competing policies after getting the benefit of full discussion unhampered by government officials.

The only way to preserve "the existence of free American institutions" is to make free institutions a living force. To ignore them in the very process of purporting to defend them, as frightened men urge, will leave us little worth defending.

We must choose between freedom and fear—we cannot have both. If the citizens of the United States persist in being afraid, the real rulers of this country will be fanatics fired with a zeal to save grown men from objectionable ideas by putting them under the care of official nursemaids.

VI Purges Are for Russian Lawyers, Not American Lawyers

> It is the obnoxious and the suspected who want
> the protection of law.——BURKE, *Letter to the Sher-*
> *iffs of Bristol on Affairs in America*

Every lawyer, on admission to the bar of his state or to that of a United States court, is required to take an oath of office in the presence of the court. Its form is prescribed by a statute or by a rule of the court. The Massachusetts law is typical.[1] It requires that whoever is admitted as an attorney shall in open court take and subscribe oaths to support the Constitution of the United States and of the Commonwealth; and also the following oath of office:

> I, (repeat the name), solemnly swear that I will do no falsehood, nor consent to the doing of any in court; I will not wittingly or willingly promote or sue any false, groundless or unlawful suit, nor give aid or consent to the same; I will delay no man for lucre or malice; but I will conduct myself in the office of an attorney within the courts according to the best of my knowledge and discretion, and with all good fidelity as well to the courts as my clients. So help me God.

A lawyer admitted to practise in the United States Supreme Court must take and subscribe this oath or affirmation: [2]

> I, ——— ———, do solemnly swear (or affirm) that I will demean myself, as an attorney and counsellor of this court, uprightly, and according to law; and that I will support the Constitution of the United States.

Nevertheless, during the Korean crisis, a new and additional oath for lawyers was recommended by the House of Delegates of the American Bar Association on September 21, 1950, in the following resolution: [3]

WHEREAS, lawyers, better than any other group in America can understand and teach others to understand the principles of our Constitution and the protections afforded by our Bill of Rights, and the fundamental conflicts between these constitutional principles and the doctrines of Communism; and

WHEREAS, The lawyers of America, by virtue of the license each has obtained to practice law, to serve courts of justice, and to advise citizens as to their legal rights, have a much greater duty than citizens generally to support the principles of the Constitution and oppose the doctrines of Communism inconsistent therewith; now therefore be it

RESOLVED, By the American Bar Association:

1. That it is not inappropriate, with world conditions as they are, that any American citizen be required to attest to his loyalty to our form of government by anti-communist oath, and that it is especially appropriate that all licensed to practise law in the United States of America be required so to do;

2. (a) That the legislature, the court or other appropriate authority of each state or territory and the District of Columbia, be requested to require each member of its Bar, within a reasonable time and periodically thereafter, to file an affidavit stating whether he is or ever has been a member of the Communist Party or affiliated therewith, and stating also whether he is or ever has been a member or supporter of any organization that espouses the overthrow by force or by any illegal or unconstitutional means, of the United States Government, or the government of any of the states or territories of the United States; and in the event such affidavit reveals that he is or ever has been a member of said Communist Party, or of any such organization, that the appropriate authority promptly and thoroughly investigate the activities and conduct of said member of the Bar to determine his fitness for continuance as an attorney;

(b) That in the event at any time later it be established that said attorney has wilfully sworn falsely to any of the facts, he should be the subject of immediate disbarment proceedings.

Although this resolution called for a uniform law setting up novel and drastic disciplinary mechanism throughout the United States, it was passed in the closing rush of the Association's annual meeting with no debate. "Patriotism is not enough," said the dying Edith Cavell. Deliberation, too, is desirable, as lawyers surely ought to know. This hasty recommendation soon evoked a vigorous protest (printed at the close of this chapter) by John W. Davis, former Justice Roberts, and twenty-four other members of the American Bar Association. The upshot was that five years have gone by without a single state adopting this oath. And, except for New Jersey which already had a non-retroactive test oath, loyalty oaths for lawyers are still unknown in the United States.[4]

Nevertheless, the objections to this measure ought to be kept fresh in the minds of American citizens. The resolution has never been rescinded. There is no telling when another emotional outburst will produce renewed efforts to get such an oath established. Moreover, the important issues are much wider than this particular proposal or than the legal profession. Many of the points I shall consider are equally applicable to many other occupations where test oaths have been required in recent years by a never-ending series of laws. Consequently, this chapter which starts with the special situation of lawyers has a good opportunity to look at the whole subject of loyalty oaths.

Any state which adopts this proposal that lawyers must periodically take a loyalty oath will be creating risks of grave injury to the careers of faithful, law-abiding lawyers, to the harmonious brotherhood of the bar, and to freedom of speech and assembly, which are among the most precious possessions in our land.

A test oath for lawyers has never been seriously considered in this country since 1867 when the United States Supreme Court killed the attempt to purge the federal and Missouri bars of Confederate sympathizers down to the day in 1950 when this resolution for a test oath was introduced in the American Bar Association by lawyers from Texas. It is indeed ironical that the bitter lessons of Reconstruction should have been thus forgotten in the largest state in the Confederacy.

Every member of the bar in every state has been admitted to practise law after a thorough examination into his legal attainments and a careful investigation into his character. Every lawyer then took an impressive oath, as set forth at the opening of this chapter, in which he promised faithfully to perform his duties in what he was constantly made to think of as a great profession. Each of us remembers that solemn moment, and its force upon our minds has increased with the running of the years. We took that oath in the presence of the full bench of judges. Often, as in my case, it was under the eyes of a father who is no longer living. Yet now the chief bar association in the United States assumes that this ceremony counts for nothing, and that the only way to save the country is to supplement that impressive oath by a piece of paper signed once a year in a bank or between telephone calls in a law office with the same perfunctory haste with which a lawyer signs an application to renew his authority to act as a notary public. How is it possible that the conscience of a lawyer who no longer cares about his solemn promise in open court to uphold the Constitution is going to be affected by the hugger-mugger of signing an affidavit? Plainly, the object of this novel oath is not to make a man a better lawyer and increase his devotion to the principles of the Constitution. The object is to find a way to get rid of a lawyer if his opinions, or those of persons with whom he associates, are thought objectionable by a large number of other lawyers and by an influential portion of the community. This is a plan to purge the American bar.

But, it will be said, the loyalty oath is aimed at Communist lawyers. Communists are bad, so the oath must be good. This does not follow at all. Communism ought to be combatted, but that does not mean that every possible suggestion for opposing communism is desirable, especially a measure which by its very terms affects all lawyers, most of whom are not Communists at all. There are well-known direct ways of dealing with lawyers who are actually engaged in a revolutionary conspiracy. They can be reached without subjecting every lawyer in the United States to filling out an annual form and without imperiling, in ways I shall soon describe, the livelihood of lawyers who are far from being Communists.

Nobody can detest Communists more than I do. I have confronted a good many of them in the United Nations at Lake Success and Geneva. Some of them are menaces, a good many others are nuisances. They are opposed to every ideal of freedom which I hold dear and on behalf of which I have argued in season and out of season for nearly forty years. As citizens rather than as lawyers we are bound to prevent them from taking over our government and our lives and destroying our freedoms; but we ought to try to do so by choosing methods which will be effective, which will not cause unnecessary harm to non-Communists, which will not impair the very freedoms which we are anxious to maintain. This test oath is not the right way to deal with Communists.

Too often we are tempted to meet totalitarianism with the weapons of totalitarianism. And this proposed test oath is just the sort of thing which was used in Hitler's Berlin and Stalin's Moscow. It seeks to purge the bar of those who do not toe the American party-line, as defined by those in power for the time being. By starting an inquisition into men's ideas, it violates David Lilienthal's principle of protection for "the integrity and dignity of the individual." By threatening honest lawyers holding somewhat heterodox views with expulsion from their sole means of livelihood, it deserves General Marshall's denunciation: "To us, a society is not free if law-abiding citizens live in fear of being denied the right to work." [5]

ANALYSIS OF THE RECOMMENDATION OF THE AMERICAN BAR ASSOCIATION FOR A LOYALTY OATH

In order to realize the consequences of the proposed test oath for lawyers, one must look carefully at what the resolution of the American Bar Association says. Its operative provisions fall into two main stages—the oath itself and the subsequent disbarment proceedings.

In the first stage, each member of the bar will be required by law to file periodically an affidavit stating "whether he is or ever has been a member of the Communist Party, or affiliated therewith" —and now comes the much vaguer second part of the oath which calls for particular attention—"and also whether he is or ever has been a member or a supporter of an organization that espouses the overthrow by force or by any illegal or unconstitutional means," of the government of the United States or any state.

The second stage involves three different proceedings, all leading toward disbarment: (1) If a lawyer refuses to take the oath, he will presumably be automatically disbarred. (2) If his affidavit reveals that he is or ever has been a member of any of the proscribed organizations, the appropriate authority will "promptly and thoroughly investigate the activities and conduct" of this lawyer "to determine his fitness for continuance as an attorney." (3) If, as will usually happen, the lawyer denies membership in any such proscribed organization, then he can be subjected to a subsequent perjury inquiry without any time-limit whatever; and if it be established that he has "wilfully sworn falsely to any of the facts," immediate disbarment proceedings are to be brought.

The First Stage in the Recommendation— The Exculpatory Oath

The American Bar Association departed very far from our cherished traditions when it proposed a procedure which would begin by setting up systematic exculpatory oaths for all members of a profession. The exculpatory oath differs greatly from the customary oath of office such as the President of the United States takes when he is inaugurated. The oath of office looks to the future. It is an affirmative promise. Its purpose is to inspire the man to keep on the job at the highest level of which he is capable. The exculpatory oath, on the contrary, is a negative disclaimer of present or past acts and present or past associations and beliefs. Its purpose is to put men out of office by the back door, without the bother of presenting charges of specific wrongdoing and supporting those charges at a regular trial.

If we scrutinize any test-oath law carefully, we see that it does two separate things: (1) It creates new grounds of ineligibility to engage in a profession, regardless of the length of time the man has been doing such work or of the way he has performed his obligations. (2) The law provides a novel way of proving these grounds of ineligibility. The mere failure to take the oath is enough to disqualify the man without any evidence having to be offered against him by any accusers.

These two aspects of exculpatory oaths are constantly getting confused. Each aspect ought to be examined all by itself, in order to get adequate consideration of possible mistakes and injustice.

Suppose, for instance, that the new grounds of ineligibility to practise law in the Bar Association resolution had not been hidden under an oath but presented more directly. Such a straightforward proposal could be summarized like this:

> There shall be four new grounds for possible disbarment:
>   1. The lawyer is now a member of the Communist Party.
>   2. He was once a member of that Party, no matter how long ago.
>   3. The lawyer is now a member of some other group (described as in the resolution).
>   4. He was once a member of such other group, no matter how long ago.

If a good many of the lawyers at the Association meeting had only realized that this was what they were really voting on, probably numerous objections would have been suggested. Some delegate would have pointed out that none of the specified disqualifications involved a crime or lack of fidelity to a client. Somebody else would have been disturbed by the *ex post facto* operation of two of the grounds of ineligibility. Others would have stressed the vagueness with which the non-Communist groups are described. In the end, it would have been sensible to put the whole thing over till the next meeting in order that such a far-reaching measure could receive prolonged thought.

Now look at the other end—the method for proving ineligibility. A given ground for disqualification may be desirable, but it does not follow that a test oath is a wise or fair way to establish the existence of this ground. For example, misappropriation of a client's funds is a well-recognized reason for disbarment. Yet most lawyers would, I believe, oppose the proposal that every lawyer should once a year take an oath that he had never used a client's money for his own benefit. Or let me give a simple illustration outside law. A football player in training can be rightly thrown off the squad for drinking. Yet the coach who forced every player to swear every Monday that he had not touched liquor during the week before would soon be called a sneak and lose his job. The test oath has some of the insidiousness of compelling a man to incriminate himself.

It is one thing for a character committee to ask a candidate for the bar to tell a good deal about himself, and quite a different matter to extort personal information from a lawyer long in practice, just out of the blue without specific charges of wrongdoing.

The traditional Anglo-Saxon method for removing a man from office after he has acquired it is to present formal charges and have a hearing before an impartial tribunal, which can summon witnesses on his behalf to rebut the charges and furnish guidance when difficult questions of law or fact arise. Many safeguards furnished by this method are absent if an officeholder is confronted with a test oath and thus forced to determine his own guilt or innocence without judicial guidance. The man's plight is especially unfair when, as in the proposed oath for lawyers, he is obliged to interpret a vague definition of the wrong which he must disclaim in order to continue his career and when he has to reach conclusions of fact although much of the relevant evidence is unknown to him and beyond his reach.

Therefore, when any new grounds for disbarment are proposed, we ought first to consider very carefully whether they would be desirable to adopt if enforced in the customary way by bar committees and judges. If so, the next question is: Why not use that well-tried procedure instead of incurring the dangers of exculpatory oaths?

The exculpatory oath was twice severely condemned as unconstitutional by a majority of the Supreme Court in 1867. Furthermore, the four dissenters on the constitutional points in each case agreed with the majority in regretting the imposition of such an oath because of the harm it did to men of good character.[6]

One case involved a provision of the Missouri constitution of 1865 forbidding any lawyer to practise and any clergyman of any religious denomination to teach, preach, or solemnize marriages, unless he had first taken an oath that he had never, among other things, manifested his adherence to the cause of the Confederate States or his desire for their triumph or his sympathy with those engaged in carrying on rebellion against the United States. A Roman Catholic priest was convicted and imprisoned for continuing to perform his religious duties without having taken the oath. The Supreme Court let Father Cummings out of jail. It held this to be an *ex post facto* law because it added new punishments to past acts, and a bill of attainder because the law-making body had made guilt of those past acts determinable without any judicial trial.

In the other case, Congress in 1865 required all lawyers practising in the United States courts to take an oath that they had never borne arms against the United States, or held office under any hostile authority, or yielded voluntary support to any pretended government within the United States which was hostile thereto. Augustus H. Garland, a leader of the Arkansas bar who had received a full pardon from President Johnson, was unable to take this oath without perjuring himself. Yet the Supreme Court allowed Garland to practise before it, ignoring the statutory oath as a retroactive punishment of him by Congress. The constitutional grounds were the same as in the Cummings case, and also that the courts and not the legislature had power to regulate qualifications for the bar.

The men in Missouri and in Congress who imposed these test oaths had much stronger reasons than we have for being disturbed about possible disloyalty among lawyers. The laws were passed toward the close of the Civil War when millions of men had been doing their best to overthrow the government of the United States by force and violence. It was certainly arguable that a lawyer who had taken an active part in an endeavor so dangerous to the nation was not fit to be a member of the bar. Nevertheless, the Supreme Court resolutely rejected this means of ensuring loyal lawyers. The Court relied on Alexander Hamilton:

> Nothing can be more repugnant to the true genius of the common law than such an inquisition into the consciences of men. . . . It substitutes for the established and legal mode of investigating crimes and inflicting forfeitures, one that is unknown to the Constitution and repugnant to the genius of our law.

There was, I say, as much reason then for fearing Confederate sympathizers in the bar as there is for fearing Communists and Communist sympathizers in the bar today. Yet were those fears realized when the test oaths were killed by the Supreme Court? Never, so far as I know, did any lawyer who would have been excluded by the test oath do anything offensive to good morals and good government. Take Augustus H. Garland himself. He had been at the forefront of the endeavor to overthrow the government of the United States by force, since he was a member of every Confederate Congress. Yet, after the Supreme Court had readmitted him to practise contrary to the intention of Congress, he conducted many important litigations with great distinction. He became Cleveland's first Attorney General. His honorable career was ended by what every lawyer would regard as the ideal death, for he was stricken while arguing a case in the United States Supreme Court.

It is true that after loyalty oaths were revived in this country during recent years and spread as they did in England three hundred years ago,[7] the Supreme Court has upheld their constitutionality in three cases, although subsequently the Court nullified a sweeping oath for teachers in Oklahoma.[8] Two of these decisions sustained Maryland and California laws enacted for the purpose of disqualifying state and city officials and employees who belonged to the Communist Party.[9] The Douds case [10] sustained the provision of the Taft-Hartley Act which required union officials to abjure present membership in that Party in order to be eligible to represent workmen in collective bargaining before the National Labor Relations Board. In the same case, however, the Justices divided three to three on a provision of the Taft-Hartley oath disclaiming specified non-Communist affiliations and beliefs, in language somewhat resembling the latter portion of the lawyers' oath recommended by the American Bar Association.

None of the three cases just described purports to overrule the great Reconstruction decisions which protected Father Cummings and Garland in their chosen professions without their taking loyalty oaths. The majority in these recent cases seems to have concentrated attention on the reasonableness of the grounds of ineligibility, and then assumed rather easily that this point settled the validity of the oaths. The other aspect of the oath—determination of guilt without a judicial trial—was somewhat slighted except by the dissenters. Moreover, it was difficult for the Court to upset these particular laws. A federal tribunal was bound to be reluctant to force states and municipalities to employ men whom they plainly did not want. The Taft-Hartley oath was intended to remedy serious evils of industrial relations, such as strikes for political or revolutionary purposes. Union officers who speak for workmen before the N.L.R.B. ought to be working to further the interests of the persons they represent and not the very different objectives of extreme radical-

ism. The Constitution puts the regulation of interstate commerce in the hands of Congress, and judges lack the training and experience which would warrant their rejection of the way Congress had chosen to meet these difficult problems. When it comes to the affairs of lawyers, there is much less reason for reluctance because judges are experts in the problems and their solution. They do know what is unwise and what would be better. They are on the home grounds. "Bred en bawn in a brier-patch!"

And it is not just a question of unconstitutionality here, any more than with other laws which restrict human rights. Lawyers should think a long time before they depart from any great tradition of liberty, even if the Supreme Court will perhaps feel unable to upset the measure because of its unwillingness to interfere with Congress or with a state's management of its own affairs. A bad law ought not to be passed just because it is possibly valid. "Test oaths, designed to impose civil disabilities upon men for their belief rather than for *unlawful* conduct" were, as Justice Black says,[11] "an abomination to the founders of the nation."

This exculpatory oath is especially bad because of the vague behavior which a lawyer must disclaim, to avoid thorough investigation of all his "activities and conduct." I leave aside for the moment lawyers who are Communists.[12] What really matters is the loyal lawyer, who is no Communist but has participated like other forward-looking men and women in unpopular enterprises, especially those irresponsibly labeled as "Communist-fronts." Here something else that Hamilton said about test oaths is very pertinent, that they "excite scruples in the honest and conscientious." Such men will occasionally refuse to take the oath. They believe (not unreasonably) that it violates at least four provisions of the very Constitution which they swore to support—the *ex post facto* clause, the bill of attainder clause, the First Amendment, and the privilege against self-incrimination in the Fifth Amendment. They consider it an unwarranted invasion of their liberties for anybody to make them declare their lawful private opinions and activities about politics and economics. So they leave the profession rather than take the oath. Such men may be called over-conscientious, but excessive scru-

pulousness is not so common among lawyers that we can afford to
drive it out of the bar.

Some experienced lawyers have told me that my apprehension
on this score is nonsensical. They insist that no honest lawyer will
decline to sign the required affidavit, and that anybody who does
have difficulties about signing is sure to be the kind of man whom
the bar is better off without. On the contrary, I believe that there
are many conscientious lawyers who will have just the worries I
have described. They will be like Samuel Taylor Glover when confronted with the Missouri test oath for lawyers at the end of the
Civil War.

Glover was an active St. Louis lawyer who had identified himself
with the emancipation of slaves from his youth up, despite the
overwhelming preponderance of proslavery sentiment in the various
states where he had lived. He was a prominent Republican in the
campaign of 1860. While it was touch-and-go whether Missouri
would secede, Glover was a leader in keeping his state in the Union.
Probably no lawyer in Missouri could have subscribed with greater
honesty to the terms of this test oath. Nevertheless Glover refused
to take it on ground of principle. He was indicted and convicted
after trial for continuing to practise without taking the oath. Luck-
ily for him, the Cummings case was decided in time to get his conviction reversed. Thereafter he became the recognized head of
the St. Louis bar, and was retained in thirty cases in the United
States Supreme Court and in 410 cases in the highest court in
Missouri.[13]

The exculpatory oaths after the Civil War almost deprived the
bar of Glover, the best constitutional lawyer of his time in the
West, and of Garland, a future Attorney General. If the American
Bar Association gets its loyalty oath adopted, nobody can predict
how many able lawyers of equal integrity will be driven out of the
profession.

Of course, most lawyers will sign whatever oath the law requires.
Here another serious objection arises, which applies to all exculpatory oaths at the present time, whether for the bar or any other
occupation, unless they are confined to actual membership in the
Communist Party. That is rarely the case. The backers of these
oaths are usually as eager as the American Bar Association was to do

more than get rid of out-and-out Communists. They are after
"subversive" groups and "fellow-travelers" too. Yet an oath framed
for that broad purpose becomes full of vague words. Consequently,
the persons required to take the oath have to guess at what it means,
and the authorities who possess power to wreck the careers of the
oath-takers can make it mean almost anything they happen to
dislike.

In order to bring out this objection to loyalty oaths generally,
look at the description of non-Communists in the Bar Association
oath. No doubt, other words could be used, but this is a fair sample.
It was drawn and indorsed by scores of leading American lawyers.
There is no reason to expect that less eminent men would produce
anything less vague than the following language:

> stating also whether he is or ever has been a member or *supporter*
> of any organization that *espouses* the overthrow . . . , *by any illegal
> or unconstitutional means* [of the government of the nation or any
> state]. . . .

Now suppose a conscientious lawyer, some of whose views are
detested by many persons in his community. He is ready to swear,
but he will be puzzled about what he is swearing to. Especially by
the words I have italicized. He has to try to remember every peaceable group with which he had any conceivable connection since
he was old enough to be a Cub Scout, and decide for himself which
he has to mention in order to escape a charge of perjury. He recalls
going to some meetings of the National Lawyers Guild while he
was in law school, but not whether he became a member. It was all
so long ago. Is he a "supporter" of the Jefferson School because
he supported some of its activities in a letter to the *New York
Times?* Or because he gave one lecture at the school on medical
testimony in automobile accident cases? And what is "espousing"
outside of marriage?

His biggest puzzle will be caused by "illegal and unconstitutional
means." It often takes years of litigation to be sure that a statute is
unconstitutional, and even then Justices disagree. How can anybody
know that a merely proposed law is an unconstitutional means of
altering the government? If the lawyer belongs to a group to persuade Congress to abolish state poll taxes as a prerequisite to voting

at elections, such a law might "overthrow" the present government of several Southern states, and many lawyers (including myself) believe that the law would be unconstitutional. Suppose he once worked in the Secretariat of the United Nations. Several Senators and some of the most influential members of the American Bar Association are constantly declaring that the United Nations is endeavoring to overthrow the government of the United States and our basic liberties by unconstitutional treaties. If officers of his state bar association fervently share this view, must he then mention the United Nations in his oath?

Some may argue that compulsory disclosure of non-Communist groups, whether the phraseology used, is satisfied if the oath-taker confines himself to "Communist-front organizations" ordered to register under the McCarran Act and to subversive groups on commonly accepted lists. Must he then name any organization of his which was red-listed by the Attorney General, often without a hearing,[14] by every Congressional and state investigating committee, and by the American Legion? Does he have to include the American Civil Liberties Union, the Fund for the Republic, and the League of Women Voters? Or shall he safely use his own judgment like a free man, and give to all these lists as much or as little weight as they deserve?

Only those who have studied the operation of sedition laws can realize how sweepingly and unexpectedly vague phrases in a loyalty oath may operate. Anything can happen under a sedition law.

The Second Stage in the Recommendation— Disciplinary Proceedings Tending Toward Disbarment

Suppose the lawyer honestly decides his organization is not within the oath and omits it, but the community would like to run him out of the bar. If the dominant lawyers in the community disagree with him about the nature of the organization, they may conclude he has "wilfully sworn falsely" to this fact and urge his disbarment. The oath is what Justice Roberts called "a dragnet which may enmesh anyone who agitates for a change of government," [15] and, what is still worse, those who have merely associated with him. Its vague phrases are an open-house invitation to fanatics and personal enemies to deprive any heterodox lawyer of his livelihood. And "wherever the test oath was in vogue, spies and informers found rewards far more tempting than the truth." [16] In particular, a lawyer who ventures to defend alleged Communists in any proceeding is very likely to be threatened with disbarment by men who would be glad to deprive such accused persons of any effective legal defense. That is exactly what happened in Missouri during Reconstruction. Several lawyers were disbarred when they ventured to represent men who were prosecuted for not taking the loyalty oath. And during the Red Menace after the First World War, some lawyers who defended radicals were disbarred.[17]

Now take a lawyer with some heterodox opinions who, when he took the oath, thought that frankness was the safest policy. He put down every organization to which he was ever related, no matter how remotely, if anybody might conceivably object to it. He may soon learn that he is not safe at all, and find himself on the road to disbarment. For the resolution says that if he belongs to a single organization within its vague definition, then the authorities shall promptly and thoroughly investigate him. They are not just to ask about his connection with this organization, but go over his whole "activities and conduct . . . to determine his fitness for continuance as an attorney." None of these "subversive" organizations are criminal. Yet he is treated like a suspected embezzler of clients' funds.

Whether an honest lawyer omits a disliked organization or mentions it, he is pretty sure to be entangled in another objectionable feature of almost all loyalty oaths—their retroactive clauses. Thus the Bar Association oath says, "or ever has been a member" with no Statute of Limitations for conduct which was not even a minor crime.

Most of us did foolish things when we were young. There were no "Communist-front organizations" while I was growing up, but I should be sorry to have a few transactions dragged into the light of day after many years. An Italian proverb says, "He who is not a radical at twenty will be a spy at forty." It is very harsh to cloud the career of a reputable lawyer with investigations and threats of disbarment because he joined some leftish group while he was in college. A law-abiding man can be grilled about an organization which he left years ago and which may have been entirely legitimate when he belonged to it. Suppose he tries to clear himself by showing that the purposes and activities of the enterprise changed after he got out of it. Think how hard this will be. He has to hunt up scanty records which are scattered over the country. He has to interview later officers of the group who are complete strangers to him and very likely labeled "subversive" even more than he is, in the forlorn hope of using them as his witnesses.

Possibly it is right to assume that a lawyer who has served his clients faithfully will come through an ordeal like this without being ousted from the profession. Whatever his fellow-lawyers do, judges will eventually dismiss the proceeding. Yet that will not undo the harm already done to his standing in the community. The big evil of this oath is not actual disbarments, but its encouragement of proceedings against lawyers whose views are disliked. No matter what the court says in the end, a man's law practice has been disrupted for months. People will be always saying, "They did think he needed to be investigated." New clients will not come to him and old clients will slip away elsewhere. Mud sticks.

Next, look at the punishment which is provided in this Bar Association resolution. The cherished American tradition is that a man shall be punished only for having done some wrongful act, either a crime or a grave breach of the duties of his occupation; the wrongful act must be clearly defined by law and definitely proved to have been committed. On the contrary, tyrannies from which our ancestors escaped and those against which we have fought valiantly in our own time punished men because of something that they might possibly do in the future. Such was the obvious purpose of test oaths in Seventeenth-Century England.[18] They excluded men from public office and the learned professions, not for any past crime or violation of duty, but because their beliefs and affiliations were considered to show that they might not perform the particular work in a satisfactory way. Of course the character test which each of us lawyers underwent before his admission to the bar did involve predictions about our subsequent performance, but why should a mature lawyer be forced to go through the same process of predictions after years of practice have proved that he always fulfils his obligations to the courts and to his clients?

Disbarment is about the worst penalty a lawyer can suffer. It deprives him of the profession to which he is devoted and of his chosen livelihood, leaving him little chance of supporting himself adequately in some other occupation. Thoughtful lawyers and judges have always been reluctant to impose such a drastic punishment even for some conduct which was plainly a reprehensible breach of professional duty. Surely, the bar should be very cautious indeed about disbarring for novel kinds of lawful behavior which have no close relation to judges or clients or to anything that a lawyer does in his office.

It is absurd to say that the lawyer who has denied membership in any proscribed organization, and then is found to belong to one of these groups, is punished for perjury and not for membership. Suppose some fanatical "dries" during Prohibition had succeeded in forcing every lawyer to swear he had not patronized a bootlegger, with penalties like this resolution. This would obviously be punishing lawyers for buying from bootleggers. Perjury is just a trick.

All this time I have been speaking of the consequences of the proposed loyalty oath to lawyers who are not Communists. Now let me say a little about the comparatively few lawyers who do actually belong to the Communist Party. Remember that men are not criminals merely by being Communists, for Congress expressly provided in the McCarran Act of 1950 that "Neither the holding of office nor membership in any Communist organization shall constitute *per se* a violation [of a specified provision of this Act] or *of any other criminal statute*." [19] I regret that any lawyer should hold Communist views, but do they render him unfit to move for a directed verdict in an automobile accident or draw a will? The necessity of earning a living forces him to spend most of his time in the same way as lawyers who are lifelong Republicans or Democrats. Everything he does in court is under the close supervision of judges, and misconduct elsewhere can be thoroughly investigated by a grievance committee. If it be argued that Communist lawyers show a marked inclination to delay and disrupt trials, this is all done in the open and they can be readily punished for contempt of court.

Even if some Communist lawyer of the milder sort I am now discussing may possibly cause some harm some day, trying to remove him by a dragnet like this oath would cause far greater harm. And if you do disbar him because of a possible future danger, what practical way is there for him to support himself and his family except by becoming an active employee of some Communist organization? Instead of making him less dangerous, you render him much more dangerous.

As for the Communist lawyers who are in fact criminally inclined, what good will a loyalty oath do? Men who are ready to start a bloody revolution will not boggle at false swearing. Spies will take a chance on a perjury prosecution. So you will not ferret out their names by this oath, and there is a pretty good chance that the F.B.I. knows their names already.

Those lawyers who believe that any member of the Communist Party is almost surely unfit to practise law ought to raise the issue squarely by proposing that being a Communist should be made a new cause for disbarment. By this method, any lawyer who was suspected of belonging to the Party would have specific charges filed before the grievance committee. Then the issues of his membership and unfitness would be tried in the usual way. This was the course urged by Charles Evans Hughes in 1920, when anxious patriots set out to have a blanket purge of left-wing Socialists from the New York legislature.[20] If there is evidence, he said, that any individuals are plotting violent revolution, "let the evidence be laid before the proper authorities and swift action be taken for the protection of the community."

The American Bar Association did take such a straightforward course in February 1951, a few months after it recommended the loyalty oath.[21] Here again, however, it did not stop with Communists. It urged the immediate disbarment of all lawyers who are members of the Communist Party "or who advocate Marxism-Leninism"—a term unknown to the law. This request appears to have fallen on stony ground.[22]

The Association was still not content to rely on normal disbarment proceedings, but flatly refused to stop recommending the exculpatory oath.[23] I have already told [24] how, when such an oath was imposed at the University of California, no damage from hypothetical Communists could have equaled the damage from actual unrest, ill will, and suspicion. Imagine the havoc if the bar of every state were thrown into similar unrest, ill will, and suspicion "periodically."

After the First World War somebody remarked that the war had not taught us to love our enemies, but at least it had taught us to hate our allies. After the Second World War we have learned to hate each other. Never before have various groups of Americans made such bitter and grave accusations against other groups of Americans. We have been tearing the community apart at a time when unity was most needed. Whatever the rest of the country does, the bar ought not to tear itself apart. We are brothers in a learned profession, even when we oppose each other in the court-room. This oath, if adopted, is going to create suspicions, occupy the time and energies of busy men, and breed constant uneasiness and perplexed anxiety and resentment not only in those who face inquiries, but also in their friends of unimpeachable loyalty.

And what do you have when you get through all the fuss that this oath will cause, the signing of papers by thousands of men each year, checking up to be sure that everybody has signed, finding a place to store the papers, and then investigations, perjury trials, dis-barment proceedings? If you get rid of a few dangerous Commu-nists, you could reach them anyway by filing specific charges. You will probably get rid of a few conscientious men like Glover, the old Missouri lawyer, and you will possibly ruin the careers of sev-eral honest lawyers whose only offense was disagreeing with many of their fellow-citizens. Suppose, however, that everybody signs and nobody is investigated. Who will be better off then?

CONCLUSION

There is one final danger in this test oath to ferret out radical lawyers. Reinhold Niebuhr says that it is always dangerous to put a weapon in the hands of your enemies which is capable of being used against yourself. It is all very well for prosperous lawyers to view this particular measure complacently. They know it will not bother them for a minute to sign it. But once you get the idea of a test oath firmly established, it can be used against all sorts of people. The current hatred of "subversives" and "fellow-travelers" may be replaced by hatred of corporate officers who make profitable contracts with the government, or, if inflation should flare up again, by hatred of sellers who raise prices, however justifiably. The lawyers for these well-to-do clients will be detested too. Then the test oath will be available in the hands of demagogues. Think how effectively it could be used to purge the bar of lawyers who are suspected of aiding rich men and big corporations to circumvent radical legislation.

Behind this test oath, I venture to think, is the notion, now rather prevalent among lawyers, that it is one of the primary functions of the legal profession to be teachers of the community about political and economic doctrines which happen to be favored by an influential portion of the bar. Consequently, lawyers ought to be drastically sifted out so that they will pour only the pure milk of the Gospel down the throats of American citizens.

No doubt, lawyers have an important influence on public opinion, but so do men in many other professions. Our main job is not teaching laymen. It is helping laymen, helping them to adjust their disputes and to conduct their affairs satisfactorily. Lawyers can best serve the American people, in current crises as always, by performing their own specialized duties to get controversies settled justly, to guide transactions wisely, and to improve the law. This is no time for them to neglect these tasks in order to turn themselves into policemen for hunting down other lawyers who have done no wrongful acts, investigating their private lives, and depriving them of their reputations and their professional careers.

We want no purge trials here.

NOTE

Statement of Twenty-six Members of the American Bar Association Opposing a Loyalty Oath for Lawyers
February 1951 [25]

The undersigned members of the American Bar Association oppose the requirement that all lawyers take a special anti-Communist oath, with periodic repetition, such as is urged upon all state authorities by the resolution adopted without debate by the House of Delegates and Assembly of the Association at the September, 1950, Annual Convention.

Every lawyer, upon his first admission to the local Bar, has been called upon to take an oath of allegiance and loyalty to the Federal and State constitutions, and adherence to honorable, professional purpose and practice. Many lawyers have taken such oaths more than once—upon admission to practice in the Federal courts, upon assuming public office, and otherwise. There is no evidence or even any charge of which we are aware, that more than an infinitesimal fraction of the approximately 200,000 lawyers throughout the United States are concealed members of the Communist Party or supporters of any subversive movement.

The requirement of this new oath, moreover, will not in our judgment reveal the disloyal in our midst, whoever they may be. The true communist or supporter of violent and illegal overthrow of the Government will, by the very nature of his belief and illegal acts, swear falsely, even at the risk of disbarment for perjury. Nor will any oath, however often repeated, deter from such belief and conduct one who is so perverted as to have already embarked upon such dirty waters. No substantial gain can result from the imposition of this oath requirement.

The existing means of discovering and punishing illegal or professionally improper conduct, by presenting specific charges and supporting evidence, are ample, in our belief, to meet any danger to our Government or disgrace to our profession. National and local law enforcement agencies, courts, bar associations, and grievance committees are fully alert to existing danger from communists in our midst, whether avowed or concealed.

We, therefore, oppose this method of intended detection as repetitious of the universally required initial professional oath, as unfounded in its implication of widespread disloyalty and illegal acts on the part of lawyers generally, and as unproductive of the hoped-for result. It violates the American tradition that suspicion of disloyalty shall not be cast upon an entire class or profession upon the chance of catching a few random delinquents. To divert or dull the force of that tradition now by a misplaced reliance on an illusory safeguard would be most unfortunate.

GEORGE W. ALGER
New York City

HORACE E. ALLEN
Springfield, Massachusetts

ERNEST ANGELL
New York City

CHARLES F. C. ARENSBERG
Pittsburgh, Pennsylvania

LAIRD BELL
Chicago, Illinois

C. C. BURLINGHAM
New York City

ZECHARIAH CHAFEE, JR.
Cambridge, Massachusetts

GRENVILLE CLARK
Dublin, New Hampshire

CYRIL COLEMAN
Hartford, Connecticut

JOHN W. DAVIS
New York City

A. CRAWFORD GREENE
San Francisco, California

FRANK W. GRINNELL
Boston, Massachusetts

JOHN L. HALL
Boston, Massachusetts

HENRY C. HART
Providence, Rhode Island

CHARLES M. LYMAN
New Haven, Connecticut

ROSS L. MALONE, JR.
Roswell, New Mexico

ROBERT McC. MARSH
New York City

GEORGE W. C. McCARTER
Newark, New Jersey

JOHN LORD O'BRIAN
Washington, D. C.

OWEN J. ROBERTS
Philadelphia, Pennsylvania

CLEMENT F. ROBINSON
Portland, Maine

WHITNEY NORTH SEYMOUR
New York City

HENRY UPSON SIMS
Birmingham, Alabama

HENRY W. TOLL
Denver, Colorado

HARRISON TWEED
New York City

BETHUEL M. WEBSTER
New York City

VII   *The Right Not to Speak*

> A right that is effective only when not needed is
> scarcely a right at all. The importance of the safety
> of the nation cannot be underestimated; equally im-
> portant is the more inclusive safety of a way of life
> which is based on principle and not expedience.——
> JUSTICE SAMUEL H. HOFSTADTER, of the New York
> Supreme Court in 1955 *

Confusion has arisen in many minds about the use and the limitations of the privilege against self-incrimination which is embodied
in the Fifth Amendment to the United States Constitution—

> nor shall any person . . . be compelled in any criminal case to be a
> witness against himself . . .[1]

One thing, however, is clear, that the privilege is universally interpreted by courts to be much broader than the literal sense of the
words just quoted. It is not merely a right to keep silent after one is
arrested on a criminal charge. The real meaning is that *a witness in
any kind of proceeding* cannot be compelled to give evidence which
might be used so as to punish him for a crime. He must not be
forced to take part in getting himself fined or put in prison or elec-
trocuted.

A witness before a legislative investigating committee, for instance, possesses this privilege, and that is the place where it has
been most often invoked in recent years. My discussion will be
largely directed to the problems which arise when a citizen summoned before a committee of the Senate or the House or a state
legislature is unwilling to answer questions.

The scope of this chapter ought to be made plain at the outset.
Its title, "The Right Not to Speak," covers the privilege against self-

* Hofstadter, *The Fifth Amendment and the Immunity Act of 1954—Aspects
of the American Way* 34 (Address to the Assn. of the Bar of the City of New
York, November 22, 1955)

incrimination and considerably more. For example, what attitude ought to be taken toward the witness who refuses to give damaging information about his former associates? Even if the law gives him no right to keep silent, does he feel a moral obligation to do so, and should the committee respect it by not pressing the question? Conversely, when a witness undoubtedly possesses the privilege, is it nevertheless sensible for him to speak out? Here, as elsewhere in this book, the main concern is not law but wisdom.

Consequently, the problems about asking and answering questions, especially outside criminal proceedings, do not stop when we find what the legal rights are. We still have to inquire whether those legal rights ought to be pushed to the limit in the particular situation. The ultimate decision can best be shaped by factors which lie deep in the life of the nation and the lives of men. We need to keep our eyes constantly on the various human beings who face these problems during a legislative investigation and after it is over. Their basic interests and their emotional attitudes diverge widely. I am reminded of the pastor who was going to preach four sermons on the Parable of the Prodigal Son from four viewpoints. "First, I'll consider the father; second the elder brother; third the younger brother. The last Sunday, I'll give the thoughts of the fatted calf." The four different viewpoints for us are: (1) the rules of law; (2) the legislative committee; (3) the university, factory, or other enterprise where the witness earns his living and wants to give the best that is in him; and (4) the witness himself, who plays the least desirable role in the entire drama.

The specific problems will be better understood if we start with the broad policies in favor of disclosure and in favor of silence. These have to be balanced against each other in fixing rules of law and in reaching wise decisions.

Policies in Favor of Disclosure

A government, in order to be efficient and just, needs to be able to learn a great range of facts from its citizens. This need is very strong in the established proceedings for charging men with definite violations of law, for jailing or bailing them to await trial, and for deciding whether they ought to be punished. Committing magistrates and grand jurors must be able to learn who deserves to be tried for a crime. It is important for judges and juries to obtain every bit of relevant evidence which bears on the prisoner's guilt or innocence, since otherwise he might be mistakenly convicted or acquitted because of a lopsided presentation of the facts. Full knowledge is also highly desirable in civil suits over damages, the ownership of land, etc., which are decided by judges with or without a jury. Therefore, the law gives to all the tribunals just mentioned the power to summon witnesses and make them answer every question which the judge in charge rules to be proper. Any witness who disobeys the judge's order can be imprisoned and heavily fined for contempt of court.

Testimony on specific issues is also often needed by administrative bodies of experts like the Interstate Commerce Commission and the National Labor Relations Board. These are frequently set up to regulate in detail the complex conditions of modern industry, etc., and to decide disputes which are not well suited for judges and juries. However, a commission, not being a court, does not itself coerce reluctant witnesses. Instead, it goes for help to a court. The usual practice is as follows: The commission can ask as many questions as it pleases and rely on willing witnesses to supply a great deal of information. Suppose a witness refuses to answer certain questions. The administrative body asks a regular court to determine his legal duty to do so. Remember that he may have good reasons for keeping silent. So the court hears lawyers on both sides. If it then decides the questions to be improper, they are dropped. If it holds them proper, the court orders the witness to answer them. After that, if he still refuses, he is punished for contempt like a disobedient witness at a criminal trial.[2]

Committees of Congress and state legislatures also need to acquire a great deal of information in order to perform their tasks well. Outside a few small areas like impeachments and election disputes where one House tries specific issues like judges, the chief tasks of Congress are to enact laws which apply to a great many citizens. These laws are more likely to be wise if the legislators have first found out a great deal about the need for them, about possible objections, and about conditions which will make contemplated provisions work well or badly. Thus the power of Congress to inform itself is an important aid to the power to make laws. Yet does it stop where the law-making power ends? The Supreme Court was once inclined toward that view, but it was repudiated years ago as unduly narrow.[3] For one thing, Congress has an obligation to be sure that the billions of dollars it takes out of taxpayers' pockets are properly spent. For another, the people can rightly look to their elected representatives to safeguard them from abuses on the part of hundreds of thousands of unelected officials. And even beyond questions about what the federal government does or could do, it is desirable for Congress to look occasionally at "the State of the Union." Suppose something is happening within our shores that Senators or Representatives consider to be a serious evil. They direct a committee to collect and digest a large mass of pertinent facts. Neither the Supreme Court nor anybody else can tell ahead of time whether the completed inquiry will show a need for federal legislation or for action by the President or for more state laws or for new efforts by private enterprises and individual citizens. At all events, Congress may be performing valuable service if it supplies readers with a thoughtful, thorough, and fair report on any vital national issue. Therefore, the informing functions of Congress probably extend to virtually all topics which affect the "general welfare of the United States."

For the sake of informing itself, each House of Congress ought to have power in its hands to coerce a recalcitrant witness who knows facts which are badly needed. Yet, to make unwilling citizens disclose their affairs and opinions and personal activities is an enormous interference with their personal integrity. When the issue at stake is the guilt or innocence of a person charged with a specific crime or the settlement of litigation, such sacrifices on the part of a witness are an almost inevitable accompaniment of the achievement of justice. In most legislative inquiries, however, the situation is quite different. The purpose is to obtain general information about a great many people. Hence facts peculiarly in the minds of a few individuals are usually far less essential than in a criminal trial or a damage suit where the issues are carefully defined. The wide range of possible questions makes a Congressional investigation resemble a warrant which does not comply with the Fourth Amendment by "particularly describing the place to be searched, and the person or things to be seized." Despite all this, the Senate and the House of Representatives ought to be able to decide when it cannot dispense with the testimony of a witness who wants to be silent. Still, it by no means follows that the two branches of Congress are wise in delegating this enormous power of coercing private citizens to every committee and every committee-member sitting alone, with respect to every witness and every question which is asked in the uncontrolled discretion of a handful of men or just one man.

That is exactly the existing situation. The law of the land now imposes on any American citizen an almost unlimited legal duty to supply any information which any sitting members of any Congressional investigating committee see fit to demand. They are not judges, but he has to give them the same obedience as to a judge. If he fails to do so and refuses to answer, the House or the Senate will have him prosecuted in a federal court for contempt. He will probably be convicted. Then he must at least pay $100 and spend a month in a common jail. His fine may go as high as $1,000 and his imprisonment may last for a year.[4]

Over and above the law, there is a moral obligation upon each witness to co-operate with his government. Whether he likes it or not, it is his government and (let us hope) the only one he will ever have. The law, for the most part, gives him no option to say, "I do not approve of this grand jury or that investigating committee; I dislike its members and its objectives; therefore I will not tell it what I know." And, quite apart from punishment for contempt, it would not ordinarily be wise or desirable for him to attempt political protests by standing silent when he is able to help his government by speaking. He assists in the administration of justice by giving testimony to a court; he assists in the regulation of business by supplying facts within his knowledge to an administrative commission; he assists in enlightening his fellow-citizens by supplying information to a legislative committee. A good deal of power to compel testimony has proved necessary to the conduct of government. It is the correlative of the guaranty to an accused in the Sixth Amendment that he shall "have compulsory process for obtaining witnesses in his favor." Consequently, any good citizen should think a long while before he refuses to give his government the facts which are requested by any of its duly established agencies. His position may indeed be very disagreeable. It is equally disagreeable for a drafted soldier to be put under an exceptionally tough sergeant. It is very burdensome to have to pay high income taxes. Nevertheless, good citizens put up with such difficulties because they have confidence in the nation as a whole and are ready to take the bitter with the sweet.

Thus there is a very strong legal obligation and a very strong moral obligation to make full disclosure. If either the law or morality makes any exceptions, they need to be framed with great care and used only after long and honest deliberation.

Policies in Favor of Silence

Efficiency is not the only test of a good government. We have the best authority for believing that governments derive "their just powers from the consent of the governed"; and this means more than the consent which is shown by voting on election day, often for the defeated candidates. It means a continuous acceptance of the action of the duly constituted authorities, even when one disagrees with them. If, however, the purposes and methods of the people in power become repulsive and hateful for a considerable number of citizens, then their obedience no longer comes from a healthy belief that we are all going the same way in the long run. Instead, obedience comes mainly from fear. That is not the kind of government of which Americans have dreamed. "I please myself," said one of the most inspiring Americans, "with imagining a State at last which can afford to be just to all men, and to treat the individual with respect as a neighbor." [5]

Consequently, it is very important that a government should, even at the sacrifice of some efficiency, perform its tasks by methods which do not shock the consciences of naturally law-abiding citizens. Regard for that principle brought about many constitutional rights. An accused man was obliged to defend himself in most criminal trials in England in the Sixteenth and Seventeenth Centuries because it was feared with some reason that if skillful lawyers were allowed, they might get many guilty men off; but the Sixth Amendment prefers to run that risk rather than let innocent men be convicted for want of counsel. Double jeopardy is prohibited, which prevents the punishment of criminals who have been mistakenly acquitted. Cruel and unusual punishments are forbidden, although these might terrorize some prospective criminals into obedience of the law.

The same insistence on decency in criminal justice produced the privilege against self-incrimination, which occupies a prominent place in the Fifth Amendment before the provision that no person shall "be deprived of life, liberty, or property, without due process of law. . . ." Every one of the seven states which adopted a bill of rights soon after Independence included this privilege; [6] and at the present time it appears in all but two state constitutions.[7] This is as close to unanimous recognition as any constitutional right is likely to obtain. And the United States Supreme Court has often emphasized its great importance. As recently as May 23, 1955, Chief Justice Warren spoke of it as "the great right which the Clause [in the Fifth Amendment] was intended to secure. . . ." [8] Equally strong support was given the privilege by two Presidents whom nobody would call mealy-mouthed idealists, Andrew Jackson and Ulysses S. Grant. Both were defying investigating committees of Congress. Andrew Jackson declared:

> You request myself and the heads of the Departments to become our own accusers, and to furnish the evidence to convict ourselves . . . .
> If you either will not make specific accusations, or if, when made, you attempt to establish them by making free men their own accusers, you will not expect me to countenance your proceedings.[9]

In spite of numerous assertions by politicians that the claim of privilege is equivalent to a confession of crime [10] the contrary is established by many Supreme Court decisions. In United States courts and most state courts, the prosecutor and the trial judge cannot even suggest to the jury that the failure of a person to take the stand or the silence of a witness gives rise to an inference of guilt.[11]

Undoubtedly, such an inference is drawn by many outside the courtroom, and very likely a great many of the persons who claim the privilege are guilty of crimes. Yet how can anybody be sure that the particular witness who keeps silent on that ground is a wrongdoer unless and until he is tried and convicted? He knows what his answer would be, but if he does not have to give it, how can anybody else know?

The possibility is always open that the witness is an innocent man, who claims the privilege because he has got into a situation where he is apparently guilty of a crime he did not commit. Take a simple illustration; readers of crime fiction could supply many more. Jones has been killed by a pistol found close to his body. Smith is called as a witness before the grand jury. He is innocent, but he was near the scene of the shooting at the time and was bitterly hostile to Jones because of a lost lawsuit. Smith is unpopular in the community, and has been in several respects an undesirable citizen. Moreover, unknown to anybody, he had taken the pistol from a neighbor's house to shoot skunks the evening before the crime and returned it unseen next morning. The case against Smith will be very black if he discloses he had possession of the pistol. So when he is asked, "Do you know anything about this gun?" he invokes the privilege. No matter if laymen jump to the conclusion that Smith is guilty, he had nothing whatever to do with the murder of Jones.

There are at least three reasons for the privilege against self-incrimination. In the first place, although it plainly interferes with short-time efficiency by making it harder to discover facts through questioning, the privilege is likely to promote long-time efficiency. When an experienced British official in India was asked why native policemen occasionally applied torture to prisoners, he remarked:

> There is a great deal of laziness in it. It is far pleasanter to sit in the shade rubbing red pepper into a poor devil's eyes than to go about in the sun hunting up evidence.[12]

If prosecutors and police could count on grilling a suspect as much as they pleased, they might not take the trouble to build up a solid case from objective proofs. Some guilty men would escape at the trial because the jury disbelieved their confessions; and, what is worse, an innocent man can get convicted on the basis of an untrue confession given under great pressure.[13]

These considerations are stressed by John H. Wigmore, who wrote the best book on Evidence:

> The truth is that the privilege exists for the sake of the innocent— or at least for reasons irrespective of the guilt of the accused. . . .
>
> The real objection [to unlimited cross-questioning of a suspect] is that *any system of administration which permits the prosecution to trust habitually to compulsory self-disclosure as a source of proof must itself suffer morally thereby.* The inclination develops to rely mainly upon such evidence, and to be satisfied with an incomplete investigation of the other sources. The exercise of the power to extract answers begets a forgetfulness of the just limitations of that power. The simple and peaceful process of questioning breeds a readiness to resort to bullying and to physical force and torture. If there is a right to an answer, there soon seems to be a right to the expected answer,—that is, to a confession of guilt. Thus the legitimate use grows into the unjust abuse; ultimately, the innocent are jeopardized by the encroachments of a bad system. . . .
>
> For the sake, then, not of the guilty, but of the innocent accused, and of conservative and healthy principles of judicial conduct, the privilege should be preserved.[14]

The privilege is even more desirable for a witness who has not yet been suspected of crime. Take, for example, a man who is called to testify in a suit between two other persons about a breach of contract:

> The witness-stand is to-day sufficiently a place of annoyance and dread. The reluctance to enter it must not be increased. Every influence which tends to suppress the sources of truth must be removed. To remove all limits of inquiry into the secrets of the persons who have no stake in the cause but can furnish help in its investigation, would be to add to the motives which now sufficiently dispose them to evade their duty.[15]

Finally, the privilege is equally valuable outside the courtroom when governmental authorities, for instance on a Congressional committee, conduct an inquisition of a person who has not yet been charged with any offense. Here again, the government will do better in the long run to pile up tangible evidence from independent sources. Indeed, it was just this method of ferreting out crimes by roving questions which brought about the creation of the legal right to keep silent, as I shall soon show.

The second reason for stoutly maintaining the right of every man not to be "compelled . . . to be a witness against himself" is that it protects us from something far worse than answering questions. Nothing else in the Constitution prevents government officials and policemen from extorting confessions from American citizens by torture and other kinds of physical brutality.

Although torture was not habitual in England as on the Continent of Europe, it was often used,[16] and Englishmen who had good reasons for detesting the government nevertheless brought torture to the American colonies. Despite its obvious tendency to make men give desired answers, even if false, in order to escape excruciating pain, torture was abandoned reluctantly because it seemed such an efficient device for detecting dangerous offenders. Thus the Puritans in Massachusetts refused to give it up entirely. Their Body of Liberties in 1641 kept it for very serious cases:

> No man shall be forced by Torture to confess any Crime against himselfe nor any other unlesse it be in some Capitall case where he is first fullie convicted by cleare and sufficient evidence to be guilty. After which if the cause be of that nature, That it is very apparent there be other conspiratours, or confederates with him, Then he may be tortured, yet not with such Tortures as be Barbarous and inhumane.[17]

We are not told what types of torture are humane.

Even when the Constitution was written, Americans were still afraid that a powerful government might be tempted to use torture. In 1788 Patrick Henry opposed the ratification of the Constitution because it had nothing like the Virginia Declaration of Rights, which included the privilege. "But Congress may introduce the practice of torturing to extort a confession of the crime." [18] The desire to quiet such objections was one reason for putting the clause against self-incrimination into the Bill of Rights.

Of course, we have long ago abolished the rack and the thumbscrew, but (as Judge Lehman of New York insisted) "the courts cannot sanction the introduction of the boxing glove in their place." [19] Yet incontrovertible proof was presented in 1931 to the Wickersham Commission from judicial opinions that policemen in various parts of the country, sometimes encouraged by prosecutors, had been employing very barbarous methods to get confessions.[20] Fortunately, the self-incrimination clause in the Fifth Amendment invalidates such confessions in United States courts if the barbarity can be proved, which is not always easy. Moreover, the partial incorporation of that clause in the Fourteenth Amendment has made it possible for the Supreme Court to reverse several state convictions based on coerced confessions, on the ground that the prisoner was getting deprived of life or liberty without due process of law.[21] And even when no physical brutality was used, the Fourteenth Amendment can be invoked by arrested men that were not taken promptly before a magistrate, who would have warned them of their right to refuse to answer incriminating questions, but were held instead by city or state policemen for prolonged grilling until they confessed.[22]

The third reason for the privilege is much more applicable to Congressional committees, who, of course, have never used physical brutality. But the reason I want to stress now is that the privilege rests on the very strong conviction of the Englishmen who established it and the Americans who put it into state constitutions and the Bill of Rights, that they did not want citizens to be condemned through evidence obtained by roving questions which had to be answered at peril of punishment for contempt. By the law of the land since Anglo-Saxon times, men were entitled to be tried on specific charges which had been framed by their fellow-citizens, who came to be called the grand jury. The Tudor and Stuart sovereigns, however, established tribunals comprising royal ministers and bishops, notably the Star Chamber and the ecclesiastical Court of High Commission. There was no jury trial and no grand jury. These bodies examined men on mere suspicion, without formally accusing them of any crime. They hoped, like Mr. Micawber, that something would turn up.

These tribunals made extensive use of the method of roving questions backed by severe penalties for refusal to answer. They found that method a powerful instrument for probing the thoughts of clergymen with inclinations toward Puritanism, and for detecting the authorship of anonymous books and pamphlets which were critical of government policies. Thus inquisition was part and parcel of the denial of freedom of religion and liberty of the press. Its victims were men who wanted to worship God in their own way and to point out their rulers' shortcomings as they saw them. Indignation flamed against the way such men were throttled through a complete departure from the tradition of the common law. They and their friends were the kind of men who went to North America and won our independence. The great popular revulsion in England against roving questions, which crystallized in the privilege, was equally strong on our shores. Therefore, the framers of our constitutions, although well aware of the need for dealing firmly with criminals, insisted that their punishment be obtained through an orderly procedure which would not shock decent people or needlessly harm innocent persons. Hence the Fifth and Sixth Amendments. Reliance was to be mainly on accusation and not on inquisition.

Chief Justice Warren in May 1955 stressed the foregoing reason why an American ought not to be condemned out of his own mouth against his will:

> The privilege against self-incrimination is a right that was hard-earned by our forefathers. . . . As early as 1650, remembrance of the horror of Star Chamber proceedings a decade before had firmly established the privilege in the common law of England. . . . To apply the privilege narrowly or begrudgingly—to treat it as an historical relic, at most merely to be tolerated—is to ignore its development and purpose.[23]

Let us look at what went on in England when government authorities were trying to force suspects to tell about thoughts and preaching and books which were objectionable to the powers that be, by both accusing themselves and disclosing other speakers or authors. Although the legal right which eventually crystallized was confined to the privilege against incriminating one's self, this chapter is also concerned with the problem of a possible moral obligation not to betray other men so that they will lose their freedom of speech and press. Consequently, it is desirable to understand the strength of the antagonism to roving questions, whether directed at the man before the tribunal or at his associates.

In 1583, Queen Elizabeth I allowed Whitgift, the Archbishop of Canterbury, to set up a permanent Court of High Commission to deal with all offenses against the Church of England. Its main energies were directed at the multiplying Puritans. It could call anybody it pleased, laymen as well as clergymen. The Court began to make use of a method of extracting information from unwilling witness, which was known as the *ex officio* oath. The witness had to swear that he would give true answers to such questions as might be put to him. He was not only forced to accuse himself, but was also liable to bring into trouble his friends, concerning whom the Court was as yet possessed of no certain information.

> The Archbishop . . . drew up twenty-four interrogatories of the most inquisitorial description, which he intended to present to all suspected persons among the clergy. They were not to be confined to inquiries into the public proceedings of the accused, but reached even to his private conversation. If the unhappy man refused to take the oath, he was at once to be deprived of his benefice [parish church], and committed to prison for contempt of the Court.[24]

Although there were forty-four commissioners, few actually took any part in the proceedings. This was practically a one-man commission. The Archbishop of Canterbury for the time being was given means of inquiry without limit. Whitgift tried to stamp out whatever doctrines he disapproved; and each of his successors felt free to impose a different test of heterodoxy. "The most terrible feature of their spiritual tyranny was its wholly personal character." [25] Whitgift drove two hundred of the best ministers from their parsonages. "It is no wonder that the Ecclesiastical Commission soon stank in the nostrils of the English clergy." [26]

When James I came to the throne, seven hundred and fifty preachers presented a petition for numerous church reforms. They asked "That the oath of *ex officio*, whereby men are forced to accuse themselves, be more sparingly used." The King called the Hampton Court Conference of Bishops, petitioners, and Privy Councillors in January 1604, and presided over it.[27] The High Commission came up for discussion:

A nameless Lord. The proceedings in that court, are like the Spanish Inquisition, wherein men are urged to subscribe more than law requireth, and by the oath *ex officio*, forced to accuse themselves, being examined upon twenty, or twenty four Articles on a sudden, without deliberation, and for the most part against themselves.

However, James treated the reformers angrily. Except for starting the great translation of the Bible, the Conference did little good. So the High Commission went on as before, getting more and more unpopular among the large dissenting groups [28] who peopled the colonies, especially when Laud was Archbishop. For instance, a Welsh clergyman was dismissed from his parish for preaching out of doors to a large assemblage. He had seen "thousands of immortal souls around me, thronging to perdition, and should I not use all means to save them?" When Thomas Shepard, later a founder of Massachusetts, was forbidden by Laud to preach, the Archbishop trembled with rage and looked at Shepard "as though blood would have gushed out of his face."

In October 1640, just as the Commission was preparing to sentence a Dissenter, a mob broke into the courtroom, tore down the benches, seized the books, and threw the furniture out of the window. Soon afterwards, the Long Parliament met and unanimously abolished the High Commission.

The roving questions of the churchmen on the Court of High Commission were so efficient in ferreting out Puritans that their method was closely imitated by royal ministers in the Privy Council who were trying to throttle the press. In 1589, soon after the Star Chamber had established a systematic censorship by limiting the number of printers and requiring every book to be officially licensed before sale, the government was greatly vexed by a series of anonymous tracts attacking the whole body of Bishops. These were appropriately signed "Martin Marprelate" and published without any license from a secret press hidden in country-houses of Puritan gentry. The royal ministers suspected that the author was John Udall, a well-born clergyman in the Church of England with Puritan views, aged about twenty-nine, a Cambridge graduate whose Hebrew grammar and dictionary made James I later describe him as "the greatest scholar of Europe." Even Udall's judges called him a learned and good man. In fact, he did not write the Marprelate tracts, but he knew who the author was and had printed two anonymous pamphlets of his own against the Bishops at the same secret press.

On December 29, 1589, the Privy Council summoned Udall to come "in the sorest weather" from his parish at Newcastle-on-Tyne, close to the Scotch border. Appearing in London two weeks later, before several nobles and lawyers and the Bishop of Rochester, Udall told them, "I have had a journey I would not wish unto my enemy." The Bishop retorted, "You may thank your own dealing in matters that you should not have meddled withal." [29]

Udall was notified that he was summoned as being Martin Marprelate. He denied this. Then the Council went on to question him about the pamphlets he had in fact written:

Lord Anderson. You are to answer concerning other books.

Udall. I hope your lordships will not urge me to any others [than the Marprelate tracts], seeing I was sent for about those. . . .

Anderson. What say you, did you make these books, or know you who made them?

Udall. I cannot answer that question, my lord.

Anderson. You had as good say you were the author.[30]

Udall. That will not follow; but if you think so, I cannot do withal. . . . My lord, I think the author, for any thing I know, did well, and I know that he is enquired after to be punished; and therefore I think it my duty to hinder the finding of him out, which I cannot do better than thus.

Anderson. And why so, I pray you?

Udall. Because if every one that is suspected do deny it, the author at the length must needs be found out.[31] . . . Besides that, if I were the author, I think that by law I need not answer.

Anderson. That is true, if it concerned the loss of your life.[32]

Udall. I pray your lordship, doth not the law say generally, no man shall be put to answer without presentment before justices [i.e. an indictment by a grand jury]. . . .

Anderson. That is law, and it is not law. . . . I tell you, by law you ought to answer in this case.

Udall. Good my lord, shew me this favour, to tell me in what book of the law I shall find it; for I profess to understand the Latin, French and English Tongues, wherein all the laws be written.

Then the baffled councillors tried to make Udall take the equivalent of the *ex officio* oath of the High Commission.

> *Anderson.* My lord of Rochester [the bishop], I pray you let us make short work with him, offer him a book; will you swear to answer to such things as shall be demanded of you in the behalf of our sovereign lady the queen?
> *Udall.* I will take an oath of allegiance to her majesty, wherein I will acknowledge her supremacy according to statute, and promise my obedience as becometh a subject; but to swear to accuse myself or others, I think you have no law for it.

Friendly persuasion was tried by Egerton, one of the Queen's chief lawyers who later became the first great Chancellor. He "had sitten all the while very soberly, noting what passed, and if a man's mind may be known by his countenance, seeming to mislike the course holden against me." Egerton "stood up, and putting off his hat to me," said:

> *Egerton.* Mr. Udall, I am sorry that you will not answer, nor take an oath, which by law you ought to do: I can assure you, your answers are like the seminary priests' answers;[33] for they say, there is no law to compel them to take an oath to accuse themselves.
> *Udall.* Sir, if it be a liberty by law, there is no reason why they should not challenge it; for (though they be very bad ones) they are subjects, and until they be condemned by law, may require all the benefits of subjects; neither is that any reason, that their answering so, should make the claim of less value for me, seeing that herein we are subjects alike, though otherwise of a most contrary disposition.

Since Udall as a Puritan was much opposed to the Jesuit priests, this insistence on maintaining their legal rights shows his unswerving devotion to government under law.

After further efforts at persuasion were met by Udall's determination "never to be mine own tormentor," the Council gave up:

> *Bishop of Rochester.* The day is past, and we must make an end: will you take the oath?
> *Udall.* I dare not take it.
> *Rochester.* Then you must go to prison, and it will go hard with you, for you must remain there until you be glad to take it.

Udall. God's will be done! I had rather go to prison with a good conscience, than to be at liberty with an ill one.

So Udall was carried off to prison, and not allowed "to have pen, ink, or paper, or anybody to speak to me." Not even his wife was admitted to talk with him in the hearing of the jailer. There he stayed for six months until put on trial for his life in July 1590. A statute enacted to suppress Roman Catholic attacks on the government was used against a Puritan. Udall was indicted for maliciously publishing a slanderous libel against the Queen, although his anonymous pamphlet was against only the Bishops.

Udall craved counsel, but was denied. After pleading "Not guilty," he requested to be tried by learned men as his peers, but accepted a jury of ordinary citizens. When he asked how many jurymen he could challenge, the judge replied: "I sit to judge and not to give you counsel." The government's only evidence consisted of written depositions by persons far from the courtroom, whom he had no chance to cross-examine. In vain did Udall assert the right, now embodied in the Sixth Amendment, "to be confronted with the witnesses against him."

Why is he not present to verify it face to face, according to law? Here is nothing but bare papers to show for evidence against me.

Sharpe, an absent accuser, wrote down that he had heard Penry (the real Martin Marprelate) say that Udall was the author of an anonymous pamphlet against the Bishops. In fact, Udall had written this pamphlet, but he indignantly protested against being hanged on hearsay evidence:

Here is one man's saying that another said so; let the Jury consider of what force this proof is. . . .

Udall's experience in the Privy Council had got him so used to claiming privilege against self-incrimination, that he went right on doing so in a regular courtroom, although no longer able to object that a grand jury and specific charges were lacking.

Judge Clarke. What say you? Did you make the Book, Udall, yea, or not! What say you to it, will you be sworn? Will you take oath that you made it not? . . . Take your oath, and swear you did it not, and it shall suffice.

Udall. . . . If I would have done so before the lords of her majesty's privy-Council . . . , I had not come hither; but I neither then might, nor may do so now, whereof I pray you let me shew a reason to the Jury. I and many more do think the Book to be good, for any thing we can find in it, and to be written in defence of a cause which we take to be most true. Now the Author is sought for, that he may be punished for some speeches that may be wrested in the Book; therefore lest he should be found (if one after another that are suspected do deny it) it is thought best every one neither to confess nor to deny, yea though we suffer some punishment, rather than the author, being found out, should suffer extremity. . . .[84]

Judge. You of the Jury consider this. This argueth, that if he were not guilty, he would clear himself, and consider well of it.[85] And then speaking to Mr. Udall, he said, Do not stand in it, but confess it, and submit yourself to the queen's mercy, before the Jury find you guilty.

Udall. My Lord, I answer, that according to my Indictment I am not guilty, every point whereof must be proved, or else the whole is false . . . and would you have me to confess a fault where there is none? No, I cannot do it, neither will I. . . .

At the last, Udall told the jurymen that they were about to consult "about the life of a Minister of the Gospel." [36] They departed. Messages came from the judges to Udall, to yield to them before the jury gave their verdict.

> Unto whom Mr. Udall replied, willing them not to trouble him with any such matter; for he was clear in his conscience and therefore he was not to accuse himself.

After the two judges had dined, the jurymen came back with a bundle of verdicts convicting some prisoners and acquitting others. Udall, they said, was guilty. The jailer was ordered to bring the prisoners early next morning, "and so for that time every man departed to his place."

> The next morning, being the 25th of July, about four of the clock, the Prisoners were brought to the bar, who stayed till the coming of the Judges: who came thither by six of the clock, or thereabouts, and called the Prisoners by their names to receive Sentence of Death: and first, they began with Mr. Udall; who, after he was called, was commanded to stand aside till anon. And then were

seven Felons that received Sentence of Death; who being taken aside, Mr. Udall was called the second time; and the Clerk of the Assizes said, "John Udall, hold up thy hand, what canst thou alledge for thyself, why thou shouldst not receive Judgment to die?"

Udall asserted his innocence and that his book was God's truth.

> *Judge.* But are you sorry that you have offended the queen's majesty?
> *Udall.* I am sorry that the course of the law hath found me to have offended.
> *Judge.* So is every thief that is condemned sorry, that his offence is found out, but not for the fact.

Still, the judges shrank from hanging an ordained clergyman of the Church of England for the sole crime of discussing church affairs in print. So Udall went back to prison for another six months and more. In February 1591, when again called up for sentence of death, he still insisted that he had been improperly convicted and refused to admit he had done wrong. So the judges condemned this scholar to die at the age of thirty. A rapid reprieve from the Queen kept Udall alive in prison. He could have gone free by acknowledging that his pamphlets were dangerous and seditious. He would only sign a statement that some passages were "so bitter and undutiful" as to deserve censure. His young wife finally coaxed him into confessing a bit more guilt than that. Then Sir Walter Raleigh, the Earl of Essex, and Lancelot Andrewes interceded for Udall. The decision on his fate was left in the hands of Whitgift, the head of the High Commission, who remained obdurate. The Archbishop of Canterbury had little awareness of human situations.

After Udall had been in prison for over two years, the Turkey Company offered to send him to Syria as clergyman for their trading-post there. Whitgift relented. The Queen signed a pardon in June 1592. Immediately afterwards, Udall fell ill from his long incarceration and died when he was only thirty-two. He was among the first of the English-speaking men who won for us the privilege against self-incrimination, and liberty of the press.

Forty-five years later, John Lilburn, a young man perhaps twenty-three, was suddenly arrested on a London street by order of the Star Chamber.[37] This was a small committee of the Privy Coun-

cil, which sat as a court without any jury and possessed an indefinite
power to deal with almost any conduct which it considered dangerous to public safety. It could inflict any penalty it chose, short of
death. During the early years of this extraordinary court, after the
long demoralization of justice in the Wars of the Roses, it performed a good service in going after powerful offenders whom
juries were afraid to convict and in making a nation-wide clean-up
of crime. By the opening of the Seventeenth Century, however, it
was directing a large portion of its energies against books which it
considered to contain dangerous thoughts. The court which Lilburn
had to face in 1637 was composed of some of the close advisers of
Charles I—noblemen, two or three judges, and Laud, the Archbishop
of Canterbury—men hardly fitted to decide impartially about an outspoken opponent of government.

Lilburn was no ripe scholar like Udall. He came from the plain
people like John Bunyan and Daniel Defoe. An apprentice to a
dealer in cloth, he had somehow picked up a good deal of dislocated
law to mix with his inborn brashness and cantankerousness. Of late
he had made a journey to Holland. The strict censorship of the
press by the Star Chamber had driven many Puritan writers to get
their books and pamphlets printed in that freer country, whence
they were smuggled over to English booksellers and readers. The
officers who arrested Lilburn loosely charged him with sending
"factious and scandalous books" out of Holland into England. This
offense he flatly denied, but refused to answer questions about anything else.

At first, he was examined by a clerk of Sir John Banks, the Attorney General, who inquired about his meeting one Hargust in
Holland.

> *Lilburn.* But why do you ask me all these questions? These are
> beside the matter of my imprisonment; I pray come to the thing for
> which I am accused, and imprisoned. . . .
> *Q.* But do you know of any that sent over any books?
> *A.* What other men did, doth not belong to me to know or search
> into; sufficient it is for me to look well to my own occasions. . . .
> *Q.* What speeches had you with Chillington [an informer against
> Lilburn and according to him a perjurer] since you came to town?
> *A.* I am not bound to tell you: but sir (as I said before) why do

you ask me all these questions? these are nothing pertinent to my imprisonment, for I am not imprisoned for knowing and talking with such and such men, but for sending over Books; and therefore I am not willing to answer you to any more of these questions, because I see you go about by this Examination to ensnare me: for seeing the things for which I am imprisoned cannot be proved against me, you will get other matter out of my examination: and therefore if you will not ask me about the thing laid to my charge, I shall answer no more: but if you will ask of that, I shall then answer you, and do answer that for the thing for which I am imprisoned, which is for sending over books, I am clear, but I sent none; and of any other matter that you have to accuse me of, I know it is warrantable by the law of God, and I think by the law of the land, that I may stand upon my just defence, and not answer to your interrogatories; and that my accusers ought to be brought face to face, to justify what they accuse me of. And this is all the answer that for the present I am willing to make: and if you ask me of any more things, I shall answer you with silence.

At this he [the clerk] was exceeding angry, and said, there would be a course taken with me to make me answer.

I told him, I did not regard what course they would take with me; only this I desire you to take notice of, that I do not refuse to answer out of any contempt, but only because . . . I am unwilling to answer to any impertinent questions, for fear that with my answer I may do myself hurt.

Clerk. This is not the way to get liberty: I had thought you would have answered punctually, that so you might have been dispatched as shortly as might be.

Lilburn. I have answered punctually to the thing for which I am imprisoned and more I am not bound to answer, and for my liberty I must wait God's time.

When Attorney General Banks had read over the clerk's report, he said to Lilburn, "I perceive you are unwilling to confess the truth."

Lilburn. My answer was to him, and so it is to you, that the thing for which I am imprisoned (which is for sending over books) I am clear, for I did not send any, and for any other matter that is laid to my charge, I know it is warrantable by the law of God, and I think by the law of the land, for me to stand upon my just defence, and that my accusers ought to be brought face to face, to justify what they accuse me of: and this is all that I have to say for the present.

Ten days or so later, Lilburn was taken to the Star Chamber office and told to enter his appearance. He said, "To what?"—no bill of charges had been filed against him. One of the clerks told him, he must first be examined and then Sir John Banks would make the bill.

> It seems they had no grounded matter against me for to write a bill, and therefore they went about to make me betray my own innocency, that so they might ground the bill upon my own words. . . .

Lilburn thereupon refused to take the Star Chamber oath, "You shall swear that you shall make true answer to all things that be asked of you: so help you God."

> *Lilburn.* Before I swear, I will know to what I must swear.

On Friday, February 9, 1638, perhaps the most momentous day in the history of the privilege, young Lilburn was taken from the Fleet prison, where Samuel Pickwick would be confined two centuries later, and brought to the bar of the Star Chamber near Westminster Hall. Beside him stood an old man of eighty-five, John Wharton, a hot-presser. An affidavit by Chillington that they had both printed Puritan books in Rotterdam was read. "A most false lye and untrue," Lilburn told the court. In fact, he said, Chillington had been caught importing books, and bought his liberty from the Bishops by agreeing to betray Lilburn into their hands. Yet the informer was not there to confront him.

> *Lord Keeper Coventry.* But why do you refuse to take the Star-Chamber oath?
> *Lilburn.* Most noble lord, I refused upon this ground, because that when I was examined, though I had fully answered all things that belonged to me to answer unto, and had cleared myself of the thing for which I am imprisoned, which was for sending Books out of Holland, yet that would not satisfy and give content, but other things were put unto me, concerning other men, to insnare me, and get further matter against me; which I perceiving refused, being not bound to answer to such things as do not belong unto me. And withal I perceived the oath to be an oath of inquiry [that is, *ex*

officio like the High Commission oath]; and for the lawfulness of which oath, I have no warrant; and upon these grounds I did and do still refuse the oath. . . .

Earl of Dorset. My lords, this is one of their private spirits; do you hear him, how he stands in his own justification?

Well, my lords, said the great prelate [*Laud*], this fellow (meaning me) hath been one of the notoriousest dispersers of libellous Books that is in the kingdom; and that is the father of them all (pointing to old Mr. Wharton).

Lilburn. Sir, I know you are not able to prove, and to make that good which you have said.

Laud. I have testimony of it.

Lilburn. Then produce them in the face of the open court, that we may see what they have to accuse me of; and I am ready here to answer for myself, and to make my just defence.

With this he was silent, and said not one word more to me; and then they asked my fellow soldier, old Mr. Wharton, whether he would take the Oath; which he refused, and began to tell them of the Bishops' cruelty towards him; and that they had had him in five several prisons within these two years, for refusing the Oath.

And then there was silence. . . .

"Our crime," Lilburn comments, "was so far from treason that it was neither against the glory of God, the honour of the king, the laws of the land, nor the good of the commonwealth: but rather for the maintaining of the honour of them all, as all those that read the books without partial affections and prejudicate hearts can witness and declare. . . ."

The Star Chamber sent both Lilburn and Wharton back to the Fleet that Friday as close prisoners with no friends admitted. There they were to stay until they took the oath. Unless they did so by Monday night, the twelfth, the Star Chamber would punish them for contempts.

On Monday Lilburn was taken to Gray's Inn, where an official of the Star Chamber tendered him the Bible to swear on.

Well, sir, said I, I am of the same mind I was; and withal I understand, that this Oath is one and the same with the High Commission Oath, which Oath I know to be both against the law of God, and the law of the land; and therefore in brief I dare not take the oath, though I suffer death for the refusal of it. . . .

So he said, he had no more to say to me; and I took my leave of him, and came away.

After that came in the old man, Mr. Wharton, who also refused.

And, as he hath told me, he declared unto him how the bishops had him eight times in prison for the refusal of it, and he had suffered the bishops' merciless cruelty for many years together, and he would now never take it as long as he lived; and withal told him, that if there were a cart ready at the door to carry him to Tyburn, he would be hanged, before ever he would take it.

And this was the day's business.

Upon the next morning, February 13, about seven a-clock, we were had to the Star-Chamber Bar again, to receive our Censure; and stood at the bar about two hours before sir John Banks came: but at last he began his accusation against us, that we did still continue in our former stubbornness.

Lilburn once more maintained his innocence:

Now, my lords, I do protest before your honours on the word of a Christian, that I did not send over these Books, neither did I know the ship that brought them, nor any that belongs to the ship, nor to my knowledge did never see with my eyes, either the ship, or any that belongs unto it. . . .

Lord Keeper Coventry. Thou art a mad fellow, seeing things are thus, that thou wilt not take thine Oath, and answer truly.

Lilburn. My honourable lord, I have declared unto you the real truth; but for the oath, it is an oath of inquiry, and of the same nature as the High-Commission Oath; which oath I know to be unlawful; and withal I find no warrant in the Word of God for an oath of inquiry, and it ought to be the director of me in all things that I do: and therefore, my lords, at no hand, I dare not take the oath. (When I named the Word of God, the court began to laugh, as though they had had nothing to do with it.)

So they spoke to the old man, my fellow-partner, and asked him whether he would take the oath. . . . He began to thunder it out against the Bishops . . . "[Their oaths] are all against the law of the land, and by [them] they deceive and perjure thousands of the king's subjects in a year. And withal, my lords, (said he) there is a maxim in divinity, that we should prefer the glory of God, and the good of our king and country, before our own lives. . . ."

So they censured us 500£. a-piece; and then stood up judge Jones, and said, "It was fit, that I being a young man, for example sake, should have some corporal punishment inflicted upon me. So my Censure was to be whipt. . . . As for the old man, in regard of his age, being 85 years old, they would spare his corporal punishment, though (said they) he deserves it as well as the other (meaning me), yet he should stand upon the pillory. . . .

Accordingly, the Star Chamber decreed that Lilburn was to be whipped through the streets, from the Fleet prison in the City of London to the pillory, which stood between the Star Chamber and the gate of Westminster Hall; both he and Wharton were to be returned to the Fleet, there to remain until they obeyed the orders to take the oath; and neither to be released until he had paid his fine of five hundred pounds, an enormous sum for an apprentice of twenty-three and a hot-presser of eighty-five, and had also given a surety bond for his future good behavior.

Wharton was released in three weeks, "being very weak, more likely to die than to live," but Lilburn remained a close prisoner until his sentence was carried out.

Upon Wednesday the 18th of April, 1638, I was cruelly whipped through the streets to Westminster (repeating several texts of Scripture as the cart went along and talking enthusiastically to the people). At the last [I] came to the Pillory, where I was unloosed from the cart, and having put on some of my clothes, went to the tavern, where I staid a pretty while waiting for my surgeon, who was not yet come to dress me; where were many of my friends, who exceedingly rejoiced to see my courage, that the Lord had enabled me to undergo my punishment so willingly.

Not surprisingly, Lilburn had a desire to retire into a private room and get away from the multitude of people, which made him likely to faint. He had not been there long when the tipstaff of the Star Chamber came to tell him that confessing his fault would save him from standing in the pillory. Lilburn still refused:

Why, Paul found more mercy from the heathen Roman Governors, for they would not put him to an oath to accuse himself, but suffered him to make the best defence he could for himself: neither would they condemn him, before his accusers and he were brought face to face, to justify, and fully to prove their accusation:[38] but the Lords have not dealt so with me, for my accusers and I were never brought face to face . . . I was condemned . . . because I would not accuse myself.

And so he went away, and I prepared myself for the Pillory, to which I went with a joyful courage; and when I was upon it, I made obeisance to the lords, some of them, as I suppose, looking out at the Star-Chamber window towards me. And so I put my neck into the hole, which being a great deal too low for me, it was very painful to me, in regard of continuance of the time that I stood on the pillory, which was about two hours; my back being also very sore, and the sun shining so exceeding hot, and the Tipstaff-man not suffering me to keep on my hat to defend my head from the heat of the sun, so that I stood there in great pain: yet through the strength of my God I underwent it with courage, to the very last minute; and lifting up my heart and spirit unto God, I began to speak. . . .

The speech, which went on for about eleven pages of fine print, denounced the oath and exhorted his hearers to resist the tyranny of the Bishops. The noise of it reverberated into the Star Chamber, in session close by.

There came a fat lawyer, I do not know his name, and commanded me to hold my peace, and leave my preaching. To whom I replied and said, Sir, I will not hold my peace, but speak my mind freely, though I be hanged at Tyburn for my pains.

So then Lilburn talked much longer until the fat lawyer came back with the Warden of the Fleet prison, who ordered Lilburn to be gagged. If he spoke any more, he would be whipped again while he stood on the pillory.

So I remained about an hour and a half gagged, being intercepted of much matter, which by God's assistance I intended to have spoken; but yet with their cruelty I was nothing at all daunted, for I was full of comfort and courage, being mightily strengthened with the power of the Almighty, which made me with chearfulness triumph over all my sufferings, not shewing one sad countenance or discontented heart.

And when I was to come down, having taken out my head out of the Pillory, I looked about me upon the people, and said, "I am more than a conqueror through him that hath loved me." *"Vivat Rex,"* Let the king live for ever; and so I came down. . . . . After I came back to the prison, none were suffered to come to me, but the surgeon to dress me. And to what I have here said and written, I set-to my name, by me, John Lilburn, being written with part of my own blood.

That same day the Star Chamber, because Lilburn during his whipping and in the pillory "audaciously and wickedly did not only utter sundry scandalous speeches, but likewise scattered divers copies of seditious Books among the people," entered a new decree:

> That the said John Lilburn should be laid alone, with irons on his hands and legs, in the Wards of the Fleet, where the basest and meanest sort of prisoners are used to be put; and that the Warden of the Fleet take special care to hinder the resort of any persons whatsoever unto him. And particularly, that he be not supplied with money from any friend. . . .

Since in those days the warden had no duty to feed his prisoners free, Lilburn passed ten days with nothing to eat. Somehow he managed to survive in prison for thirty months until November 3, 1640, the day the Long Parliament met.

Lilburn presented a petition that same day and was immediately freed—the first person, he says, to be set at liberty. In May 1641, the House of Commons resolved:

> That the Sentence of the Star-Chamber given against John Lilburn is illegal, and against the Liberty of the subject; and also bloody, cruel, wicked, barbarous, and tyrannical.
>
> That reparation ought to be given to Mr. Lilburn for his imprisonment, suffering, and losses sustained by that illegal sentence.

Three months later, Parliament wiped out his enemy the Star Chamber forever.

Four years went by before the Lords concurred with the Commons in erasing all the Star Chamber proceedings and awarding Lilburn three thousand pounds, of which (he says) he got very little. Meanwhile he went on to fight in the Civil War and defy the House of Lords, the House of Commons, and Oliver Cromwell, until he left prison for the last time at forty-one. So great was his popularity that his protests in the Star Chamber had an almost immediate impact on the regular courts. By the end of Charles II's reign in 1685, the doctrine that no man is bound to incriminate himself in any court was judicially accepted. No single person did so much as "Freeborn John" to bring about the constitutional right of American citizens not to be forced to convict themselves out of their own mouths.

Hardly had the privilege become recognized in England than it was asserted in Pennsylvania. William Bradford was a pioneer printer in the colonies, from whom, many years later, Peter Zenger learned his trade. In 1689, when he was twenty-six, the Charter of Pennsylvania, granted eight years before, was printed for the first time by Bradford in an unauthorized anonymous pamphlet, instigated by a citizen who wished to apprize the settlers of their rights. Suspecting who was responsible, Governor Blackwell summoned Bradford before the Provincial Council for examination:

> *Governour.* . . . I desire to know from you, whether you did print the Charter or not, and who set you to work?
> *Bradford.* Governour, it is an impracticable thing for any man to accuse himself; thou knows it very well.
> *Governour.* Well, I shall not much press you to it, but if you were so ingenuous as to confess, it should go the better with you.
> *Bradford.* Governour, I desire to know my accusers; I think it very hard to be put upon accusing myself.
> *Governour.* Can you deny that you printed it? I do know you did print it, and by whose directions, and will prove it, and make you smart for it, too, since you are so stubborn. . . .
> *Bradford.* . . . Let me know my accusers, and I shall know the better how to make my defence.[39]

Soon afterwards, Bradford went back to England, partly because he was weary of being harassed by the leaders of the government, but he did return next year and then moved in 1693 to New York.

Several features of these early cases deserve attention.

First. Observe how often the objectors to roving questions relied on traditional requisites of criminal procedure, along with the privilege. Where is the grand jury, they indignantly protest; it ought to determine that there is probable cause for charging a man for a specific offense known to the law, before he is put on trial. Why don't the officials bring in witnesses who dare to accuse him to his face? He's not their witness. He doesn't have to disclose any supposed wrongdoing until the grand jury has found something definite to question him about— And perhaps not even then, he begins to assert. Thus the privilege against self-incrimination ties right in with other safeguards of a fair trial. It supplements in an important way the guaranty of a grand jury at the start of the Fifth Amendment, and the provisions in the Sixth Amendment entitling the prisoner "to be informed of the nature and cause of the accusation" and "to be confronted with the witnesses against him." Those are the long-established methods of proving him guilty. That is the job of the government officials. And they cannot make him do their job for them.

Second. The claim of a right not to incriminate one's self or other men is closely linked with liberty of speech and press. In every instance just recounted, the investigators were trying to suppress books, pamphlets, or opinions which they disliked. And the men who kept silent were usually guilty. Most of the ministers haled before the Court of High Commission were in fact Puritans. Udall and Bradford had published the books about which they refused to answer. Perhaps Lilburn did help smuggle books—what was he doing in Holland if not that? A remark made long ago about the *ex officio* oath is very pertinent:

> The real truth was that those who disliked the oath had usually done the things of which they were accused, and which they regarded as meritorious actions, though their judges regarded them as crimes. People always protest with passionate eagerness against being deprived of technical defences against what they regard as bad law.[40]

The point is that the suspects I have been describing used the privilege as a way of protecting themselves and their friends from being punished for what (they believed) ought not to be punishable. They wanted the kind of freedom of worship and speech and press which we possess in the United States today. We possess them because these men and others like them stood up for the legal rights they had and also for some they did not have but only imagined.

Of course, the obstinate silence of persons who are suspected of theft or murder does not mean that the laws against theft or murder ought to be repealed. The situation is different, however, when the men who refuse to testify are valuable artisans like Bradford or outspoken lovers of liberty like Lilburn or scholars like Udall. What sort of law is this which turns into criminals a large number of persons who respect the lives, property, and welfare of others? When such men are ready to risk bodily suffering or imprisonment or death, rather than co-operate with their government in ferreting out forbidden intellectual activities, then it is high time for the whole community to consider whether the law is trying to punish what ought to be left alone.

Third. The battle is not to the strong. The investigators seemed, at the close of every case, to be having it all their way. Yet by relying on force and ignoring human values, they aroused widespread detestation and destroyed the consent of the governed, on which government is built. Although Udall died, Puritanism flourished. The Bishops drove hundreds of ministers from their pulpits in parish churches. Then half the families in England left the pews in parish churches, never to return. Whitgift in the High Commission and nobles in the Star Chamber triumphed over their victims. Pretty soon there was no more High Commission and no more Star Chamber, and the nobles were exiled in France. Lilburn was whipped, but only five years later Laud was beheaded. The Royal Governor harried Bradford out of Philadelphia. Yet unauthorized political printing went on, Independence Hall stands close to the site of Bradford's press, and where are the royal governors? It would be well if many persons who ask roving questions today would remember the High Commission and the Star Chamber and the colonial Governor of Pennsylvania, and profit by their example.

Finally, the refusal to respond to roving questions is sometimes backed by strong moral convictions, even if not by law. Most of the suspects I have been quoting based their silence on grounds outside the limits of the modern privilege against self-incrimination. Bradford was the only one who showed any accurate comprehension of that privilege. Udall and Lilburn were groping around for it—that is about all one can say. And they relied more on the absence of specific formal charges and government witness than on anything like the privilege. Also they were all the time refusing to incriminate others. Udall's steadfast unwillingness to answer questions about associates whose actions he considered meritorious went beyond the Fifth Amendment, though not beyond American traditions. Plainly these men were not sound lawyers. Yet they possessed something better than legal knowledge—faith in freedom of the spirit. And that is just what their adversaries fatally lacked. Udall, Lilburn, and Bradford had the insight and courage to show us the serious weaknesses, whether legal or moral, of fishing-expeditions into the minds of men.

What seems to me a proper adjustment between the two sets of conflicting policies can be summarized in three propositions:

1. The witness's legal duty of disclosure is limited by his legal rights to keep silent, including the privilege against self-incrimination.

2. Nevertheless, he may feel that he ought not to exercise this legal privilege because of wisdom and a moral obligation to cooperate with the government.

3. Conversely, the witness may feel that his legal duty to answer questions is outweighed by moral considerations in which he firmly and sincerely believes. Such a sincere belief has no weight in a law court; but, whether one agrees with him or not, it should receive careful consideration from persons who are not bound to enforce his legal duty, and especially from the heads of the enterprise where he does his normal work and earns his living.

The first proposition will be discussed forthwith. The second, which is fairly obvious, requires little attention. The third proposition appears to me very important. It will occupy the last part of the chapter.

The Law

The legal obligation of a citizen to communicate facts at the request of the government is very strong. Consequently, there are only two legal grounds on which a duly summoned witness can escape punishment for refusing to answer questions, apart from matters which do not concern this chapter. For example, I leave out the obligation of a lawyer not to betray the confidence of his client, and the inability of a wife to report what her husband has said to her because compulsory disclosure would poison the intimacy of marriage. And, although the Supreme Court has not yet made the First Amendment a protection for witnesses before Congressional committees,[41] it seems probable that there are some questions which, if asked by such a committee, could be safely ignored, *e.g.*, How did you vote last November? To how many girls have you proposed? Do you often quarrel with your wife? Which of your children do you love the most? What are the terms of your will? Do you believe in God? And if so, why?

First. The legal duty of disclosure does not extend beyond the lawfully authorized purpose of the particular proceeding.[42] For instance, a witness called by the prosecution in a trial for murder does not have to tell whether he owes his landlord for several months' rent. If the question which seems irrelevant is asked in a courtroom, the witness or his lawyer can get an immediate ruling from the presiding judge about his right to keep silent. If he is testifying before a grand jury, he can at once seek a similar ruling from the judge who is in charge though not sitting in the grand jury room. If the dubious question comes from the Interstate Commerce Commission (or some other administrative body), the witness, as already explained,[43] can temporarily say nothing and wait for the commission to get a court order. It is very significant that in all those types of inquiries where exact facts on specific issues are very important, the witness is never obliged to decide for himself whether he needs to answer, at the risk of going to prison if he decides mistakenly. Instead, he can keep silent without fear until one or more independent, impartial judges listen to his objections and then pass on the rightness of the question. If the court rules against it, nothing at all happens. Only after the court has upheld the question and commanded the witness to speak, does his silence become punishable.

The situation is quite different under the common practice of legislative committees. Although a committee usually needs rather general information, it can make a witness decide at his peril whether a distasteful question is outside the scope of the inquiry.

For example, suppose that a director of a manufacturing company with many sizable defense contracts is asked by the Senate Committee on Government Operations to tell what relations he ever had with any organization on the Attorney General's list. Must he answer? That is a difficult point for any witness, or for his lawyer if he is allowed to have one.[44] As for the committee chairman, "It is not permitted to the most equitable of men to be judge in his own cause." [45] Yet the witness cannot get any decision from a court at the time when he most needs it. He must either obey the chairman's order to answer the question, or else be in deep trouble.

For, if a witness keeps silent when he reasonably believes a question to be improper, the Senate will automatically vote to have him prosecuted for contempt. So a man whose whole previous life has been irreproachable goes on trial for a crime. No doubt, he will be cleared in the end if the court agrees with what he decided in the committee-room, but only after spending his savings on legal expenses, raising a defense fund, going through months of undesirable publicity, the agony of a trial and perhaps a protracted appeal. And he is lucky if he has not lost his salary meanwhile, and possibly his job.

Or his decision in the committee-room turns out to have been wrong. Then he is fined and sent to prison for a mistake of law. When he comes out, neither his own institution nor any other may want to employ a jailbird. Therefore, the court's decision on the relevancy of a committee's question comes far too late to give the witness any real help. If he could have got it during the committee hearings, he would ordinarily have obeyed the judge and answered. As things are, however, he never had a chance to obey a judge. He is merely punished by a judge for disobeying a legislator.

A business corporation is not forced to disobey a possibly invalid statute and risk a heavy fine as the only way to test constitutionality. Instead, the Due Process Clause is held to entitle the corporation to ascertain its rights and duties as soon as possible without incurring any penalty for resorting to an impartial court.[46] A single human being has a much greater need for rapid judicial determination of the validity of an order which does not come, like a statute, from the whole law-making branch of the government, but only from a few members of one House. The witness's legal right not to answer irrelevant questions from a legislative committee is plain, but asserting that right is dangerous. Suppose that the law told every pedestrian injured by an automobile, "You have a right to make the motorist pay your hospital bills if he was driving negligently. If you sue him and lose, you'll go to prison for six months as a criminal."

Whatever the proper solution, there ought to be some effective way for the courts to protect the legal rights a citizen has against disclosing his thoughts and private affairs.[47]

The second solid legal ground for keeping silent is the constitutional privilege of the witness not to incriminate himself.

There are several current misconceptions about this privilege. One is that when the critical question is asked, the witness is the sole judge of the tendency of an answer to bring about his punishment. This is not altogether true. A court shares in the job. The witness can be required, under pain of being in contempt, to disclose enough to the court to show a real possibility that an answer will tend to convict him, whether rightly or wrongly, of a crime. The answer may not disclose the whole offense, but does it furnish proof of a link in the chain? Chief Justice Taft said while still a lower-court judge:

> It must appear to the court, from the character of the question, and the other facts adduced in the case, that there is some tangible and substantial probability that the answer of the witness will help convict him of a crime. . . . "[The] danger to be apprehended must be real, with reference to the probable operation of law in the ordinary course of things, and not merely speculative. . . ."[48]

Manifestly, this is a delicate business. The witness alone knows how he would answer the question if forced to do so. To oblige him to reveal his answer in order to avoid giving it would obviously be absurd and make the privilege worthless. He ought not to be required to supply the prosecution with some useful evidence in the process of demonstrating the incriminating character of the answer sought. Hence, a court must decide when the witness has gone far enough to show he is in peril, and then let him stop right there.

Suppose that a legislative committee asks the critical question. Its incriminating character is not to be finally passed on by the committee. The witness is entitled to a judicial decision on the point. Here again, postponement until a contempt prosecution months or years later is unfortunate. An immediate request by the committee for a court order to answer would provide a much more satisfactory procedure for everybody concerned.

There is only one ground for the privilege: The facts which the answer would disclose must subject the witness himself to some reasonable danger of getting convicted and punished for a criminal offense, for example, spying or a violation of the Smith Act. Fear of a perjury prosecution, perhaps even if he tells the truth, is not an excuse, because the facts disclosed by his prospective answer will not in themselves be a link in proving that crime. Mere embarrassment is not an excuse. Fear of social disgrace or loss of his job is not an excuse. A sense of sportsmanship toward suspected associates is not an excuse; the Fifth Amendment grants no legal right to protect one's friends. If a man feels that he has a personal code compelling this reticence, he must pay for his scruples by standing the punishment which society prescribes in the law, to the extent which the authorities see fit to impose it.

This, however, is not the whole story. Suppose that a true answer would actually endanger the witness, but he does not care a bit about that; he claims the privilege because he does not want to help get his friends into trouble. For example, a professor is asked by a Congressional committee in 1955, "Were you a member of the Communist Party in 1948?" He believes that his admission of that fact will be supplemented by false testimony from professional ex-Communists, and thus it might very likely be an important link in bringing about his conviction under the Smith Act. Yet, if nobody else were involved, he would run that risk and co-operate with the government by answering, "Yes; but I never did anything except listen to speeches at two meetings; and I got out in June 1950 because their talk about Korea made me sick." Still, he apprehends that the committee would follow up this reply by demanding the names of other men who were members with him, and so he keeps silent to avoid betraying them and perhaps making them lose their present positions in various colleges.

Here the claim of the privilege is valid. The law gives a witness the right to withhold an answer which would incriminate him. So long as that essential element exists, he can exercise his right for any reasons which he deems satisfactory. This was squarely decided by Taft in the lower-court case already quoted.[49] Several men were on trial for a conspiracy to transmit lottery tickets across state lines. Another man was questioned about their activities and claimed the privilege. The government argued that he did so in bad faith, because his purpose was not to protect himself from a future prosecution but merely to save his associates from getting convicted at this very trial. Even so, Taft held, the witness's silence could not be punished as contempt:

> We do not understand any of the American authorities to go so far as to hold that where, from the evidence and the nature of the question, the court can definitely determine that the question, if answered in a particular way, will form a link in the chain of evidence to establish the commission of a crime of a witness, the court should inquire into the motive of the witness in pleading his privilege.

In my opinion, Taft was quite right. Law is too rough and ready an instrument to base distinctions on such complicated and delicate matters as the mental and emotional processes involved in a man's reasons for asserting an undoubted constitutional right. It is consequently unsound for some lawyers to say that a college professor is *ipso facto* dishonest and a liar if he sets up the privilege in order to shield his friends and not himself. He has a legal right to keep silent, whatever his reasons, *so long as the danger of his being convicted for crime is there.*

In the same way, it is entirely lawful for a witness to base his refusal to answer *an actually incriminating question* on the privilege when his main reason for silence is fear of a perjury prosecution or sheer terror of being bumped off.[50] And, so long as the facts in his answer do tend toward convicting him, it makes no difference that he is confident of being acquitted. How can he or anybody else be sure what a future jury will do?

Difficult problems arise when a witness is asked by a Congressional committee, "Are you now or have you ever been a member of the Communist Party?" The McCarran Act of 1950, which was discussed at length in Chapter V, has a section providing:[51]

> Neither the holding of office nor membership in any Communist organization by any person shall constitute per se a violation . . . of any other criminal statute.

This language diminishes the danger of a conviction under the Smith Act when the witness's answer would be in effect, "Yes, I did belong to the Party for five years, but never advocated the overthrow of the government by force and violence, or took the slightest part in urging or planning any sort of unlawful action." Consequently, it is arguable that such a witness has no privilege and will be punishable for contempt if he keeps silent.

Yet suppose this witness fears, with good reason, that he will be prosecuted and convicted under an anti-Communist statute in his own state, which makes bare membership in the Party a prison offense. Several states have enacted laws of that sort; some go far beyond the Smith Act. It is not clear whether this witness could then be protected by the McCarran Act. When it says that he has not violated "any other criminal statute" does this refer only to some other *federal* statute like the Smith Act, or does it include a state statute too? [52] And quite apart from the McCarran Act, does a committee of Congress have to grant the privilege to a witness before it because he will incriminate himself under a state law? The United States courts do not need to pay attention to anything except the danger of getting convicted for a federal crime.[53] Still, Congress possibly has a wider obligation to recognize the privilege. Its informing power, as I have already argued, extends to almost anything affecting the welfare of American citizens. If Senators can investigate state crimes and local juvenile delinquency under the glare of television, as the Kefauver Committee did, how can they shut their eyes to the fact that a witness who answers their questions will soon find himself in a state prison? [54]

Go back to federal dangers under the Smith Act from an answer disclosing only past Communist membership with colorless conduct. Such limited association with Communists may not be a crime all by itself, but it may bring about a conviction under the Smith Act if the government adds other evidence. The Supreme Court in 1950 upheld the privilege of a witness who refused to tell a federal grand jury whether she knew the names of the officers of the Communist Party of Colorado, whether it had ever employed her, and whether she had custody of its books.[55]

Indeed, a witness runs a considerable risk if he answers any question about Communist affiliations, even though it calls for facts which seem harmless in themselves. He may then find that he has lost his privilege of silence altogether, and must either tell the rest of the facts, however damaging to him under the Smith Act, or else go to jail. Once the witness starts down the road of self-incrimination, he has to follow it to the finish, wherever it goes. He cannot pick and choose among the questions. Judge Learned Hand remarks,[56] "The privilege is to suppress the truth, but that does not mean that it is a privilege to garble it."

In 1948, another witness before a federal grand jury in Colorado, Mrs. Rogers, testified that she had been treasurer of the Communist Party of Denver until eight months previously, when she turned over the membership lists and the record of dues to somebody else. Then she balked, and was taken before the judge in charge of the grand jury:

> *The Court:* Now what is the question?
> *The Prosecutor:* Who has the books and records of the Communist Party of Denver now? Who did Mrs. Rogers give those books up to . . . ?
> *The Court:* Do you care to answer that question, madam?
> *Mrs. Rogers:* I do not.
> *The Court:* What?
> *Mrs. Rogers:* I do not, and that's what I told them.
> *The Court:* Why won't you answer?
> *Mrs. Rogers:* I don't feel that I should subject a person or persons to the same thing that I'm going through.
> *The Court:* It is the order or finding of the Court that you should answer those questions. Now, will you do that?
> *Mrs. Rogers:* No.[57]

Next day, again before the Court, she asserted: "I do have a right to refuse to answer these questions, on the basis that they would tend to incriminate me. . . ." Thereupon, the judge sentenced her to four months' imprisonment for contempt. The Supreme Court affirmed her conviction, holding that her incriminating answers to some questions waived her privilege as to any more. Chief Justice Vinson said that the opposite decision would "open the way to distortion of facts by permitting a witness to select any stopping place in the testimony."

Yet the dissent by Black, joined by Frankfurter and Douglas, shows how this doctrine puts witnesses in a bewildering dilemma. How can they be sure of the proper place to cease answering? Justice Black remarked:

> On the one hand they risk imprisonment for contempt by asserting the privilege prematurely; on the other they might lose the privilege if they answer a single question.

And Dean Griswold points out that the investigators lose information they might otherwise obtain:

> As a consequence of this case, witnesses who have legitimate fears of prosecution, but who might be willing to cooperate as far as they could, are induced (if not actually compelled) to refuse to answer any questions at all.[58]

If I were consulted by a prospective witness who contemplated the possibility of claiming the privilege or wanted to keep silent for any other reason, I should give him two pieces of advice:

First. "It is not only a legal requirement, but also by and large a principle of wisdom and good citizenship for an individual called before a court, a grand jury, an administrative commission, or a legislative investigating committee, to answer questions frankly and honestly. The constitutional privilege to keep silent is an exception to your legal obligation to testify; but even when the legal privilege is available, there are times when it is best not to exercise it. For one thing, although the law is plain that you do not admit guilt by claiming this right to silence, the law cannot control the effect on public opinion. The fact that you feel it necessary to refuse information to a government agency on the ground that it will incriminate you, inevitably casts a shadow on your reputation, whether fairly or not. Also you hurt the enterprise where you work, and you will perhaps imperil your job there"—a matter to be discussed later.

Second. If this prospective witness is in a situation of especial difficulty, where he has strong reasons for taking advantage of the privilege—and this does occasionally happen—then I would urge him to remember that the privilege is a complex and technical subject. "If you attempt, when questioned, to decide for yourself the legality or the wisdom of asserting a right to remain silent, you are as ill-advised as the layman in serious pain who doses himself with home remedies. Therefore, if you are at all doubtful about the desirability of answering questions, you should feel that it is essential for you to obtain the professional counsel of a lawyer, to whom you ought to disclose all the facts as soon as possible."

THE CONGRESSIONAL COMMITTEE

Now I turn from legal rights to considerations of fairness, integrity, and wisdom as they apply to the three sets of human beings involved in the problems of a legislative inquiry—the committee, the witness, and the enterprise where he works.

Every Congressional investigating committee would be wise to keep in mind what was said, in May 1955, by Chief Justice Warren, a man with firsthand experience in governing. After recognizing the wide scope of the power of Congress to inform itself and the American people, he went on:

> But the power to investigate, broad as it may be, is also subject to recognized limitations. It cannot be used to inquire into private affairs unrelated to a valid legislative purpose. Nor does it extend to an area in which Congress is forbidden to legislate. Similarly, *the power to investigate must not be confused with any of the powers of law enforcement; those powers are assigned under our Constitution to the Executive and the Judiciary.*[59]

It is true that the courts are unlikely to interfere if a committee violates these limitations. Regard for the separation of powers is very strong. A judge is not going to enjoin a Senator from coercing a witness into answering undesirable questions.[59a] Still, when men in high authority cannot be controlled by anybody else, that is all the more reason for them to control themselves. For instance, the Supreme Court Justices know that their decisions will not be corrected by anybody, and this very fact makes them reach those decisions with a deep sense of responsibility. Congress and the members of its committees have a corresponding obligation to impose upon themselves the cautionary limitations just quoted, especially the final italicized words.

A Congressional committee sits to make laws and get general information. It has no duty to enforce law. It is not a court to decide issues of guilt or innocence.[60] It is not a police force; its room in the Office Building of the Senate or House is not a police station where suspects are brought in order to determine who ought to be arrested and prosecuted and, if possible, made to suffer penalties established by law for a crime defined by law. Above all, it is not a tribunal to inflict extra-legal punishments like social disgrace and loss of private employment for alleged misconduct which is not a crime under any statute.

I once heard a former counsel of the House Un-American Activities Committee liken it to a grand jury. Hardly anything could be farther from the truth. A witness in the grand-jury room is questioned by and before men like himself, chosen by lot from his fellow-citizens, usually in his own neighborhood. In a Congressional committee-room he faces strangers clothed with power—legislators and a group of government officials. The grand jury is guided by a judge, who is available to decide questions affecting the legal rights of a witness at short notice. The witness before a committee of Congress will not see a judge until he is put on trial for contempt after months or years. The questions the witness has to answer in the grand jury are ordinarily directed toward the specific purpose of deciding where somebody should be later tried by twelve men and a judge on definite charges of a crime; under the Bill of Rights, it is an essential stage in due process of law. The questions by Senators or Representatives rove over everything, and need prepare for nothing. Finally, the questioned man speaks to the grand jury in secret, and if he has to disclose very painful facts, he knows that his listeners will keep those facts secret. Contrast a Congressional committee where, ordinarily, he is asked to bare his life to a crowd of spectators in the room, and often to millions of other Americans at their television or radio sets. Even in executive sessions, a secret is about as safe as at a ladies' bridge-club. The chairman, at the close, gets whatever he wishes into newspaper headlines, and sometimes brings in guests to watch the proceedings. One Senator admitted thirteen students from a neighboring women's college because "the girls simply wanted to know how the committee operated in closed sessions." [61] Imagine the consequences if anybody gave college girls a chance to see how a grand jury works.

Apart from unusual situations like Teapot Dome where a specific combination of actual legal wrongs was unearthed, leading to criminal prosecutions, court proceedings for the recovery of government property, and the resignations of members of the Cabinet, the purpose of a Congressional investigating committee is to obtain information on broad subjects. Consequently, coercion of testimony appears much less necessary than in a grand jury, a criminal trial, a damage suit, or the Interstate Commerce Commission. It seems possible, then, that willing witnesses are likely to supply much of the information which most Congressional committees need in order to render adequate reports on wide problems. The Wickersham Commission in 1929-1931 was given no power at all to order witnesses either to appear or to answer questions, and yet it published six volumes of great value, whose importance was unfortunately hidden from the public by the absurd initial report which showed the complete breakdown of Prohibition and then, with only one courageous vote to the contrary, recommended its continuance. English Royal Commissions illuminate all sorts of national matters without being able to subpoena evidence.[62]

No doubt, as shown early in this chapter, Congress must have in reserve the power to compel unwilling witnesses to give information which it really needs. No doubt, too, Congress ought to be the sole judge of its own need. Yet I respectfully suggest that Congress should pay more attention than in the recent past to the process by which the need for coercing witnesses is determined. For its choice of proper methods matters greatly to freedom.

"Legislatures are guardians of the liberties of the people in quite as great a degree as the courts." These words of Holmes [63] are often quoted by judges as a reason why courts should do nothing to protect those liberties, but his words ought to be often repeated by Senators and Representatives as a reason for doing something. Men chosen by the people have a greater responsibility than anybody else to watch over the liberties of the people. Important among those liberties is the freedom of a citizen to stay home, minding his own affairs and to keep those affairs to himself. Congress interferes enormously with that freedom when it orders a citizen, without his consent, to drop everything and spend hours or days disclosing his affairs to strangers. Of course, Congress may properly require such sacrifices *when the loss of freedom is outweighed by the value of the information which cannot be obtained unless compulsion is used.* Nevertheless, Congress ought to realize how great those sacrifices are, and not let them be demanded mechanically or carelessly or at the arbitrary will of a single man. Whenever coercion is contemplated, the vital question is always the need of Congress to get information not otherwise obtainable, and not the desirability of getting re-elected or getting an individual disgraced or in jail. The process comprises three successive decisions:

(1) Before the investigation begins, is it worth while to make it at all and if so, can it be only carried on fruitfully by a grant of the powerful weapon of subpoena? The whole Senate or the whole House ought to have in mind current conditions about the need to investigate a particular subject when it considers allowing a few of its members to coerce a great many American citizens. Instead, the decision cutting so deeply into freedom was reached years ahead of any specified investigation, by the blanket provisions of the Legislative Reorganization Act of 1946? [64] Congress now says to a dozen committees, "Go ahead and extract answers about anything, as much as you please, any time."

(2) When a witness refuses to answer a question during the investigation, the committee has to decide whether to press for an answer. Although the witness is not excused legally by the fact his disclosures will cause trouble for him with his church, his lodge, his union, his employer, his university, or his conscience, still the members of a committee ought to avoid ordering him to disgrace himself unnecessarily, for instance, when "most of the information sought to be elicited concerning his activities was already in the hands of the committee" [65] or could easily be obtained from willing witnesses and official sources, such as the Federal Bureau of Investigation. It is always a matter for good judgment whether to force a witness to go against his deep moral convictions. Thus, most lawyers and judges are very reluctant to coerce a doctor into betraying the confidences of a patient, in violation of professional ethics, even

though he has no legal right to keep them secret.[66] Senators and Representatives might well display a similar caution when confronted by an equally conscientious witness.

At all events, freedom is deeply involved in the question whether the need of testimony from *this* witness is so great as to justify shutting him up in jail. That is too delicate and important a decision to be entrusted to a single member of a Congressional committee. It would be wise to have three members always present when a possibly unwilling witness is questioned. This is not just a matter of representing two political parties or divergent views about civil rights. My point is that any three men sitting together in the same room will check each other from abusing power. It is only human for a man "drest in a little brief authority" to get angry at ordinary fellows who thwart his will. Then, he is tempted, if alone, to say things which he would keep inside his head if he had two colleagues beside him whose respect he wanted to retain. There is much less scope for personal vendettas. Of course, this suggested rule for three sitting members is burdensome, for Congressmen and Senators have many other tasks. Still, if an investigation is not important enough to command the steady attendance of three Senators or three Representatives, then it is not important enough to have the power to put citizens in jail.

Whatever the size of the committee, its rulings (as already suggested) do not settle the legal rights of a witness satisfactorily. Hence I hope that Congress will consider whether it would be a serious obstruction to its important task of informing itself if it adopted the practice of the Interstate Commerce Commission and requested a court to order the witness to answer specific questions.[67] Such a course might be helpful to the committee. If a judge immediately found a particular kind of question to be proper, several witnesses might often obey him and answer at once instead of waiting until the outcome of a prosecution for contempt years later.

(3) After the investigation is over, the House or the Senate as a whole has to decide that a witness who refused to answer should be prosecuted. The statute [68] aims to give Senators or Representatives who do not belong to the committee an opportunity for a genuine exercise of judgment. Is a genuine judgment now made, or does the Senate or the House act as a rubber-stamp and, without a single

dissenting voice, authorize every prosecution for which its committee asks, no matter how conscientious the witness, how solid his claim of privilege against self-incrimination, or how irrelevant the questions to which answers were refused?

Congress might some day care to ask whether all the committees investigating radicalism since 1938 yielded the kind of information Congress really needs about the dangers from communism inside the United States. These committees have been constantly trying to ferret out individual criminals and start them on the road to the prison gate. Yet, so far as I can recall, not a single person is in prison for spying or sabotage or urging violent revolution, because of evidence dug up in a committee investigation. The committees do boast of helping convict a few men of perjury by lying to save themselves, while public suspicion grows that more than a few of the committee's own witnesses have been lying to harm and imprison others. The most notable achievement of the investigators consists of sending a great many people to jail for crimes which would never have been committed at all except for the investigations. Congress has cited more witnesses for contempt during the last two and a half years than during the preceding ninety-two.[69] The committees did not unearth the offenses, they created them. Is Congress proud that it has turned scores of previously law-abiding citizens into criminals?

While the investigating committees have been thus trying to do law-enforcement, they have neglected big problems about the dangers from domestic communism. How many persons belong to the Communist Party? Why did they become Communists? What makes a large number soon stop being Communists? Do spies and saboteurs and active revolutionists usually belong to the Communist Party, or work outside it? Instead of supplying the country with trustworthy answers to these serious problems, the published reports devote much of their space to denouncing individuals who have done useful work in or out of government service, and whom hardly any serious-minded citizen believes to be dangerous. The committees have cried, "Wolf" so often that few would get alarmed even if a genuine wolf appeared now and then in their rather inaccessible pamphlets. A scholarly survey of the House Committee on Un-American Activities reaches the conclusion:

> One can read through the hearings and reports and learn almost nothing about the larger aspects of the threat offered by subversive agents to a democratic society in a world in revolution.[70]

Therefore, anybody who wants reliable and significant information about the real danger from Communists in the United States will go to books like *Where We Came Out* by Granville Hicks (1954) and Morris Ernst's *Report on the American Communists* (1952).

Finally, Congress might well inquire whether these investigating committees have been doing a satisfactory public-relations job. It is very important that a government should be on good terms with its citizens. I am not talking about Communists, but about the large number of questioned persons who had got out of the Party or never been in it. The grilling and jailing of these non-Communists has made a bad impression on thousands of citizens. One of the main purposes of a nation is to encourage the good life. Hence government agencies should be very reluctant to make individuals live what is for them a bad life, by asking them to help undermine freedom of thought and freedom of speech.

The Witness

Hitherto I have tried to advise the witness who is about to testify, and have stated the general rule that it will be wise for him to answer questions. How about somebody in our own times, like Udall or Lilburn, who is already in trouble for refusing to speak? We are no longer concerned about what the committee and the courts should do. They are through with him. The question now is: How ought this silent witness to be regarded for the rest of his life by the American public and by employers, present or prospective? To use picturesque language, I have been urging people to keep away from the edge of a precipice. Here is a man who has fallen over the top and is sitting on a ledge twenty feet below. Shall he be pushed off or helped up?

A few hours of testifying are a far less significant test of the witness's character than the many years he lived before that. However, attention is bound to be focused on those few hours. The way to deal fairly and squarely with the witness who has kept silent is to try to put yourself in his place during the entire time after he was summoned by the committee. Then, if you refused to answer as he did, would you feel guilty of wickedly obstructing the government?

The first thing to keep in mind is the environment in which a witness has to make difficult decisions. Ask yourself whether you would behave well under these conditions:

> There were, in close proximity to the witness, television cameras, newsreel cameras, news photographers with their concomitant flashbulbs, radio microphones, a large and crowded hearing room with spectators standing along the walls. The concentration of all these elements seems necessarily to disturb and distract any witness.[71]

In the next place, it is very hard for anybody who has not been at the receiving end of an investigation to realize what an agitating experience it is, both before and during the hearing. The investigated suspect is worse off in some ways than the accused man at a criminal trial, who only has to clear himself of one sharply defined offense. The suspect must be prepared to defend almost everything he ever did or thought. If he is an honorable man, he is under a steady strain trying to satisfy himself as well as the committee of the rightfulness of any action of his which happens to bob up in the roving questions. Small wonder, then, that a scholar, let us say, sometimes makes answers and decisions not to answer which, when put into cold type, appear unwise or evasive to university trustees who have never been grilled. The landsman smoking quietly at his own fireside in a howling gale has no notion how calm and sensible he would be aboard a lobster-boat washed by green seas.

Moreover, before condemning the witness for the way he responds to a disagreeable question, remember he was under what United States Circuit Judge Martin calls "a triple threat": [72]

> [1] Answer truly and you have given evidence leading to your conviction for a violation of federal law; [2] answer falsely and you will be convicted of perjury;[73] [3] refuse to answer and you will be found guilty of criminal contempt and punished by fine and im-

prisonment. In our humble judgment, to place a person not even on trial for a specified crime in such predicament is not a manifestation of fair play.

Consider the witness who braves the third threat just mentioned, by keeping silent. He has left the Communist Party or never belonged to it. His refusal to reveal associates is unsupported by the law. He bases his silence on moral grounds, which many of those who are to pass judgment on him reject. Yet the point I want to bring out is that such a man today is often as sincere as Udall or Lilburn long ago. Like the obstreperous Francis Jenkes before the Privy Council, he firmly believes that "to name any particular person would be a mean and unworthy thing." [74]

Among many interesting contemporary examples of this sincerity,[75] listen to two witnesses before the Permanent Subcommittee on Investigations of the Senate Committee on Government Operations.

The first is Professor Wendell Furry,[76] a physicist at Harvard, who was questioned by Senator Joseph R. McCarthy of Wisconsin on January 15, 1954. Mr. Furry was a former Communist who had left the Party. When first called before this Committee in November 1952, he claimed the privilege against self-incrimination because (as he said) "innocent people who feel the threat of false, mistaken or overzealous prosecution because of unpopular opinions have every right to invoke this protection." Subsequently, he came to think that for him to continue to claim this constitutional privilege would bring undue harm to himself and to Harvard. So he waived his privilege by the prepared statement read at the opening of his 1954 examination:

> *Mr. Furry:* I now intend to give this committee all the evidence it may legitimately seek concerning my own activities and associations. I hope that by telling my own political history I can help to dispel suspicion and contribute to public understanding.
>
> Experience has taught me that the inquiry is likely to concern other persons than myself. I feel obliged to state now that I shall respectfully refuse to answer questions that bring in the names of other people. I wish to make it clear, however, that if I knew of any person whose conduct as I saw it was criminal, I should feel bound to reveal the facts. I am not seeking to protect the guilty from pro-

secution. I wish merely to shield the innocent from persecution.

The Chairman: You will be ordered to answer the questions that we ask you.

We asked you the last time that you were here whether or not you had discussed your secret radar work with members of the Communist Party. You refused at that time and said that you were refusing because you felt your answer might tend to incriminate you. Do you want to change that answer today?

Mr. Furry: I certainly do, sir. I am not claiming any constitutional privilege. There were some members of the Communist Party employed in the laboratory where I was employed [at MIT during the war, where classified material was handled]. By my observation they were among the more security minded members of this laboratory. They never in any way departed from the rules, to my knowledge, or showed any inclination to regard any outside connections, including that with the Communist Party, as having any bearing on their work. They were devoted to the war effort, they work loyally, and I shall not reveal their names. . . .

The Chairman: Now, as to the professor who was a Communist and worked with you in the radiation laboratory whom you have identified as now teaching in an American university, let me ask you this question: Is this university Harvard?

Mr. Furry: No, sir, it is not.

The Chairman: Is it MIT?

Mr. Furry: Sir, I cannot answer all these questions going through the list of American universities one by one. I will make the statement that it is not MIT, but I think I will have to refuse to answer if you keep on listing different places. I mean, this would be a way of identifying the man finally. It would be a game of 20 questions. . . .

The Chairman: If we refer your case over to a grand jury, will you give the names of the six Communists who were working with you in the radar laboratory?

Mr. Furry: No, sir, I would give them to a grand jury only if the grand jury were investigating actual crimes, not crimes of opinion but actual crimes, of espionage, sabotage or that sort of thing. I would give them, certainly, if they were involved there. . . .

The Chairman: Do you know of any one connected with Harvard who is or was a member of the Communist Party?

Mr. Furry: Sir, I am not sorting people for the committee. . . .

The Chairman: To me it is inconceivable that a university which has had the reputation of being a great university would keep this type of a creature on teaching our children.

The second witness who refused to disclose his associates is Senator Joseph R. McCarthy.[77] When brought before his own committee less than four months later, he was equally insistent on a moral obligation to hide names, although he also relied on a non-existent legal right.[78] The Senator was testifying on May 6, 1954, about a short document, which falsely purported to be a letter from J. Edgar Hoover to General Bolling but was really a garbled version of a highly secret F.B.I. memorandum:

> *Mr. Jenkins* (counsel for the committee): I want to ask you . . . to tell this committee . . . all of your knowledge with respect to the two-and-a-quarter-page letter, particularly where you obtained possession of it, when you obtained possession of it, whence it came. . . .
>
> *Senator McCarthy:* First let me make it clear, Mr. Jenkins, and Mr. Chairman, that I will not under any circumstances reveal the source of any information which I get as chairman of the committee. One of the reasons why I have been successful, I believe to some extent, in exposing communism is because the people who give me information from within the Government know that their confidence will not be violated. It will not be violated today. . . . I want to make it very, very clear. I want to notify the people who give me information that there is no way on earth that any committee, any force can get me to violate the confidence of those people.[79]

Here, which is very unusual, the Congressional committee respected the witness's determination to conceal his associates although he did not set up the privilege against self-incrimination. Both cases re-enforce the main theme of this chapter, that the privilege is only part of the important problems raised by refusal to answer questions. A court in a contempt proceeding can consider only legal rights, but there is no such rigid fence around the thinking of other persons. When they evaluate the witness's conduct, they ought to examine especially the strength and nobility of his reasons for keeping silent.

The Enterprise Where the Witness Works

Nobody has a greater duty to look at the moral convictions of a witness than the heads of the enterprise where he works. He is their man. Committees and courts are concerned with only a few hours torn out of context, but the enterprise has received years of his life before he took the stand and he will contribute to its welfare during many more years, unless his career is cut short by companions with whom he has labored long and, in most cases, well. When the heads of his enterprise are forced to take cognizance of his behavior in the committee-room, they should put into the scales all those years of service and the whole man.

It will be convenient if I concentrate on one kind of enterprise, the university, where I have seen the problems at both ends, during forty years of teaching, and membership on the governing boards of another institution. A good deal of what is said can be readily applied to other enterprises like factories, government departments, and schools.

What ought a university to do about one of its professors after he has got into trouble for refusing to answer questions from a legislative committee?

My starting-point is that this is not a decision about constitutional rights but about the fate of a teacher. Each case ought to be decided by the educational authorities on its individual merits, including the teacher's long performance in his classroom and his study, as well as his brief behavior in the committee-room. There should be no blanket rule of dismissal for silence.

Of course, high moral character is one of the elements in a good teacher. Still, a man can sometimes be at odds with the law and yet possess high moral character. Socrates and Galileo are two examples. A third is the professor who parks his car on the wrong side of the street.

A great deal has been said lately about the imperative necessity of exterminating "disloyalty" in colleges and universities. There is a real danger from domestic revolutionaries, but when governmental authorities and the public undertake to do battle against "disloyalty" they are spreading their fire over too wide a front instead of carefully aiming at the enemies who most need shooting down. The concept of "disloyalty" is so vague and hard to define that it is unsuitable for use by a jury deciding whether to send a man to prison or by university trustees deciding whether to turn a professor out in the cold. Even when the word is not just a label we paste on anybody whose economic and political views we dislike, "disloyalty" is nothing but a state of mind, which in some people sometimes leads to bad acts. No doubt, it is an objectionable state of mind, but so is stupidity.

The law does not battle against stupidity at large and try to cure it by punishments, not at least where adults are concerned. Instead, the law selects one precise form of stupidity called "negligence" which it can handle successfully in the courtroom. Otherwise it leaves stupidity to be remedied by individual experience and arguments from other men. In the same way, we might profitably break down the vague concept of disloyalty, and select for punitive action only the particular manifestations of hostility to our government which are capable of precise statement and are really dangerous to the nation, or in the case of a professor, to his university.

Two specific purposes seem worth carrying out. One is to protect the nation from espionage, sabotage, and revolutionary plots. If trustees suspect that a professor is engaged in anything like that, then report him to the police or the prosecutor and let the law take its course. Men without judicial experience or power to subpoena witnesses have no business deciding whether a professor has committed a crime.

The other specific purpose is to maintain among professors a proper standard of fitness for the work they are to do. This *is* the concern of educational authorities. Whenever they are asked to discharge a professor because of his refusal to answer questions, the issue is not "disloyalty" but *fitness*.[80] Of course, the extent of a teacher's devotion to the government is an element in considering his fitness, but it is only one element among others, such as intelligence, originality, good health, sobriety, and care not to "slop over." A shortage of one element may be outweighed by a big supply of another, as when a man who publishes little is appointed because of his extraordinary power to make his students enthusiastic over ideas and skilled in testing their soundness. Hence, intellectual and emotional antagonism to the powers that be is not a fatal defect for a professor, any more than for a businessman between 1933 and 1953. A man's fitness to teach depends on *all* his qualities, just as it did before Congress began investigating radicals. If the heads of any enterprise allow themselves to be preoccupied with the single element of "loyalty," they will steadily expand their inquiries until they bring in a host of personal matters which have a very remote bearing upon fitness. Trustees, faculty, and graduates get so busy disputing whether Professor X is a fellow-traveler that his inspiring lectures and readable scholarship are rarely mentioned.

A good question for trustees to ask each other is: "Would we have ever thought seriously of dismissing this teacher if he had not been called by a Congressional committee?" President Harold Taylor of Sarah Lawrence College aptly says:

> The man who in every respect has shown himself to be worthy of his post over a long period of time does not suddenly become a different person because of his refusal to answer political questions in public.[81]

Two concrete situations will show how legal rights and sound academic policy may not coincide.

First. Consider a case where the legal rights are indisputable. The professor has properly claimed the constitutional privilege against self-incrimination. Nevertheless, I can see why most university authorities feel that they cannot let the matter rest there. Although, as already stated, the privilege is not an admission of guilt, many persons have probably claimed it without being innocent. Widespread public belief that this is always so hurts the university's reputation. And some doubt is inevitable. University authorities are unlikely to want an actual offender on the campus. Consequently, it seems quite natural and proper for the president of the university to ask the professor to clear up the mystery in a confidential conversation. "Won't you tell me what you wouldn't tell the committee? What were your real reasons for keeping silent?"

The professor owes it to his university to give this explanation *if* he can safely assume that it will all be kept secret. Yet can he? Perhaps the committee learns about this conversation. Then it summons the president. "What did the professor tell you in your office that day?" The president would have no privilege, no legal right whatever. Yet how can he run a university if professors can't rely on his promises of secrecy? So I assume that the president would say nothing, and risk going to jail for contempt. Indeed, the spectacle of a few university presidents behind bars for refusing to answer questions which decent men don't ask would be a great contribution to liberty.

Suppose that the professor does talk freely to the president. If he admits present membership in the Communist Party, then the prevalent policy against having Communists on faculties will put him out at once. However, Communist professors are scarce as hen's teeth. It is not they who present the problems which are bothering most universities. The rest of this chapter will deal only with non-Communists. If such a man confidentially discloses facts which leave his scholarship, teaching ability, and moral character unsullied, then he ought to go on doing a good job.

Even if the professor remains as silent in the president's office as he was before the committee, I hope that the educational authorities would not automatically dismiss him, but make some independent investigation, by conversations with his friends and so on, in order to learn whether his reasons for claiming the privilege were discreditable.

The various Harvard teachers who claimed the privilege in the spring of 1953 were willing to explain their action to the university authorities. Nobody with a permanent appointment was dismissed. My only disagreement is with some of the reasoning of the Harvard Corporation. It described the claim of the privilege as "grave misconduct." As one who has sworn allegiance to the Constitution, I think this a very inappropriate phrase to apply to the use of a right given by the Constitution.[82]

Second. The professor keeps silent without any legal right. Suppose a professor named Ajax, who was never a member of the Communist Party or any affiliated organization. In 1938 when he was doing graduate work, he engaged in many social activities with Miss Bluejeans and Mr. Cockfight who both belonged to the Party. A Congressional committee in 1955 asks Ajax two questions: (a) Were you a member of the Communist Party in 1938? (b) Did you then know any Communist graduate students and who were they? He has no chance whatever of being convicted under the Smith Act or any other law. Yet he has strong reasons for keeping silent. He knows that Miss Bluejeans has told the committee that he was a Communist in 1938; he is afraid that if he truthfully denies that fact, he will be prosecuted for perjury. The leading witness against him will be Miss Bluejeans, who has attained great glory with the public by denouncing her former friends and may easily get him convicted. He refuses to answer the other question, because of unwillingness to harm his friend Cockfight, who left the Party years ago and is doing valuable research in a distant university. Ajax's institution learns of his actual motives for keeping silent. Ought it to discipline him?

Let us start by supposing that the committee did nothing to Ajax or that a jury acquitted him. When the law has not punished him for going outside his legal rights, why should his university do so? Perhaps his first reason was unwise, but if a lack of good judgment in practical matters were a cause for dismissing professors, most universities would have very small faculties indeed. The second reason, though legally bad, is ethically supportable, as much for him as for Udall and Lilburn long ago.

Consider the other alternative. The committee disallows Ajax's claim of privilege, but he still remains silent. The prosecution for contempt follows, in which he is convicted by a jury for his silence on both questions. He appeals and inevitably loses. He spends six months in jail. Without urging the university to treat this period as a sabbatical on full pay, I want to inquire what ought to happen when he gets out.

Here is a man who has been in jail for a statutory crime. Does this make him automatically unfit to teach? Or should the university go on getting the benefit of his great abilities and a character which has been unimpeachable apart from this one affair? The University of South Carolina in 1820 chose as a professor of chemistry, and soon as its president for fourteen years, Thomas Cooper, who had served six months in prison under the Sedition Act of 1798. He was a pioneer teacher of political economy, established the first medical school and the first insane asylum in the state, and embodied most of the "noblest hopes and aspirations" of his age.[83]

I fully realize the difficulties of distinguishing among the crimes which carry prison sentences. I should not excoriate the educational authorities who discharged Ajax, but I should honor those who decided to keep him. His fears about answering the first question were by no means baseless; and if he had been mistakenly convicted for perjury, the university would be in the same quandary it is now. As for the other question, all American schoolboys are brought up on the maxim that it is a dirty business to peach on your comrades. Most of us would disregard that maxim when asked about burglary or counterfeiting. Yet is it moral turpitude to refuse to betray persons into social obloquy and possible financial ruin on account of their former political activities or their "dangerous thoughts"? [84] Is it wicked to give greater scope to the noble ideals of freedom of speech than the Supreme Court does? The desire to shield a friend from a detestable kind of attack is not automatically inconsistent with high moral character.

CONCLUSION

Our country has been going through the same experience as in the days of the Fugitive Slave Law. Many citizens have been brought face to face with governmental activities which though clearly legal are detestable. Sensitive men are placed in the dilemma of either doing things they believe wrong or else being law-breakers. When Garrison and the men on the Underground Railroad helped slaves to escape, this sort of law-breaking was differentiated from burglary and arson by many thoughtful men at the time and by the judgment of history.

Still, these abolitionists did break the law. And every kind of law-breaking has evil effects. Anybody who contemplates disobeying the law, no matter how noble his motives, faces a very grave responsibility.

A very grave responsibility also confronts a government which year after year carries on campaigns to suppress the spread of ideas and turns decent productive people into jailbirds solely for not opening their mouths. Since 1938 the two Houses of Congress by harassing and imprisoning authors, journalists, playwrights, actors, and teachers, not to mention hard-working secretaries and bookkeepers, have produced very little information and an enormous wastage of time, money, energy, and liberty.

"They broke the law, didn't they?" That sends me back to a law-breaker 110 years ago, who for not paying his poll tax in protest against slavery, found himself in the Concord jail:

> As I stood considering the walls of solid stone, two or three feet thick, the door of wood and iron, a foot thick, and the iron grating which strained the light, I could not help being struck with the foolishness of that institution which treated me as if I were mere flesh and blood and bones, to be locked up. I wondered that it should have concluded at length that this was the best use it could put me to.[85]

VIII   The Freedom to Think

If a man does not keep pace with his companions,
perhaps it is because he hears a different drummer.
Let him step to the music which he hears, however
measured or far away.——THOREAU, *Walden*

If the universities had not recently brought the social sciences into
the curriculum, they would have saved themselves a lot of trouble.
Their freedom would have been attacked very little in the Twentieth Century. The struggle between the natural sciences and religion ended in an armistice decades ago. Geology no longer battles
against Genesis, and evolution can be taught with impunity outside
Tennessee and Mississippi. New theories and discoveries in physics,
chemistry, and biology are enthusiastically heralded. They may
enable us to save sick men by the hundreds or slaughter well men by
the hundreds of thousands. They may bring about inventions which
will add to our comfort and help the advertising business. As for
the humanities, innovation has always been welcome since Homer
said, "Men ever love the song that rings newest in the ear." If universities had only stuck to the classics, professors of Latin and
Greek might have imparted radicalism to their students by insisting
that the Conspiracy of Catiline was a frame-up by Cicero just as the
Reichstag Fire was a frame-up by Hitler, or injected Fascist ideas
into lectures on the *Republic* of Plato. Most people would not have
known what they were talking about and nobody would have cared.

No such obscurity awaits the professor who indulges in heterodox
views about economics, government, international affairs, or law.
He occupies the front page of newspapers beside bank robbers. Columnists bracket him with spies. The lightning he keeps attracting
does not spare the university where he works. If it protects itself
from the storm by sending him away, it will often lose the teaching
and research of a distinguished scholar, and it will surely demoralize
his colleagues and lessen its future power to recruit a strong faculty.

236

Yet, if the university dares to retain the unpopular professor, it, too, will become a favorite target for professional patriots. The sources of indispensable funds may perhaps dry up, and many parents of desirable undergraduates, present or potential, will be honestly disturbed. One of the great calamities of these angry attacks on disliked ideas in universities is that they distract the heads of an institution from their vital task of facilitating thought and ask them to stifle thought.

People are inclined to regard the multiplication table as characteristic of all education—something which is just so and not otherwise, which once learned stays with you through life. When a professor expresses to his class ideas about politics or economics with which the critics disagree, they think it just as bad as telling boys and girls that seven times nine is sixty-one. Of course there is a core of indubitable knowledge in education, but most of the teacher's task consists in imparting methods for understanding what is still unknown and for dealing with it wisely. The best kind of education was what Mark Twain got as an apprentice pilot on the Mississippi. After he had learned all the shoals and points in the river from St. Louis to New Orleans, he found that many of them had changed. He had to learn them all over again; and better yet, he had to know how to be perpetually acquiring information through which he could predict those changes.

Mistakes are easier to make in such a process than in the communication of an established body of knowledge. Yet it is absurd to assume that such mistakes will warp the minds of students for life.

This is one reason why citizens at large are scared about teachers. They think that students believe what they hear in college. Did these anxious folk do that when they were in college themselves? They are like Mr. Dooley—"I remember when I was a little boy, but I don't remember how I was a little boy." They have forgotten what it was like to be young.

Undergraduates do not believe all that their professors tell them, even if it happens to be right. A great many teachers of economics in colleges in my boyhood were for low tariffs, but students who went out of their classrooms into business were soon protectionists. A former Secretary of State told me, while he was in law school, that what worried him about education at Yale was that most of his classmates were rapidly becoming just like their fathers. The frequent fear of citizens that radical professors produce radical students is not borne out by my experience. The most fertile nursery of Socialists I have known was the classroom of Professor Thomas Nixon Carver, a conservative of the toughest fiber. He was determined to be more than fair to economic theories with which he disagreed, but his lectures made socialism so unattractive that undergraduates, in and out of his courses, started the Harvard Socialist Club to combat his influence.[1] Around 1910 the club was flourishing. One member, John Reed, is buried in the walls of the Kremlin. Another member was Walter Lippmann. Boys and girls do not really think always like their teachers, nor do they necessarily go on thinking like themselves when in college. Life wears us all down.

The capacity of citizens to adjust themselves wisely to changes is particularly urgent in matters of government, law, economic transactions, and other areas of the social sciences. Even if there were no new inventions, we should be foolish to expect ideas to stay as they are, however satisfactory we now find them. In Greece, science did nothing between the Persian Wars and the death of Socrates to increase man's mastery over nature, and yet established ways of life kept breaking down. "There was always considerable hell in Hellas." The Industrial Revolution was barely under way when Blackstone wrote his *Commentaries*. He thought he was expounding a solidified body of law, when in fact law was changing faster than it had done for centuries. Men are always bound to rethink their relations with each other. This tendency is enormously accelerated by the arrival of inventions which alter their daily lives. President Eisenhower of Columbia told his students, "In this life we don't know what is around the corner."

Still, the response of a society to change may be merely drifting. Newly suggested political, social, and economic devices usually meet a stubborn resistance. In any event, it is hard to shape them wisely to fit the facts. Sometimes a community fails to see the need for new methods of conducting its affairs even though that need is great. The Industrial Revolution caused an immediate, enormous, and never-ending growth of metropolitan areas, whose problems could not possibly be handled efficiently by the old simple, overlapping governments of counties, townships, and cities in a particular region like Greater New York. And yet it was decades before men began asking what kind of government ought to replace those which had hopelessly broken down.

In the United States today institutions are not frozen, nor are they so anywhere in the free world from which we must seek allies. As the newly independent nations of Asia plan their governments, we ought not to be shocked if they decide to govern themselves in ways which are somewhat unfamiliar to us. The numerous problems the American people face at home or in their relations with other countries call for inventiveness and wisdom on the part of the few who propose solutions and of the many who decide whether to accept or modify or reject them. Devotion to tradition is useless here. The inevitability of change requires our unyielding maintenance of the principle of open discussion, not only for ideas and persons we like but also for those we detest.

This brings me to what I want to say most. The universities of the United States are taking an indispensable share in the work of continuously testing, readjusting, and improving the machinery of human relations, and nobody else can do what they do. Of course, a great deal of this work will always be carried on by the active men in the field such as politicians, journalists, lawyers, judges, and businessmen. They have an experience, a sense of what is possible and other qualities of mind which are rare among professors. Still, no matter how shrewd the practical men are, they are absorbed in a crowded succession of immediate tasks; and this leaves them far less time than professors have for taking long views. Few social problems are wholly novel. One may seem so to the man in the field, but the professor is likely to have encountered something resembling it during his researches. At least he knows where to look for it. He is like a specialist consulted by a family doctor about a baffling illness. The specialist hunts up medical case-records of decades ago. He discovers how similar symptoms were diagnosed and treated, and what was the outcome. Moreover, the teacher's task of making difficulties plain to undergraduates fits him to translate technicalities into language which is intelligible to any thoughtful layman.

In former times in England and the United States there were a considerable number of able men outside universities who had sufficient leisure to take long views of society and put them into books. Remember the influence exerted by Jeremy Bentham and Walter Bagehot. John Stuart Mill did not even go to college. Most of the great American historians of the Nineteenth Century held no professorships. However, with high taxes and modern pressures we can no longer count on getting the help we need from such independent men. No doubt, there will still be an occasional farsighted columnist like Walter Lippmann, an occasional part-time historian like Douglas Southall Freeman. But the major contributions to comprehensive thinking about the problems of society will have to come from the universities. Think of Adam Smith at Glasgow, Blackstone at Oxford, Wythe the teacher of John Marshall at William and Mary, Thomas Cooley at Michigan, William Graham Sumner at Yale, Woodrow Wilson at Princeton, Frank Taussig at Harvard, not to mention many more dead scholars and those who, happily, are serving us today.

In comparison with the natural sciences, the social sciences are handicapped by the almost complete impossibility of experimentation. One cannot try out a new tax law, for instance, with the intention of discarding it if it works badly. Voters refuse to be guinea-pigs. Thorough thinking in advance is about the only way to discover whether a legal or political reform is desirable or bad. The universities are the appropriate place for a good deal of this necessary thinking.

The professor in a social science performs his indispensable task in several different ways. He writes himself. He teaches the writers of the future. Still more important, he trains potential politicians and voters to deal wisely and well with the problems which they will have to face. And the classroom discussions teach him as well as his students; he discovers the weak spots in his views and puts them into print more clearly than if he wrote in isolation.

What I am saying about the indispensable task of a university applies to all universities in the United States, public or endowed, and particularly to the former. As taxes rise, endowed universities lose and state universities gain. The fact that these public universities are ultimately controlled by legislatures ought to be irrelevant to their performance of the indispensable task of supplying long views about the problems of society. The government pays judges, but it does not tell them how to decide. An independent state university is as essential to the community as an independent judiciary. Legislatures make it possible for scholars to think and teach. There the political part in education should end. When he who pays the piper insists on calling the tune, he is not likely to get much good music.

For many decades the American universities have been performing their indispensable task. All of a sudden they are gravely hampered in carrying it out by current fears of radicalism. There is no class of people more injured by repression than teachers. If you confine the teaching in his thinking, what do you leave him? That is his job, to think. Universities should not be transformed, as in Nazi Germany, into loud-speakers for the men who wield political power. If they are deprived of freedom of thought and speech, there is no other place to which citizens can confidently turn for long views about public issues. Here and there some courageous writer or speaker may still make himself known, but such men are no substitute for the present systematic creation and communication of ideas which take place in our universities.

> Ye are the salt of the earth: but if the salt have lost his savour, where withal shall it be salted?

Without attempting any exhaustive presentation of current efforts to block the indispensable task of universities, I want to speak of three kinds of attacks on professors who express unwelcome views about the social sciences. Right away let me make it plain that I am not writing about professors who are really Communists. Only a handful of such men have been discovered among university teachers during all the investigations by Congress and state legislatures. Many university presidents have announced that they will not hire or keep a Communist on their faculties. The Federal Bureau of Investigation is well informed about members of the Communist Party. There is plenty of federal legislation to take care of dangerous revolutionaries on or off the campus.

What began years ago as an onslaught on a few Communist scholars has been long since transformed into an onslaught on a great many scholars who are not Communists, but who are suspected of holding views which happen to be unpopular with an influential number of citizens.

Let me give some concrete illustrations. The University of Colorado was urged to dismiss an economist for favoring a Missouri Valley Authority like the TVA. A prominent alumnus of Harvard Law School refused to give any money for its new dormitories unless the leading American astronomer was turned out of Harvard Observatory for presiding over a meeting at the Waldorf of scientists and other thinkers from all over the world, including (with our government's definite sanction) some from the Soviet Union. No evidence was offered that the astronomer was a Communist. The regents of the University of California expressly said that none of the numerous distinguished professors they discharged were Communists. In California, too, a professor's textbook on American history was denounced because he wrote that the Supreme Court reacted to the wishes and thinking of the people when it eventually held New Deal legislation to be constitutional. This, said the critic, was subtly hidden Communist propaganda; in fact the Court decides cases free of such pressures.

The first and most far-flung attack on freedom in the social sciences is modeled on *The Red Network* by Elizabeth Dilling, who ended her career by being tried under the Smith Act among a mass of anti-Semites and Nazi sympathizers. The attack takes the form of an enormous amount of talk about the membership of professors in so-called subversive organizations. The word "subversive" has no precise definition in American law. It is as vague as "heretical" was in the medieval trials which sent men to the stake. Some government official or some group of politicians classifies an organization as subversive, and a university is thereupon urged to dismiss every professor who ever had any connection with that organization.

While dealing with the registration of "Communist-front organizations" under the McCarran Act in Chapter V, I spoke of the great dangers to our national life from efforts to interfere by law with the shaping of public opinion through associations formed for all sorts of purposes. The dangers from such interference are all the greater when the objectionable label of "Communist-front" or "subversive" is pinned on an enterprise by successive Attorney Generals of the

United States or by various Congressional and state investigating committees which, unlike the Subversive Activities Control Board, do not feel under a duty to grant a thorough hearing to the enterprise before condemning it.

When it comes to depriving professors of their lifetime careers because of membership in a "subversive" organization, there are often weak links in the chain of reasoning of the attackers.

First, the characterization of the particular organization as subversive is a delicate task, which is rarely undertaken in a judicial manner. Clearly legitimate purposes may be mingled with purposes which are objectionable to many Americans. Some men join for the legitimate purposes and others for the objectionable purposes. Legislative investigating committees tend to assume that a few Communists in the organization are enough to condemn it as a whole. One of them remarked, "How much poison does it take to make a cup of coffee harmful?" [2] In fact, the mere membership of a professor in an organization has little significance until one knows whether he was one of the radicals or one of the conservatives or simply mailed a small check to further the legitimate purposes and went back to reading a learned book.

Anything can happen when people get started on this business of outlawing groups, not for any crimes committed by either the group or any of its members, but for having some vaguely bad ideas or some vaguely bad members.

Another weak link is the determination of the professor's membership in a stigmatized organization. It is not a matter of record like being a stockholder in a business corporation. Or take a club. A man is elected to it, he pays regular dues, he resigns in order to stop his dues; but in these propaganda enterprises, joining and leaving are very informal and dues are either loosely collected or nonexistent. If one comes to dislike new associates or new purposes, he just stops doing anything; there is no particular reason for taking the time and trouble to write a letter of resignation. Often the alleged member has no knowledge of belonging to the organization at all. Somebody inside it put his name on its mailing list, which gets into the hands of a legislative committee, and that's enough. I am red-listed by the House Un-American Activities Committee in the National Federation of Constitutional Liberties and the Veterans of the

Abraham Lincoln Brigade. My only relation with these two groups was to open some envelopes and put the stuff right into my waste-basket without bothering to reply.

Finally, I come to the worst weakness of this red network. Suppose a professor did undoubtedly sign a petition to the President to pardon some Communist whom he thought to be unjustly imprisoned, or joined the National Lawyers Guild when he was too young to get into the American Bar Association, or gave twenty dollars to help refugees from Franco Spain get medical care. This is only one aspect of that professor's activities. It took only a small fraction out of one working day. You need to know a great deal more about the man before you can determine his real outlook on politics and society.

The legislative investigating committees rarely bother to find out this "great deal more" about the man they classify as subversive. Take just one example. They red-list the late Charles A. Beard, the historian. He was so objectionable a man that the California schools were urged to throw out a textbook on *Our Constitution* because the bibliography cites Beard, who "has been affiliated with [five] Communist-front organizations." [3] One was the Non-Partisan Committee for the Re-election of Vito Marcantonio to Congress. The others were equally short-lived affairs, gotten up to file a petition in Washington or appear at Congressional hearings on a specific subject. No mention of Beard's long membership in the American Political Science Association and the American Historical Association; he was one of only two scholars who served as president of both these learned societies. No mention of *The Rise of American Civilization* or his dozen other books. Yet these lists are used, with no independent verification, by columnists and infuriated alumni as if they possessed the accuracy of a financial rating by Dun & Bradstreet.

It is high time for a group of trustworthy men to evaluate this red network. Let them take all the non-Communists who have been labeled as "fellow-travelers" and "subversive" on these lists. Tell American citizens how many persons are really dangerous to the safety of the nation out of a total which includes Beard, Ed Murrow, Frank Lloyd Wright, Frank P. Graham, Lin Yutang, Roscoe Pound, and James Bryant Conant.

The whole thing ought to be put into the incinerator. No more government by gossip.

The second attack on universities is the rapidly increasing practice of singling out teachers in public and endowed institutions for test oaths and compulsory declarations of loyalty.[4] Thus to regard all professors as potential transgressors is an insult to law-abiding and hard-working men and women. Teachers were once esteemed in American communities, but now they are treated *en masse* as if they were peculiarly inclined to betray their country. Alexander Hamilton, whom nobody would call a radical, denounced the exculpatory oath which was designed to root out Tories in New York: [5]

> It was to excite scruples in the honest and conscientious, and to hold out a bribe to perjury. . . . Nothing can be more repugnant to the true genius of the common law than such an inquisition into the consciences of men.

These test oaths for teachers are a subtle way of enforcing upon them the view which happens to be dominant for the time being. They revive a detested practice used in England in the Seventeenth Century to impose religious uniformity upon teachers.[6] They combine insult with futility. No really revolutionary professor would boggle at taking them. If they get rid of anybody, it is "the honest and conscientious" as Hamilton said.

The Massachusetts Loyalty Oath, enacted in 1935 in response to assertions that the schools and colleges of the commonwealth were riddled with Communists and traitors, has not ferreted out a single teacher with the slightest taint of disloyalty. In the subsequent twenty years, only five teachers and professors have failed to take the oath. What is especially significant is that these five men and women had served for years with unquestioned devotion. They stopped their lifework because they were sensitive people who thought it wrong to be forced to swear that they possessed the common virtues of decent citizens.

Some supporters of loyalty oaths cannot understand why professors who are far from being Communists should object to swearing, "I am not a member of the Communist Party or any other organization which advocates the overthrow of the government by force and violence." If it's true, why not say so? Why all this fuss?

Scholars object to being forced to plead "Not guilty" before any evidence of guilt is produced. They object to making a public avowal of their loyalty and their allegiance to the pursuit of truth, when these qualities ought never to have been doubted. Picture the parallel situation of a loyal wife whose suspicious husband demands a public assertion—at a dinner party in their home—that she has never been unfaithful to him. "If it's true, why not say so?"

If we are going to revive the abomination of exculpatory oaths, why stop at one profession and one kind of objectionable behavior? Why not extend the device to other occupations and other offenses? Let us require every Congressman to swear that there were no illegal practices at his election and that he has never accepted a bribe or taken a kickback out of the salary of his secretary. Let us require every lawyer to swear that he has never solicited clients by ambulance-chasing, every doctor that he has never performed an abortion, and every businessman that he has never violated the antitrust laws. Imagine the indignation which these proposals would raise from men who see no harm in teachers' oath laws. Yet these offenses are far more frequent in the respective occupations than disloyalty among teachers, and they are at least as injurious to society.

It is high time to stop this persistent probing of the patriotism of professors and schoolteachers. We teachers have a difficult job and perhaps we are not doing it very successfully, but we shall surely do it worse when misguided people are constantly tearing us up by the roots to see whether we are growing straight or crooked.

Lastly, I want to speak of the attack on scholars at the frontiers of the United States. Our government, seven years ago, signed the Universal Declaration of Human Rights, which proclaims "freedom . . . to seek, receive, and impart information and ideas . . . regardless of frontiers." This freedom embodies the experience of centuries. Many notable contributions to the art and literature of the world have been made by men who wrote or published in countries not their own—Dante, Locke, Montesquieu, Voltaire, Rousseau, Heine, and Mazzini. Foreign scholars have enriched thought at universities ever since Erasmus sojourned at Cambridge.

Of late years, they have gathered at many international conferences with great benefit to intellectual and practical progress.

The values just described will be hard to obtain if our government continues its present inhospitality to traveling thinkers on the ground of their real or supposed political opinions. Men with original ideas to give the world do not fall into orthodox patterns. If they did, they would probably be unable to tell us anything new. The writer who complies strictly with established views is usually not worth listening to.

We have come a long, long way from Thomas Jefferson, whose name is so frequently invoked by the politicians who have brought about the present laws of the United States. He invited professors from abroad to the University of Virginia, which (he wrote) "will be based on the illimitable freedom of the human mind. For here we are not afraid to follow truth wherever it may lead, nor to tolerate error so long as reason is left free to combat it." [7] Our government is repudiating the spirit of Jefferson just at the time when it is more important than ever before that the free countries of the world should pool their intellectual resources for the sake of preserving their freedom and increasing human welfare.

The doors of the United States are now locked on both sides. When American scholars are asked to lecture at European universities or attend important conferences, their passports may be denied by subordinate officials or delayed so long that the object of the journey is wrecked. Linus Pauling, former president of the American Chemical Society and winner of the 1954 Nobel Prize in Chemistry, was invited to take part in a discussion of the structure of proteins at the Royal Society in London on May 1, 1952. Pauling applied for a passport on January 24. Through the efforts of Senator Wayne Morse, he finally got it—on July 15. Ten weeks too late for the Royal Society meeting! [8]

Some recent court decisions have compelled the State Department to issue passports which were refused unreasonably.[9] Still few scholars can afford to spend time and money on a lawsuit in order to go to Europe.

Meanwhile, some of the most distinguished thinkers in free countries have been refused visas to enter the United States and help us advance our knowledge. According to a very measured and painstaking examination of such cases in the *Bulletin of Atomic Scientists* for October 1952,[10] none of the many excluded foreign scholars there discussed would have been dangerous to the United States if admitted, and not one had the remotest tinge of communism. The natural sciences are the chief sufferers from this policy, but the social sciences are by no means left free. Michael Polanyi, for example, is Professor of Social Studies at Manchester in England. Polanyi was among the distinguished scholars whom Princeton gathered at its bicentenary in 1946, but in 1951 he was not allowed to return to the United States to occupy the chair of Social Philosophy at the University of Chicago. The adamant American consul never looked at any of Polanyi's writings.

Visas are not always denied, only delayed without reasons. "I waited, but nothing happened." "Weeks and months elapsed without an answer." Anybody who has been shocked by Menotti's opera *The Consul* will find its scenes re-enacted in offices which fly the Stars and Stripes.

The restoration of freedom of movement for journalists, creative writers, scientists, and other scholars can be accomplished without modifying the general immigration laws of the United States. These are primarily designed to determine the character of our permanent population. The restrictions are framed with regard to aliens who wish to settle in new homes here for the rest of their lives and eventually become citizens. The present national policy as to such persons is that they must not differ very much from the mass of our population. It was not the policy which brought over Roger Williams and built up the colonies and the states, but it is firmly established now. My point is that restrictions which may be suitable for intending settlers are undesirable and needless for scholars who wish to come here for a short time.

The obstacles to free trade in ideas are not satisfactorily removed by the provision of the existing law which allows the Attorney General to issue exceptional dispensations to a few temporary visitors. Such special favors take a long time, and they are a shabby recognition of the good which distinguished thinkers and writers from our side of the iron curtain can bring to the intellectual life of the United States. Each proposal to disregard our immigration laws for the sake of benefiting some individual may possibly raise an outcry among Congressmen and columnists.

Consideration of this matter by intelligent writers in the press with the help of our leading learned societies might shape public opinion and eventually persuade Congress to place temporary visitors to the United States in a separate category from permanent settlers. When a foreigner is not going to stay here, we do not really need to worry about his present or past political and economic views or his present or past membership in various organizations, so long as he himself will not do any bad acts during his visit. The only real question is: Will this scholar endanger the public safety if we let him in? Proof submitted directly to high authorities in Washington by an American university or learned society that it has arranged for the scholar to give lectures or attend conferences here ought to go a long way to satisfy this test. The institution which thus sponsored the visa would feel a moral responsibility for the proper behavior of its guest. There would be no need for a distinguished scholar to be grilled by a consul, no need for long delays while many letters crossed the Atlantic, little or no occasion for publicity.

Anybody who regards this simple procedure as perilously hospitable to "subversive" foreigners ought to remember that Great Britain, France, Italy, and most other countries of free Europe require no visas whatever for a visiting American. He just needs a passport to get in and stay in, so long as he behaves himself. Yet those countries are three thousand miles nearer to the Soviet Union and its satellites than we are. If they are willing to take a chance on our citizens, why are we afraid to take a much smaller chance on theirs?

But that is not the way things are now. Although the situation has become somewhat better than in 1952 and continues to improve, it is still a good deal worse than it ought to be. For example, a conference on High Energy Nuclear Physics was held in Rochester, New York, on January 31, 1955, with the Atomic Energy Commission and the Office of Naval Research among its sponsors. Winners of the Nobel Prize and several other distinguished scientists, whose discoveries were the basis of a large portion of the discussions, were invited but did not come because of visa difficulties.

We, the people of the United States, are shutting out quiet thinkers who are anxious to come among us to help us treat leukemia and breast cancer, and to aid us in many different ways to develop valuable ideas for an industry and our welfare. Russia hangs an iron curtain along its frontiers and China a silken curtain. The government of the United States has been doing its best to put around our shores a curtain of solid ivory.

Very little needs to be added to what was said in the preceding chapter about a fourth current attack on teachers through legislative investigations and subsequent prosecutions for perjury or contempt. The professors put under questioning have not always acted wisely, but those who have not been under fire (as I was years ago) can have no understanding of the mental turmoil it causes to a teacher and the difficulty of keeping one's poise. These cases are striking illustrations of the words of Spinoza:

> Laws directed against opinions affect the generous-minded rather than the wicked, and are adapted less for coercing criminals than for irritating the upright. . . . What greater misfortune for a state than that honourable men should be [treated] like criminals . . . ? [11]

The public has worried far too much about a single objection to professors; it applies at most to only a handful of them, whom the federal government can catch through its own machinery if that be necessary. There are many reasons besides communism which make a professor a poor teacher. Most important of all, the public would do well to think about the kind of professors we do want in a university.

Professors are different from the general run of people. They ought to be different. Most people think in order to take action. Professors ought to think for the sake of thinking.

The real danger to our colleges and universities is not from radical teachers—or conservative teachers—but from uninspiring teachers, men who can't get over the footlights, dispensers of branded canned goods. The greatest need is for teachers who will produce eagerness of spirit among young men and women and the ability to deal in after life with what is around the corner. Such a spirit is best nurtured by a teacher who can have untroubled periods of time when "the wind bloweth where it listeth" and, in the words of Hobbes: "Thoughts run [seeking] as a spaniel ranges in the field, till he finds a scent." Helmholtz, the great scientist, declared on his seventieth birthday: "Happy ideas have never come to me at my working table. They come particularly rapidly during the slow ascent of wooded hills on a sunny day."

Nothing kills such a spirit in a university like a systematic campaign of suppression. Thinking and research stop while everybody discusses the latest investigation or the next. Grief over the dismissal of friends, efforts to protect other friends from being the next victims, trying to raise money to pay lawyers to defend a colleague who is under fire, drafting and redrafting a faculty statement of principles, going to alumni for support, interviewing trustees or regents, fears for one's own prospects, lengthy examination of old letter-files and diaries and account books to disprove alleged affiliations with subversive groups, loss of faith in the educational authorities who are saving themselves by more and more concessions to the foes of freedom—how is an untroubled mind possible any longer? "The quiet and still air of delightful studies" has been transformed into the shouts of the battlefield.

A Czech said after the Communists took over his country: "We must be neither good nor bad, we must be careful." Most unhappy of all are those professors and administrators who keep aloof from the campus conflict and play safe. They become ashamed of themselves for doing nothing to maintain what, in their hearts, they know to be a great principle.

> Because we move
> And breathe, and say a few complacent words
> With tongues that are afraid to say our thoughts,
> We think we are alive. But we are dead.[12]

Thirty years ago I was on the receiving end of an academic investigation for heterodox writing, and I know what a great encouragement it has been to feel absolutely assured that the authorities of Harvard will never dismiss a professor because of his honestly held opinions, whether expressed in or out of the classroom. For the sake of having a university do its special and essential work well, it is worth while to run the risk of whatever injuries may come from a few men on its faculty with objectionable ideas.

The time has come to strike back. Not just individual professors brought under fire and easily picked off like an isolated sentry. They ought not be allowed to feel like the young State Department man in Europe who explained to me why he was resigning. "I haven't been attacked yet, but I know that if I am attacked, not a single person in Washington will raise a finger in my defense." In contrast I thought of what Mr. Lowell told me, after he had warded off the Wall Street lawyers who sought my dismissal: "I had to protect my front."

To presidents, trustees, regents, alumni, I say, "This is your fight."

Despite proper anxieties about future gifts and student enrollments, I believe a university which proclaims its devotion to freedom and lives up to it will attract farsighted givers and young men and women who are worth teaching. It is easy to underestimate the admiration which American citizens feel toward courage.

The issue is whether the unusual man shall be rigidly controlled by the usual men.

No more concessions. We will not bow down in the House of Rimmon. We will not take breakfast in the Schine apartment.

The time has come for the universities of the United States to stop retreating and carry the war into Africa. We ought to educate more than our students. "We must educate our masters"—the legislators and the citizens who in the end make educational institutions possible. We need to persuade them to minimize the dangers of heterodoxy and be ready, as Jefferson was, to take a calculated risk. We need to convince them of what they have forgotten—the importance of intellectual freedom, if we are to have the kind of country most loyal Americans desire. We need to make our fellow-citizens realize that freedom is not safety, but opportunity.

IX   With Full Liberty in Religious Concernments

Fight, and say what you feel; say more than words.
Give men to know that even their days of earth
To come are more than ages that are gone.
Say what you feel, while you have time to say it.
——Saint Paul, in EDWIN ARLINGTON ROBINSON,
The Three Taverns *

High above Providence the statue of Roger Williams looks across to the Capitol of the community he founded, and to the words carved over its portal which proclaim the driving purpose of his life: *To hold forth a lively experiment that a flourishing civil state may stand and be best maintained with a full liberty in religious concernments.*[1]

Not even a Rhode Islander will assert that this ideal originated with Roger Williams and the Charter of 1663. In the square at Rouen where Jeanne d'Arc died in agony and often near other fires, a few thoughtful men and women must have wondered whether it was right to do such things in the name of God who bade us love one another. For example, a hundred years before the Rhode Island Charter, after the Unitarian Michael Servetus had been burned at Geneva under the domination of John Calvin, an obscure Protestant teacher at Basle, Sébastien Castellion, published in 1554 his *Treatise on Heretics*, which declared:

> The time has come to put an end once and for all to this folly that it is necessary to torture and kill men merely because they have other opinions than the powers that be. No, Michael Servetus has not been burned by the will of Christ, but at the order of John Calvin, for Christianity would be sullied by such an act. Killing a man is not upholding a religious principle—it is killing a man.

* Robinson, *Collected Poems* (New York: The Macmillan Company, 1947), p. 469. Copyright by The Macmillan Company, N. Y., and quoted by their permission.

But that is as far as Castellion got. He could write but he could not do anything about it. Indeed, because he objected to this torture of the heretic Servetus, Castellion was immediately accused of being a heretic himself and the only way he escaped being burned at Basle like Servetus at Geneva was dying suddenly of a fever.

In his ideal of soul liberty Roger Williams had precursors, but he was the first to bring this ideal down to earth, even though only to a few hundred square miles around Narragansett Bay. As the patent lawyers say, he reduced the invention to practice. Other men had dreamed of "full liberty in religious concernments." He made the dream work.

His experiment has succeeded beyond his wildest hopes. From a few scattered shacks of hewn logs beside a lonely river, it has spread over a nation of one hundred and sixty millions, spread to England which he left to seek freedom, to most of Western Europe, to newly independent India, and to great islands in the South Pacific which no white man saw until long after Roger Williams died. His experiment is commonplace today, just as the laborious experiments in the transmission of messages without wires, which taxed the genius of Hertz and Marconi, are commonplace to any schoolboy who tinkers with a radio set.

Yet for Roger Williams there was nothing commonplace about his experiment. It was dangerous to him personally, as bitter experience had shown; and, in the opinion of almost all rulers and wise thinkers in 1636, it was sure to ruin any country which was silly enough to try it. And no other government in 1636 had the audacity to make the trial. Roger Williams stood alone in his act of faith then as he stands alone now on the brow of Prospect Terrace.

When he came to Rhode Island Europe was in the midst of the longest and bloodiest of all religious wars. The happy era of toleration which had been begun in France by Henry of Navarre was breaking down in constant struggles between the Huguenots and the Crown, and soon after Williams died, it was to be cruelly ended by the Revocation of the Edict of Nantes. Protestant lands had their own kinds of persecution. Even Holland, where the Pilgrims found refuge, was torn during Roger's boyhood by a bitter religious quarrel in which one of her noblest patriots, John of Barneveldt, was publicly beheaded.

His ideal of "full liberty in religious concernments" was equally alien to England where he was born. John Milton went farthest in his direction when the *Areopagitica* passionately argued for an uncensored press, and yet Milton would have denied freedom of publication to Roman Catholics. The actual English laws, of course, lagged far behind Milton as long as Roger Williams lived. Ever since the beginning of the reign of Queen Elizabeth everybody was debarred from every kind of public office unless he took the Oath of Supremacy, swearing that the sovereign was the only supreme governor in "all spiritual or ecclesiastical things" and that no foreign prelate had any "ecclesiastical or spiritual authority" in England. It was impossible for any honest Roman Catholic to take this oath and it was also repulsive to many loyal Protestants who were not members of the Church of England.

When the dissenting sects came into power during the Civil War, they were just as intolerant as their former adversaries. Before anybody could hold public office or be a teacher, he had to subscribe to the Solemn League and Covenant, in which he swore to endeavor to extirpate "church governments by bishops and whatsoever shall be found contrary to sound doctrine and power of godliness," in addition to a virtual promise to support the cause of Parliament against the Cavaliers.

The tables turned again when Charles II was restored. In 1662, the year before Rhode Island got her Charter, Parliament required every person conducting "public worship" in England to use the Book of Common Prayer. And it obliged every teacher in Oxford and Cambridge and every schoolmaster keeping any public or private school, and every person instructing or teaching in any house or private family as a tutor, to take a new test oath, declaring that he belonged to the Church of England, Bishops and all; that it was "not lawful, upon any pretence whatsoever, to take arms against the King"; and "there lies no obligation upon me or any other person from the Solemn League and Covenant . . . and the same was in itself an unlawful oath. . . ." It was indeed perilous for any Englishman to love to teach in the middle of the Seventeenth Century. Regardless of his mastery of his subject and his ability to prepare his students for life, he was obliged to alter his religious and political beliefs with every shift of power.

Such, when Rhode Island obtained her Charter, was the unhappy situation in England of every Roman Catholic and every Protestant who did not thoroughly approve of all the doctrines and all the practices of the Church of England. But this was not the worst. The English statute-book in 1663 contained an Act of Parliament passed two centuries and a half before in the reign of Henry IV. This bore the cheerful title *De Heretico Comburendo*—For the Burning of Heretics. Stirred up in 1401 against the embryo Protestants called Lollards, Parliament had provided that "no one either openly or secretly shall preach, or teach or impart anything, or compose or write any book, contrary to the Catholic faith or the decisions of Holy Church, or anywhere maintain schools for such nefarious doctrines and opinions," and also that no one should favor anybody who did any of these things. And if any person is convicted before the local Bishop or his delegates of the said nefarious doctrines, opinions, and heretical and erroneous instruction, etc., then he will be turned over to the civil authorities. The sheriff of the local county or the mayor of the nearest town is to receive such persons and "shall have them burned before the people in some prominent place, so that such punishments shall inspire fear in the minds of others and prevent such nefarious doctrines and opinions, or their authors and protagonists from being supported or in any way tolerated against the Catholic faith, the Christian religion and the decisions of Holy Church—which God forbid!"

For more than a century this statute made life uncomfortable for the Lollards and their Protestant successors. Then the Catholics became the underdogs, and discovered that they were imparting "nefarious doctrines . . . contrary to the Catholic faith and the decisions of Holy Church," which was now the Church of England. Eventually Catholic laymen ceased to be in practical danger of death so long as they kept reasonably quiet. No such policy of neglect was extended toward the few audacious persons who were neither good Protestants nor good Catholics. In 1612, when Roger Williams was nine years old, two Unitarians were burned alive under the Act of 1401. During the Puritan Interregnum the milder penalty of hanging was barely escaped by another Unitarian and by a poor mad Quaker who declared that he was God and insisted on making an entry into Bristol in the manner of Palm Sunday. The fiery statute of 1401 was still in force in 1663, when Rhode Island got her Charter.

Fifteen years later, Parliament in a mood of modernism repealed the Statute for the Burning of Heretics. Religious liberty thus scored a signal victory, but in the same year of 1678 hatred of the Roman Catholics burst out more savagely than for a century past.

An ex-Catholic named Titus Oates appeared before legislative investigators and accused prominent Roman Catholics of engaging in a far-flung conspiracy to kill the King and take over the government. There is a familiar ring to the following passage in the old book:

> On October 24th [1678], Titus Oates was examined in the House of Commons six or seven hours, at the end of which he was several times, and with great strictness, interrogated, *Whether he knew anything more of the plot?* He solemnly answered that he did not. But notwithstanding Oates's solemn asseveration of his not knowing any more, he soon began so much to abound with newer discoveries that some began to doubt his veracity.

Several other ex-Catholics then came forward to add corroboration or fresh details to the terrifying history of the Popish Plot. A magistrate, who had taken the affidavit of one of these renegades was found murdered one night in a lonely lane. Even to this day it is a mystery who killed Sir Edmund Berry Godfrey, but the populace of 1678 had no doubts whatever on the subject. The Papists had done it, and nothing was too bad for them. Every Catholic in London was ordered to go ten miles out of the city within a fortnight. No Catholic was allowed to sit in either the House of Commons or the House of Lords. The Prime Minister, a zealous Protestant, was impeached for being "Popishly affected" and concealing the plot. Several Jesuit priests were seized, tried, and put to death. Five Roman Catholic nobles were sent to the Tower, where one of them died and three stayed for five years in fear of trial. The fifth, a poor old Viscount, convicted on the testimony of Oates and other ex-Catholics, was tried and sentenced to be hanged, drawn and quartered; but by the mercy of the House of Commons he was permitted to die "only by having his head severed from his body."

All this perjury and murderous hysteria in the name of religion took place while Roger Williams was still alive, and so did the bloody persecution of Presbyterians in Scotland which Scott pictures in *Old Mortality*.

For this terrible record of European persecutions, every faith must bear the guilt, with a few exceptions like the Quakers. Some killed more because they had bigger opportunities, but every group would justify its actions by saying, "You'ld do this to us if you had the chance." We are all miserable sinners.

Roger Williams was in his grave two hundred years before "full liberty in religious concernments" at last prevailed in England and Scotland and the island immediately to the west.

After the Revolution of 1688, which Churchmen had won with the help of Dissenters, toleration did indeed gradually gain ground. Even the Roman Catholics were left pretty much alone, except for the outbreak of mob violence in London under Lord George Gordon which Dickens narrates in *Barnaby Rudge*. Nevertheless, many legal handicaps were still imposed on those who did not belong to the Established Church. They could not teach or study at Oxford or Cambridge, because they were unwilling to sign the Thirty-nine Articles of faith in the Prayer Book. Neither Catholics nor Jews could sit in Parliament. In 1739 a Jew left money by will to establish a synagogue. One of the ablest of English judges decided that this legacy was illegal because it promoted "a religion contrary to the established one"; and the King then ordered the money turned over to support a Church of England preacher in a home for abandoned children.

In Ireland, as might be expected, the situation of Roman Catholics was far worse. A statute of 1695, which was not repealed until after the battle of Yorktown, enacted:

> That no person whatsoever of the popish religion shall publickly teach school, or instruct youth in learning, or in private houses teach or instruct youth in learning within this realm from henceforth— upon pain of twenty pounds, and also being committed to prison . . . for the space of three months for every such offence.

In the same year Roman Catholics were also forbidden to own a horse worth more than five pounds. In 1782 they did at last get leave to own satisfactory steeds and were also graciously permitted to teach school, so long as they had no Protestant pupils and obtained a license from the local Anglican Bishop, which could be revoked at any time. Even then Roman Catholics were forbidden to erect or endow any university or college or to have any endowed school in Ireland.

In the Nineteenth Century and long after our own First Amendment was adopted, the ideal of Roger Williams was gradually realized in the land of his birth. Parliament admitted Catholics in 1829 and Jews in 1858. The final step did not come until my own lifetime. In 1886, after a tremendous struggle, an agnostic succeeded in taking the seat in the House of Commons to which he had been elected three times.

In the American colonies and the ensuing United States, religious freedom came a good deal faster, and yet obstacles lingered longer than we usually appreciate.

When Williams was expelled from Massachusetts in 1635 for asserting, among other things, "that the civil power of a state could have no jurisdiction over the consciences of men," and founded his new settlement the following spring with a view to its becoming "a shelter for persons distressed for conscience," no such ideals were embodied in law in any other colony. This was still true in 1647, when the Rhode Island Code provided: "Otherwise than what is . . . herein forbidden [breaches of the peace, etc.], all men may walk as their consciences persuade them, every one in the name of God."

The first grant of power to colonize in America, given to Sir Humphrey Gilbert in 1578, declared that any laws made should not be "against the true Christian faith or religion now professed in the church of England," which (if he had ever settled anywhere) might have made trouble for Roman Catholics and Dissenters. The Virginia Charter of 1609 required all settlers to take the Oath of Supremacy (already described) before leaving England, in order to prevent any persons affected with the superstitions of Rome from passing to the colony. The Patent to the Council of New England in 1620, under which the Pilgrims came over, had similar language; and the later Plymouth Patent from the Council declared the colony to be "a pious worke which may especially tend to the propagation of religion and the great increase of trade to his Majesty's realmes." In the Massachusetts Bay Charter, there is nothing on religion, oddly enough in view of the immediate theocracy in Salem and Boston, except a statement that the conversion of the Indians was the principal purpose of the settlement. The Dutch grant of New York in the same year contemplates something like an established church when it directs the patroons and colonists "to endeavor to find out ways and means whereby they may support a Minister and Schoolmaster, that thus the service of God and zeal for religion may not grow cool and be neglected among them." The early articles of association among the inhabitants of Connecticut merge religious and political affairs completely in their plans for "settling civill government according to God," and like the Massachusetts statutes limit voters and officeholders to church members. By 1641 the Massachusetts legislature was regulating the establishment of new churches and taking from the Bible a list of capital crimes, which condemns to death those who "have or worship any other god, but the lord god. . . ." In 1643 the New England colonies formed the New England Confederation, from which Rhode Island was purposely left out, and declared:

> we all came into these parts of America, with one and the same end and ayme, namely, to advance the Kingdom of our Lord Jesus Christ, and to enjoy the liberties of the Gospel, in purity with peace. . . .

Maryland, founded by Roman Catholics and desirous of attracting Protestant settlers as well, was more tolerant, but less so than Rhode Island. The Maryland Charter of 1632 makes no reference to soul liberty, and gives no indication whatever of its undoubted purpose of providing a new home for many Englishmen who certainly did not belong to the Established Church. It does speak of Lord Baltimore's "being animated with a laudable and pious zeal for extending the Christian Religion and also the Territories of our Empire," and mentions the conversion of savages; and then it goes on to give Baltimore power to erect churches, which are to be "consecrated according to the ecclesiastical laws of England," which would definitely forbid a Roman Catholic place of worship. Maryland's great achievement came later in the colony's Toleration Act of 1649. This declares that

> No person professing to believe in Jesus Christ shall from hence-forth bee any waies troubled . . . in respect of his or her religion nor in the free exercise thereof. . . .

Here is liberty of worship for all except Unitarians, atheists, etc., but nothing to prevent the use of public revenues for the support of a particular church. In fact, Virginian influence eventually established the Church of England over the Maryland line.

The Rhode Island Charter set a new pace. Although the later documents from the King and Proprietors never quite caught up with it, they did repeatedly insert liberal provisions on behalf of those who were prevented by conscience from conforming to the ceremonies of the Church of England. Thus the proprietary grant in 1677 to West Jersey, a Quaker region, stated "That no men, nor number of men upon earth, hath power or authority to rule over men's consciences in religious matters . . ." and went on to assure the free exercise of religious worship. Just why authorities who could be so intolerant in England, Scotland, and Ireland were so liberal overseas is one of the most fascinating problems of history, but so it was.[2]

Nevertheless, freedom of religion usually had a string to it. The royal instructions of William III in 1692 to a new Governor of New York, Fletcher, directed: "And you are to permit a liberty of conscience to all persons, *except papists* . . ." Even William Penn, in giving Pennsylvania its Charter of 1701, which lasted till the Revolution, limited freedom from molestation to persons "who shall confess One almighty God, the Creator, Upholder and Ruler of the World . . . ," thus excluding Deists and freethinkers. The last colonial charter, from George II to Georgia in 1732, provided for "a liberty of conscience allowed in the worship of God, to all persons . . . and that all such persons, *except papists*, shall have a free exercise of their religion. . . ."

I am reminded of what Oliver Cromwell said while he was besieging a town in Ireland. This Catholic community offered to surrender upon the sole condition of freedom of conscience. Years earlier Cromwell had declared, "All that believe have the real unity, which is most glorious because inward and spiritual." Yet now Cromwell replied:

> As to freedom of conscience, I meddle with no man's conscience; but if you mean by that, liberty to celebrate the mass, I would have you understand that in no place where the power of the Parliament of England prevails shall that be permitted.

Liberalized by felling trees and building log-cabins with men of many different faiths, the colonists outside Rhode Island had gradually come to believe in liberty for most beliefs, but not yet for those which were detested or strange to them. But not for Roman Catholics, but not for atheists, but not for Unitarians. "I believe in religious freedom, but—"

For Roger Williams there was no "but." He welcomed the Jews to Newport and gave the Quakers a refuge from being hanged in Boston, even though he disagreed so strongly with their views that he rowed down the whole of Narragansett Bay to persuade them of their errors. No doubt he would have given hospitality to Catholics as well, if any of them had come. It was in his spirit that, when the first factories were built in Bristol and the workmen from Ireland and Italy had as yet no place of worship, the rector of the Episcopal church invited a priest to use his altar for saying mass.

After Independence the constitutions adopted by all the new states, except Rhode Island and Connecticut, give constant recognition to freedom of worship. And yet the "buts" are there. Liberty to go to one's own church or no church at all without penalties was a great gain accomplished, but not enough if the unmolested worshiper was disqualified from public office or obligated to pay money for the support of a faith which he did not share. In Virginia, South Carolina, and Massachusetts the constitutions allowed support of a particular church from the public revenues, and New Hampshire gave similar help to Protestant ministers and religious teachers generally. Delaware, North Carolina, and Pennsylvania imposed religious tests on officeholders.

Even as late as 1790, the Pennylvania Constitution recognized only a person, "who acknowledges the being of a God, and a future

state of rewards and punishments. . . ." Roger Williams had wiped
the slate clean, and the first state to follow his example was Virginia
in 1785. Her Act for Establishing Religious Freedom, which
Thomas Jefferson regarded, on his tombstone, as a greater achievement than being President of the United States, declared in part:

> WHEREAS Almighty God hath created the mind free; that all at-
> tempts to influence it by temporal punishments or burthens, or by
> civil incapacitations, tend only to beget habits of hypocrisy and mean-
> ness, . . . that it tends only to corrupt the principles of that religion
> it is meant to encourage, by bribing with a monopoly of worldly
> honours and emoluments, those who will externally profess and con-
> form to it; . . . that to suffer the civil magistrate to intrude his
> powers into the field of opinion, and to restrain the profession or
> propagation of principles on supposition of their ill tendency, is a
> dangerous fallacy, which at once destroys all religious liberty, because
> he being of course judge of that tendency will make his opinions the
> rule of judgment, and approve or condemn the sentiments of others
> only as they shall square with or differ from his own; that it is
> time enough for the rightful purposes of civil government, for its
> officers to interfere when principles break out into overt acts against
> peace and good order; and finally, that truth is great and will prevail
> if left to herself, that she is the proper and sufficient antagonist to
> error, and has nothing to fear from the conflict, unless by human
> interposition disarmed of her natural weapons, free argument and
> debate, errors ceasing to be dangerous when it is permitted freely
> to contradict them. . . .

These principles of Jefferson's were, with the energetic help of
James Madison, written into the United States Constitution. That
instrument makes no mention of God. The oath prescribed for the
President is very different from the usual officeholder's oath of the
Eighteenth Century in England or America, and the last operative
clause in the original Constitution forbids religious tests for other
officers of the United States. In 1791 the First Amendment began:
"Congress shall make no law respecting an establishment of religion
or prohibiting the free exercise thereof. . . ."

The work of Roger Williams was nearly complete, but not quite.
Only the national government was as yet dedicated to the separation

of Church and State. Any of the states were still free to have an established church, and Massachusetts and Connecticut kept theirs until after the Nineteenth Century had begun. Any state could, if it wished, impose all sorts of restrictions on liberty of worship, although fortunately none of them did so, and minor restrictions on heterodoxy were gradually removed, such as the inability of atheists to testify in court. Still, the possibility of state interference with religious freedom continued until 1940, when the Supreme Court first held that religious liberty was part of the "liberty" of which, according to the Fourteenth Amendment of 1868, no person can be arbitrarily and unreasonably deprived by a state.[3] And the total application of the First Amendment to the states was finished only nine years ago, when the Court decided that it would also be an unconstitutional deprivation of "liberty" for a state in a sense to have "an establishment of religion" by using the money of taxpayers for what the Court considered religious purposes.[4]

We of Rhode Island should not take any credit to ourselves for this ultimate victory of the noble ideal in our Charter. It would be hard to prove that most inhabitants of this colony and state had been by nature more tolerant than those in neighboring communities. We were simply magnificently fortunate that our founder was Roger Williams. With a different sort of beginning, we might have been as other men were.

It is also wise to remember that the ideal of Roger Williams was not the only possible noble ideal for a state. Other men of high character have dreamed of a state founded on religious unity where this unity formed an integral part of its laws and administration, where the church and the government would be, as it were, two sides of the same shield. The Puritans cherished such an ideal and through it, despite all their faults, they achieved a cohesiveness which was long lacking in Rhode Island. In a way Rhode Island paid a high price for Roger Williams. For example, many of its towns, instead of being closely knit communities of men with a common purpose, were only geographical areas. In Massachusetts, practically every township has a central village of the same name, but in Rhode Island there is no village named Gloucester in Gloucester, no village named Exeter in Exeter, etc. I question whether

thoughtful voters in Massachusetts would have complacently ac-
quiesced for decades in the very limited suffrage which, in Rhode
Island, preceded the Dorr War. The separatism which made religious liberty possible renders political achievement very difficult.

As an example of this other noble ideal, I recall that one of the
main reasons why the university in which I teach was founded out
of public revenues was to provide a theological seminary. Compare
with the words on the Rhode Island State House this inscription on
the principal gate of Harvard:

> After God had carried us safe to New England and wee had
> builded our houses, provided necessities for our livelihood, reard
> convenient places for God's worship, and settled the civill govern-
> ment, one of the next things we longed for and looked after was to
> advance learning and perpetuate it to posterity dreading to leave
> an illiterate Ministry to the churches when our present ministers
> shall lie in the dust.

This same noble ideal had a wider expression in the third article
of the Massachusetts Declaration of Rights of 1780:

> As the happiness of a people, and the good order and preservation
> of civil government, essentially depend upon piety, religion, and
> morality; and as these cannot be generally diffused through a com-
> munity, but by the institution of the public worship of God, and of
> public instructions in piety, religion, and morality:— Therefore
> to promote their happiness, and to secure the good order and
> preservation of their government, the people of this common-
> wealth have a right to invest their legislature with power to author-
> ise and require, and the legislature shall, from time to time, authorise
> and require the several towns, parishes, precincts, and other bodies
> politic, or religious societies, to make suitable provision, at their own
> expence for the institution of the public worship of God, and for
> the support and maintenance of public protestant teachers of piety,
> religion, and morality, in all cases, where such provision shall not
> be made voluntarily.

This article has long been gone from the Constitution of the Commonwealth of Massachusetts, and I assume that nobody would willingly revive its full form. We have made our choice and chosen
the dream of Roger Williams. It was not a choice between a good
dream and a bad dream, but between a good dream which on the

whole works and a good dream which occasionally turned into the nightmare of the burning of Servetus in Geneva and the hanging of Mary Dyer on Boston Common. Sometimes nostalgia for what we have given up creeps over us. Men sometimes lament, for instance, that our public schools are godless. Suppose we admit frankly that this is a loss to the public schools, that one very important part of our nature has to be wholly neglected in the place where we receive much of the shaping of our characters and minds. It is a price to pay, but we must look at all which we have bought thereby. We cannot reject a portion of the bargain and insist on keeping the rest. If the noble ideal of the Puritans had persisted, there would be no godless schools in Massachusetts and there would be nobody in her churches except Congregationalists. Through the choice which all of the United States has made, it becomes possible for men of many different faiths to live and work together for many noble ends without allowing their divisions in spiritual matters to become, as in the old days, unbridgeable chasms running through every aspect of human lives.

One thought more. The framers of the First Amendment did not limit freedom of the spirit to our convictions on supernatural concerns. In the rest of the First Amendment they extended the freedom of the spirit to cover the speculations and expressions of men on other affairs which are of intense concern. Here, too, the unobtainable ideal of an enforced unity presents great dangers. No heterodox economic or political views on the part of our citizens are so perilous to us as stuffed shirts, men who are not able to think or do not dare to think. The ideal of Roger Williams is not an ideal for religious concernments alone. It is continued for the America of today by the thought which Justice Robert Jackson uttered:

> Our forefathers found the evils of free thinking more to be endured than the evils of inquest or suppression. . . . I cannot believe that they left open a way for legislation to embarrass or impede the mere intellectual processes by which those expressions of belief are examined and formulated. This is not only because individual thinking presents no danger to society, but because thoughtful, bold and independent minds are essential to wise and considered self-government.[5]

X Strengthening Liberty in All Countries

Then, with new vision of unwonted scope,
They lifted up their eyes to the hills of hope.
——MARK ANTONY DeWOLFE HOWE, *The Known
Soldier* (For the Day of Woodrow Wilson's Burial) *

For the first time in history, a serious endeavor is actively going forward to safeguard the basic liberties of men and women everywhere inside their own countries. The International Covenant on Human Rights, now getting drafted in the United Nations, will obligate the governments which sign it to protect the fundamental freedoms of their own citizens, as well as foreigners within their borders.[1] The hope is that all nations will eventually become parties to the Covenant.

This is a long-time task which raises many difficult problems. The present chapter will discuss a few of them, both on account of the importance of the Covenant itself and because they throw a good deal of light on the nature of freedom in our own country, on the extent to which it can be effectively promoted by law, on the question of what limitations of freedom are desirable.

Revolutionary as the project of the Covenant appears, it is the outcome of much experience. Since the close of the First World War, many nations have made agreements for the control of internal situations causing grave harm abroad. Take two examples: Countries producing opium have signed treaties which set up limitations and supervision upon the amount of poppies grown within their borders. The International Labor Office at Geneva has during many years brought about Conventions whereby many governments promise to make specific improvements in labor conditions within their borders. Opium and goods produced on starvation wages can be exported, so other countries have a reasonable interest in their regulation.

* Howe, *Sundown* (Boston: Little Brown & Company, 1955), p. 61.

Tyranny can be exported too. Witness the fate of Austria in 1938, and the double doom of Czechoslovakia in 1939 and 1948. A despot is inclined to overrun his frontiers. Moreover, he supplies an example for others to copy; Hitler and then Franco imitated Mussolini. Fortunately, freedom can also be exported. Religious toleration in Holland influenced the colonization of Plymouth and the eventual establishment of religious liberty in England. South American countries became republics in imitation of us. Canada acquired self-government because the British had the sense to profit by what had happened in the United States. The provision of Article IV of our own Constitution, "The United States shall guarantee to every State in this Union a Republican Form of Government, . . ." confirms the proposition that any free state is deeply concerned in having free neighbors.

Moreover, infringements on human rights inside a country are a potent cause of international hostility, which may ripen into war. As far back as 1898, our war with Spain was primarily due, not to the sinking of the *Maine*, but to the bad treatment given by the Spanish government in Cuba to its own subjects. There could hardly be a better demonstration that no nation lives to itself alone.

Everybody recognizes that a treaty can obligate one government to protect aliens who have come into its territory from the other nation. The people of any nation are concerned in the welfare of their fellow-citizens in another land. But other bonds besides a common nationality create an acute interest in human rights inside a country. Roman Catholics in New York lament the plight of Roman Catholics in Warsaw. Milton, a Protestant in England, wrote a sonnet "On the Late Massacre in Piedmont." Professors in Amsterdam passed a resolution condemning the treatment of professors in Nazi Germany, and their action was indorsed by professors in American universities. Trade unionists in any country are anxious to promote the welfare of trade unionists in other countries.

Out of such lessons from history, especially from the terrible years after Hitler attained power in 1933, came the provision of the Atlantic Charter, which President Roosevelt and Prime Minister Churchill signed at Newfoundland four months before we entered the Second World War:

Sixth, after the final destruction of the Nazi tyranny, they hope to see established a peace . . . which will afford assurance that *all the men in all the lands may live out their lives in freedom from fear and want. . . .*[2]

In the Declaration by United Nations, issued on New Year's Day, 1942, soon after Pearl Harbor, the countries engaged in the struggle for victory over Hitlerism subscribed to the purposes and principles of the Atlantic Charter.[3] Even two years before this, the State Department had begun discussions of what Mr. Roosevelt called "the kind of peace that will lighten the troubles of the world." Now, at his request, Secretary of State Cordell Hull set up a thorough organization on Post-war Foreign Policy, comprising members of Congress and qualified private citizens as well as his own officials. This group soon envisaged the creation of a permanent "United Nations Authority" and then steadily developed plans which culminated in the San Francisco Conference.[4] As early as March 14, 1942, consideration was given to the problems of a possible bill of human rights; and before the year ended a careful draft for this was completed, which anticipates the Draft Covenant in important respects.[5] In August 1943, ten staff officers drew up a proposed "Charter of the United Nations," with a clause in which the member nations agreed "to give legislative effect to the Declaration of Human Rights annexed to this Charter."[6]

Eventually, it was decided that the Charter, unlike our Constitution since 1791, should not contain a Bill of Rights.[7] Instead of bothering the San Francisco Conference with this difficult job on top of its many pressing tasks, the Department began preparing broad provisions to go into the Charter on the protection of human rights. In addition, UN machinery would be set up to hammer out the desired fundamental document without being rushed.[8] It is unnecessary to review the hard work which was done by our officials and our delegates to the Conference in order to get the essential elements of this new plan ready for consideration at San Francisco.[9] A brief statement went into the Dumbarton Oaks Proposals, that the Organization should "promote respect for human rights and fundamental freedoms."[10] The important changes and expansions of this clause at San Francisco were either suggested by the United States Delegation or embodied in the amendments which were jointly proposed by the governments of the United States, United Kingdom, Soviet Union, and China, after ten days of consultation.[11]

As a result of all this work by American citizens in and out of the government, the Charter contains at least seven specific references to human rights.[12] The most important is in Article 55:

> With a view to the creation of conditions of stability and well-being which are necessary for peaceful and friendly relations among nations based on respect for the principle of equal rights and self-determination of peoples, the United Nations shall promote: . . .
>
> c. universal respect for, and observance of, human rights and fundamental freedoms for all without distinction as to race, sex, language, or religion.

In Article 56 all members pledge themselves to take joint and separate action in co-operation with the Organization to achieve the purpose set forth above. And Article 68 orders the establishment of a commission "for the promotion of human rights"—the only body below the Councils which is specifically mentioned in the Charter, aside from the Military Staff Committee.

Secretary of State Stettinius, the chairman of our delegation,[13] reported to the President about all these human rights provisions: [14]

> Finally, no sure foundation of lasting peace and security can be laid which does not rest on the voluntary association of free peoples. Only so far as the rights and dignity of all men are respected and protected, only so far as men have free access to information, assurance of free speech and free assembly, freedom from discrimination on grounds of race, sex, language, or religion and other fundamental rights and freedoms, will men insist upon the right to live at peace, to compose such differences as they may have by peaceful methods, and to be guided by reason and good-will rather than driven by prejudice and resentment. The United States, as a nation which takes pride in its free institutions, is particularly interested in the promotion, through international means, of human rights throughout the world. . . .
>
> In no part of the deliberations of the Conference was greater interest displayed by the group of American consultants, representing forty-two leading American organizations and groups concerned

with American foreign relations [including the American Bar Association [15]] than in the opportunity afforded to extend the enjoyment of human rights and basic freedoms to all peoples. They warmly endorsed the additions to the statement of objectives. Beyond this they urged that the Charter itself should provide for adequate machinery to further these objectives. A direct outgrowth of discussions between the United States Delegation and the consultants was the proposal . . . to provide for a commission on human rights. . . .

The unanimous acceptance of this proposal may well prove one of the most important and significant achievements of the San Francisco Conference. . . . [The] commission on human rights will have the opportunity to work out an international bill of rights which can be submitted to member nations with a view to incorporation in their fundamental law, just as there is a Bill of Rights in the American Constitution.

Thus the Covenant began in the minds of numerous fellow-citizens of ours and they drew its main outlines.[16] That, of course, does not affect the merits or demerits of the way UN delegates from many countries, including our own, have subsequently formulated some particular right or handled a perplexing matter, almost always with the approval of the United States government. There are differences of opinion about such questions of detail, but the events just narrated make one thing plain. The idea of the Covenant and its general scheme are as American as apple pie.

When many bright hopes of 1945 were growing dim, our country abandoned the leadership in the field of human rights which we had held since the Atlantic Charter. The present Secretary of State told Congress in 1953 that the United States would not sign the Covenant.[17] Nobody had asked us to sign it, and years of redrafting were still ahead before it reached final form. Evidently the removal of all American objections on specific points would make no difference. Mr. Dulles intended to repudiate everything his predecessors had done to bring about a treaty of just this kind on behalf of fundamental freedoms.

Yet this loss of faith does not render the problems of the Covenant meaningless. Never is a long day. Far greater changes in American foreign policy have taken place than would be involved in our reappearance at the forefront of the endeavor to strengthen liberty in all countries. And no matter how long our government remains aloof, private citizens here can, through thinking and discussion, help to bring about eventually a wise and workable treaty on behalf of those human rights which can be effectively protected by international action.

Moreover, the ultimatum may not have been a decision on the merits of the Covenant. It was issued at a time when widespread misconceptions of that proposed UN treaty were all mixed up with a strong demand for the Bricker Amendment to cut down the constitutional power of the nation to enforce treaties.[18] That dangerous proposal would impair the ability of our government to make and carry out all sorts of international agreements which have nothing to do with human rights. These are essential for the North Atlantic Treaty Organization, reciprocal commercial privileges, and other vital matters. So perhaps the Administration felt that it was good practical politics to throw the Covenant like a baby to the wolves in order to save the Constitution from being mangled. Once the Bricker Amendment is out of the running, the government will be more likely to revive interest in the Covenant, especially if popular misconceptions about it have been counteracted by discussion. They will tend to dwindle away if American citizens can be persuaded to look with open eyes at what the Draft Covenant is actually trying to accomplish, and not at what its bitter enemies say about it.

> If hopes were dupes, fears may be liars;
> It may be, in yon smoke conceal'd,
> Your comrades chase e'en now the fliers,
> And, but for you, possess the field.

The really important thing is for the United Nations to take a great deal of time before completing the Covenant. Despite the fact that in the autumn of 1955 the Human Rights Commission regards its work as finished and the provisions are undergoing revision in the Assembly, I believe that it would be a bad mistake for the Assembly to open the Covenant for signatures until several years hence. The wisest course would be for all UN bodies to take the Covenant off the agenda and lay it on the table until 1958 at the earliest.

In the first place, so long as the Covenant lacks the prestige of support from the United States, the largest freedom-loving country, it will limp along like an automobile with one cylinder missing.

Moreover, even if the United States were willing to sign, such a postponement would be desirable. It is too soon for the Covenant to do much good. An international guaranty of human rights cannot work with the effectiveness of law during the present troublous period of settling down after the most devastating war in history. Already the promises to protect fundamental freedoms, which were made in 1947 by Rumania, Bulgaria, and Hungary in their peace treaties,[19] have been badly broken. This shows the futility of such international obligations unless they are to be performed in a more orderly world than now exists. The Covenant is for the better years ahead.

Thus there is no need whatever for speed. Why not take advantage of the fact that there is plenty of time? Recognize frankly that the present text is unsatisfactory, and then take a long vacation from detailed work on the Covenant. That will probably give the world a better treaty in the end. The document has reached the stage where what is required is not more drafting and revising, but more thinking at large. Writers often find themselves imprisoned inside the pages they have already produced. The only thing to do then is to burst out of the cell into the open air for a while; on returning, everything looks differently. Horace knew this when he advised poets to lay their verses aside for nine years. Without any such long wait as that, a substantial postponement of the Covenant would give a fruitful opportunity to get away from words and phrases and ask some basic questions all over again about how far we can really expect that human rights inside nations will be made safe by international efforts. Some of the answers which those questions received when the Commission began its work may not seem so sound as they did then, because bitter experiences since 1946 have brought about a clearer understanding of the difficulties of turning aspirations into law. During the suggested long vacation, hard thinking about main problems can be carried on, not only by UN delegates and government officials, but also by forward-looking men and women in all countries, including our own.

After this long vacation, the Human Rights Commission would

be able to look at the whole enterprise with fresh minds. This might make the Commission feel in 1958 that some provisions it had approved before 1955 ought to be eliminated as undesirable. One such possibility will be considered in my Problem 1, later in this chapter. And surely it was a bad blunder for recent drafts like the text now before the Assembly to tangle up fundamental freedoms with political rights.[20] This is like block-booking in the movies. A nation might be persuaded to comply with decent standards of administering justice and to respect those spiritual and intellectual liberties which have been cherished for centuries, but now it will not be able to agree to do so without also obligating itself to subject its own system of government to international control. For example, it must promise to introduce universal suffrage, which, although it may be desirable for a country to adopt voluntarily, cannot be classed as a fundamental human right; it did not exist in Great Britain or most of the United States until after the First World War. France and Switzerland are leaders in civil rights, but they might not sign a treaty obliging them to give women the vote. There might be a reasonable chance of getting habeas corpus and the elements of a fair trial established in several Oriental countries, if they did not have to take them in the same package with representative government and periodic elections. For years the Commission was doing a practical sensible job which had real possibilities of success. Of late, however, its members have lost the sense of what things are possible. By attempting to do almost everything at once, they are likely to get nearly nothing. Men who spend their working hours in glowing fantasies, had better knock off and take a rest-cure.

The Americans who conceived the Covenant started an important enterprise. They knew, as Secretary Stettinius said, that "freedoms cannot be attained by declarations and resolutions alone. Hard work extending over many years will be necessary, and long-range planning." [21] The two main tasks are to write a treaty which many nations will sign, and to have its promises carried out after they are made. Neither task can succeed until the Commission changes its attitude and the world becomes more peaceful. Thinking about the Covenant needs to go on, but it is too dark now for any more intensive work. There is no hurry. We ought to put off this important enterprise till we get clear weather.

Some people will think these cogitations about an unfinished UN document a waste of time, because (so they keep telling us) the United Nations is dying if not already dead, and the causes of death were evident at its birth to anybody with common sense. It was always just a lot of talk anyway. Lake Success could never have succeeded. The only way to preserve our freedoms is by battalions, not ballots. Nobody can say at the moment that these prophets of doom are mistaken, but I find it encouraging to read what wiser thinkers than they wrote early in our Civil War about the rapidly approaching death of the Constitution of the United States. That, too, was a great endeavor to bind men together despite the disrupting force of separate sovereignties. While it was undergoing terrific strains like the Charter of the United Nations today, Walter Bagehot wrote in October 1861:

> It will be easy to show that the Constitution of the United States is now failing from the necessary consequences of an inherent ineradicable defect. Such an institution is only adapted to circumstances exceptionally favourable. Each State is in some sense a centre of disunion. The Supreme Court was excellent upon minor points; it has been useless upon the greatest. What worse method of electing a ruler [the President] could by possibility have been selected? It almost always insures the selection of untrained and unknown mediocrity. Under the American Constitution, there was no opportunity for a great statesman.
>
> The steadily augmenting power of the lower orders in America has naturally augmented the dangers of their Federal Union. It places the entire control of the political action of the whole State in the hands of the common labourers, who are of all classes the least instructed. The American Union will fall, if it does fall, little regretted. The American Constitution was, in its very essence, framed upon an erroneous principle. They left the sovereign people, sovereign still.[22]

Bagehot did not foresee Gettysburg or the Gettysburg Address.

Even if our hopes are dashed by the dissolution of the United Nations, some fresh organization of many countries is bound to emerge in its place. The shrinkage in transportation and communications, the linkage of interests of diverse peoples, will continue to exert powerful pressures against any lasting return to the international anarchy of disconnected governments which existed before 1914. When the new unification comes, whether it be world-wide or limited to freedom-loving nations, then problems are certain to revive how best to protect human rights internationally. Of course, the problems may not take exactly the same form under different conditions of union, but they will be there in essence just the same.

THE UNIVERSAL DECLARATION OF HUMAN RIGHTS AND THE DRAFT COVENANT

In order to make clear the problems of the Covenant, something must be said about its general scope and its relation to the other activities of the Human Rights Commission.

The Commission comprises one representative from each of eighteen different nations, always including the United States and the other four great powers. Its first chairman, who headed the work on the Covenant through several sessions, was Mrs. Eleanor Roosevelt. A prominent American lawyer considers the Covenant dangerous because Mrs. Roosevelt is not a lawyer, and all the other members of the Commission were, surprisingly, foreigners.[23] Anybody who took the trouble to visit a session of the Commission would see at least one lawyer from the State Department constantly at hand behind Mrs. Roosevelt's chair. And every word in every draft of every article of the Covenant has been gone over with a fine-tooth comb in Washington by several government lawyers. What Mrs. Roosevelt contributed to the Human Rights Commission were qualities very few lawyers possess. She has vision and imagination. She has an eager desire to do her part in bringing about a better world without sacrificing a single vital American interest.

The main task given the Commission by its UN superiors was to draft an International Bill of Rights. Almost at once the Commission decided to split this task into two documents: a short declaration of principles, and an elaborate treaty or covenant enforcing those principles so far as practicable.

The Universal Declaration of Human Rights [24] would not be

binding as law but would present the main ideals of human rights and freedoms in order to inspire everybody, whether in or out of governments, to work for their progressive realization. The best analogy, suggested by Arthur Holcombe,[25] is to the phrases Jefferson and his associates put into the Declaration of Independence—"all men are created equal," "certain unalienable rights . . . among these are life, liberty and the pursuit of happiness." As Lincoln said:

> They meant simply to declare the right, so that enforcement of it might follow as fast as circumstances should permit. They meant to set up a standard maxim for free society, which should be familiar to all, and revered by all; constantly looked to, constantly labored for, and even though never perfectly attained, constantly approximated. . . .[26]

The Commission finished the Declaration and it was promulgated by the UN Assembly on December 10, 1948. Two of its characteristics need to be kept in mind because of their importance for the present discussion of the Covenant. *First*, the Declaration presents the "rights" (ideals or aspirations) in absolute terms. For example, the "right" to life has no qualifications recognizing that killing is allowable in self-defense, in execution for very serious crime, or in warfare. *Second*, the range of "rights" is much wider than in the long familiar fundamental documents in Western civilization, such as the United States Constitution, our state constitutions, and the French *Déclaration des Droits de l'Homme et du Citoyen* of 1789. Almost all the rights safeguarded by our Constitution [27] are in the UN Declaration. In addition, it contains what may conveniently be called "social and economic rights"—to adequate food, clothing and housing; to education; to social security and unemployment relief; to health and medical care; to rest and leisure and sharing the cultural life of the community.

The second document planned by the Commission was a Covenant, which would bind the nations which signed it to carry out, by their own laws, some of the ideals in the Declaration. Such a treaty would necessarily concern the relations between each signatory government and its own citizens, but this would not be inconsistent with the paragraph of the UN Charter which says: [28]

> Nothing contained in the present Charter shall authorize the United Nations to intervene in matters which are essentially within the jurisdiction of any state. . . .

A nation can always consent by a treaty to abrogate a portion of its sovereignty. The outstanding example of the domestic jurisdiction has always been the regulation of immigration into a country. Yet a treaty by the United States with Italy about the immigration of Italians is plainly valid under both our Constitution and international law. This article in the Charter refers merely to what the United Nations can do of its own accord, in the way of issuing orders to nations and putting them on the carpet. Of course, it does not wipe out the long practice of nations to make treaties which affect laws inside their territories, e.g., inheritance of local land by or from aliens, the right of aliens to engage in business, establishment of special courts for aliens, etc. In recent peace treaties, already mentioned, several nations promise to maintain freedom of religion and speech for everybody within their borders.[29] Furthermore, the Charter expressly enables the United Nations to initiate treaties on human rights and to act as a clearinghouse for every sort of treaty; and its agencies can be utilized to assist in the administration of treaties by the consent of the parties which sign them.[30]

The Covenant may be in the throes of drafting for some time yet, so I shall ignore all questions about the phrasing used in any particular past draft. The main outlines have been sufficiently established to raise the problems I shall discuss about what an international treaty on fundamental freedoms may wisely seek to accomplish.

The Draft Covenant, looked at in the large, differs from the Declaration in two important ways: *First,* this proposed treaty necessarily avoids absolutist definitions and states each right with careful qualifications. No nation would ratify the Covenant if the right to life wiped out the privilege of self-defense and if freedom of speech and press turned every libel action into a breach of international good faith.[31] *Second,* except in one draft several years ago,[32] the Covenant omits the social and economic rights and confines the promised legal protection to long-recognized liberties.

The Covenant is framed as a treaty among many nations, by which each signer is to promise all the others that legislation will be enacted [33] and other specified legal steps taken toward assuring the various fundamental rights described in the body of the document to all persons inside its territory, without any distinctions based on race, color, sex, or religion. These rights are to be enjoyed at least to the extent of the minimum standards set forth. But any nation may always go *above* the minimum standard if it wishes. The Covenant is to contain a provision emphatically stating that it must not be interpreted to reduce the rights and freedoms inside a nation which signs it.[34] Therefore, the Covenant will leave any nation completely at liberty to have a constitution and laws which give more freedom than its international standard requires. But it must not give less.

For the most part, the rights chosen for protection in the various drafts of the Covenant correspond pretty closely to those mentioned in the United States Constitution and our state constitutions,[35] *e.g.*, life, habeas corpus, various aspects of a fair trial, immunity from *ex post facto* laws, and freedom of religion, speech, press, and assembly. Jury trial is inevitably left out since many countries in the United Nations do not have this institution of ours. A more controversial problem, considered later, is raised by the failure of the Covenant to say anything about property rights. Another problem, at the opposite extreme, is whether the Covenant includes more of our traditional rights than is desirable.

In one important respect, the Covenant goes beyond our national and state constitutions. It promises to protect the enumerated rights, not only against national, state, and local governments, but also against violations by private citizens. Thus it differs from our Due Process Clauses in the Fifth and Fourteenth Amendments; but memory of Nazi gangs in Germany before Hitler got office and in neighboring countries before he invaded them is a persuasive argument for this extension.[36]

Each of several articles in the body of the Covenant takes up a single human right (or a group of human rights) and tells what, in this particular respect, each nation promises other nations that it will assure to all individuals within its territory. Various aspects of several rights are elaborated and almost every definition is accompanied by a description of laws which a signatory nation may have if it wishes, without breaking international good faith. Such qualifications are, as I have already pointed out, indispensable. The draftsmen of the permissive limitations have taken care and assiduously kept in mind the type of restrictions on basic rights which have been customarily recognized as necessary by a good many freedom-loving countries. Of course, in framing minimum standards for twenty or more nations, it is impossible to make an article embody the exact law of any single country. Lord Ellenborough's famous question comes to mind: [37] "Can the island of Tobago pass a law to bind the rights of the whole world?" Furthermore, conditions of public safety, economic stability, and popular attitudes vary considerably among the potential signatories of the Covenant, and a nation like ours may be able to afford a much larger amount of freedom than some other governments. Hence the wisest course is to do what the Covenant does—set minimum standards which all nations can fairly be asked and expected to attain, while leaving any nation completely at liberty to go as far above these standards as its people may desire.

An important problem, to be taken up soon in this chapter, is whether the various rights ought to remain in full force during grave emergencies or be sacrificed to some extent.

After the articles on substantive rights will come provisions establishing machinery for dealing with possible breaches of the international promise to protect these rights. I shall speak again of this problem of enforcement. Finally, several articles will have to deal with general matters like how the Covenant is to be signed, that twenty nations must sign before it is to take effect, how it is to be amended, and the special situations of federal nations like ours and of nations with colonies like Great Britain and France.

The document I have just outlined presents many difficult problems. Some concern the way the Covenant fits into our own constitutional and federal system. I have fully discussed those questions elsewhere,[38] and they are not immediately pressing in view of the current indifference of our government to this enterprise. So nothing needs to be said about them here except to state that only what Justice Holmes called "an intelligence fired with a desire to pervert" [39] could find in the Draft Covenant any obligation to have laws which are prohibited by any clause of the United States Constitution. The widespread popular belief that the Covenant would take away our cherished liberties is totally mistaken. Indeed as I already explained the Covenant declares exactly the opposite, that it does not lessen the liberties in any nation.[40]

Five problems affecting every nation will be considered. Their interest extends beyond the Covenant, because they will arise in almost any effort to promote fundamental freedoms inside countries by international action, whether it be undertaken by many nations or by only two nations agreeing with each other. The five problems are: (1) Should the enterprise attempt to establish almost all of the traditional rights or only the few which can be most effectively enforced? (2) Should property rights be included? (3) What should be done about emergencies? (4) What machinery should be set up for handling violations of human rights? (5) Should "economic and social rights" be included?

PROBLEM 1. SHOULD A COMPREHENSIVE TREATY LIKE THE COVENANT INCLUDE ALL THE FUNDAMENTAL FREEDOMS OR ONLY A FEW?

Whatever happens to the Covenant, any treaty which seeks to protect several fundamental freedoms at the same time is pretty certain to employ the same basic method of stating each right in rather broad language, following the pattern of our Bill of Rights and the constitutions of other freedom-loving countries. Indeed, it is practically impossible for such a comprehensive treaty to deal with specific concrete situations, because that would make it as bulky as an income tax law.

If any human right is valuable, there is a strong impulse to put it into the treaty. Yet the nature of the treaty and the way it operates may make this unwise. Perhaps the proper place to use this particular right for international purposes is somewhere else. A saw is a good thing, but not to shave with.

Consequently, it is desirable to look more closely at what I call the method of the Covenant. An unavoidable feature of it is that the presentation of each affirmative right has to be followed, as I have already shown, by qualifications or limitations. The treaty must state the ways in which a signatory nation is able, without being a violator, to have laws which somewhat cut down the right, if it so desires and its own constitution permits this. Very few fundamental rights are absolute in domestic law, and a treaty also has to face the facts of life.

For a concrete illustration, take freedom of speech. In spite of the inestimable values of open discussion, newspapers are made to pay for libels; sellers of pornographic books are put in jail; infringers of copyright are enjoined and forced to pay damages. Therefore, if a treaty like the Covenant is to include free speech, the situations just mentioned cannot be ignored. They have to be taken care of somehow. And that obliges the draftsmen to insert express limitations in the article on freedom of speech and press.

It is true that the First Amendment does not mention any limitations. It just says "Congress shall pass no law. . . ." Yet the limitations are there just the same. Chief Justice Vinson summarizes the actual scope of constitutional free speech by saying that "this is not an unlimited, unqualified right, but . . . the societal value of speech must, on occasion, be subordinated to other values and considerations." [41] In accordance with this principle, courts allow the apparently absolute prohibition in the First Amendment to be cut down by familiar rules of the common law and by the affirmative powers of Congress. Thus men are fined for profanity in streetcars and pay damages for slander; Eugene Debs was imprisoned for what he said about our entering the First World War; indecent books are barred from the mails or seized by the customs; and anarchists have been deported for what they merely thought.

Now, this device of judicially implied limitations upon an apparently absolute freedom is obviously impossible for an international treaty like the Covenant. It stands by itself. It cannot take anything for granted. The framers cannot assume a background of familiar law, because the agreement is intended to bind many nations, each of which has its own sort of law. And so with all the other rights to be protected. Every nation which signs the treaty has to be told in express language what kinds of laws it can have without breaking its promise. Nothing can be left out. Therefore, the limitations on freedom of speech, which are understood without being mentioned in a domestic constitution, need to be spelled out carefully in a treaty provision on free speech.

Remember that a treaty like the Covenant is not just describing an ideal situation in Utopia. It is prepared with the hope that it will be signed by most of the countries in the United Nations. Otherwise it will be words and not law. Consequently, it has to frame the kind of promises which governments can reasonably be expected to make. If, for example, the promise to maintain free speech leaves no opening for a government to punish a person who betrays its secret plans for jet planes, there is very little prospect that any nation will sign it. And so with every other right. In order to get the treaty accepted by many countries, it is essential for it not to prevent any nation from enacting or continuing *all* restrictions on freedom which are regarded as customary and proper by the governments of free societies.

Furthermore, getting the promises signed is not enough. They will be just pious hopes unless they are kept, down the years. For that, they must be the sort of promises which the officials and the people of a nation will be ashamed to violate. A breach of a treaty cannot be penalized with vigor and sureness like the breach of a private contract. Enforcement machinery will exist (which I consider in Problem 4) but external sanctions against a national government involve cumbrous procedure. It seems unlikely that any international sanction short of war will be very effective in checking repeated governmental violations of a specified human right if they are caused by a strong feeling in the particular country that the treaty obligation endangers public safety. In matters like this, it is unwise to induce a government to tie its hands very tightly. The result may simply be that it will untie them whenever its people feel an urgent need for the kind of law which it imprudently promised not to pass. And other nations are not likely to object very much, especially if they consider that the treaty right ought to have been qualified so as to allow this legislation. In any event, history shows many instances where violations of treaties which were far more harmful than infringements of a citizen's freedom failed to evoke any protest; thus our government said not a word in 1936 when Hitler marched into the Rhineland in breach of our peace treaty with Germany fifteen years before. This shows how undependable external sanctions are.

Therefore, the main reliance has to be on what Dicey calls *internal* sanctions.[42] The promise to maintain each human right in the treaty has to be the kind of promise which most good citizens within a country will want to carry out because they believe it to be a fair and desirable promise. A few men in the United Nations and a piece of paper cannot do very much to prevent a strong government from breaking promises which both its officials and its people intensely dislike. In short, the whole Covenant rests largely upon willingness to obey.

All this shows how very hard it is for an international enterprise to undertake to protect a great many fundamental freedoms at once. Interminable and bitter controversies arise about the qualifications of each right. If these limitations are narrowly stated, the treaty will get few signers. Even these will not pay much more attention to it than a motorist does to a thirty-mile speed limit on a four-lane highway. If, instead, the limitations try to cover every legitimate restriction of the right, they are likely to be unbearably long or else so vaguely phrased as to whittle the right down to little or nothing. The situation recalls the Irishman who wanted a gun that would shoot just high enough not to hit his dog and just low enough to miss his cow.

This makes me conclude that only a few of the important human rights belong in this kind of treaty. The rest call for different methods of international protection. For there are two classes of traditional rights. This is a fact I want to hammer in. The difficulties about qualifications are very much greater in one class than in the other. For instance, they are enormous for freedom of speech and press. It is what I shall call a Blurry Right. In the First Amendment and in the Covenant, the very wide range of the qualifications causes great uncertainty about how much is protected. On the other hand, many rights in the Constitution fell into an entirely different class. They are Bright Rights. The qualifications are either nonexistent, or few and well-established by experience. The right of habeas corpus has only one qualification; it can be suspended during rebellion or invasion. Bills of attainder and *ex post facto* laws are absolutely forbidden. Double jeopardy in criminal cases is always wrong. There are no limitations on the right of an arrested person to be informed of the charges against him, to be confronted with his accusers, to obtain witnesses in his favor, and to have the help of a lawyer.

Only the Bright Rights, I believe, are suitable for protection in a treaty like the Covenant. All those just mentioned involve either safeguards against wrongful imprisonment or the essentials of a fair trial. If international action can make sure of these indispensable liberties, a very great deal will have been achieved. Years ago, a wise refugee scholar insisted that "personal inviolability" was what most needed insertion in an International Bill of Rights.

> Restriction and control of lettre-de-cachet procedures is the very core of civil liberty. All the other freedoms of the most generous bill of rights may stand destitute of meaning, as long as individuals can be detained indefinitely by police action without appeal.[43]

When unfair trials can be conducted and imprisonment is possible without explanation or redress, other forms of liberty are gone. A man in jail cannot discuss or publish or assemble or enjoy property or vote. The appropriateness of these Bright Rights for the Covenant is demonstrated by their satisfactory presentation in numerous drafts. Nations that sign the treaty will know plainly what they have promised. Violations are comparatively easy to detect and investigate and prove. There is little room for those endless arguments which muddle almost every inquiry into alleged violations of liberty of speech and press, about the iniquities of speakers and writers and the terrible dangers to morals or public safety.

Therefore, I strongly urge that, in the drastic revision of the Covenant which I have suggested, only the Bright Rights should be retained. Possibly some non-procedural rights belong in this class, *e.g.*, the right to life, and the prohibition of slavery and involuntary servitude. Still, the Covenant would be most effective if it were confined to procedural safeguards like habeas corpus and the essentials of a fair trial. At all events, the Blurry Rights ought to be thrown overboard. It may seem queer for a persistent advocate of freedom of speech to say it is out of place in a Covenant on Human Rights. Yet the conclusion is forced upon me because years of devoted labor, by scores of lovers of freedom, have ended by producing an article on free speech which will do very little good.

International protection for freedom of speech and press ought to be given by a different kind of treaty. Instead of abstract principles, it should produce specific measures. What I have in mind is illustrated by the Convention on the International Transmission of

News and the Right of Correction,[44] adopted by the UN Assembly on May 13, 1949, and then unwisely put on the shelf at a time when it might have obtained many signers. This Convention facilitates the entry of foreign correspondents into a country, enables them to work there more effectively, and reduces the evils of censorship if it exists. Also it provides an intelligent method for a government to disseminate replies to news reports which it considers erroneous.

The distinction between the Covenant and this News Convention resembles the difference between moonlight and a flashlight. The language of a free speech article in the Covenant is more glowing, but it is so far away that you cannot be sure of what you are looking at. With the flashlight you've got something. You can hold it close to what you want to see. The Covenant is like a man saying to his bride, "With all my worldly goods I thee endow." The News Convention is like his more prosaic statement, "You are going to get seventy-five dollars a month as a dress allowance."

The Englishman's right not to be put in jail unless charged with a crime remained a Blurry Right, dependent on the pleasure of the King and his ministers, until 1679 when Parliament made it bright by the flashlight of the Habeas Corpus Act. The First Amendment is inspiring like the moon, but freedom of speech and freedom of assembly are Blurry Rights, nevertheless. Contrast the definite though smaller rights of Jehovah's Witnesses to distribute pamphlets without a city license, of motion pictures not to be subjected to baseless censorship, of citizens to assemble in public parks to discuss public questions. All these are Bright Rights because the Supreme Court has used the flashlight of a specific decision.

There is a similar opportunity for more specific international agreements to operate like flashlights. For example, a treaty assuring "freedom of religious worship" may in fact amount to much less than a treaty which promises to permit one Catholic church, one Protestant church, and one synagogue in each of four cities.

Such limited practical agreements seem far wiser to me than the determination of UN bodies to put every traditional right into the Covenant. Those who aim their arrows at the stars may shoot higher than those who aim at the trunk of a tree, but the tree does get hit.

PROBLEM 2. SHOULD PROPERTY RIGHTS BE INCLUDED IN A TREATY
LIKE THE COVENANT?

The Covenant says nothing about the right to property. It offers
no protection against deprivation of property without due process
of law, or unreasonable searches and seizures, or the taking of land
and things for public use without just compensation. Strong objections to this total omission of property have been voiced by some
American lawyers and by Charles Malik of Lebanon, as chairman
of the Human Rights Commission.

The decision to leave property out of the Covenant was not a
denial of its importance. The Universal Declaration of Human
Rights places it among the ideals which constitute "a common
standard of achievement for all peoples and nations" and which
ought to be given "universal and effective recognition and observance." "Everyone has the right to own property," declares Article
17, and "No one shall be arbitrarily deprived of his property."

Therefore, if what the hostile critics of the Covenant desire is a
tribute to property from the United Nations, this has been already
given. The proper place for a tribute is in the Declaration, not in
the Covenant. Certainly very little in the way of legal protection
would be accomplished if the Covenant merely repeated the phrases
just quoted. Yet is it possible to say anything more definite?

The fact that a human right is important does not automatically
mean that it belongs in the kind of treaty which the Covenant is.
The real issue, as I showed in Problem 1, is whether the right is
capable of being stated in general terms so as to do any good.

Suppose that the Commission set out to protect property rights
broadly. Just what words would be effective? It could not simply
copy our phrase, "without due process of law" for the governments
of other nations would not know what it meant, and even our Supreme Court Justices are rather uncertain. Or consider the provision drafted by the State Department in 1942 in a possible bill of
rights for the unborn United Nations: [45]

> No person shall be deprived of . . . property except in accordance
> with humane and civilized processes provided by law.

This would give the legislators in each promising nation a very
wide scope for taking away property, so long as it was done politely.

The essential point to remember is that conceptions about the relationship between the ownership of property and other factors in human welfare vary greatly among the countries which, it is hoped, will sign the Covenant. Imagine trying to frame an article on the right to property which would satisfy the American bar, the supporters of nationalization in Great Britain, Socialist Sweden, and Tito of Yugoslavia. The only result would be endless dissensions.

Doing nothing is much the wisest course. The omission will have no effect within the United States—we can go on protecting ownership and free enterprise as fully as we desire, under the terms of the Fifth and Fourteenth Amendments. So far as other countries go, it is tremendously important for the United States to do its best to bring about and strengthen some of the rights which are in the Covenant now, like the abolition of forced labor, the essentials of a fair trial, habeas corpus. Why bother about property if we can help stop the knock on the door at 3 A.M.?

PROBLEM 3. WHAT OUGHT TO BE DONE ABOUT EMERGENCIES?

If there is to be a Covenant on Human Rights at all, I do not see how it can ignore the problem of emergencies like a big paralyzing strike, a hurricane or flood, an armed revolt, the Nazi invasion of France, and the Battle of Britain. Emergencies were not left out of our Constitution. The Philadelphia Convention permitted the "Privilege of the Writ of Habeas Corpus" to be suspended "when in Cases of Rebellion or Invasion the Public Safety may require it." And further emergency powers have sometimes been exercised by our government, as when the freedom of movement of enemy aliens is restricted in wartime. In the Second World War, citizens of Japanese descent were evicted from their homes and kept in concentration camps in the desert.[46] The Defence of the Realm Acts in Great Britain in both World Wars and the French state of siege offer other illustrations from freedom-loving nations. No doubt, abuses may occur as they did when Lincoln suspended habeas corpus in the Civil War. Yet it is impossible to word the Covenant so as to prevent such abuses and it will be fatal to word it so as to deny any emergency powers.

The solution of the emergency problem in several drafts of the Covenant [47] does not seem to give governments greater leeway than has been the practice in democratic countries; and some international safeguards against abuses are provided. In an emergency, a signatory nation will not be violating its obligations to other signers if it takes measures which limit liberties to the extent strictly required by the exigencies of the situation. Nevertheless, it can abrogate only some of the traditional freedoms. For example, it is allowed to make arrests more easily than in normal times and keep people in custody without trial, as we did on the West Coast in 1942. It can limit freedom of speech and press, but not freedom of religion, no matter what the emergency. It is not released from its promises to ensure the right to life and abstain from cruel and unusual punishments. It cannot have slavery or peonage, although it may impose compulsory labor, as might obviously be necessary in a bombed city. Moreover, it must not discriminate on grounds of race, color, sex, etc., and not do anything incompatible with its obligations under international law, which would include treaties about the treatment of war prisoners or resident foreigners. Finally, if any signatory nation does avail itself of the emergency provision, it must immediately inform the Secretary-General of the United Nations about the rights which have been temporarily suspended; and it must also tell him of the date on which it restores these rights. This gives other nations ample opportunity to complain if the derogation of human rights in a particular nation goes on indefinitely.

This solution may not be perfect, but it is sensible. Observe that it does not compel a nation to take any of the emergency measures described. It simply leaves each signer free to respond to the emergency in a manner which is determined by its own national constitution and the judgment of its own rulers. Under the Covenant, as always in history, the barrier against the unwarranted exercise of emergency powers must be found in the kind of people who get put into high office and elected to legislatures.

PROBLEM 4. WHAT INTERNATIONAL MACHINERY SHOULD BE SET UP FOR HANDLING VIOLATIONS OF HUMAN RIGHTS?

When a state in this country takes away a fundamental human right, the Fourteenth Amendment enables the victim to go to the United States courts for relief. There he may get his wrongful conviction reversed, the official action enjoined, or the statute declared invalid. Moreover, the Civil Rights Acts can be used to imprison some state officials who have outrageously infringed constitutional rights.[48] No similar powerful sanctions are available in the United Nations. Its single court at The Hague would never have the time to decide cases of alleged breaches of a comprehensive treaty on human rights. And no international body is likely to be empowered to punish individual violators of a treaty. Therefore, machinery of a new kind has to be devised in order to enforce the Covenant.

The present plan [49] is to set up a Human Rights Committee of nine, not more than one from a single nation. The members will be chosen by the International Court of Justice at The Hague from a panel of names submitted by the nations who have signed the Covenant. The Committee is to meet at UN headquarters or in Geneva, and act on any complaints of violations of the Covenant.

The procedure is to be largely conciliatory. When any signatory nation complains that some other signer is not giving effect to a provision of the Covenant, the nation which is alleged to be breaking its international promise must within three months explain its conduct to the complaining nation, telling about its laws, the remedies taken, etc. If the matter is not adjusted to the satisfaction of the two countries concerned, then either of them can refer it to the Human Rights Committee. The Committee is to ascertain the facts and try to help the nations involved to reach a friendly solution to the matter on the basis of respect for human rights in accordance with the Covenant. Finally, the Committee will draw up a report on the whole case, sending it to the UN Secretary-General and the disputing nations.

The methods just outlined for enforcing the Covenant are pretty mild. No punishment of the offending nation, military or economic, is proposed. Publicity is to be the only sanction against a recalcitrant violation of human rights. Moreover, the victims cannot register any complaint against their own alleged wrongdoing government; they must find some other government to initiate proceedings for their benefit. Since this is the provision which has aroused the most controversy, I shall confine myself to it.

Who ought to have a standing as plaintiff before the international tribunal which will investigate alleged violations and report its findings? The most extreme proposal would permit individuals to file complaints with the tribunal and be heard. An intermediate proposal would exclude private complainants, but give a right of initiative to a list of organizations approved by the United Nations as deserving this privilege. Examples might be the American Federation of Labor-C.I.O., the World Federation of Churches, the Roman Catholic Church, and various other well-known and reputable associations devoted to the protection of women, children, Jews, Negroes, and other classes of people who are especially liable to be exploited or oppressed. But our own government and many others in the United Nations think it wiser to limit proceedings, as in the World Court at The Hague, to complaints filed by one government against another government.

Underlying this controversy is the undeniable fact that the Commission on Human Rights is already receiving hundreds of letters yearly from individuals and organizations about governmental infringements of rights such as the Covenant defines, and about governmental inactivity in the face of widespread private infringements of those rights. This fact is used as ammunition by both sides. The supporters of the present scheme ask how the Human Rights Committee can possibly deal with "all the oppressions that are done under the sun." The Committee will have a manageable burden of work, they say, if it entertains only litigation between governments. The advocates of a wider scope for investigations point to the shame of leaving the vast proportion of these multitudes of possible victims unhelped, and remind us that governments are notoriously unwilling to step into trouble on behalf of the weak until there are enough weak men of a particular sort to transform themselves into a strong pressure group. Usually, if the victims can speak only through a government, they will be voiceless. With effect can their sympathizers quote the entire passage from Ecclesiastes:

> So I returned, and considered all the oppressions that are done under the sun; and behold the tears of such as were oppressed, and they had no comforter; and on the side of their oppressors there was power; but they had no comforter.

The real issue, it seems to me, is how far the international tribunal will be capable of being more than a mere comforter. How many victims of widely separated and very different types of oppressions can a handful of UN officials adequately investigate in a year, so that each of their reports will be respected by "the opinions of mankind" and actually help restore the freedom which has been taken away?

Some familiarity with previous investigations of violations of human rights has made me rather pessimistic. Whichever conclusion is reached by the inquirers, it always seems to satisfy only the side which it upholds, and does not much shake the views of the other side. The American Association of University Professors each year investigates a few complaints that some professor has been discharged in violation of academic freedom. Every inquiry involves a large amount of time and labor. Despite endless conscientious care, the university authorities almost invariably accuse the A.A.U.P. investigators of failure to talk with the right people, of foregone conclusions, of Communistic leanings, and so on and so on. Not once (so far as I recall) has a vindicated professor been reinstated. The Wickersham Commission set up a committee, to which I belonged, to investigate the "third degree"—the compulsory eliciting of confessions. We spent $40,000 and two years on the job.[50] Yet our report was greeted by the police with two answers which they regarded as conclusive: first, there wasn't any third degree; and second, they couldn't do their work without it. Or take an instance where the inquirers concluded that there had been no denial of fundamental human rights.[51] How many people who believed Sacco and Vanzetti to be innocent changed their minds after reading the report of the Lowell Commission?

Those were all investigations made inside the United States, a fairly homogenous country, by men reasonably familiar with the complex of conditions surrounding the alleged violations and facing few language difficulties. How much greater success in forming public opinion can we expect from UN investigators who travel thousands of miles into a strange country with a foreign language? Will they have power to summon witnesses and make them talk against their will? Can they assure witnesses of permanent protection, should they testify against their own government? Each job is going to be a very tough one, and it may be wise to select a very few of the worst and most far-flung oppressions rather than give half-baked reports on scores of cases.

Concentration of justiciable complaints in outraged governments does, therefore, have the advantage of obtaining a thorough sifting of the innumerable accusations, many of which (we must remember) are sure to be palpably baseless and others trivial. In disbarment proceedings in this country, the court which ultimately decides does not hear all complaints. Instead, it leaves them to be sifted by the grievance committee of a bar association, which then presents the few complaints deemed to involve probable cause of guilt of unprofessional practices.

Yet, although the Human Rights Committee ought never to be asked to take a case until somebody else has made sure that it is well grounded, I am not quite sure that this sifting function should be monopolized by foreign governments—foreign, that is, to the country where the alleged violations occurred. Every complaint will then create an international incident; it is bound to produce serious tensions between the complaining nation and the accused nation. Consequently, the decision by the foreign government whether to complain or not and the vigor with which it presses the case against the accused government may easily be swayed by politics rather than justice. Suppose, for instance, that the Covenant had gone into force several years ago, that Argentina and the United States had both signed it, and that our government was asked to initiate proceedings against Argentina before the Human Rights Committee for violating freedom of expression by silencing the great newspaper, *La Prensa*. Was not our course of action bound to be influenced by the extent of our need to keep on good terms with Argentina, the possibility of a dictators' deal between Perón and Stalin, and similar factors? Then, might it not be good if, instead, proceedings could have been initiated by some recognized organization of journalists like the American Society of Newspaper Editors? Such a body would be able to sift complaints with the same professional spirit as a bar association grievance committee and undertake the presentation of the most urgent complaints without being bothered by diplomatic and military anxieties.

Therefore, my tentative suggestions on this problem are: (1) Individually initiated complaints must continue to be ruled out because their volume would make it well-nigh impossible for the Human Rights Committee to work effectively. (2) There may be considerable value in allowing complaints to be filed, not only by signatory nations, but also by approved associations which have been put on a picked list by the Economic and Social Council or some other appropriate organ of the United Nations.

Still, if such non-governmental organizations have a standing to start UN investigations into violations of human rights, two serious difficulties may arise. First, the question of what organizations are on the approved list is almost sure to cause bitter heartburnings and resentments. Second, the chosen organizations will have to act under a very grave sense of responsibility and exercise great restraint in their selection of complaints. Racial and religious organizations are not more impartial than the National Association of Manufacturers, and, like it, they sometimes assert their own interests at the cost of broader considerations. In short, the admission of some private associations and not others to a privileged position in public affairs is always a delicate and dangerous matter.

PROBLEM 5. WHAT OUGHT TO BE DONE ABOUT ECONOMIC, SOCIAL, AND CULTURAL RIGHTS?

Our Constitution does not mention economic, social, and cultural rights. For lawyers they are ideals rather than rights, since they are not enforced by the courts until they have been embodied in affirmative legislation, e.g., about public schools, unemployment relief, and social security. However termed, they have received much attention in the United Nations. As already stated, they are included in the Universal Declaration of Human Rights as ideals, but are kept out of the Draft Covenant, where, apart from a few exceptions like universal suffrage, legal protection is confined to the rights and freedoms which were embodied in our national and state constitutions, after they had developed in England and the colonies during the long struggle which began with Magna Carta. The aspiration for these familiar civil liberties was expressed in the English Revolution of 1688 and the American Revolution, and reached boiling-point in the French Revolution of 1789. Our forefathers felt little need to assert the rights to work, food, clothing, housing, and so forth. They took them for granted. Leave a man alone in a country with abundant unoccupied land, give him an axe and a rifle, and he could take care of himself and his family—get food from game and a few crops on cleared soil, clothing from skins and spun wool, shelter under the stars or in a log-cabin. A. B. Guthrie, Jr.'s novel, *The Big Sky*, shows the extreme self-reliance of the men who asked nothing of government but occasional help against the Indians, and his *Way West* describes their ability to manage their own affairs when groups did begin to form. Eventually, national defense grew more urgent, courts became necessary to settle disputes, and officials had to be set up and kept from abusing their powers, but outside such narrow areas a man's life was in his own hands.

The crowded conditions of Europe and the Industrial Revolution produced an appetite for a new set of rights, at least as early as the French public workshops of 1848. The fact that man is a thermodynamic machine which has to be stoked to run became increasingly evident to political thinkers.[52] Of what use is the right to vote or talk freely when a man is starving? Of what use a fair trial when he has to steal bread in order to stay alive? The boiling-point of the new rights, which would protect men from such disasters, was reached in the Russian Revolution of 1917. Yet, regardless of communism or hatred of communism, these new rights have gone on spreading and found milder manifestations in the Labor government of England, in Australia and New Zealand, in the 1950 Constitution of India, and the current legislation of all of Western Europe. The Constitution of Japan declares:

> All people shall have the right to maintain the minimum standards of wholesome and cultured living.[53]

These words were written in the headquarters of General Douglas MacArthur.

The old-fashioned liberties are as precious as ever, but they are no longer enough. A man left alone cannot save himself. He would merely be out of a job, starve because meat and grain are not transported, freeze because coal and oil do not arrive in his city. The duties of government have ceased to be merely negative —to protect its citizens from enemies foreign and domestic, including tyrannical officials. They are also affirmative—to help keep running the thermodynamic machine of each human being and the equally complex interadjustments of a great aggregate of human beings.

There is nothing un-American about all this, even though the Constitution of the U.S.S.R. declares the right to work, the right to rest and leisure, the right to maintenance in old age, the right to education.[54] Macaulay's famous letter on Jefferson predicted that these new social and economic ideals would cross the Atlantic as soon as free land was exhausted. The long years after 1929 etched those ideals into us with indelible acid. Opinions may differ among politicians how best they can be realized, but Republicans and Democrats alike strive for them more eagerly than they seek to promote freedom of speech or the old-fashioned right of an accused person to be confronted with the witnesses against him. There may be no brief paragraphs in our constitutions about the rights to work, to rest and leisure, to maintenance in old age, to education, but those ideals are spread over hundreds of pages of the United States Statutes at Large and the statute-books of all the states, and we have been willing to spend billions of dollars in order to weave those ideals into the fabric of American life.

Consider what one state is doing to gratify the economic, social, and cultural wants of its inhabitants:

> The State of New York is in the mineral water business, and like other manufacturers pays a tax on the product to the United States; directly or through one of her subordinate elements she runs a surprising collection of businesses; one of her cities owns and operates one of the busiest railroads in the nation; she is authorized to engage in the gas and oil business; she runs amusement parks; she builds and rents dwellings; she lends money at interest; she sells water, electricity, and gas; she runs schools, colleges, universities, hospitals, a radio broadcasting station; and she owns at Saratoga as luxurious a resort hotel as ever inspired a writer of advertising-copy.[55]

The aspirations of Americans do not stop at the three-mile limit. Franklin Roosevelt's vision of freedom from want for all the men in all the lands took concrete form in plans for the United Nations,[56] as early as December 1942, and was eventually transmuted under the leadership of Eleanor Roosevelt into the many specific ideals of the Universal Declaration of Human Rights. Especially notable is Article 25:

Everyone has the right to a standard of living adequate for the health and well-being of himself and of his family, including food, clothing, housing, and medical care and necessary social services, and the right to security in the event of unemployment, sickness, disability, widowhood, old age or other lack of livelihood in circumstances beyond his control.

The purpose here is not to put everybody in every nation on public relief and have all doctors hired by the state. Government is only one of the forces pulling together. If private energy and thrift and private generosity to the less fortunate can give a country the essentials of decent living, with no gaps left for taxpayers to fill, the promises of the Declaration will be amply fulfilled.

In view of the intense devotion of peoples and governments in our time to diffusion of economic, social, and cultural welfare, it is not surprising that great pressure was brought on the Human Rights Commission to include the new "fundamental rights" in the Covenant as well as the Declaration.[57] The General Assembly on December 4, 1950, passed, over the opposition of the United States and by a rather narrow margin, a Resolution telling the Commission to add articles on economic, social, and cultural rights to the old-fashioned freedoms already set forth.[58]

Respectfully, I venture the opinion that this Resolution asked the Commission to spoil its own work. Social security, unemployment relief, a just wage, education, adequate rest and leisure, health, food, clothing, housing, and medical care are all objects of the greatest importance, but they do not belong in a document which deals mainly with the protection of rights through proceedings in domestic courts and international tribunals. The 1950 Indian Constitution wisely recognizes this truth by having two separate categories of human rights. The old-fashioned types are made legally binding and supreme over legislatures, as in our Constitution; but the social, economic, and cultural rights are presented in a separate article entitled "Directive Principles of State Policy," which expressly states they are not binding as law but great ideals at which legislators should constantly aim.[59] This presentation as ideals is the equivalent of the Universal Declaration of Human Rights. In this Indian Constitution and also in Western countries, these economic, social, and cultural rights are promoted by methods quite different from the court procedures customarily available to protect life, freedom from arbitrary arrest, a fair trial, freedom of speech and religion, and other constitutional rights which have long been recognized. For one thing, food, medical care, etc., for everybody require communities of considerable wealth.

After a single attempt, in 1951, to crowd these two unlike sets of objectives into a single document,[60] the Human Rights Commission wisely decided to return to its original plan and keep the new types of rights out of the Covenant on which it had long been working. Unfortunately, it did not merely leave the economic and social rights in the Declaration where they best belong. It had to obey the orders of the Assembly somehow. So it gave birth to twins, and the 1955 Assembly had before it *two* Draft Covenants on Human Rights. In addition to what in this chapter is *the* Covenant, now renamed as the "Draft Covenant on Civil and Political Rights," there is a "Draft Covenant on Economic, Social and Cultural Rights." The implementation of these rights is even milder than the machinery described in Problem 4 for handling traditional rights. Every state which signs is to send to the Economic and Social Council reports of the progress made in achieving observance of the various ideals of full employment, adequate living standards, education, and so on, either through private enterprise and private organizations or by governmental action. The Council will make this information available for use by the Human Rights Commission and the Assembly. This is much like the method long employed in the International Labor Organization for carrying out treaties which promise to raise wages, shorten hours, and otherwise improve working conditions.

This is all right in itself, but "First things first." To get better protection for the traditional human rights, especially a fair trial and freedom from illegal imprisonment, is a far more pressing task than trying to stop unemployment, increased medical care, and multiply schools and teachers by putting words on paper. If a nation is prosperous, it is going to look after the social and economic ideals without a treaty. If it is poor, it cannot carry out its promises, however glowing; the proper remedy is Point Four or some other kind of direct help from richer countries. And if there is any need for the information in the projected reports, enough of it can be easily obtained by already available methods.

Moreover, putting out two far-reaching documents together is likely to ruin both. This is exactly what happened when the Assembly tied the excellent News Convention to a futile treaty about freedom of speech in the abstract. Everybody got confused. Opponents of the News Convention talked about the faults of the treaty until most people got disgusted with the whole business, and the immense support from American newspapers, which the Convention had received at first, all evaporated.

The original Covenant which seeks to strengthen civil rights in all countries is a great enterprise, as I keep insisting, but it has gone off the tracks. The job of getting it rightly repaired is going to be very difficult. Besides the problems I have discussed, there are many more. The main thing is to concentrate all energies on that job. Get this Covenant in such thoroughly good shape that it will be adopted, not only by the United States and other nations where liberties are at a high level, but also by governments which need jacking up. And the hard work will not end when the treaty begins to operate. During the early years of enforcement, all sorts of obstacles will have to be overcome.

Not until this Covenant works well, should something else be attempted. The United Nations may lose everything by trying to do everything at once. It is like the fable of the crow with a cheese in his mouth, who started talking about getting a second cheese and dropped the one he had.

The United Nations is a new organization and international supervision of human rights inside countries is a new endeavor. Organizations like men grow gradually in strength, and should beware of multiplying tasks in advance of tested powers. The members of the Human Rights Commission and the Assembly who insist on getting every human right into some plan for international action might well pay heed to the words of Edmund Burke:

> Alas! they little know how many a weary step is to be taken before they can form themselves into a mass which has a true political personality.[61]

Conclusion

There are plenty of reasons for discouragement about the Draft International Covenant on Human Rights, but every once in a while I like to recall what one of the high officials in the State Department said to me, the first time that I went to Washington after I was appointed to the UN Sub-Commission on Freedom of Speech and of the Press: "Don't be in a hurry. This is a job for twenty-five years."

Americans, while looking at the Covenant, should always remember that it is not, for the most part, a document which will have any effect on domestic law in the United States. Its main purpose is to gain more freedom in countries which have too little now, and to hold the line in countries which might be tempted to increase suppression. One can argue that the minimum standards here fixed are rather low and ought to be made higher. It would be very pleasant indeed if it were immediately possible to bring every conceivable signatory nation up to the high level of fundamental human rights which fortunately has long prevailed in our land. Yet that is obviously impossible. As one of the wisest of Americans remarked about demanding that all the countries in the world should at once adopt by treaties our wide scope of freedom of the press:

> Such demands would be unrealistic, since a free press is integrated into the whole social organism; an international organization cannot go so far as to determine what shall be internal social structures of the participant nations.[62]

The result, for example, of trying to make the entire complex of Supreme Court decisions about the First Amendment into law for the world would be that only a few nations would sign the Covenant, and those few would not need it. The countries where there is really some chance of helping to get *some* freedom of the press, although not so much as ours, would stay out and remain just as they are now. The freest nations are in the position of scoutmasters trying to teach the running high jump to boys who have never left the ground for more than a few inches. *We* can jump five feet, let us say, but if we set the cross-bar there, what good will it do? This lofty expectation may cause a momentary happiness in the raw recruits, but they will soon miss the bar altogether or crack through it, and jump no more. To begin at three feet may be over-indulging, when they really could surmount three feet, six inches, but we shall be erring on the safe side. We shall not be lowering our own standards for we can go on jumping five feet whenever we please, and we shall encourage a good many to do better than ever before. Even if three feet be too easy, once they have learned the trick, they will want to go higher and raise the bar of their own accord.

To change the image again, I think of a wise secondhand bookseller in Providence on his eightieth birthday, describing his lifelong policy: "I always tried to size a man up and sell him the best book *he* would buy." In the field of human rights, anything gained is something gained.

XI Free Speech in the United Nations

> Even if the breath of hope which blows on us
> from that New Continent were fainter than it is and
> harder to perceive, yet the trial (if we would not
> bear a spirit altogether abject) must by all means be
> made. For there is no comparison between that
> which we may lose by not trying and by not suc-
> ceeding; since by not trying we throw away the
> chance of an immense good; by not succeeding we
> only incur the loss of a little human labour. But as
> it is, it appears to me . . . that there is hope enough
> and to spare, not only to make a bold man try, but
> also to make a sober-minded and wise man believe.
> —Francis Bacon, *The Novum Organum*

The biggest fact in the world today is the United Nations. This
is said with full awareness of limitations and shortcomings. For the
first time in history practically all the countries in the world are
meeting frequently to discuss their affairs, and acting even more
frequently through smaller bodies. It is characteristic of human
nature that we have hardly got what we have dreamed about for a
long time when some people say that it is no good and start wanting
something quite different. Perhaps the Charter of the United Nations *is* like the Articles of Confederation. But our ancestors did not
start planning a new Constitution within a few years after the first
Continental Congress met. No, they put all their strength behind
the Continental Congress and the Confederation. And so the Confederation achieved our freedom and it gave men from the various
states the experience of working together on their common concerns. Out of that experience grew a more perfect Union. I want
to speak about the similar experience of working together in the
United Nations.

Despite all we hear about the veto as a fatal obstacle to accomplishment, the United Nations has many areas where no veto can be

raised. One of these is the settlement of problems of freedom of speech, in which I had the good fortune to participate some years ago. The situation has not altered enough since to outmode the reflections which then took shape about the channels and chances for world-wide growth of understanding among men of different nations.

My observations began in May 1947 at Lake Success in the Sub-Commission on the Freedom of Information and of the Press, a small group of twelve experts chosen from different countries. Although each member's government must approve his serving, he does not act under orders from that government but is, for the time being, an official of the United Nations. He receives much help from the permanent officials of his own State Department or Foreign Office, and naturally pays considerable respect to the wishes of his government. Otherwise his work might come to naught when it is reviewed by bodies higher up in which his government is directly represented. In the end, however, he decides for himself what is best in the interest of the United Nations. Thus while the Sub-Commission met, we were citizens of the world. This power of independent judgment produced a strong sense of common responsibility. We became accustomed to working together. We met each other often in pairs or small groups at lunch at Lake Success and at dinner in New York, where troublesome matters of phraseology were sometimes straightened out during the evening. Because of the general mastery of English, pieced out by tolerable French, linguistic barriers hardly existed. Simultaneous translation facilitated the exchange of views at the conference table. Several members had legal training, relevant to the tasks of drafting, including the chairman, G. J. Van Heuven Goedhart from the Netherlands, now UN High Commissioner for Refugees and then chief editor of a large Amsterdam newspaper. The members who were not lawyers were experienced in journalism. Regardless of some sharp differences of opinion, the Sub-Commission was an admirable and enjoyable working unit. Nothing draws human beings closer to one another than association in difficult tasks—whether it be a rough cruise or marriage or drafting an important legal document. When the Sub-Commission suspended work in June, all of us (including our Soviet colleague) parted with real liking and regret. When we met again in January 1948, it was like coming back to college after summer vacation and rejoining old friends.

Then in the spring of 1948, I went to Geneva as one of five delegates of the United States to the Conference on Freedom of Information. This was a much larger gathering, comprising over two hundred delegates from more than fifty nations. It was called by the General Assembly, and the tasks it was to undertake had been arranged by the Sub-Commission. The Conference sat for five weeks. Most of its work was done in four committees, to each of which every nation could send a delegate. I was assigned to Committee IV on law. Its chairman was Sir Ramaswami Mudaliar from India, who had previously, as the first chairman of the Economic and Social Council, done much to block out the work this important body might profitably perform.

Many members of Committee IV were lawyers, and others were government officials with lawyerlike minds. The conditions of work were different from those in the Sub-Commission. At Geneva we were delegates of our respective governments, bound to act in consultation with our co-delegates and the permanent officials in the national group, and subject to directives cabled from the home capital. Each nation tended to act as a separate unit. There was little opportunity (as in the Sub-Commission) for progress through informal meetings of a few men from diverse countries who had got to know each other intimately. At sessions, instead of twelve men sitting close together around a single table, forty or more delegates in Committee IV occupied at least half a dozen tables with the chairman and other committee officers behind a raised desk. So one had the sense of addressing a mass meeting rather than trying to persuade individuals. Indeed, the speaker knew that there was little use in convincing his listeners, since the real decisions were usually not made by them but by hundreds of people outside the room. The necessity of a long interval for translating each speech broke the continuity of discussion, although it had the advantage of giving an opponent plenty of time to collect his thoughts for a reply. There was no danger of blurting out the first idea that came to mind, as with simultaneous translation. A final contrast to the atmosphere in the Sub-Commission was caused by the intervening *coup d'état* in Czechoslovakia, which produced a considerable strain right through the Geneva Conference. Despite all these obstacles, the members of Committee IV developed a notable *esprit de corps*. They wasted little time on eloquent and prolonged denunciations of other countries, but "made a noise like a lawyer" and kept steadily at work on rather tedious tasks with a common attitude toward problems of law and draftsmanship.

One significant observation at both the Sub-Commission and the Conference was how little embarrassment arose from the differences between the law of Continental Europe and the Anglo-American law. Lawyers were lawyers, in whichever system they had been trained. In the area of international freedom of information, at any rate, they understood each other and knew the same craftsmanship.

There is no need to say much about the documents we adopted in the Sub-Commission and the Conference, or the precise issues on which we voted.[1] The main purpose of this chapter is to give the thoughts which came to me while we were working together.

President Lowell once remarked to me that one of a man's main jobs is to tell the eddy from the stream. The international tension which has disturbed our own people so much is, I believe, an eddy; the United Nations is the stream. Much of the tension arose from waiting for treaties of peace to be concluded with Japan, Austria, and Germany. Sir John Evatt of Australia wrote in 1948 when he was President of the General Assembly:[2] "Although the primary function of the United Nations is to maintain world peace, paradoxically there is as yet no world peace to maintain." Still, each of these peace treaties was a temporary affair, however difficult. It had to end some time. It was not the job of the United Nations, which goes on. I listened to more war talk from the taxi driver coming from South Station in Boston to our home in Cambridge at the end of April 1948 than I had heard during seven weeks in Europe. The Geneva Conference did not waste time on fears about the future. Like the men of the Continental Congress we had a job to do and we did it.

The most important fact about the Geneva Conference and about all other international efforts toward liberty of news and opinions is the common heritage of European civilization. Since 1492 this civilization has spread to all of America and to the portions of the

British Empire which were settled by Europeans. China and India, too, although they have their own civilizations, possess a great many of the ideas which are fundamental in this common European heritage.[3] At the Conference the Chinese and Indian delegates seemed much closer to us than the Russian delegates. It was easier to talk to them, not only in trying to settle disputed matters but also about wholly non-controversial topics around the dinner table.

Out of this common heritage grew the great ideal of freedom of information. The Sub-Commission and the Conference put it into these words:

> Everyone shall have the right to freedom of thought and expression; this right shall include freedom to hold opinions without interference and to seek, receive and impart information and ideas by any means and regardless of frontiers.[4]

But words alone cannot make that ideal meaningful to us. It grips us because it is embodied in the lives of men.

To me the inspiring symbol of freedom of information is the Reformation Monument in Geneva. There against the bastion of the Old City stand forth the men to whose leadership—imperfect though some of them were—we of all creeds owe the liberty of the spirit we now possess: Calvin and Henry IV of France, William of Orange, Knox and Cromwell, the founders of Rhode Island and Plymouth, Germans and Swiss, and a valiant Hungarian. Here, indeed, is freedom regardless of frontiers.

These leaders of the past belong to the brotherhood of men of all lands whose lives are devoted to freedom of thought and utterance. And the ranks of that brotherhood are never closed. Our Czech colleague on the Sub-Commission, Lev Sychrava, who helped Masaryk found the Republic of Czechoslovakia, was deprived of his editorship by the Nazis and spent six years in Buchenwald. Soon after we said good-bye to him in New York, he was torn from his newspaper by the Communists and driven into exile, "because he was a little too critical of the new regime." The life of freedom comes from men who have loved freedom more than life.

We in the United States are, I venture to think, somewhat forgetful that we are not the only country on earth which cherishes liberty of thought and speech. Roger Williams and the Pilgrims appear on the Reformation Monument alongside thinkers from many other nations. The First Amendment to our Constitution ought to be viewed against its European background. When, soon after V-J Day, a large number of prominent American newspapermen urged UN action in the field of liberty of information, they were a bit inclined to assume that such action would result in our ideas of freedom of the press being taken over bodily by all other countries. However, when the United Nations did act at Lake Success and Geneva, other countries were anxious for us to take over some of their ideas. This came as an unpleasant surprise to several of our leading editors and publishers,[5] and the cry was taken up by a small group of lawyers who vigorously oppose almost everything that the United Nations has proposed for the protection of human rights. They started in denouncing as totalitarianism whatever UN decisions about the press they happened to dislike, entirely ignoring the fact that these decisions were made in the face of bitter totalitarian opposition. The decisions came from men within the common heritage—William Benton, publisher and later Senator, Erwin Canham of the *Christian Science Monitor*, Sevellon Brown of the *Providence Journal*, Oveta Culp Hobby, publisher of the *Houston Post* and afterwards Secretary of Welfare, Harry Martin, president of the American Newspaper Guild, British Labor officials, editors of great newspapers in Scotland and Canada, Pertinax, the chief columnist in France, leaders in the struggle of India for independence, men who conducted underground newspapers in Norway and Holland at the risk of their lives. Yet it was said of their work by Senator Bricker,[6] "It is impossible to imagine a more legal basis for the most repressive measures of atheistic tyranny." The absurd idea has spread across the United States that every free government in the United Nations except our own is trying to throttle the press.

It is stupid to behave as if the world consisted of just Russia and the United States. During the years since the Second World War they have happened to be the only two nations with great military strength and a stable economy, but that is pretty much beside the point when you are dealing with the free flow of news and opinions. A very important aspect of the common heritage is that it comprises many nations and that the smallness of some of them does not matter much. Where freedom is at stake, the weight of Holland or

Switzerland is out of all proportion to its size. Hence the Geneva Conference was a very different place from the Security Council where size and brute power are decisive factors. At Geneva, delegates from many nations which share the common heritage with the United States knew that their contributions to that heritage have been as significant as our own. In the long run the problems of the world cannot be solved by either bombs or money. Ideas will be the weapons.

Therefore, we should constantly build upon this common heritage. Within the countries which derive from it, disagreements about details should, so far as possible, be subordinated to the unity of principles. The solution of international problems of freedom of speech and press is a long hard task. There are bound to be honest differences of opinion inside the United Nations, and outside it among American newspapermen and lawyers. When such disagreements do occur, they should be discussed, not with imputations of sinister motives, but with a constant sympathetic understanding of the difficulties involved. It is good to know right from wrong—it is also essential to distinguish between the great and the small. Disputes about the best way to attain a deeply cherished freedom ought not to be exaggerated into disputes about the fundamental ideal itself. The perpetuation and strengthening of the common heritage is the surest way to the kind of world we want.

The Soviet Union lies outside the common heritage. It derives from Byzantium and the Tartars. Russia did not participate in the long experience of Western Europe in the Papacy, the Holy Roman Empire, chivalry, representative assemblies, merchant cities, the Revival of Learning, the Reformation and the religious wars which at last taught the wisdom of toleration. Occasional hospitality toward Western ideas, as under Peter the Great and Alexander I, was often followed by strong oscillations toward its own special civilization, exemplified of late by the return of its capital from St. Petersburg to Moscow. This persistent isolationism and the overpowering effect of the endless plain are as much responsible as the Marxian ideology for the difficulties of doing business with the Russians.[7] Travelers long before Lenin wrote of similar difficulties:

The rulers take good care to keep out any foreign influence which might alter national customs [1588].

In Russia secrecy presides over everything. . . . . You are allowed to communicate only with the top men [1839].[8]

The Russians *are* different and difficult. So far as my experience goes, I see no prospect of common ground for several years ahead. Certainly the obstacles will not be removed by a cordial handshake and a smile. Speaking from my own knowledge of them, I think that the trouble in working with them is not entirely due to a conflict of ideologies and national ambitions. They appear to lack the experience which comes to every American lawyer and businessman and director of a charity or a club, an experience in give-and-take—sitting down over a draft and trying to have it say what will make it work. Often with us everybody intends the same thing, and the differences are only about the form of expression. Possibly in their own concerns the Russians have proceeded on the principle of all or nothing, while we have gone on the belief that half a loaf is better than no bread. The more they have of this experience of compromise and collaboration—and there is plenty of it in the United Nations—the easier it will be to separate true divergences from mere misunderstandings and quickly remove the latter.

As for the satellite states in the United Nations—these included Yugoslavia at the time of the Geneva Conference [9]—they followed the Soviet lead like children playing "Simon says up" whereas the United Kingdom could never count on Canada or Australia or South Africa. Still, there was some room for differentiation among the satellites. The Ukraine and Byelorussia are simply loose pieces of the U.S.S.R., as much a part of it as big states like New York and Texas are part of the United States. Yugoslavia, even before Tito's defection, did not seem at all the same. Though also lying outside the common heritage, it derives from Turkish rule. Many of its citizens have been in the United States. My Yugoslav associate at Geneva had been a parachutist in our army. They know more truth about American conditions than most Russians—more than they cared to admit at Geneva. The Poles and the Czechs are in still another category. Their countries have been part of the common heritage since the Middle Ages. Although at the Conference they echoed the Russians' ideology, I found their cultural background much closer to ours and could carry on an animated conversation with them on plenty of safe topics. Time may show that the Soviet system *overextended*, as the businessmen say, when it obliged Poland and Czechoslovakia to take orders from Moscow. A rigid rule which has been unquestioningly accepted by the descendants of Russian peasants, schooled to docility by centuries of absolutism, may not work so smoothly in these two strongholds of spiritual independence now cut off from the European civilization in which they have played such proud roles.

The big problem as I see it is to bring the Union of Socialist Soviet Republics into the common heritage of Western thought. To expect the abandonment of all Russian traditions would be foolish, but the Russian peoples might eventually come to get along with us as easily as do the Indians and (until lately) the Chinese and yet, like them, preserve ways of their own. It would not be the first time that Russia grew weary of isolation and became much more like the rest of Europe. My guess is that the process will not be a one-way street running solely in our direction. They will learn from us, but we shall also learn from them.

Meanwhile, is it possible to establish good will and fruitful relations between peoples so far apart in their ways of life as those of the U.S.A. and the U.S.S.R.? A story from Herodotus comes to mind:

> There is a country beyond the pillars of Hercules which the Carthaginians are wont to visit. As soon as they arrive, they unlade their wares and dispose them after an orderly fashion along the beach. Then they return aboard their ships and raise a great smoke. The natives see the smoke, come down to the shore, and lay out to view as much gold as they think the worth of the wares. Then the natives withdraw to a distance.
>
> The Carthaginians come ashore and look. If they think the gold enough, they take it and go their way; but if it does not seem to them sufficient, they go aboard ship and wait patiently. Then the natives come back and add more gold, till the Carthaginians are content. Neither party deals unfairly by the other. The Carthaginians never touch the gold till it comes up to the worth of their goods. The natives never carry off the goods until the gold is taken away.[19]

The Carthaginians and the West Coast Africans understood nothing of each others' religion or habits of life. They had not a word of language in common. And yet they accomplished together what they wanted because the Carthaginians knew how to "wait patiently."

Despite the present difficulties of dealing with the Soviet Union and its satellites *inside* the United Nations, the world would be much worse off if they were outside. Secretary Marshall's strong arguments to Congress soon after the Geneva Conference established that point as to high political and military matters.

> The suggestion that a revised United Nations, or some form of world government, should be achieved, if necessary, without those nations which would be unwilling to join, deserves special attention. Such a procedure would probably destroy the present United Nations organization. The result would be a dispersal of the community of nations, followed by the formation of rival military alliances and isolated groups of states. This result would weaken us and expose us to even greater dangers from those who seek domination of other states.[11]

I venture to add a few observations about the value of the continued presence of the Slav states in UN bodies which are concerned with fundamental freedoms, particularly the flow of news and ideas.

While we were working at Lake Success in January 1948, a friend asked me whether the stream which now separates us from the Russians could be crossed. "Yes, lower down or higher up; but not where we stand now." Lower down, if it becomes possible to go below the leaders to the ordinary men of both countries, who get on together so much better than the leaders do—remember how the common soldiers of the two armies met on the Elbe. Higher up, if the debate can be lifted by the leaders above the level of short-run considerations. But at the point on the stream where both countries are at present, the most we can hope is to be able to talk to each other across the torrent.

And that is made easy by periodic UN meetings. Whatever our present troubles, we do not have the added difficulty of arranging special conferences. Whenever our representatives go to the Headquarters in New York or to Geneva, the Russians are there too. The physical opportunity for adjustment exists whenever the will to adjust happily makes its appearance. A Soviet Union outside the United Nations would be beyond speaking distance.

It is especially important that these periodic chances for mutual acquaintance should happen in the area of ideas as well as of military and political matters. The chief causes which keep these two nations apart are, as already said, differences in ideas. To lessen those differences is thus the best remedy for the serious antagonism which threatens to throw the lives of the young into the kind of world no sensible person would desire for them. And we cannot rely on methods which in the past made peoples know each other better—active private trading, frequent visitors back and forth between the two countries for recreation and study, the ample exchange of contemporary literature and art. Those channels are still badly blocked between Russia and the United States. All the more need for the UN channel.

Paradoxical though it may seem, the totalitarians were more of a help than a hindrance to the promotion of liberty of the press. Not in their own countries, of course, where the official decrees regulating every phase of newspapers and books and everything else made the censors whom Milton and Tolstoy denounce seem sloppy amateurs. But this suppression would go on just the same if the Slav states were out of the United Nations. What I have in mind is the effect of the Slavs' presence on the countries within the common heritage.

Toward the end of the Geneva Conference, I was talking with one of the younger State Department advisers about what would have happened if the Slav states had not been there. Running over the important actions of the Conference, we soon exploded the notion which was coming across the Atlantic from the press at home, that the solid Soviet bloc of six votes had swung several critical decisions their way. Instead, the six Slav states were usually in a minority of six. They had not picked up a single vote outside the Iron Curtain—beyond the line their armies reached in 1945. They could invade, but not persuade. On the few occasions where the Soviet bloc formed part of the majority, the numerous countries voting with them would have had a majority anyhow. Therefore, I suggested, the results of the Conference would have been just what they were, if the Slav states had stayed away. With this my State Department friend vehemently disagreed. It would have made a big difference, he insisted. The results would have been much worse, because without the Slavs the Western countries would have quarreled a great deal more among themselves, the way they did at Versailles. In fact, he pointed out, the repeated Soviet attacks on the free press had made the rest of us close up our ranks. Our differences of opinion seemed less important when compared with the gulf between our view of the purposes of the press and that of the Soviets. Consequently, many desirable measures had been ironed into shape which would otherwise have come to nothing. I feel sure that my State Department friend was right. The fresh realization given by the Slavs of what it would mean to lose liberty of the press helped the Conference to start the work of making this fundamental freedom stronger in the rest of the world.

Stronger and clearer. We faced the Soviet picture of the press as an instrumentality of the government, and they kept asserting that the government is completely identical with the people. The purpose of the press, they said, is to produce the particular type of society which "the people" decides to be desirable. This view, so far from our conception of newspapers, is easier for Americans to understand if we ask whether public schools and state universities ought to be a similar instrumentality of the government. Is it the teachers' job to shape students' mind into a mold approved by the taxpayers? Or ought they to develop intelligence for handling the unforeseeable conditions of many years ahead? The Slavs also differed from us by insisting that the principal obligations of the press ought to be legal obligations, while we said that, except in a few narrow areas like libel and pornography, the only obligation should be moral. Both sides agreed that newspapers ought to seek the truth, but the Soviet bloc wanted to make new kinds of crimes out of many newspaper statements if a tribunal of "the people" found that these were falsehoods. For instance, they repeatedly urged that the law ought to punish the spreading of false and distorted reports which promote war or national hatred or religious hatred or racial hatred. (When the Greek delegate suggested listing *class hatred* too, the Soviet delegate balked and reasoned like John Stuart Mill.) The obstinacy of the Slavs in presenting their views of newspapers, in season and out, forced the delegates from free countries to reconsider our own views of liberty of the press. We had to reformulate the creed of Milton and Jefferson, and make it more precise to suit problems of the Twentieth Century.

In particular, the necessity of rebutting the Soviet insistence upon legal obligations made us more aware of the moral obligations of the press. The principle that freedom is inseparable from responsibility could not be ignored, although it is not mentioned in the First Amendment. We began asking ourselves new questions. Just what are the moral responsibilities of the press? Do they extend beyond gathering facts and printing them "objectively"? The Conference answered "Yes" and declared:

> That it is the moral obligation of the press and other agencies of information to seek the truth and report the facts, thereby contributing to the solution of the world's problems through the free interchange of information bearing on them, promoting respect for human rights and fundamental freedoms without discrimination, fostering understanding and co-operation between peoples, and helping maintain international peace and security.[12]

The Conference refused to let these purposes remain merely pious hope. Though keeping their enforcement as much outside law as ever, it brushed aside the old plea of newspaper owners, broadcasters, and movie producers that their own consciences and the pecuniary intake are the sole tests of their performance. Instead, it declared that professional organizations should encourage the fulfilment of the moral obligations of the press, and that the observance of those obligations can also be effectively advanced by the persons whom the press serves, "provided that news and opinion reach them through a diversity of sources. . . ."

This cogent summary of responsibilities was hardly what the Slav delegates wanted, but some of the credit for it must go to their presence, nevertheless.

There is, however, one subtle danger from the participation of the totalitarians in such UN gatherings. Because they are so vociferously antagonistic to our conceptions of freedom, a verbal battle soon develops during which the difficult and delicate problems of the relationship between press and public are soon forgotten. What started as an exploring party splits into the two sides of a Kentucky feud. The Soviet formulations of the principle of freedom of the press are so outrageous to Western thinking that we are tempted to demolish them and stop. Yet an international meeting on the press, if it is to be fruitful, ought to consider, not only the censorship and other tight controls in totalitarian nations, but also disturbing situations and important new problems in freedom-loving countries.

What is the nature of these important new problems? Think first of some old problems of press freedom: Even if the state usually keeps its hands off the press, what objectionable publications may it properly subject to law? How, in that event, should the law operate—through a censor, a jury, or a judge? These are familiar questions and they are never fully answered. Yet recently the focus of interest in the West has shifted from the *scope* of freedom of the press to the *use* of that freedom in the countries where it does exist.[13] What do the citizens of a free society need to receive from their press? Are they getting it now? If not, what methods can wisely be employed to make the press better? We have begun worrying about the way some press lords are using their freedom to publish reckless inaccuracies, about trends toward monopoly within cities and regions, about the low level of our radio programs, about the desire of powerful enterprises in this country to swamp the native cultures of other countries with American movies and magazines and press services, about the possibility that irresponsible gigantic headlines might help bring about an unnecessary war. Or take what Geoffrey Crowther, the editor of the *London Economist*, called the $64 question: How are you going to change the judgment of the readers who now create such enormous circulations for newspapers which are so far below the standards of their best competitors? Even if these journals read by five or ten millions are really giving the public what it wants, nevertheless it is not what the public needs in order to make wise political decisions which deeply affect the welfare of everybody. How then can the public come to *want what it needs?* There is no sense in improving a newspaper if people will stop buying it. Is it possible in a democracy for more and more men to insist on buying the best?

Questions like these were much in the minds of the men at Lake Success and Geneva, although they rarely got aired in the conference chambers. Delegates from the free countries were tempted to keep silence about such disquieting matters. They felt that any concession of weaknesses in their own press was like furnishing ammunition to the enemy. Experience left no doubt it would be used against us in some later Russian excoriation of American newspapers. The Slavs presented their press as perfect. So we made out our press to be much nearer perfection than it really is. The Russians spent an hour each day pointing out the sensationalism and inaccuracies of our press and what they described as "censorship" by millionaire owners. We retorted at length about the uniformity of ideas in the Soviet press and its censorship by government officials. Each side kept repeating its own position—what the Geneva newspapers called playing over worn phonograph records. The cold war becomes the scold war.

Often at Lake Success and Geneva I was reminded of the story of the Oxford dons who were composing a letter inviting Queen Victoria to visit their college. The draft began: "Conscious as we are of our shortcomings—" A sarcastic colleague suggested that it would be much more accurate to say: "Conscious as we are of one another's shortcomings—"

Such an attitude may be natural, but it is unproductive. Here were many distinguished experts on the press from the various parts of the world. It was an opportunity to learn more about problems, even if the time had not yet come to solve them. It would have been a first step toward results if representatives from each side had given honest firsthand information about some significant aspects of their own system. Suppose the Russians told what use is actually made of the article in the Soviet Constitution which purports to give every writer access without charge to a printing-press and plenty of paper.[14] Suppose the Americans described the difficulties of reaching a satisfactory solution of the problem of the ownership of radio stations by newspapers. This sort of thing practically never happened at Lake Success or Geneva. A bushel of argument to a grain of fact about the speaker's own country. Plenty of facts about the other fellow's country—all damaging. But denunciations do not open the way to the fruitful exchange of ideas.

Doubtless, even under the best conditions, an international gathering with all sorts of political implications cannot be expected to conduct inquiries with the dispassionate spirit of a congress of astronomers. Still, there are degrees of heat and it is a pity for controversy to become unnecessarily warm. The constant altercations in the Sub-Commission and the Conference kept these bodies from contributing as much as their members were capable of giving toward the solution of the new problems about the press which now confront nations within the common heritage. I hope that future UN bodies on the press will deal with these questions better than we did. For the future of the common heritage depends on bringing these problems closer to solution.

The common heritage of freedom-loving nations faces today over a century after its fundamental liberties were solidified through the American and French Revolutions, the same great question which a wise English historian says Protestantism was called upon to solve during the early years of the Thirty Years' War, a century after Luther and Calvin brought liberty of thought into the common heritage. It is "the eternal question which presents itself to all who have embraced freedom in any form. Would they regard their liberty as a means by which to grasp the conception of a higher order than they had known before?" [15]

Freedom *from* something is not enough, as I have already said— it must be freedom *for* something. What is the press of the common heritage going to do with the opportunity bestowed on it by the First Amendment and similar constitutional protection in other countries?

The national interests of many peoples beside the Slavs interfered at the Conference with the immediate accomplishment of measures which were internationally desirable. For example, the ability of the people of one country to learn about the people of another country depends greatly upon the ease with which journalists are allowed to pass international frontiers. There has been especial difficulty in getting correspondents into Communist countries and keeping them there. But when the Conference tried to do something about this, the Slavs pointed out that it was even harder for the correspondents of Communist newspapers to get into the United States. The joke is that Soviet correspondents, who are *prima facie* the most to be feared, get in automatically since they are part of the Soviet government and have diplomatic passports. Yet a solitary reporter from a Paris Communist newspaper runs into trouble at once, and a Venezuelan editor, with a long and distinguished career in orthodox politics, cannot accept an invitation to attend a seminar at the Columbia School of Journalism because he was a Communist years ago.

In the Geneva Conference, this policy of ours cropped up to plague us at every turn. The United States delegation unanimously asked Washington to admit foreign journalists regardless of their opinions, so long as they were not personally dangerous. The government has thus far refused to make any such concession. So in Geneva we didn't get to first base. This chance of lifting the Iron Curtain was thrown away.

Such conflicts between international and national purposes are bound to occur in the United Nations. They are like the conflicts between national and state interests in Congress. When the present discriminatory taxes on oleomargarine are in peril, should a Wisconsin Senator care more for some thousands of dairymen in Wisconsin or for millions of consumers all over the United States who are now forced to pay a high price for a healthful food? As life is, no representative at an international conference can reasonably be expected to ignore entirely his own government and people. If he does not consider conditions and consequences in his own country, who will?

The vital thing in such a conflict, if there is to be real international progress, is to *consider the international purposes first*. If you begin with your own national interests, you may never get further. So forget for the time being what is good for your own country and ask only what solution would be best for the international situation. What would you favor doing if you lived somewhere else—in a country which was not affected at all? After you have decided on the best solution for international purposes, then ask whether it has to be changed here or there to take care of the special needs of your own country. Perhaps you will find that these can be taken care of more easily than would have seemed possible if you had kept them in the forefront of your mind all the time.

This I call the Dartmouth Library approach. The story is that when the trustees set up a committee to design the present library, they asked, "How much money can we spend?" "We're not going to tell you. Think just about the kind of library which will best meet the needs of Dartmouth students and professors forty years ahead." That's what the committee did. Their plan was turned over to the estimators. It would cost, say, seven millions. Then only did the trustees say, "All we have is five millions." They told the committee to go over the original plan and see what could be lopped off from it to save two millions. So the committee cut down their first plan and the library was built at the allotted cost. The point is that Dartmouth got a better five million dollar library because the committee started by planning for Dartmouth, instead of planning for five million dollars.

The spirit of a world organization depends on the presence within it and the encouragement outside it of men and women who take this approach of looking long and steadily at the central problem, ahead of home concerns, whose thinking does not stop at their own borders, who see things in the large—*sub specie aeternitatis*. What most gives me hope is meeting so many of such persons in the United Nations—Sir Ramaswami Mudaliar, the Prime Minister of Mysore; Carlos Romulo of the Philippines, who proposed the Conference and was its president; from Holland, Van Heuven Goedhart, chairman of the Sub-Commission and of the most important committee at Geneva; from Belgium, Fernand Dehousse, Professor of International Law at Liége, who made some of the ablest legal arguments I have ever heard; Evatt of Australia; from our own country, Erwin Canham, editor of the *Christian Science Monitor*, and Eleanor Roosevelt.

Out of the working together of men and women like these, and many more of the same vision whom I do not know, can come the world of which we dream. Not the world some now picture to us as inevitable where every country is to be like a perpetually beleaguered city, diverting all its inhabitants and resources and thoughts into preparations for an attack which may never come. That, I believe, is the eddy. The deep and abiding emotions of the race will pull peoples out of this psychosis hanging over from the worst of all wars into the natural course of life where we can watch children grow up, cultivate our gardens, and cherish "the long hope, the towering dream"—*le long espoir et les vastes pensées*. The true symbol of our life is Thanksgiving Day—the generations of men and the harvest, not Memorial Day.

The greatest international story is the story of Pyrrhus. When he was about to start across the Adriatic to fight the Romans, an old philosopher at his court asked: "What will you do after you have conquered Rome?" "Next I'll take over Sicily." "And then?" "It's only a step to annex the Carthaginians." "And then?" "Next, Greece." "After all this you won't have anything left to conquer, so what will you do?" "We'll go home and have a grand banquet with wreaths of flowers on our heads." "*But you can do that now.*" We do not have to defeat Russia and shatter most of the cities on earth and put an army of occupation into Siberia and dispute with Great Britain and Germany over the peace treaty, in order to form a successful international organization. We can do that now if we will only put into it all our hearts and minds.

This is my picture of the United Nations as I have looked at it. As Cromwell directed the man who painted his portrait, I have put in all the warts I saw. We should not expect too much or too soon. Like the Carthaginian traders we have to learn to wait patiently. Institutions like children grow under the care of men and women. We can wisely watch over the United Nations as we watch over our children, remembering the counsel of the Prophet Isaiah:

> For precept must be upon precept, precept upon precept; line upon line, line upon line; here a little, and there a little.

The basic problem is for persons to learn to live together—husbands and wives, workers and managers, Negroes and whites, the many nations of the earth. The difficulties must not be minimized. When the local contractor in the little Maine village where we go for the summer engaged workmen from the next village, there was outcry against him for employing "foreigners." This illustrates the friction which will have to be overcome between inhabitants of different countries and different parts of the world. A large portion of international trouble comes from the instinct which led Dr. Johnson to say that the experience of a lifetime had taught him most foreigners are fools. Stamp down this instinct, come to know them, and you find they are not very different from the men you meet at home socially or in your working career. Some foreigners will still be pikers, but so are some Americans.

To make the United Nations work, governments must stop playing the old game of territorial grabs and armament races and begin playing a new game. National rivalry now is like sailors fighting each other while the ship labors against a gale. There is no simple solution. We ought to be patient and remember that cathedrals are rarely built by a single generation. We have to know much and hope much.

The real enemies of mankind are not in some special region of earth but in the conditions all men face—famine, disease, ignorance, injustice, greed, cruelty, abuse of power, and mental unbalance. The dark places of the mind are nearer than we think. Hitler and his associates are only one example of this. There is the terrifying danger that political and social organization and human understanding cannot develop fast enough to cope with the advance of science and invention.

To preserve the integrity and dignity of the individual human being through ever-increasing complexities is a baffling task. Yet it is our task. As DuPont de Nemours wrote from France to Jefferson: "We are only snails with the peaks of the Andes to climb. By God, we must climb!"

NOTES

Footnotes to Chapter I: *Watchman, What of the Night?*

1. See Chafee, "Charles Evans Hughes," 93 Proceedings of the American Philosophical Society 267 (1949). The five cases mentioned were Tot v. United States, 319 United States Reports 463 (1943); United States v. Lovett, 328 *id.* 303 (1946); United States v. Cardiff, 344 *id.* 174 (1952); Bolling v. Sharpe, 347 *id.* 497 (1954); United States *ex rel.* Toth v. Quarles, 350 *id.* 11 (Nov. 7, 1955). The First Amendment has never resulted in a decision declaring an Act of Congress unconstitutional or reversing a federal conviction.
2. Brown v. Board of Education, 347 United States Reports 483 (1954); Bolling v. Sharpe, 347 *id.* 497 (1954).
3. Contrast the reversal of convictions in Moore v. Dempsey, 261 *id.* 86 (1923) with Frank v. Mangum, 237 *id.* 309 (1915), where the mob had its way. Justice Holmes dissented in the earlier case, and spoke for the majority eight years later.
4. See Pollak, Stern, and Chafee, "Report on Lawlessness in Law Enforcement," 4 *Reports of National Commission and Law Enforcement* (Wickersham Commission) (1931); Chafee, "Remedies for the Third Degree," 148 Atlantic Monthly 621 (1931).
5. See McNabb v. United States, 318 United States Reports 332 (1943); and the 1944 statement and memorandum of the Bill of Rights Committee of the American Bar Association, reprinted in 2 Chafee, *Documents on Fundamental Human Rights* 474-546 (1951).
6. A religious conscientious objector, duly classified as such by his draft board and of high moral character, was refused admission to the Illinois bar. *Re* Summers, 325 United States Reports 561 (1945), 4 Justices dissenting. Any conscientious objector is ineligible for any public office by 42 Louisiana Revised Statutes (1950) §32.
7. See Arthur E. Sutherland, "Due Process and Disestablishment," 62 Harvard Law Review 1306 (1949).
8. John Bunyan, *The Pilgrim's Progress,* end of Part I.
9. Eleanor Bontecou, *The Federal Loyalty-Security Program* 105 (1953). With the possible exception of a single charge of contributing to the defense of a person indicted in the Canadian spy case, Miss Bontecou reports (*Ibid.*) that, among the eighty-five loyalty cases chosen by her at random for detailed study (*Id.* 101n.) "not one was found which involved charges of treason, sedition, espionage, sabotage, or advocacy of the overthrow of the government by force or violence, and no such cases were reported by the agency officials interviewed."

   Richardson's testimony is in *State Dept. Loyalty Investigation,* 81st Cong., 2d Sess., Hearings before (Tydings) Subcommittee of Senate Foreign Relations Committee, Part I, 409 (April 5, 1950). The statement as to Fort Monmouth is based on a mimeographed report, *The Fort Monmouth Security Investigations, August 1953-April 1954* (Washington: The Federation of American Scientists, April 25, 1954).

10. This is probably a big overestimate, but I have let it stand in order not to minimize the danger. J. Edgar Hoover, head of the F.B.I. says there are now about 21,500 Communist Party members in the United States. Boston Traveler, Dec. 5, 1955, p. 15, col. 1.

11. 18 United States Code (1951) §2385. The Smith Act was discussed soon after its passage in Chafee, *Free Speech in the United States* 462-90 (1941).

12. *Id.* §2384. The latest case under this statute was in Puerto Rico in 1937. Albizu v. United States, 88 Federal Reporter, 2d Series, 138 (C.C.A. 1st, 1937).

13. The 1954 Act will be discussed at various points in Chap. V.

14. See the McCarran Subversive Activities Control Act of 1950, 64 U.S. Statutes at Large 987, §§22-25; and the McCarran Immigration and Nationality Act of 1952, 66 *id.* 163, §§101(15), 212, 214, 221, 222, 241-244.

15. Schachtman v. Dulles, 225 Federal Reporter, 2d Series, 938 (D.C. Appeals, June 23, 1955).

16. See "Government Exclusion of Foreign Political Propaganda," 68 Harvard Law Review 1393 (1955).

17. See Chafee, *Free Speech in the United States* 190n (1941), for the situation before 1929, the terms of the 1929 Act, and decisions thereunder.

18. For an account of Mr. Cairns' work, see 1 Chafee, *Government and Mass Communications*, Chap. 12 (1947).

19. *Op. cit., supra* note 16.

20. The hearings and reports of this committee are carefully examined and summarized by Professor Robert K. Carr of Dartmouth in his *The House Committee on Un-American Activities, 1945-1950* (1952).

21. 98 Congressional Record 1701 (March 3, 1952). For the duties of this committee, see 60 U.S. Statutes at Large 816 (Aug. 2, 1946).

22. Carr, *op. cit., supra* note 20, 55-79.

23. *Id.* at 56.

24. N.Y. Times, June 15, 1953, p. 1, col. 8.

25. Executive Order 9835, 12 Federal Register 1935 (Mar. 25, 1947), is reprinted at p. 275 in Bontecou, *op. cit., supra* note 9, which is a thorough and scholarly study of the administration of the program until July 1952. President Eisenhower on April 27, 1953, issued Executive Order 10450 altering the loyalty program. This is printed in 3 Code of Federal Regulations (1953 Supp.) p. 73. See also 5 U.S. Code Ann. (1950) §22-1 ff.

26. *Id.,* preamble to Executive Order 9835. The bracketed numerals have been inserted and emphasis supplied.

27. N.Y. Times, Oct. 19, 1954, p. 12, col. 2.

28. In a statement published in Science, December 1954.

29. On this list, see Bontecou, *op. cit., supra* note 25, Chap. 5. She reprints the full list at 352, probably as it stood in 1953.

30. Executive Order of March 21, 1947, reprinted *Id.* 280; emphasis supplied.

31. Chief Judge Swan, in United States v. Remington, 191 Federal Reporter, 2d Series, 246 (C. A., 2d, 1951). See also Kutcher v. Gray, 199 *id.* 783, at 787 (D.C. App. 1952); Rudder v. United States, 226 *id.* 51, at 53 (D.C. App. 1955).

32. Joint Anti-Fascist Refugee Committee v. McGrath, 341 United States Reports 123 (1951).

33. 18 Federal Register 2619 (May 5, 1953).
34. Schachtman v. Dulles, *supra* note 15. On this group, see Bontecou, *op. cit., supra* note 25, at 202n, 357, 358.
35. *Id.* 173n, 354. The anti-Communist magazine, Counterattack, had demanded that this group be put on the list.
36. Browder v. United States, 312 United States Reports 335 (1941).
37. See *The States and Subversion,* edited by Walter Gellhorn (1952), summarizing state and local activity in California, Illinois, Maryland, Michigan, New York, and Washington, with a general view. More detailed volumes on several of these states have also been published by the Cornell University Press under the supervision of Robert E. Cushman.
38. A Pennsylvania sedition law was held unconstitutional on this ground in Commonwealth v. Nelson, 377 Pennsylvania Reports 58 (1954). Even if the Supreme Court reverses this decision, that will not affect the unwisdom of state anti-Communist laws.
39. Gerende v. Board of Supervisors, 341 United States Reports 56 (1951), holding Maryland oath constitutional.
40. Garner v. Board of Public Works, 341 *id.* 716 (1951), holding Los Angeles oath constitutional.
41. Wieman v. Updegraff, 344 *id.* 183 (1952), unanimously holding Oklahoma oath unconstitutional.
42. American Communications Assn., C.I.O. v. Douds, 339 *id.* 382 (1950), majority held part of oath in Taft-Hartley Act constitutional, and Court split evenly on rest of oath.
43. Vernon's Texas Revised Civil Statutes (1951) art. 2908(b), enacted in 1949.
44. Held constitutional in Dworken v. Callopy, 91 North Eastern Reporter, 2d Series, 564 (Ohio Common Pleas, 1950).
45. N.Y. Times, July 9, 1955, p. 31, col. 2, as to New York City.
46. California Laws (1953) c. 1503, p. 3114.
47. 42 United States Code Annotated (1954 Cumulative Pocket Part) §1411c, enacted in 1953. The requirement of a certificate was held to violate the First Amendment in Lawson v. Housing Authority, 70 North Western Reporter, 2d Series, 605 (Wisconsin, 1955). Other state cases are divided. See Alanson W. Willcox, "Invasions of the First Amendment Through Conditioned Public Spending," 41 Cornell Law Quarterly 12, at 47, n. 143 (1955); Note, "Constitutionality of Denying Federal Housing to Members of Subversive Organizations," 53 Columbia Law Review 1166 (1953); note, 69 Harvard Law Review 551 (1956).
48. Housing Authority v. Cordova, 279 Pacific Reporter, 2d Series, 215, at 218 (1955).
49. 62 Purdon's Pennsylvania Statutes Annotated (1954 Pocket Part) §2509.
50. Danskin v. San Diego Unified School Dist., 28 California Reports, 2d Series, 536 (1946), holding law unconstitutional. Two judges out of seven dissented.
51. Maurice I. Goldbloom, *Civic and Political Status* 6 (pamphlet reprinted from *The American Jewish Yearbook* (1954).
52. N.Y. Times, Aug. 16, 1955, p. 25, col. 2. See *Id.,* Aug. 2, 1955, p. 13, col. 3.
53. Alabama Acts (1953) Act No. 888, p. 1196; 17 Vernon's Annotated Revised Civil Statutes of Texas (1955 Annual Pocket Part) Title 110A, art. 6252-7, §3, enacted in 1953. See 6 Alabama Law Review 131 (1953). The Alabama

Law became inoperative after being held unconstitutional by a lower court from which no appeal was taken. American Book Co. v. State Board of Education (Montgomery Cty., Alabama, May 1954).

54. Louisiana Laws (1950) Act No. 284, p. 477 (July 4, 1950).
55. Barsky v. Board of Regents, 347 United States Reports 442 (1954), 3 Justices dissenting. On the previous conviction, see Barsky v. United States, 167 Federal Reporter, 2d Series, 241 (D.C. App. 1948), one judge dissenting.
56. N.Y. Times, Apr. 30, 1955.
57. See Chafee, *How Human Rights Got Into the Constitution,* Chap. 3 (1952), on the importance of the Habeas Corpus Clause.
58. Williamson v. United States, 184 Federal Reporter, 2d Series, 280, at 282 (C.A., 2d, 1950). Two slight omissions are not indicated.
59. McCarran Act, §§101-116; 50 United States Code Annotated (1951) §§811-826. This law and its effect are summarized in 2 Chafee, *Documents on Fundamental Human Rights* 629.
60. See Chafee, *op. cit., supra* note 59, at 631-32.
61. Justice Murphy, dissenting in Korematsu v. United States, 323 United States Reports 214, at 241 (1944).
62. *Ibid.,* quoting from the Final Report on Japanese Evacuation from the West Coast, by General J. L. De Witt, who was in charge.
63. See "The Constitutional Prohibition of Bills of Attainder: A Waning Guaranty of Judicial Trial," 63 Yale Law Journal 844 (1954).
64. *Supra* in text at note 13.
65. Cummings v. Missouri, 4 Wallace (U.S.) Reports 277 (1867), priest; *Ex parte* Garland, 4 *id.* 333 (1867), lawyer.
66. See the dissenting opinion of Justice Douglas, in Harisiades v. Shaugnessy, 342 United States Reports 580, at 598 (1952). The majority held a retroactive deportation law constitutional. The McCarran Act of 1950 added many more retroactive causes for deportation.
67. Olmstead v. United States, 302 *id.* 438, at 470 (1928).
68. 47 United States Code (1953) §605, enacted in 1934.
69. Nardone v. United States, 302 United States Reports 379 (1937).
70. For this case of Judith Coplon and other instances of wire-tapping see Max Lowenthal, *The Federal Bureau of Investigation,* 323-28, 434-37 (1950). See Nathaniel Weyl, *The Battle Against Disloyalty* 212-18 (1951).
71. S. R. Gardiner, 1 *History of England, 1603-1642,* Chap. 4.
72. Bontecou, *op. cit., supra* note 25 at 248-49.
73. N.Y. Times, Nov. 29, 1955, p. 1, col. 7.
74. 8 United States Code Annotated (1953) §1252.
75. Williamson v. United States, *supra* note 58.
76. Carlson v. Landon, 342 United States Reports 524 (1952), a 5-4 decision.
77. 8 United States Code Annotated (1954 Cumulative Pocket Part) §1481(a) and (a)(9). See "The Expatriation Act of 1954," 64 Yale Law Journal 1164 (1955).
78. See my Foreword to Alan Barth, *The Loyalty of Free Men,* at xv-xvi (1951).
79. On the importance of procedure in the loyalty program, see the letter signed by four Harvard Law School professors in N.Y. Times, Sunday, Apr. 13, 1947, editorial page. This was mainly written by my colleague Milton Katz.

80. See 5 John H. Wigmore, *Treatise on Evidence*, §1395 (3d ed., 1940).
81. See Bontecou, *op. cit.*, *supra* note 25, at 214-15, 248, with a very interesting long quotation from Hale.
82. Address to the B'nai B'rith Anti-Defamation League, N.Y. Times, Nov. 24, 1953, p. 20, cols. 4-5.
83. *Supra* note 24. For other eloquent expositions of liberty, see Mr. Eisenhower's letter to the American Library Association at Los Angeles, N.Y. Times, June 27, 1953, p. 26, col. 4; and his telegram to the Commission on Religious Organizations, *Id.*, July 10, 1953, p. 1, col. 1.
84. At pages 105-06 of Brief for Respondents (the government) in John P. Peters v. Oveta Culp Hobby, No. 376, Supreme Court of the United States, October Term, 1954. The case was decided for Dr. Peters, without considering this point, in 349 United States Reports 331 (1955). But see the concurring opinion of Justice Douglas, at 350-51:

    "Dr. Peters was condemned by faceless informers, some of whom were not known even to the Board that condemned him. Some of these informers were not even under oath. None of them had to submit to cross-examination. None had to face Dr. Peters. So far as we or the Board know, they may be psychopaths or venal people, like Titus Oates, who revel in being informers. They may bear old grudges. Under cross-examination their stories might disappear like bubbles. Their whispered confidences might turn out to be yarns conceived by twisted minds or by people who, though sincere, have poor faculties of observation and memory."
85. See Acknowledgments, *supra*.

Footnotes to Chapter II: *Why I Like America*

1. Archibald MacLeish, "Empire Builders," in *Collective Poems, 1917-1952*, (Boston: Houghton Mifflin Co., 1952), p. 75.
2. Walter Prichard Eaton, "Saving New England," 145 Atlantic Monthly 614, at 615 (May 1930).
3. Charles A. Beard, *The Republic* (New York: The Viking Press, Inc., 1943), p. 200.
4. 101 Congressional Record, reporting session of July 14, 1955, at pp. 9081, 9082, 9083-4.
5. See, for example, Chap. III *infra*, in the text at note 80.
6. Burke, *Reflections on the Revolution in France*, in 3 *Works* 359 (Boston, 1899).
7. See his life by William MacDonald in 2 *Dictionary of American Biography* 612 (1929).
8. Concurring opinion in Whitney v. California, 274 United States Reports 357, at 372 (1927).
9. The complete statement is in the N.Y. Times, Feb. 5, 1947.
10. The complete statement is in *Id.*, Mar. 15, 1947.

Footnotes to Chapter III: *Forty Years with Freedom of Speech and of the Press*

1. Frank B. Ober, "Communism vs. the Constitution: The Power to Protect Our Free Institutions," 34 American Bar Assn. Journal 645, at 742, and note 44 (1948).
2. Dennis v. United States, 341 United States Reports 494, at 510 (1951).
3. Gitlow v. New York, 268 *id*. 652 (1925). See also the majority opinion in People v. Gitlow, 234 New York Reports 132 (1922).
4. Chafee, *Free Speech in the United States*, 51-52 (1941), slightly rephrased.
5. Nelles, *Espionage Act Cases, with certain others on related points—"New Law in Making as to Criminal Utterances in Wartime"* (National Civil Liberties Bureau, New York, 1918). See especially the Analysis of Holdings, pp. i-ii.
6. See the opinion of Justice Holmes in Commonwealth v. Peaslee, 177 Massachusetts Reports 267 (1901); Beale, "Criminal Attempts," 16 Harvard Law Review 491, at 501 (1903).
7. Schenck v. United States, 249 United States Reports 47, at 52 (1919).
8. Meiklejohn, *Free Speech: And Its Relation to Self Government*, Chap. II (1948); reviewed by Chafee, 61 Harvard Law Review 891 (1949).
9. These figures are based on Reports of the Attorney General for 1918 and 1919. See Chafee, *Freedom of Speech*, 387 ff. (1920).
10. Fiske v. Kansas, 274 United States Reports 380 (1927).
11. Masses Publishing Co. v. Patten, 244 Federal Reporter 535, 540 (S.D. N.Y., 1917), reversed in 245 *id*. 102 (C.C.A. 2d, 1917).
12. Chafee, "Freedom of Speech," 17 New Republic 66, 67 (Nov. 16, 1918).
13. For example, Meiklejohn, *op. cit., supra* note 8, at least as to all discussion of public issues.
14. N.Y. Penal Law, §§160-166, first enacted in 1902.
15. Act of Oct. 16, 1918, c. 186, 40 Statutes at Large 1012, retained in all subsequent immigration legislation in more drastic form.
16. Colyer v. Skeffington, 265 Federal Reporter 17 (Mass. 1920), reversed as to only a few prisoners, who did get a fair hearing, in 277 *id*. 129 (C.C.A. 1st, 1922).
17. N.Y. Times, Jan. 10, 1920.
18. Chafee, *Freedom of Speech* 307 (published Nov. 30, 1920), stating that the searches and seizures made by the Lusk Committee were contrary to the provision of the N.Y. Constitution against compulsory self-incrimination. This was flatly contrary to 4 Wigmore, *Treatise on Evidence* (1st ed. 1905) §2264.
19. Gouled v. United States, 255 United States Reports 298 (Feb. 28, 1921).
20. Gitlow v. New York, 268 *id*. 652 (1925).
21. People v. Gitlow, 234 New York Reports 132, at 158 (1922).
22. *Progressive Democracy: Addresses and State Papers by Alfred E. Smith*, ed. by Henry Moskowitz (1928) 270-84.
23. For the text of this 1919 Act and further details, see Chafee, *Free Speech in the United States* 326-42.
24. These decisions are all discussed at length in Chafee, *Free Speech in the*

United States 357-66, 375-98. They are Stromberg v. California, 283 United States Reports 359 (1931); Near v. Minnesota, 283 *id.* 697 (1931); Grosjean v. American Press Co., 297 *id.* 233 (1936); De Jonge v. Oregon, 299 *id.* 353 (1937); Herndon v. Lowry, 301 *id.* 342 (1937).

25. Lovell v. Griffin, 303 *id.* 444 (1938); Cantwell v. Connecticut, 310 *id.* 296 (1940); and many subsequent decisions.
26. Thornhill v. Alabama, 310 *id.* 88 (1940); Carlson v. California, 310 *id.* 106 (1940); and several subsequent decisions.
27. Hague v. Committee for Industrial Organization, 307 *id.* 496 (1939).
28. West Virginia State Board of Education v. Barnette, 319 *id.* 624 (1943). This overruled Minersville School District v. Gobitis, 310 *id.* 586 (1940), which had sustained the compulsory flag salute. The Bill of Rights Committee filed briefs in both cases, as friends of the Court (*amici curiae*).
29. Cases cited *supra* notes 25 and 28.
30. Cases cited *supra* note 26.
31. Times-Mirror Co. v. Superior Court, 314 United States Reports 252 (1941); Pennekamp v. Florida, 328 *id.* 331 (1946); and later cases.
32. Julian Boyd, "Subversive of What?" Atlantic Monthly, Aug. 1948, p. 19.
33. 10 *Writings of Thomas Jefferson* 175 (Washington ed. 1903). For a more accurate copy of the letter quoted, see Library of Congress Quarterly Journal of Current Acquisitions, No. 2, 1944, pp. 3-8.
34. Cantwell v. Connecticut, *supra* note 25.
35. Grosjean v. American Press Co., 297 United States Reports 233 (1936).
36. A. F. of L. v. Swing, 312 *id.* 321 (1940); and other cases.
37. Cases cited *supra* note 31; Bridges v. California, 314 United States Reports 252 (1941).
38. See the account of this affair in 1 Chafee, *Government and Mass Communications* 318-20 (1947).
39. Hartzel v. United States, 322 United States Reports 680 (1944).
40. These three addresses are reprinted in a book, *The Next War* (Harvard Alumni Bulletin Press, Cambridge, Mass., 1925).
41. 75 Reports of American Bar Assn. 441 (1950). Earlier and later volumes publish other reports of the Bill of Rights Committee. These show a striking contrast between the activities of the committee during the Period of Achievement (ending in 1945) and its concerns since V-J Day.
42. Act of June 28, 1940, c. 439, secs. 2-5; 54 Stat. 67. Secs. 2 and 5 are now 18 U.S. Code (1948) §2385.
43. *Infra* Chap. V, p. 122.
44. The most careful 1920 estimates were by Gordon Watkins of the University of Illinois, "The Present Status of Socialism in the United States," 124 Atlantic Monthly 821 (Dec. 1919). Attorney General Palmer, in November 1919, gave the figure of 60,000 "radically inclined individuals" of whom a complete history had been gathered and classified by the Radical Division in his Department. Three months later he quoted the secretary of the Communist Party for 50,000 members. This did not include members of the Communist Labor Party.
    The 1955 estimate by Mr. Hoover is given *supra*, Chap. I, note 10.
45. Cooke, *A Generation on Trial* 17-18 (1950).
46. For the legislative history of the Smith Act, see Chafee, *Free Speech in the United States* 463-67 (1941).

47. Act of Sept. 22, 1950, c. 1024. The McCarran Act is discussed at length in Chap. V *infra.*
48. See for example the passage quoted in the text of this chapter at note 1.
49. *Supra* note 47, sec. 4(a). See *infra* Chap. V.
50. See, for example, Massachusetts General Laws, chapter 264, §23, as amended in 1951.
51. See the full discussion in "Passport Refusals for Political Reasons: Constitutional Issues and Judicial Review," 61 Yale Law Journal 17 (1952); Chafee, *Three Human Rights in the Constitution,* Chap. III (1956); Reginald Parker, "The Right to Go Abroad," 40 Virginia Law Review 853 (1954). See *supra* Chap. I, p. 23.
52. *Supra* note 47, secs. 100-117. See *supra* Chap. I, p. 31.
53. *Infra* Chap. V, p. 143.
54. Important recent cases include Rogers v. United States, 340 United States Reports 367 (1951); American Communications Assn. v. Douds, 339 *id.* 382 (1950); Gerende v. Board of Supervisors, 341 *id.* 367 (1951); Garner v. Board of Public Works, 341 *id.* 716 (1951); Bailey v. Richardson, 341 *id.* 918 (1951), equally divided Court; Adler v. Board of Education, 342 *id.* 485 (1952).

   However, a notable case of protection of an organization against redlisting without a hearing was Joint Anti-Fascist Refugee Committee v. McGrath, 341 *id.* 123 (1951); and the Court set aside, on technical grounds, the action of officials in disqualifying a distinguished medical investigator for disloyalty without confronting him with the witnesses against him, Peters v. Hobby, 349 *id.* 331 (1955). A state loyalty oath was held unconstitutional in Wieman v. Updegraff, 344 *id.* 153 (1953). The privilege against self-incrimination before Congressional committees was vigorously enforced in the Quinn, Emspak, and Bart cases, 349 *id.* 159, 190, 219 (1955).
55. Dennis v. United States, 341 United States Reports 494 (1951). For a defense of this abdication, see Richardson, "Freedom of Expression and the Function of Courts," 65 Harvard Law Review 1 (1951).
56. *Supra* note 46.
57. These words were used about the Smith Act by Justice Frankfurter, concurring in Dennis v. United States, 341 United States Reports at 550 (1951). But see *supra* note 46.
58. State legislation in 1919 and 1920 is reviewed in Chafee, *Free Speech in the United States,* 163-68, and indexed by states, *id.* 574-97 (1941). The Smith Act is discussed, *id.* 462-89.
59. Report of Kerr Committee, quoted by Justice Black in Lovett v. United States, 328 United States Reports 303, at 311, note 3 (1946). This case is discussed in Chafee, *Three Human Rights in the Constitution,* Chap. II (1956).
60. *Supra* note 47, secs. 103(a), 104(a)(1). It is unlikely that "reasonable ground" allows judges to override the officials. Similar language in a British statute for the internment of citizens turned out to be meaningless. If the officials ruled that a man ought to be shut up, the courts took it for granted that they had "a reasonable ground" for doing so. That ended the matter. See Liversidge v. Anderson, Law Reports [1942] Appeal Cases 206.
61. This disbarment resolution was adopted by the House of Delegates in February 1951. 37 American Bar Assn. Journal 313 (1951).

62. *Supra* note 51.
63. California Legislature, 1948 Regular Session, Third Report Senate Investigating Committee on Education. See the alphabetical index to "subversive" writers at 48.
64. Dennis v. United States, 341 United States Reports 494, at 501 (1951).
65. 18 United States Code (1948) sec. 2384, first enacted in 1861 and continued to date. As to the single individual who thinks up a rebellion all by himself, does no unlawful act, and nothing happens, see Chafee, *op. cit., supra* note 58, at 147.
66. 8 *The Writings of Thomas Jefferson* (ed. P. L. Ford, 1897) 3.
67. Quoted by Alan Barth, *The Loyalty of Free Men* 203 (1951).
68. *Id.* 216.
69. For concrete illustrations of what happens in legislative investigating committees, see the Cornell University studies cited in Chap. I, notes 20 and 37.
70. In the administration of the loyalty program, lack of confrontation with accusers is still more probable. See Edgerton, J., dissenting, in Bailey v. Richardson, 182 Federal Reporter, 2d Series, 46, at 67 (D.C. App. 1950); affirmed by equally divided Court, 341 United States Reports 918 (1951). See also Peters v. Hobby, *supra* note 54; *supra* Chap. I, pp. 34-37.
71. Proceedings against Mr. Francis Jenkes, 6 Howell's *State Trials* 1189, at 1194 (1676). The case is narrated in Chafee, *How Human Rights Got Into the Constitution,* Chap. III (1952).
72. See United States v. Remington, 191 Federal Reporter, 2d Series, 246 (2d Circuit, 1951); 208 *id.* 567 (1954), Learned Hand dissenting.
73. The original indictment was quashed by Judge Youngdahl in United States v. Lattimore, 112 Federal Supplement 507 (Dist. Col. 1953); affirmed in 215 Federal Reporter, 2d Series, 847 (D.C. App., 1954). The second indictment was quashed by the same judge, 127 Federal Supplement 405 (1955), see also 125 *id.* 295 (1954).
74. See *supra* Chap. I, p. 33. Among the numerous decisions in favor of Bridges are Bridges v. Wixon, 326 United States Reports 135 (1945); Bridges v. United States, 346 *id.* 209 (1953); United States v. Bridges, 133 Federal Supplement 638 (Cal. July 29, 1955).
75. Adler v. Board of Education, 342 United States Reports 485 (1952).
76. McAuliffe v. New Bedford, 155 Massachusetts Reports 216, at 220 (1892).
77. See Brown, *The French Revolution in English History,* index *sub* "Spies"; Hammond, *The Skilled Labourer, 1760-1832,* Chap. XII on Oliver the Spy (1919).
78. Testimony of Nowell, N.Y. Times, Apr. 19, 1949, p. 14, col. 4; testimony of Angela Calomiris, *id.* Apr. 29, 1949, p. 11, col. 1; testimony of Blanc, *id.* May 14, 1949, p. 8, col. 1, and *id.* May 18, 1949, p. 19, cols. 3-4.
78a. See judges' characterization of government witnesses who were ex-Communists in United States v. Flynn, 130 Federal Supplement 412 (S.D. N.Y. 1955); United States v. Bridges, 133 *id.* 638, at 641-8 (N.D. Cal. 1955). See also Jencks v. United States, 226 Federal Reporter, 2d Series, 553 (5th Circ. 1955).
79. Harold J. Gallagher, "American Liberalism at the Crossroads," 36 American Bar Assn. Journal 813, at 814 (1950).
80. Barrett, *The Tenney Committee: Legislative Investigation of Subversive Activities in California* (Ithaca, 1951), pp. 214-15, 235.

81. Palmer, "The Totalitarianism of Mr. Justice Holmes: Another Chapter in the Controversy," 37 American Bar Assn. Journal 809 (1951), citing numerous similar attacks on Holmes.
82. See the survey of "Civil Liberties" by M. I. Goldbloom in *The American Jewish Yearbook*, (1955); Luther A. Huston, "Survey of 50 Loyalty Cases Implies Evaluation Flaws," N.Y. Times, Aug. 15, 1955.
83. Several of these matters are summarized by Richard L. Strout, "Court Cleans up Security Debris," Christian Science Monitor, Aug. 12, 1955.
84. A recent decision is Superior Films v. Dept. of Education, 346 United States Reports 588 (1954).
85. Peters v. Hobby, *supra* note 54.
86. See the Lattimore cases on perjury, *supra* note 73; and on passports, Schachtman v. Dulles, 225 Federal Reporter, 2d Series, 938 (Dist. of Col. Appeals, 1955).

Footnotes to Chapter IV: *Does Freedom of Speech Really Tend to Produce Truth?*

1. Act of 3 Henry IV (1401), reprinted in Stephenson & Marcham, *Sources of English Constitutional History* 274 (1937). For the repeal of this Act, see *Id.*, 556. The statute is further discussed in Chap. IX *infra*.
2. 1 United States Statutes at Large 596.
3. Carlyle, "The Present Time" in *Latter-Day Pamphlets* (1850).
4. See the passages which are indexed at 628-29, under SPEECH, FREEDOM OF, *Arguments*.
5. *The Trial of John Peter Zenger* (pamphlet in Pantaleoni Collection, Harvard Law School) 35.
6. Frank H. Knight, "Economic Theory and Nationalism," in *The Ethics of Competition and Other Essays* 304, 323, 302 and 353 (New York: Harper & Brothers, 1935).
7. Dissenting opinion in Abrams v. United States, 250 United States Reports 616, at 630 (1919). See Chafee, *Free Speech in the United States*, Chap. IV (1941).
8. Louis Blanc, 1 *Letters on England* 438 (London, 1866).
9. Near v. Minnesota, 283 United States Reports 697 (1931). See Chafee, *op. cit.*, *supra* note 7, 375-81.
10. Herodotus, *History*, Book VII, Chap. 10.
11. Funeral Oration of Pericles, in Thucydides, *The Peloponnesian War*, Book II, Chap. 6.
12. *Supra*, p. 78.
13. Burstyn v. Wilson, 343 United States Reports 495 (1952).
14. 14-18 (1947). See the whole of this small book; and Chafee, *Government and Mass Communications*, Chaps. I, XXIV, XXV (1947).
15. Knight, *op. cit.*, *supra* note 6, at 355.
16. Edwin Arlington Robinson, *The Master (Lincoln)*. Copyright by The Macmillan Company, N.Y., and quoted by their permission.
17. *The Critique of Pure Reason*. Chap. 1, sec. 2.

18. Simone Weil, *Waiting for God* (London: Rutledge & Kegan Paul, Ltd., 1951).
19. Spinoza, "Theologico-Political Treatise," Chap. 20, in 1 *Chief Works* (tr. Elwes, 1908) 263.
20. Burke, *Letter to the Sheriffs of Bristol on America*, in *Collected Works* (7th ed. Boston, 1881) 229.
21. *Supra* pp. 95-97.

Footnotes to Chapter V: *Freedom and Fear*

1. The original text of the McCarran Act of September 23, 1950, chapter 1024, can be found in 64 United States Statutes at Large 987ff. Only §§1-17, 32, are discussed in this chapter (as the text explains); these cover twenty-six pages in 50 United States Code Annotated (1951) §§781-796, 798. The revised text of the sections which were amended by the Communist Control Act of 1954, *infra* note 3, is given in 50 United States Code Annotated (1954 Cumulative Pocket Part) §§781-796, 798, *passim.*

   All my references to the McCarran Act are to sections of the Act as passed and amended, and not to the very different section-numbers in the Code.

2. The Alien Registration Act of 1940 is discussed at length in Chafee, *Free Speech in the United States*, Chap. 12 (1941). Section 2 (the Smith Act) is treated there at pp. 462-85.

3. "The Communist Control Act of 1954," 64 Yale Law Journal 712 (1955).

   The text of this Act of August 24, 1954, chapter 886, can be found in 68 United States Statutes at Large 775ff. The portions which amend sections of the McCarran Act are included in the revised text of that Act, *supra* note 1. The wholly new provisions of §§2-5 of the 1954 Act are reprinted in 50 United States Code Annotated (1954 Cumulative Pocket Part) §§841-844.

4. McCarran Act, §§101-116. See Chap. III *supra*, in text at notes 57-62.

5. These two types are defined in the McCarran Act, §3(3)(4).

   The 1954 Act, §§7-11, adds a third type, "Communist-infiltrated organizations." The Subversive Activities Control Board is empowered to determine that any labor union belongs to this type, but registration is not ordered. The main purpose of the amendment was probably to prevent such unions from representing workmen in collective bargaining and other proceedings before the National Labor Relations Board; but members of a "Communist-infiltrated organization" are subjected to several other damaging consequences, the same as for members of a "Communist-front organization."

   Before this 1954 Act, the labor unions themselves were doing a pretty good job of handling Communists in their ranks. Also the Taft-Hartley Act required officers of unions to take an anti-Communist oath in order to represent workmen before the NLRB. The question whether this new legislation is necessary or desirable involves problems of labor relations which fall outside the scope of this book.

6. A maximum fine of $10,000 on the organization which fails to register; the same fine and a maximum of five years imprisonment for every officer or

member who has an obligation to do the registering. Every day of failure is a separate offense. McCarran Act, §15(a)(b).

7. A member of a "Communist-action organization" is also obligated to register if the organization has not done so or if it has left his name off the list. The maximum criminal penalties on a member who violates this requirement are $10,000 fine and five years in prison for every day he delays. McCarran Act, §§8, 15.

8. McCarran Act, §§7, 15.

9. McCarran Act, §§6, 15(c). Members of "Communist-action organizations" and any official who knowingly issues a passport to one are liable to the same punishments.

10. Chap. VIII *infra*.

11. McCarran Act, §11. The same provisions apply to "Communist-action organizations."

12. *Id.*, §10. The same provisions apply to "Communist-action organizations."

13. *Id.*, §5(a)(1)(B).

14. *Id.*, §5(a)(1)(C). As to the definition of "defense facility" and the direction for publication of the list of such facilities, see *id.*, §3(7); §5(b). For criminal punishments, see §15(e).

15. Chap. III *supra*, in text at notes 75, 76.

16. The veto message is printed in full in N.Y. Times, Sept. 23, 1950.

17. These two statutes are now 18 United States Code (1951) §§2384, 371.

18. 18 *id.* §2387. The statute and case mentioned in the text are discussed in 1 Chafee, *Government and Mass Communications* 375-77 (1947).

19. *Supra* note 2. The most significant provisions of the Smith Act are now in 18 United States Code (1948) §2385. It was held constitutional, at least against officers and organizers of the Communist Party, in Dennis v. United States, 341 United States Reports 494 (1951). See Chap. III *supra*, in text at notes 55-58.

20. See Chafee, *Free Speech in the United States* 462-85 (1941).

21. 18 United States Code (1950) §§791-7. The death penalty in peace was added in September 1954. 18 *id.* (1954 Cumulative Pocket Part) §794.

22. See, for example, 18 *id.* (1950) §§1382-3.

23. 18 *id.* (1951) §§2151-56.

24. McCarran Act, §4(b)(d).

25. *Id.*, §5(2)(b). Apparently no Secretary of Defense has paid any attention to this order that he publish a list of defense plants, etc.

26. 18 United States Code (1951) §§1461, 1717. On denial of second-class rates, see the Milwaukee Leader case, 255 United States Reports 407 (1921).

27. 22 United States Code (1952) §§611-621; 18 *id.* (1951) §2386. See Chafee *op. cit.*, *supra* note 20, at 434.

28. The percentage is only 1/60 of 1 per cent in 1955, by J. Edgar Hoover's estimate of 21,500 Communists and the World Almanac's estimate of the total U.S. population as 162,187,000. See Chap. III *supra*, note 44.

29. 9 Annals of Congress 2991-2 (February 25, 1799).

30. Chap. III *supra*, in text at notes 1-3.

31. See, in Chap. III *supra*, the portion entitled "The Period of Struggle and Criminal Prosecutions, 1917-1920."

32. The account of the work of the Board is based on *Subversive Activities Control Board: Fourth Annual Report* (1954), and on the draft of part of

its forthcoming Fifth Annual Report for the fiscal year ending June 30, 1955. These reports are required to be submitted to Congress by McCarran Act, §12(c).

33. 50 United States Code Annotated (1954 Cumulative Pocket Part) §843.
34. Communist Party of America v. Subversive Activities Control Board, 223 Federal Reporter, 2d Series, 531 (Dist. Col., Dec. 23, 1954), with Judge Bazelon dissenting. See also his interesting opinion at a preliminary stage in Communist Party of America v. McGrath, 96 Federal Supplement 47 (Dist. Col. 1951). The arguments in the Supreme Court and questions by Justices are recounted in 24 U.S. Law Week 3141 (Nov. 22, 1955).
35. International Workers Order, Inc.; American Slav Congress; Committee for a Democratic Far Eastern Policy.
36. Council on African Affairs, Inc.; United May Day Committee; Washington Pension Union; California Labor School.
37. Congress appropriated $350,000 to the Board during the fiscal year 1954 and it spent $236,484. Besides the five members who received $15,000 apiece, it employed a staff of twenty-seven persons. *Subversive Activities Control Board: Fourth Annual Report* 11-12 (1954).
38. See Chap. X *infra*, Problem 3, What Ought to be Done About Emergencies?
39. United States Constitution, Article I, section 9.
40. 34 George III, c. 54, reprinted in 2 Chafee, *Documents on Fundamental Human Rights* 365 (1951).
41. An opinion that all the registration provisions of the McCarran Act are constitutional was rendered to the American Bar Association by John W. Davis. The same conclusion was reached by my colleague Arthur E. Sutherland, "Freedom and Internal Security," 64 Harvard Law Review 383 (1951). He relies on a case upholding a New York statute requiring the Ku Klux Klan to register its members. Bryant v. Zimmerman, 278 United States Reports 63 (1928).
42. Act of December 26, 1785, 12 Hening's Statutes at Large of Virginia (1823) c. 34, page 84.
43. Masses Publishing Co. v. Patten, 244 Federal Reporter 535, at 540 (N.Y. 1917).
44. In a recent passport case, Judge Fahy said, "The right to travel, to go from place to place as the means of transportation permit, is a natural right subject to the rights of others and to reasonable regulation under law." Judge Edgerton added: "Freedom to leave a country or a hemisphere is as much a part of liberty as freedom to leave a State [inside our nation]." Schachtman v. Dulles, 225 Federal Reporter, 2d Series, 938 (Dist. of Col. Appeals, June 23, 1955).
45. United States Code Annotated (1954 Cumulative Pocket Part) §786(d)(6), amending §7(d) of the McCarran Act.
46. McCarran Act, §1(b). This clause was inserted by a Senate Amendment. 2 U.S. Code Congressional Service (1950) 3900. See Sutherland on this clause, 64 Harvard Law Review at 400-1,407.
47. Archibald MacLeish, "Brave New World," in his *Collected Poems, 1917-1952*, (Boston: Houghton Mifflin Co., 1952) p. 142. The poem is addressed to Thomas Jefferson.

48. If the reviewing court finds that additional evidence is desirable, it may order the Board to hear it. McCarran Act, §14(a).
49. McCarran Act, §12. The salary was originally $12,500, but was raised by the 1954 Act.
50. During the fiscal year ending June 30, 1955, the three Republican members of the Board were Chairman Thomas J. Herbert, lawyer, Attorney General of Ohio for six years and then Governor; Harry P. Cain, formerly Mayor of Tacoma and Senator from Washington; and David J. Coddaire, lawyer, formerly Assistant Attorney General of Massachusetts and member of the U.S. Maritime Commission. The two Democratic members were Miss Kathryn McHale, long Professor of Education at Goucher College, who has written much on education and psychology and been active in the American Association of University Women and the U.S. National Committee for UNESCO; and Watson Miller, who had served for many years as Director of the American Legion Rehabilitation Commission, and was Commissioner of Immigration and Naturalization when he was appointed to the Board.
51. N.Y. Times, Jan. 16, 1955.
52. *Commonwealth of Australia: Report of the Royal Commission on Espionage,* paragraphs 310, 316, 380 (1955). Long excerpts from this Report were published in N.Y. Times, Sept. 15, 1955.
53. See the information about the publications of the American Flag Committee, the Christian Educational Association (which publishes a semi-monthly magazine, Common Sense), the Philadelphia Committee for Nationalist Action, and the National Blue Star Mothers of America, in the recent report of the American Legion's Special Investigating Committee to Study UNESCO, which is largely reprinted by the Christian Science Monitor (Sept. 8, 1955) page 9. Such organizations are there characterized as Hate Groups and Patrioteers for Profit.
54. *To Secure These Rights* 51-52, 164 (1947).
55. See 2 Chafee, *Government and Mass Communications* 489-94 (1947).
56. The looseness of membership in the kind of enterprises which are frequently termed subversive is discussed in Chap. VIII *infra.* The McCarran Act contains no definition of "member" although the word is used in numerous provisions; and it does not provide for an authenticated list of members of "Communist-front organizations" as it does for "Communist-action organizations." However the annual report is to include all officers, contributors, and persons to whom money is paid for work in the organization. In the absence of any legal test of membership, all such persons are presumably members.

   The Communist Control Act, §5, has some puzzling provisions about membership in the Communist Party or a successor of a similar nature, but these plainly do not concern membership in a "Communist-front organization."
57. See Chap. VIII *infra* for the situation in ordinary life. The McCarran Act in §§7(g) and 13(b)(i) does have a procedure by which persons incorrectly listed as members of a "Communist-action organization" or as officers of either type of organization can get their names stricken after considerable trouble.

   The 1954 Act repeals a provision of the McCarran Act, §5(g), which did give a member or officer of either type of organization an opportunity to withdraw from the organization promptly after it was ordered to register.

58. McCarran Act, §14(f)(4). The preceding text of §14(f) reads:
In determining whether any organization is a "Communist-front organization," the Board shall take into consideration—

(1) the extent to which persons who are active in its management, direction, or supervision, whether or not holding office therein, are active in the management, direction, or supervision of, or as representatives of, any Communist-action organization, Communist foreign government, or the world Communist movement . . . ; and

(2) the extent to which its support, financial or otherwise, is derived from [the same specified bodies]; and

(3) the extent to which its funds, resources, or personnel are used to further or promote the political objectives of [the same specified bodies];

59. See McCarran Act, §3(4), quoted *supra* p. 120.

60. Gellhorn, "Report on a Report of the House Committee on Un-American Activities," 60 Harvard Law Review 1193 (1947).

Footnotes to Chapter VI: *Purges Are for Russian Lawyers*

1. Mass. General Laws (1931) c. 221, §38.
2. Rules of the Supreme Court, Rule 2; at the end of Title 28, United States Code Annotated.
3. 36 American Bar Assn. Journal 972 (1950).
4. *New Jersey*, in 1949, before the Bar Assn. resolution, established an oath disclaiming present belief in or advocacy of "the use of force, or violence, or other unlawful or unconstitutional means, to overthrow or make any change in the government" of the nation or state; and also disclaiming present membership in any organization with such purposes. 41 New Jersey Statutes Annotated (1954 Cumulative Annual Pocket Part) §§1-1, 1-3. This is required of every lawyer before admission, but not periodically like the Bar Assn. oath. The same law applies to all kinds of elected and appointed officeholders, including legislators and judges, and also to candidates. This oath was held unconstitutional as to candidates and elected persons, but valid as to teachers. Its validity for lawyers and judges has not been decided. It is in fact taken on admission to the New Jersey bar.

A thorough search by George L. Johnston of Harvard Law School has found no other state requiring lawyers to take any kind of exculpatory oath.

Three states have dealt with the problem of Communist or radical lawyers in more direct ways. *California* in 1951 made present advocacy of the overthrow of the government "by force, violence, or other unconstitutional means" a ground for exclusion from admission to practise and for disbarment or suspension. *Maryland* in 1952 imposed the same consequences on "a subversive person"; this includes existing membership in any "subversive organization." (Both phrases were defined in the 1949 state sedition law to involve present advocacy of overthrow or alteration of the government "by revolution, force, or violence.") *Illinois*, without any statute, allowed a character committee to ask an applicant for the bar whether he was a member of the Communist Party. *In re* Anastaplo, 3 Illinois Reports, 2d Series, 471 (1954). Similar questions are probably asked by character committees in other states.

5. The statements by Lilienthal and Marshall were printed more fully in Chap. II *supra*, in the text at notes 9 and 10.

6. Cummings v. Missouri, 4 Wallace (United States) Reports 277 (1867); *Ex parte* Garland, 4 *id.* 333 (1867).

7. See Chap. IX *infra*, pp. 255-56.

8. Wieman v. Updegraff, 344 United States Reports 183 (1952).

9. Gerende v. Board of Supervisors, 341 *id.* 56 (1951) (present membership only); Garner v. Board of Public Works, 341 *id.* 716 (1951) (including past membership during five years before the law, but while it was proscribed by a city ordinance).

A Maryland law expressly provides for the exclusion from admission or disbarment of a lawyer who is charged with being presently "a subversive person" (see note 4 *supra*). No court has passed on this clause. Apparently Maryland does not require lawyers to take a test oath, although elective and appointive officers of the state, municipalities, etc., must do so.

10. American Communications Assn. v. Douds, 339 *id.* 382 (1950).

11. Dissenting opinion, *In re* Summers, 325 *id.* 561, at 576 (1945).

12. These are considered *infra* pp. 173-75.

13. See the life of Glover by Leland O. Howard, 7 *Dictionary of American Biography* 332 (1931); The Murphy and Glover Test Oath Cases, 41 Missouri Reports 339 (1867).

14. See *supra* Chap. I, pp. 27-29.

15. Herndon v. Lowry, 301 United States Reports 242, at 263 (1937).

16. Justice Black, dissenting in American Communications Assn. v. Douds, 339 *id.* 382, at 447 (1950).

17. See Chafee, *Free Speech in the United States* 359, 554 (1941).

18. *Supra* note 7.

19. McCarran Act, §4(f). The provision of the Act here referred to is §4(a), creating a new political crime. See Chap. V *supra*, p. 142. The language I have quoted is hard to reconcile with some prosecutions under the Smith Act. Does "any other criminal statute" include state legislation against Communists? See Note, 66 Harvard Law Review 327 (1952). Compare Adams v. Maryland, 347 United States Reports 179 (1954).

20. Chap. III *supra*, in text at note 17.

21. 37 American Bar Assn. Journal 312-313 (1951).

22. Only California and Maryland passed laws to disbar Communists, and these said nothing about "Marxism-Leninism." See *supra* note 4.

23. 37 American Bar Assn. Journal 318-320 (1951).

24. *Supra* Chap. III, in text at note 68.

25. 37 American Bar Assn. Journal 123 (1951). The statement was written by Ernest Angell, one of the signers. The Association of the Bar of the City of New York approved a report and resolution to the same effect. This is reprinted in full, 37 *id.* 124 (1951).

Footnotes to Chapter VII: *The Right Not to Speak*

1. The classic exposition of the privilege is in 8 John H. Wigmore, *A Treatise on the Anglo-American System of Evidence* . . . , §§2250-2284 (3d ed. 1940). The contemporary situation is discussed at length by Erwin N. Griswold, *The Fifth Amendment Today* (1955); Telford Taylor, *Grand Inquest: The Story of Congressional Investigations*, Chap. 7 (1955). Other portions of Taylor's book will be found useful.
2. Interstate Commerce Commission v. Brimson, 154 United States Reports 447, at 468-479, 485-489 (1894); and other authorities cited in 8 Wigmore *op. cit., supra* note 1, §2195, note 6.
3. See the important article by J. M. Landis, "Constitutional Limitations on the Congressional Power of Investigation," 40 Harvard Law Review 153 (1926); McGrain v. Daugherty, 273 United States Reports 135 (1927).
4. 2 United States Code (1954 Pocket Part) §192.
   This power to compel witnesses to answer questions is automatically conferred on every standing committee of the Senate by the Legislative Reorganization Act of 1946, which gives the same power to the House Un-American Activities Committee; but the House itself has to give the subpoena power to any of its other committees. See §§134(a) and 121(q) of the Act; 2 United States Code (1954 Annual Pocket Part) §190b and note to §192. For reasons for this difference between the Senate and the House, see Taylor, *op. cit., supra* note 1, at 232-3.
5. H. D. Thoreau, *The Duty of Civil Disobedience* (1848).
6. Virginia (June 12, 1776); Delaware (September 21, 1776); Pennsylvania (September 28, 1776); Maryland (November 1776); with some qualifications; North Carolina (December 1776); Massachusetts (1780); New Hampshire (1784). Georgia, New Jersey, New York, and South Carolina had no bills of rights before 1791. Connecticut and Rhode Island did not adopt constitutions until the Nineteenth Century.
7. Iowa and New Jersey are the two exceptions; but Iowa upholds the privilege by judicial decisions, and New Jersey puts it in a statute. Some state constitutions qualify the privilege so that the failure of the accused to take the stand can be made a ground for adverse comment by the prosecutor or trial judge. See the full list of references in 8 Wigmore, *op. cit., supra* note 1, §2252, note 3.
8. Emspak v. United States, 349 United States Reports 190, at 195 (1955).
9. Quoted by Taylor, *op. cit., supra* note 1, at 193. For Grant, see *Id.* 196.
10. An example is quoted by Taylor, *op. cit., supra* note 1, at 184-85.
11. 8 Wigmore, *op. cit., supra* note 1, §2272; Wilson v. United States, 149 United States Reports 60, at 67-68 (1893). Such an inference is permitted in a few states. Wigmore, *ibid.* and note 7 *supra*. Even so, it is just an indication of guilt to be weighed with the testimony on both sides.
12. J. F. Stephen, quoted by 8 Wigmore, *op. cit., supra* note 1, §2251, at page 312.
13. For a striking example of an untrue confession by an innocent feeble-minded youth, see Homer S. Cummings, "State vs. Harold Israel," 15 Journal of Criminal Law & Criminology 406 (1924). For other examples, see E. M.

Borchard, *Convicting the Innocent* xvii-xviii (1932); and the Report cited *infra* note 19, at 181-87.

14. Wigmore, *op. cit.*, *supra* note 1, §2251. Emphasis as in the original.

15. *Ibid.*

16. A. Lawrence Lowell, "The Judicial Use of Torture," 11 Harvard Law Review 220 and 290 (1897).

17. Paragraph 45, reprinted in 1 Chafee, *Documents on Fundamental Human Rights*, 83-84, among many extracts from this code.

18. 3 Elliot's Debates 447-8 (2d ed., 1836). Some immaterial omissions are not indicated.

19. Dissenting, with Cardozo, in People v. Doran, 246 New York Reports 409 (1927). See 4 National Commission on Law Observance and Enforcement: Report on Lawlessness in Law Enforcement, at 58-60 (1931).

20. *Id.*, 52-83. Sample cases are Ziang Sung Wan v. United States, 266 United States Reports 1 (1924); Bell v. State, 180 Arkansas Reports 79 (1929); Williams v. State, 83 Texas Criminal Reports 532 (1923); Lang v. State, 178 Wisconsin 114 (1922).

21. See, for example, Harris v. South Carolina, 338 United States Reports 68 (1949).

22. The leading case is Ashcraft v. Tennessee, 322 *id.* 143 (1944).

23. Quinn v. United States, 349 United States Reports 155, at 160-61 (1955).

24. S. R. Gardiner, 1 *History of England, 1603-1642*, Chap. 1.

25. J. R. Green, 2 *History of the English People*, Book VI, Chap. 6 (1880).

26. *Ibid.*

27. The Millenary Petition and the Conference are in 2 Howell's *State Trials* 69. Quoted passages are at 90-91, 86. See also 1 Gardiner, *op. cit.*, *supra* note 24, Chap. 4.

28. See 10 Gardiner, *op. cit.*, *supra* note 24, Index *sub* "High Commission, Court of."

29. Udall's examinations, trial, etc., are fully printed in 1 Howell's *State Trials* 1271. See also his life by Sidney Lee in 58 *Dictionary of National Biography* 4 (1890).

30. Observe the inference of guilt from refusal to answer.

31. Compare the reasons given by Professor Furry for refusing to play the game of Twenty Questions. *Infra* p. 227.

32. Here is an early recognition of the privilege against self-incrimination, to a very limited extent. Lord Anderson's statement was quoted by Udall to the judge who later tried him for a capital offense, but the point was brushed aside. 1 Howell's *State Trials*, at 1288-89.

33. The Jesuit priests of English birth who dared to come from the Continent to minister to Roman Catholic families were treated like the spies of a foreign power and executed when caught. See the life of the heroic Father Edmund Campion by Thompson Cooper in 8 *Dictionary of National Biography* 398 (1886).

34. See *supra* note 31.

35. See *supra* note 30.

36. This was one of the earliest cases to raise the central problem in the trial of Peter Zenger, whether the criminality of the publication was a question for the court or for the jury. Udall and a lawyer shouting among the spectators vainly urged that the jury should decide the whole issue of his guilt, but the

judges told the jury to decide only whether he wrote the pamphlets. See the account of the Zenger trial in Chafee, *Freedom of Speech and Press* 35-40 (Freedom Agenda, 1954).

37. The trial of Lilburn and John Wharton is printed in 3 Howell's *State Trials* 1315. See Lilburn's life by C. H. Firth in 33 *Dictionary of National Biography* 243 (1893).

38. Acts xxv, 16. See Chafee, *How Human Rights Got Into the Constitution* 73-74 (1952).

39. Quoted by Griswold, *op. cit., supra* note 1, at 5-6; from John William Wallace, "An Address Delivered at the Celebration by the New York Historical Society . . . of the Two Hundredth Birth Day of Mr. William Bradford . . ." 49-50 (Albany, 1863). See also the life of Bradford by Victor H. Paltsits, 2 *Dictionary of American Biography* 563 (1929); R. Carter Pittman, "The Colonial and Constitutional History of the Privilege against Self-incrimination in America," 21 Virginia Law Review 763, at 785 (1935).

40. J. F. Stephen, quoted in 8 Wigmore, *op. cit., supra* note 1, §2251, at pp. 311-12.

41. See the dissenting opinions in United States v. Rumely, 345 United States Reports 41 (1953).

42. United States v. Rumely, cited *supra* note 41. See also United States v. Corliss Lamont, 18 Federal Rules Decisions 27 (S.D. N.Y. 1955); and cases cited *infra*, note 76. Compare United States v. Harvey O'Connor, 135 Federal Supplement 590 (D.C., 1955).

43. *Supra* p. 181.

44. See Griswold, *op. cit., supra* note 1, at 46-47, on counsel in inquiries.

45. Pascal, *Pensées.*

46. Justice Peckham said as to state laws imposing railroad freight rates: "The company, in order to test the validity of the acts, must find some agent or employé to disobey them. . . . The necessary effect and result of such legislation must be to preclude a resort to the courts . . . for the purpose of testing its validity. The officers and employés could not be expected to disobey any of the provisions of the acts . . . at the risk of such fines [up to $5,000] and penalties [imprisonment up to five years] being imposed upon them, in case the court should decide that the law was valid." *Ex parte* Young, 209 United States Reports 123, at 144-148 (1908).

The later cases of Beal v. Missouri Pacific R.R. Corp., 312 *id.* 45 (1941), and Douglas v. Jeannette, 319 *id.* 157 (1943), show a growing reluctance to declare state action unconstitutional merely because its validity has to be tested at risk of a single prosecution with penalties; but this does not affect what has been quoted by Justice Peckham about the unfairness of making men go to jail as the price of testing their rights. Our concern is not constitutionality, but wisdom.

47. A possible solution is discussed *infra* p. 222.

48. *Ex parte* Irvine, 74 Federal Reporter 954, at 960 (U.S. Circ. Ct., Ohio, 1896). Taft quotes at the end from Wharton, *Criminal Evidence.* The whole opinion will repay reading. See also Chief Justice Marshall in Aaron Burr's Trial, 25 Federal Cases 38, at 40 (Circ. Ct., Va., 1807).

49. *Ex parte* Irvine, *supra* note 48, at 964.

50. See United States v. St. Pierre, 128 Federal Reporter, 2d Series, 979, at 980 (2nd Circ. 1942).
51. McCarran Act, Section 4(f). It is very difficult to reconcile the words quoted in the text with the conviction for mere membership in United States v. Lightfoot in the Northern District of Illinois in February 1955. This was affirmed on appeal. To the same effect is Scales v. United States, 227 Federal Reporter, 2d Series, 581 (4th Circ., Nov. 7, 1955).
52. See Adams v. Maryland, 347 United States Reports 179 (1954).
53. United States v. Murdock, 284 *id.* 141 (1931). Conversely, a state court will not give the privilege to a witness in danger of a federal conviction. See Jack v. Kansas, 199 *id.* 372 (1905).
54. See United States v. Di Carlo, 102 Federal Supplement 597 (Ohio, 1952); and other recent cases in U.S. district courts.
55. Blau v. United States, 340 United States Reports 159 (1950).
56. United States v. St. Pierre, 132 Federal Reporter, 2d Series, 837, at 839-40 (2d Circ., 1942). This involved further vicissitudes of the witness who was afraid he would be bumped off, *supra* note 50.
57. Rogers v. United States, 340 United States Reports 367 (1951).
58. Griswold, *op. cit., supra* note 1, at 23. See also Taylor, *ibid.,* at 199-201.
59. Quinn v. United States, 349 United States 155, at 161 (May 23, 1955). Emphasis supplied.
59a. See Fischler v. McCarthy, 117 Federal Supplement 643 (S.D. N.Y., 1954).
60. This point is fully discussed in my Foreword to Alan Barth, *The Loyalty of Free Men* xi-xviii (1951).
61. N.Y. Times, Feb. 20, 1954, p. 7, col. 5. On executive sessions, see Taylor, *op. cit., supra* note 1, at 244-47.
62. A recent Royal Commission on Capital Punishment heard much testimony in the United States, where compulsion was obviously impossible. See the account of Royal Commissions in Taylor, *op. cit., supra* note 1, at 285ff.
63. Missouri, Kansas & Tennessee R.R. v. May, 194 United States Reports 267, at 270 (1904).
64. *Supra* note 4.
65. Aiuppa v. United States, *infra* note 72, at 296.
66. In about half the states, the physician has no legal privilege. The rest give it by legislation. 8 Wigmore, *op. cit., supra* note 1, §1380.
67. This helpful suggestion is made by Taylor, *op. cit., supra* note 1, at 260.
68. 2 United States Code, §192.
69. Bazelon, concurring with Judge Edgerton in Quinn v. United States, 203 Federal Reporter, 2d Series, 20, at 37 (Dist. of Col. App., 1952).
70. Robert K. Carr, *The House Committee on Un-American Activities, 1945-1950,* at 130 (1952).
71. Judge Schweinhaut, in United States v. Kleinman, 107 Federal Supplement 407, at 408 (Dist. of Col., 1952). The capitalization is changed, and omissions are not indicated.
72. Aiuppa v. United States, 201 Federal Reporter, 2d Series, 287, at 300 (Court of Appeals, 6th Circuit, 1952). The bracketed numbers are inserted by me to indicate the three threats. One omission is not indicated.
73. And a perjury conviction may follow even if he answers truthfully; the witness may expect, with good reason, that the jury will disbelieve the

truth, being persuaded by government witnesses who hate him and are themselves perjurers.

74. *Supra* p. 92.

75. See also the reasons given to the House Committee on Un-American Activities by Lillian Hellman, author of *The Children's Hour* and *The Little Foxes,* for not supplying names. N.Y. Times, May 22, 1952, p. 15, col. 1; quoted in Emerson & Haber, *Political and Civil Rights in the United States* 455 (1952).

76. The facts are taken from *Reprint of Stenographic Transcript of Hearings: Permanent Subcommittee on Investigation . . . , Boston, Massachusetts, January 15, 1954* (printed at the Harvard University Printing Office) p. 18-39. Some omissions are not indicated.

Mr. Furry's case is now (Dec. 1955) pending in the courts, which will probably decide whether questions about Harvard and the Massachusetts Institute of Technology are outside the scope of the Committee on Government Operations. See *supra* Chap. I, in text at note 21; Chap. VII, in text at notes 42-47.

In a related case, questions about Communists at Harvard were held to be outside the scope of the same committee. United States v. Kamin, 135 Federal Supplement 382 (Mass., Nov. 2, 1955). For similar reasons, the Court later acquitted the defendant on charges of failure to say whether he knew any Communists working in private defense plants. N.Y. Times, Jan. 6, 1956.

77. N.Y. Times, May 6, 1954, p. 22, col. 8.

78. See note 79 *infra.*

79. Senator McCarthy went on to assert that he had the same legal right as an F.B.I. agent not to disclose his informants. But the situations were wholly different. A legal rule (not mentioned elsewhere in this chapter) prevents a defense lawyer, while examining a policeman or prosecutor, from forcing the witness to answer such questions as, "Who tipped you off to arrest my client?" (See the explanation and judicial statements about this rule in 8 Wigmore, *op. cit., supra* note 1, §2374.) The rule encourages citizens to give the proper law-enforcing agency needed facts, which they might withhold unless afforded some protection against undesired publicity. However, the F.B.I. already had the facts contained in the 2½ page document. There is no policy in favor of encouraging a government official to violate the law by passing F.B.I. secrets without any authority from his superiors to a legislative committee, which has no power of law enforcement. (See Chief Justice Warren, quoted in the text of this chapter at note 59.) On the contrary, Congress has made such a disclosure punishable by imprisonment up to ten years. 18 United States Code (1950) §793(d). Finally, the tribunal can order the witness to disclose his informants when that is desirable to attain justice. Therefore, Senator Mundt was mistaken in ruling that he had no power to make the witness tell who gave him the F.B.I. document, although it may have been wise not to press for an answer.

Senator McCarthy would have been on much solider legal ground if he had said that his answer might help get him convicted for the crime of deliberately retaining a secret document, *Id.* §793(e), and invoked the Fifth Amendment.

80. In order not to complicate the discussion, I omit questions about tenure

and the extent to which the faculty should participate with the governing board in dismissing a professor (whether with or without tenure).

81. Taylor, "The Dismissal of Fifth Amendment Professors," 300 Annals of the American Academy of Political and Social Science 79 (July 1955).

82. See Opinion of the Justices, 126 North Eastern Reporter, 2d Series, 100 (Massachusetts, April 13, 1955), advisory opinion that it would be in direct contradiction of the state constitution to make the claim of privilege exclude a man from teaching in any university or school, public and private.

A helpful analogy is furnished by court decisions refusing to disbar a lawyer because he claimed the privilege. Matter of Kaffenburgh, 188 N.Y. 49, at 52-53 (1907); Matter of Grae, 282 N.Y. 428, at 434-5 (1940); Sheiner v. State, 82 Southern Reporter, 2d Series, 657 (Florida, July 29, 1955), full discussion of effect of claim of privilege before Congressional committee.

83. See the life of Cooper by Dumas Malone, 4 *Dictionary of American Biography* 414 (1930). Contrast the case in note 84 *infra*.

84. Consider the refusal of Dr. Barsky to reveal the names of contributors to the Joint Anti-Fascist Refugee Committee, in the case cited *supra* Chap. I, note 55.

85. Thoreau, *The Duty of Civil Disobedience* (1848).

Footnotes to Chapter VIII: *Freedom to Think*

1. See Professor Carver's letter and my reply in the Atlantic Monthly (Mar. 1955) 23.

2. Edward L. Barrett, Jr., *The Tenney Committee: Legislative Investigation of Subversive Activities in California* 121 (1951).

3. *Third Report: California Senate Investigating Committee on Education* 60-61 (1948).

4. See *supra* Chap. VI for a discussion of loyalty oaths in general, especially as applied to lawyers.

5. Quoted by Justice Field in Cummings v. Missouri, 4 Wallace (United States) Reports 277 at 331 (1867).

6. See *infra* Chap. IX.

7. Quoted in Alan Barth, *The Loyalty of Free Men* 203 (1951).

8. See Pauling's account of this experience in "American Visa Policy and Foreign Scientists," 8 Bulletin of Atomic Scientists 253 (October 1952).

9. See *supra* Chap. III, note 86.

10. This is reviewed at length by me in 101 University of Pennsylvania Law Review 703 (1953).

11. *Theologico-Political Treatise*, c. 20.

12. Edwin Arlington Robinson, *Nicodemus*, from *Collected Poems* (New York: The Macmillan Company, 1937), p. 1161. Copyright by The Macmillan Company, N.Y., and quoted by their permission.

Footnotes to Chapter IX: *With Full Liberty of Religious Concernments*

1. The Rhode Island Charter and other colonial documents mentioned in this chapter are reprinted in 1 Chafee, *Documents on Fundamental Human Rights* (1951).
2. On this problem, see Chafee, *How Human Rights Got Into the Constitution,* Chap. II (1952).
3. Cantwell v. Connecticut, 310 United States Reports 296 (1940).
4. Everson v. Board of Education, 330 *id.* 1 (1947).
5. Dissenting in American Communications Assn. v. Douds, 339 *id.* 382, at 442 (1950).

Footnotes to Chapter X: *Strengthening Liberty in All Countries*

1. Readers wishing to see the full text of one of the numerous successive drafts for the Covenant will find the 1951 draft reprinted in 3 Chafee, *Documents on Fundamental Human Rights* 966 (1952). Of course, this text is not final. It is the only draft containing provisions about social, economic and cultural rights; the desirability of including these rights is discussed in my Problem 5. Several problems of the Covenant not considered in this chapter are examined in my three articles cited *infra* in Chap. XI, note 1. See a short list of references on Human Rights in the United Nations, Chafee, *op. cit., supra,* 947; and a fuller bibliography in 95 Proceedings of the American Philosophical Society at 488 (October 1951).
2. Emphasis supplied. The text of the Declaration of Principles (Atlantic Charter) of Aug. 14, 1941, is printed in Leland M. Goodrich & Edward Hambro, *Charter of the United Nations: Commentary and Documents* 569 (2d ed. 1949). This book contains several other basic documents.
3. *Id.* 570. This Declaration added religious freedom, and spoke of complete victory as essential "to preserve human rights and justice *in their own lands* as well as in other lands. . . ." (emphasis supplied).
4. The authoritative source on the actions by our government leading to the formation of the United Nations is *Postwar Foreign Policy Preparation, 1939-1945.* Dept. of State Publn. 3580, General Foreign Policy Series 15 (1950). See its index *sub* Human rights.
5. *Id.* 115-16, with full text at 483.
6. *Id.* 530. See also 175-76.
7. Lawyers will observe that the Covenant resembles the Fourteenth Amendment rather than our Bill of Rights, which was adopted to restrict a strong central government. The weak central government by the United Nations needed no limitations outside the Charter itself. The Covenant restricts the powers of member states, somewhat like the Fourteenth Amendment. Of course, consent is necessary by signing the treaty.

8. Goodrich & Hambro, *op. cit., supra* note 2, at 97.
9. *Op. cit., supra* note 4, especially at 321, 327, 386; and the references cited *infra* note 11.
10. Chap. IX, Section A(1). Goodrich & Hambro, *op. cit., supra* note 2, at 580.
11. The U.S. amendments and the joint amendments are printed in full in *op. cit., supra* note 4, at 679 and 681. On the consultations, see *Id.* 438-48. On events at San Francisco, see *The United Nations Conference at San Francisco: Selected Documents*, Dept. of State Publn. 2490, Conference Series 83 (1945). The Committee on Economic and Social Cooperation appears at 23, 28, 127-29, 200, 215, 618, 636ff. See also Report cited *infra* note 14.
12. UN Charter, Preamble; Art. 1(3), purposes of UN; Art. 13(1)(b), Assembly; Art. 55(c), economic and social co-operation, and see Art. 56; Art. 62(2), Economic and Social Council; Art. 68, Human Rights Commission; and Art. 76(c), international trusteeship system. All these specific references with other relevant provisions of the Charter are printed in 3 Chafee, *op. cit., supra* note 1, at 948.
   The Charter is printed in full by Goodrich & Hambro, *op. cit., supra* note 2, at 582; and in 59 United States Statutes at Large, 1031 (1945). It was signed by fifty governments on June 26, 1945, ratified by the Senate by eighty-nine votes to two, and proclaimed by President Truman as effective on October 24, 1945.
13. The other members were Cordell Hull (Senior Adviser); Senators Tom Connally and Arthur H. Vandenberg; Representatives Sol Bloom and Charles A. Eaton; Harold E. Stassen; and Virginia C. Gildersleeve.
14. *Charter of the United Nations: Report to the President on the Results of the San Francisco Conference* (June 26, 1945), Dept. of State Publn. 2349, Conference Series 71, at 110-11, 114, 118-19.
15. The President of the Bar Association, David A. Simmons, was an especially strong supporter of human rights among the consultants. See his article, "The San Francisco Conference," 31 American Bar Assn. Journal 332, at 378 (July 1945). See also Simmons, "The Right to be Let Alone," 36 *id.* 711 (Sept. 1950). All the consultants are listed by Secretary Stettinius in his Report, *op. cit., supra* note 14, at 262-66.
16. Contrast with the facts just set forth the frequent insistence by enemies of the Covenant that an international bill of rights is outside the purposes of the United Nations; that anybody who supports the Covenant is "not in sympathy with the basic principles of our form of government"; and that it embodies "the political philosophy and policies of the Soviet state" (which, in fact, has taken very little interest in the Covenant).
17. Treaties and Executive Agreements: Hearings . . . 83d Cong., 1st Sess., on S.J. Res. 1 Proposing an Amendment to the Constitution . . . (Feb. 18-April 11, 1953) 825.
   Mr. Dulles said: "Therefore, while we shall not withhold our counsel from those who seek to draft a treaty or covenant on human rights, we do not ourselves look upon a treaty as the means which we would now select as the proper and most effective way to spread throughout the world the goals of human liberty to which this Nation has been dedicated since its inception. We therefore do not intend to become a party to any such covenant or present it as a treaty for consideration by the Senate."

18. See Sutherland, "Restricting the Treaty Power," 65 Harvard Law Review 1305 (1952); same, "The Bricker Amendment . . . ," 67 *id.* 281 (1953); Chafee, "Amending the Constitution to Cripple Treaties," 12 Louisiana Law Review 345 (1952).

 Lawyers will be interested to observe that, in fact, the Covenant on Human Rights is one of the very few treaties which would not be affected by the Bricker Amendment. (1) The clause invalidating unconstitutional treaties, which are void anyway, has no bearing on an entirely constitutional treaty, see *infra* p. 280. (2) The clause forbidding self-executing treaties does not apply to a treaty which will not be self-executing, but will require implementing legislation from Congress and the states, see *infra* note 33. (3) The clause preventing Congress from so legislating outside its domestic powers will not apply because the Covenant provides that any implementing legislation which is appropriate for state action under our constitutional processes will be passed by state legislatures, see Chafee in [1951] Wisconsin Law Review 623.

19. Extracts from these peace treaties are printed in 3 Chafee, *Documents on Fundamental Human Rights* 954 (1952).

20. Draft Covenant on Civil and Political Rights (approved by the Commission on Human Rights, at its tenth session, February-April 1954) Article 23. Several other provisions in this draft, which were added since the 1951 draft, *supra* note 1, also overload the instrument objectionably.

21. Report cited *supra* note 14, at 119. Some slight omissions are not indicated.

22. Bagehot, "The American Constitution in the Present Crisis," 3 *Works* (Barrington ed., 1915) 349 at 350, 359, 366-68, 378, 384. The order of passages has been somewhat shifted, and omissions between passages are not indicated.

23. Frank E. Holman, "An International Bill of Rights: Proposals have Dangerous Implications for United States," 34 American Bar Assn. Journal 984 (1948); same, "Treaty Law-Making," 36 *id.* 707 (1950).

24. This is reprinted in 3 Chafee, *Documents on Fundamental Human Rights* 956 (1952).

25. Holcombe, *Human Rights in the Modern World* 27 (1948).

26. Lincoln, 1 *Complete Works* (ed. Nicolay & Hay, 1920) 232. The speech was at Springfield, Illinois, June 26, 1857.

27. The Declaration does not mention jury trial, bearing arms, or immunity from having troops quartered. Protection of property is made an ideal by Article 17, but nothing specifically corresponds to the Fourth Amendment on searches or seizures or the eminent domain clause in the Fifth Amendment.

28. UN Charter, Article 2(7). This is discussed by Chafee, 14 Law and Contemporary Problems 545, at 557 (1949); and by Goodrich & Hambro, *op. cit., supra* note 2, at 110-21.

29. *Supra* note 19.

30. UN Charter, Articles 1(4), 13(1), 59, 62(3)(4).

31. See the discussion of the need for qualifications of the various rights in Chafee, *op. cit., supra* note 28, at 567-70 (1949).

32. On this 1951 draft, see *supra* note 1.

33. Lawyers will be interested to observe that the Covenant is not intended to be self-executing and operate automatically as law in the United States, as

do most of our treaties. Federal and state legislation will be required to implement the Covenant. See Chafee, *op. cit., supra* note 28, at 558-65. The UN Charter is also not self-executing. Sei Fujii v. State, 38 California Reports, 2d Series, 718 (1952). This nullifies an erroneous decision to the contrary by a lower court.

34. This is made plain by Article 5(2) of the 1954 draft cited *supra* note 20. See the fuller discussion of this point in Chafee, [1951] Wisconsin Law Review 389, at 390-91, 402 and note 24, 454-56. The 1954 draft uses new language in place of a word which caused much controversy in the corresponding provision in Article 18(2) of the 1951 draft.

35. See the detailed comparison between the rights in the Covenant and those in the U.S. Constitution in Chafee, *op. cit., supra* note 34, at 400-12.

36. For numerous references on this point, see Chafee, 95 Proceedings of the American Philosophical Society 471, at 473, note 8.

37. Buchanan v. Rucker, 9 East Reports 192, at 194 (Eng. 1808).

38. See my articles cited in Chap. XI, note 1.

39. Paraiso v. United States, 207 United States Reports 368, at 372 (1907). On the constitutionality of the Covenant, see Chafee, *op. cit., supra* note 34, at 453-73.

40. *Supra* p. 279.

41. Dennis v. United States, 341 United States Reports 494, at 503 (1951).

To the same effect, though I disagree with much else in Chief Justice Vinson's opinion, see *supra*, the opening pages of Chap. III and the close of Chap. IV.

42. Edward V. Dicey, *Law of the Constitution* (8th ed., 1915) 77-79. See also Bagehot, *The English Constitution*, 5 *Works* (Barrington ed., 1915) 136-37.

43. Arnold Brecht, "European Federation—the Democratic Alternative," 55 Harvard Law Review 561, at 563, 579-83 (1942).

44. This Convention is reprinted in *These Rights and Freedoms* 182-97 (United Nations Dept. of Public Information, 1950).

45. *Op. cit., supra* note 4, at 483.

46. See the informative article by Dorothy S. Thomas, "Some Aspects of Japanese-American Demography," 94 Proceedings American Philosophical Society 459 (1950). The Supreme Court cases are reprinted with other material in 2 Chafee, *Documents on Fundamental Human Rights* 587-628.

47. Article 2 in 1951 draft, cited *supra* note 1; article 4 in 1954 draft, cited *supra* note 20.

48. These cases are reviewed in Chafee, [1951] Wisconsin Law Review at 412-22.

49. Articles 33-59 in 1951 draft, cited *supra* note 1; articles 27-48 in 1954 draft, cited *supra* note 20. See also the numerous references on enforcement machinery in Chafee, *op. cit., supra* note 36.

50. 4 *Report of National Commission on Law Observance and Enforcement* 13-261 (Govt. Printing Office, 1931). See Chafee, "Remedies for the Third Degree," 148 Atlantic Monthly 621 (1931).

51. See 1 Chafee, *Government and Mass Communications*, Chap. 7 (1947).

52. There are interesting passages in F. S. C. Northrop, *The Meeting of East and West* at 250, 494 (1946).

53. Articles 25, 27. See other economic and social rights in articles 23-28. The

provisions on human rights in this Japanese Constitution are printed in 3 Chafee, *Documents on Fundamental Human Rights* 917 (1952).

54. Communist influences on the Covenant are charged by William Fleming, "Danger to America: The Draft Covenant on Human Rights," 37 American Bar Assn. Journal 739 (1951). Also, he says (at 795) that the right to equal pay for equal work (which is in article 23 of the Universal Declaration signed by the U.S.) "was denied by Christ almost two thousand years ago" in the parable of the laborers in the vineyard. Any employer who today gave a day's wages to those who came at the eleventh hour might have trouble with his union.

55. Arthur E. Sutherland, "Private Government and Public Policy," 41 Yale Review 405, at 407 (Spring 1952).

56. The State Department 1942 draft for a UN bill of rights said: "All persons who are willing to work, as well as all persons who through no fault of their own are unwilling to work, have the right to enjoy such minimum standards of economic, social and cultural well-being as the resources of the country, effectively used, are capable of sustaining." *Op. cit., supra* note 4, at 483.

57. References on this question are cited in Chafee, *op. cit., supra* note 36, at note 25.

58. N.Y. Times, Dec. 5, 1950.

59. For this portion of the Indian Constitution, see Chafee, *Documents on Fundamental Human Rights* 943 (1952). A similar scheme appears in General MacArthur's Japanese Constitution, last part of article 25. *Id.* 921.

60. The 1951 draft of the Covenant is reprinted in Chafee, *op. cit., supra* note 59, at 966. For the presentation of economic, social, and cultural rights, see 976-81.

61. Quoted by John Morley in "Burke," 4 *Encyclopaedia Britannica* (11th ed., 1911) 832.

62. Reinhold Niebuhr, quoted in 2 Chafee, *Government and Mass Communications* 483 (1947).

Footnotes to Chapter XI: *Free Speech in the United Nations*

1. The following articles of mine deal with these issues: "Legal Problems of Freedom of Information in the United Nations" (1949) 14 Law and Contemporary Problems 545; "Federal and State Powers under the Covenant of Human Rights," [1951] Wisconsin Law Review 389 and 623; "Some Problems of the Draft International Covenant on Human Rights," 95 Proceedings of the American Philosophical Society 471 (October 1951). See also *United Nations Conference on Freedom of Information, Geneva, Switzerland, March 23-April 21, 1948: Report of the United States Delegates* (Dept. of State Publn. 3150).

2. Evatt, *The United Nations* 49-51 (1948).

3. This statement as to China may be somewhat affected by the establishment of a Communist regime on the mainland since the Geneva Conference; but many Western ideas must still persist among Chinese.

4. The passage quoted is the Conference draft for what is now Article 19 of

the Universal Declaration of Human Rights. In giving the article its final form, the Economic and Social Council replaced "means" in the last line by the barbarous word "media." Also, besides saying "has" instead of "shall have," it altered "freedom of thought" for the worse into "freedom of opinion."

5. See, for example, the editorials, "UN and Free Press" in Editor and Publisher (Feb. 7, 1948), and "The UN and the Press" in the N.Y. Daily News (Jan. 31, 1948), with a cartoon "The Gift of Bracelets."

6. 97 Congressional Record 8257 (July 17, 1951). His entire remarks run from 8254-8263. Other denunciations by lawyers and journalists are quoted in [1951] Wisconsin Law Review at 461 and note 186.

7. Edward Crankshaw, *Russia and the Russians* (New York: The Viking Press, Inc., 1948).

8. *Voyageurs Etrangers en Russie: du X au XX siecle.* Textes choisis et présentés par Michel Forstetter 58, 144-45 (Vevey, 1947). The quoted statements are by Giles Fletcher, ambassador from Queen Elizabeth to the Czar Fedor, and the Marquis de Custine.

9. The four other member satellites were Ukraine, Byelorussia, Poland, and Czechoslovakia. (The Czech *coup d'état* in February 1948 came between the second session of the Sub-Commission and the Geneva Conference.) In addition, four satellites which were not members of the UN were represented at Geneva—Albania, Bulgaria, Hungary, and Rumania. Their representatives could speak but not vote.

10. Paraphrased from *The History of Herodotus,* translated by George Rawlinson (New York: The Dial Press, 1928) Book IV, p. 263.

11. "Strengthening the United Nations: Statement by George C. Marshall, Secretary of State" (made before House Foreign Affairs Committee, May 5, 1948). Dept. of State Bull. Vol. XVII No. 463 (May 16, 1948) 623, at 625.

12. Resolution No. 1, reprinted at pp. 25-26 of the *Report of the United States Delegates,* cited at the end of note 1 *supra.*

13. See *A Free and Responsible Press: A General Report on Mass Communication.* By the Commission on Freedom of the Press (1947) 3-29.

14. Article 125 of the Soviet Constitution of 1936, reprinted in Chafee, *Documents on Fundamental Human Rights* 915.

15. S. R. Gardiner, 5 *History of England, 1603-1642* (1901 ed.) 169.